Boy Scouts of America

The Official Handbook for Boys

Seventeenth Edition

BOY SCOUTS OF AMERICA

COSIMOCLASSICS

NEW YORK

"The scout badge is not specifically intended
to represent either the fleur-de-lis or an arrowhead,
although it resembles both, It is a modified form of the sign
of the north on the mariner's compass, which is as old
as the history of navigation. The Chinese claim its use among
them as early as 2634 B.C. and we have definite information
that it was used at sea as early as 300 A.D. Marco Polo brought
the compass to Europe on his return from Cathay. The sign
of the north on the compass gradually came to represent
the north, and pioneers, trappers, woodsmen, and scouts,
because of this, adopted it as their emblem. Through centuries
of use it has undergone modification. Now we have taken
its shape as that of our badge, which is further distinguished
by a shield and the American Eagle superimposed."

—from "Significance of the Scout Badge"

BOY SCOUT CERTIFICATE

This is to certify that . . . .

of . . . . State of . . . .
       Street and City or Town address

Age . . . . Height . . . . Weight . . . .

is a member of . . . . Patrol, of Troop No . . . .

. . . .
                         Scout Master

SCOUT HISTORY

Qualified as **Tenderfoot** . . . . 191. .

Second Class Scout . . . . 191. .

First Class Scout . . . . 191. .

Qualified as **Life Scout** . . . . 191. .

Qualified as **Star Scout** . . . . 191. .

Qualified as **Eagle Scout** . . . . 191. .

Qualified as **Associate Scout** . . . . 191. .

Qualified as **Veteran Scout** . . . . 191. .

Awarded **Honor Medal** . . . . 191. .

Registered with National Headquarters . . . . 191. .

Re-registered . . . . 191. .

Re-registered . . . . 191. .

Re-registered . . . . 191. .

Re-registered . . . . 191. .

Qualified for Merit Badges

Subject	Date	Subject	Date
Agriculture	————	Handicraft	————
Angling	————	Horsemanship	————
Archery	————	Interpreting	————
Architecture	————	Leather Working	————
Art	————	Life Saving	————
Astronomy	————	Machinery	————
Athletics	————	Marksmanship	————
Automobiling	————	Masonry	————
Aviation	————	Mining	————
Bee Keeping	————	Music	————
Bird Study	————	Painting	————
Blacksmithing	————	Pathfinding	————
Bugling	————	Personal Health	————
Business	————	Photography	————
Camping	————	Physical Development	————
Carpentry	————	Pioneering	————
Chemistry	————	Plumbing	————
Civics	————	Poultry Keeping	————
Conservation	————	Printing	————
Cooking	————	Public Health	————
Craftsmanship	————	Safety First	————
Cycling	————	Scholarship	————
Dairying	————	Sculpture	————
Electricity	————	Seamanship	————
Firemanship	————	Signaling	————
First Aid	————	Stalking	————
First Aid to Animals	————	Surveying	————
Forestry	————	Swimming	————
Gardening	————	Taxidermy	————

PREFACE

The Boy Scout Movement has become almost universal, and wherever organized its leaders are glad, as we are, to acknowledge the debt we all owe to Lieut.-Gen. Sir Robert S. S. Baden-Powell, who has done so much to make the movement of interest to boys of all nations.

The BOY SCOUTS OF AMERICA is a corporation formed by a group of men who are anxious that the boys of America should come under the influence of this movement and be built up in all that goes to make character and good citizenship. The affairs of the organization are managed by a National Council, composed of some of the most prominent men of our country, who gladly and freely give their time and money that this purpose may be accomplished.

In the various cities, towns, and villages the welfare of the boy scouts is cared for by local councils, and these councils, like the National Council, are composed of men who are seeking for the boys of the community the very best things.

In order that the work of the boy scouts throughout America may be uniform and intelligent, the National Council has prepared its "Official Handbook," the purpose of which is to furnish to the patrols of the boy scouts advice in practical methods, as well as inspiring information.

The work of preparing this handbook has enlisted the services of men eminently fitted for such work, for each is an expert in his own department, and the Editorial Board feels that the organization is to be congratulated in that such men have been found willing to give their time and ripe experience to this movement. It would be impossible adequately to thank all who by advice and friendly criticism have helped in the preparation of the book, or even to mention their names, but to the authors whose names are attached to the various chapters we acknowledge an especial obligation. Without their friendly help this book could not be. We wish especially to express our appreciation of the helpful suggestions made by Daniel Carter Beard.

We have carefully reëxamined and approved all the material which goes to make up this edition of the handbook, and have

v

tried to make it as complete as possible; nevertheless, no one can be more conscious than we are of the difficulty of providing a book which will meet all the demands of such widely scattered patrols with such varied interests. We have constantly kept in mind the evils that confront the boys of our country and have struck at them by fostering better things. We have considered the needs which the development of the Scout Movement seems to demand and have sought to provide for such changes. Our hope is that the information needed for successful work with boy scouts will be found within the pages of this book.

In these pages and throughout our organization we have made it obligatory upon our scouts that they cultivate courage, loyalty, patriotism, brotherliness, self-control, courtesy, kindness to animals, usefulness, cheerfulness, cleanliness, thrift, purity, and honor. No one can doubt that with such training added to his native gifts the American boy will in the near future, as a man, be an efficient leader in the paths of civilization and peace.

It has been deemed wise to publish all material especially for the aid of scout masters in a separate volume known as "The Scout Masters' Handbook."

We send out our "Official Handbook," therefore, with the earnest wish that many boys may find in it new methods for the proper use of their leisure time and fresh inspiration in their efforts to make their hours of recreation contribute to strong, noble manhood in the days to come.

THE BOY SCOUTS OF AMERICA

WILLIAM D. MURRAY, } Editorial Board.
FRANK PRESBREY,

OFFICERS OF THE NATIONAL COUNCIL

Honorary President: Woodrow Wilson
Honorary Vice-President: William H. Taft
Honorary Vice-President: Theodore Roosevelt
Honorary Vice-President: Daniel Carter Beard

President: Colin H. Livingstone, Washington, D.C.
Vice-President: Mortimer L. Schiff, New York, N. Y.
Vice-President: Milton A. McRae, Detroit, Mich.
Vice-President: Benjamin L. Dulaney, Bristol, Tenn.
Vice-President: Arthur Letts, Los Angeles, Cal.
Vice-President: A. Stamford White, Chicago, Ill.

National Scout Commissioner, Daniel Carter Beard, Flushing, L. I., N. Y.
Treasurer: George D. Pratt, New York City, New York.
Chief Scout Executive: James E. West, N. Y. City.

MEMBERS OF EXECUTIVE BOARD

Term ends March, 1918	*Term ends March*, 1919	*Term ends March*, 1920
Jeremiah W. Jenks	G. Barrett Rich, Jr.	Robert Garrett
Franklin C. Hoyt	Milton A. McRae	John H. Nicholson
Daniel Carter Beard	George D. Porter	Colin H. Livingstone
George D. Pratt	John Sherman Hoyt	Charles C. Jackson
Charles D. Hart	Frank Presbrey	Ernest P. Bicknell
A. Stamford White	William D. Murray	Charles P. Neill
Mortimer L. Schiff	F. L. Seely	Benjamin L. Dulaney

vii

An Act to Incorporate the Boy Scouts of America, and for Other Purposes

Be it enacted by the Senate and House of Representatives of the United States of America in Congress assembled, That Colin H. Livingstone and Ernest P. Bicknell, of Washington, District of Columbia; Benjamin L. Dulaney, of Bristol, Tennessee; Milton A. McRae, of Detroit, Michigan; David Starr Jordan, of Berkeley, California; F. L. Seely, of Asheville, North Carolina; A. Stamford White, of Chicago, Illinois; Daniel Carter Beard, of Flushing, New York; George D. Pratt, of Brooklyn, New York; *Dr. Charles D. Hart. Philadelphia. Pa.; Franklin C. Hoyt, Jeremiah W. Jenks, Charles P. Neill, Frank Presbrey, Edgar M. Robinson, Mortimer L. Schiff, and James E. West, of New York, New York; G. Parrett Rich, junior, of Buffalo, New York; Robert Garrett, of Baltimore, Maryland; John Sherman Hoyt, of Norwalk, Connecticut; Charles C. Jackson, of Boston, Massachusetts; John H. Nicholson, of Pittsburgh, Pennsylvania; William D. Murray, of Plainfield, New Jersey; and George D. Porter, of Philadelphia, Pennsylvania, their associates and successors, are hereby created a body corporate and politic of the District of Columbia, where its domicile shall be.

SEC. 2. That the name of this corporation shall be "Boy Scouts of America," and by that name it shall have perpetual succession, with power to sue and be sued in courts of law and equity within the jurisdiction of the United States; to hold such real and personal estate as shall be necessary for corporate purposes, and to receive real and personal property by gift, devise, or bequest; to adopt a seal, and the same to alter and destroy at pleasure; to have offices and conduct its business and affairs within and without the District of Columbia and in the several States and Territories of the United States; to make and adopt by-laws, rules, and regulations not inconsistent with the laws of the United States of America, or any State thereof, and generally to do all such acts and things (including the establishment of regulations for the election of associates and successors) as may be necessary to carry into effect the provisions of this Act and promote the purposes of said corporation.

SEC. 3. That the purpose of this corporation shall be to promote, through organization, and coöperation with other agencies, the ability of boys to do things for themselves and others, to train them in scoutcraft, and to teach them patriotism, courage, self-reliance, and kindred virtues, using the methods which are now in common use by boy scouts.

SEC. 4. That said corporation may acquire, by way of gift, all the assets of the existing national organization of Boy Scouts, a corporation under the laws of the District of Columbia, and defray and provide for any debts or liabilities to the discharge of which said assets shall be applicable; but said corporation shall have no power to issue certificates of stock or to declare or pay dividends, its object and purposes being solely of a benevolent character and not for pecuniary profit to its members.

---

*Omitted by error in bill which passed Congress.

SEC 5. That the governing body of the said Boy Scouts of America shall consist of an executive board composed of citizens of the United States. The number, qualifications, and terms of office of members of the executive boards shall be prescribed by the by-laws. The persons mentioned in the first section of this Act shall constitute the first executive board and shall serve until their successors are elected and have qualified. Vacancies in the executive board shall be filled by a majority vote of the remaining members thereof. The by-laws may prescribe the number of members of the executive board necessary to constitute a quorum of the board, which number may be less than a majority of the whole number of the board. The executive board shall have power to make and to amend the by-laws, and, by a two-thirds vote of the whole board at a meeting called for this purpose, may authorize and cause to be executed mortgages and liens upon the property of the corporation. The executive board may, by resolution passed by a majority of the whole board, designate three or more of their number to constitute an executive or governing committee, of which a majority shall constitute a quorum, which committee, to the extent provided in said resolution or in the by-laws of the corporation, shall have and exercise the powers of the executive board in the management of the business affairs of the corporation, and may have power to authorize the seal of the corporation to be affixed to all papers which may require it. The executive board, by the affirmative vote of a majority of the whole board, may appoint any other standing committees, and such standing committees shall have and may exercise such powers as shall be conferred or authorized by the by-laws. With the consent in writing and pursuant to an affirmative vote of a majority of the members of said corporation, the executive board shall have authority to dispose in any manner of the whole property of the corporation.

SEC. 6. That an annual meeting of the incorporators, their associates and successors, shall be held once in every year after the year of incorporation, at such time and place as shall be prescribed in the by-laws, when the annual reports of the officers and executive board shall be presented and members of the executive board elected for the ensuing year. Special meetings of the corporation may be called upon such notice as may be prescribed in the by-laws. The number of members which shall constitute a quorum at any annual or special meeting shall be prescribed in the by-laws. The members and executive board shall have power to hold their meetings and keep the seal, books, documents, and papers of the corporation within or without the District of Columbia.

SEC. 7. That said corporation shall have the sole and exclusive right to have and to use, in carrying out its purposes, all emblems and badges, descriptive or designating marks, and words or phrases now or heretofore used by the Boy Scouts of America in carrying out its program, it being distinctly and definitely understood, however, that nothing in this Act shall interfere or conflict with established or vested rights.

SEC. 8. That on or before the first day of April of each year the said Boy Scouts of America shall make and transmit to Congress a report of its proceedings for the year ending December thirty-first preceding, including a full, complete, and itemized report of receipts and expenditures, of whatever kind.

SEC. 9. That Congress shall have the right to repeal, alter, or amend this Act at any time.

Approved, June 15, 1916.

WHAT IS A BOY SCOUT?

A Glimpse of the Life of the Boy Who "Belongs"

A SCOUT! He enjoys a hike through the woods more than he does a walk over the city's streets. He can tell north or south or east or west by the "signs." He can tie a knot that will hold, he can climb a tree which seems impossible to others, he can swim a river, he can pitch a tent, he can mend a tear in his trousers, he can tell you which fruits and seeds are poisonous and which are not, he can sight nut-bearing trees from a distance; if living near ocean or lake he can reef a sail or take his trick at the wheel, and if near any body of water at all he can pull an oar or use paddles and sculls; in the woods he knows the names of birds and animals; in the water he tells you the different varieties of fish.

A scout walks through the woods with silent tread. No dry twigs snap under his feet and no loose stones turn over and throw him off his balance. His eyes are keen and he sees many things that others do not see. He sees tracks and signs which reveal to him the nature and habits of the creatures that made them. He knows how to stalk birds and animals and study them in their natural haunts. He sees much, but is little seen.

A scout, like an old frontiersman, does not shout his wisdom from the housetops. He possesses the quiet power that comes from knowledge. He speaks softly and answers questions modestly. He knows a braggart but he does not challenge him, allowing the boaster to expose his ignorance by his own loose-wagging tongue.

A scout holds his honor to be his most precious possession, and he would die rather than have it stained. He knows what is his duty and all obligations imposed by duty he fulfills of his own free will. His sense of honor is his only taskmaster, and his honor he guards as jealously as did the knights of old. In this manner a scout wins the confidence and respect of all people.

A scout can kindle a fire in the forest on the wettest day and he seldom uses more than one match. When no matches can be had he can still have a fire, for he knows the secret of the rubbing sticks used by the Indians, and he knows how to start a blaze with only his knife blade and a piece of flint. He knows, also, the danger of forest fires, and he kindles a blaze that will not spread. The fire once started, what a meal he can prepare out there in the open! Just watch him and compare his appetite with that of a boy who lounges at a lunch counter in a crowded city. He knows the unwritten rules of the campfire and he contributes his share to the pleasures of the council. He also knows when to sit silent before the ruddy embers and give his mind free play.

A scout practises self-control, for he knows that men who master problems in the world must first master themselves. He keeps a close guard on his temper and never makes a silly spectacle of himself by losing his head. He keeps a close guard on his tongue, for he knows that loud speech is often a cloak to ignorance, that swearing is a sign of weakness, and that untruthfulness shatters the confidence of others. He keeps a close guard on his appetite and eats moderately of food which will make him strong; he never uses alcoholic liquors because he does not wish to poison his body; he desires a clear, active brain, so he avoids tobacco.

A scout never flinches in the face of danger, for he knows that at such a time every faculty must be alert to preserve his safety and that of others. He knows what to do in case of fire, or panic, or shipwreck; he trains his mind to direct and his body to act. In all emergencies he sets an example of resourcefulness, coolness, and courage, and considers the safety of others before that of himself. He is especially considerate of the helpless and weak.

A scout can make himself known to a brother scout wherever he may be by a method which only scouts can know. He has brothers in every city in the land and in every country in the world. Wherever he goes he can give his signs and be assured of a friendly welcome. He can talk with a brother scout without making a sound or he can make known his message by imitating the click of a telegraph key.

A scout is kind to everything that lives. He knows that horses, dogs, and cats have their rights and he respects them. A scout prides himself upon doing "good turns," and no day in his life is complete unless he has been of aid to some person.

A scout does not run away or call for help when an accident occurs. If a person is cut he knows how to stop the flow of blood and gently and carefully bind up the wound. If a person is burned his knowledge tells him how to alleviate the suffering. If any one is dragged from the water unconscious, a scout at once sets to work to restore respiration and circulation. He knows that not a minute can be lost.

A scout knows that people expect more of him than they do of other boys and he governs his conduct so that no word of reproach can truthfully be brought against the great brotherhood to which he has pledged his loyalty. He seeks always to make the word "Scout" worthy of the respect of people whose opinions have value. He wears his uniform worthily.

A scout knows his city as well as he knows the trails in the forest. He can guide a stranger wherever he desires to go, and this knowledge of short-cuts saves him many needless steps. He knows where the police stations are located, where the fire-alarm boxes are placed, where the nearest doctor lives, where the hospitals are, and which is the quickest way to reach them. He knows the names of the city officials and the nature of their duties. A scout is proud of his city and freely offers his services when he can help.

A scout is a patriot and is always ready to serve his country at a minute's notice. He loves Old Glory and knows the proper forms of offering it respect. He never permits its folds to touch the ground. He knows how his country is governed and who are the men in high authority. He desires a strong body, an alert mind, and an unconquerable spirit, so that he may serve his country in any need. He patterns his life after those of great Americans who have had a high sense of duty and who have served the nation well.

A scout chooses as his motto "Be Prepared," and he seeks to prepare himself for anything—to rescue a companion, to ford a stream, to gather firewood, to help strangers, to distinguish right from wrong, to serve his fellowmen, his country, and his God—always to "Be Prepared."

CONTENTS

HANDBOOK FOR BOYS

CHAPTER I

SCOUTCRAFT*

Aim of the Scout Movement

The aim of the Boy Scouts is to supplement the various existing educational agencies, and to promote the ability in boys to do things for themselves and others. It is not the aim to set

Organizations using scout idea

up a new organization to parallel in its purposes others already established. The opportunity is afforded these organizations, however, to introduce into their programs unique features appealing to interests which are universal among boys. The

*Note: This chapter is the work of a number of committees of experts and officers of the National Council.

Special credit should be given Sir Robert Baden-Powell for permission to use material in "Scouting for Boys"; to John L. Alexander for editorial work, and the Minute Tapioca Company for use of the illustrations by Gordon Grant.

3

method is summed up in the term Scoutcraft, and is a combination of observation, deduction, and handiness, or the ability to do things. Scoutcraft includes instruction in Safety First methods, First Aid, Life Saving, Tracking, Signaling, Cycling, Nature Study, Seamanship, Campcraft, Woodcraft, Chivalry, Patriotism, and other subjects. This is accomplished in games and team play, and is pleasure, not work, for the boy. All that is needed is the out of doors, a group of boys, and a competent leader.

What Scouting Means

In all ages there have been scouts, the place of the scout being on the danger line of the army or at the outposts, protecting those of his company who confide in his care.

The army scout was the soldier who was chosen out of all the army to go out on the skirmish line.

The pioneer, who was out on the edge of the wilderness guarding the men, women, and children in the stockade, was also a scout. Should he fall asleep, or lose control of his faculties, or fail on his watch, then the lives of the men, women, and children paid the forfeit, and the scout lost his honor.

But there have been other kinds of scouts besides war scouts and frontier scouts. They have been the men of all ages who have gone out on new and strange adventures, and through their work have benefited the people of the earth. Thus, Columbus discovered America, the Pilgrim Fathers founded New England, the early English settlers colonized Jamestown, and the Dutch built up New York. In the same way the hardy Scotch-Irish pushed west and made a new home for the American people beyond the Alleghenies and the Rockies.

Peace Scouts

These peace scouts had to be as well prepared as any war scouts. They had to know scoutcraft. They had to know how to live in the woods, and be able to find their way anywhere, without other chart or compass than the sun and stars, besides being able to interpret the meaning of the slightest signs of the forest and the foot tracks of animals and men.

They had to know how to live so as to keep healthy and strong, to face any danger that came their way, and to help one another. These scouts of old were accustomed to take chances with death, and they did not hesitate to give up their lives in helping their comrades or country. In fact, they left everything behind them, comfort and peace, in order to push forward into the wilderness beyond. And much of this they did because they felt it to be their duty.

These little-known scouts could be multiplied indefinitely by going back into the past ages and reading the histories and stories of the knights of King Arthur, of the Crusaders, and of the great explorers and navigators of the world.

In camp

Wherever there have been heroes, there have been scouts, and to be a scout means to be prepared to do the right thing at the right moment, no matter what the consequences may be.

The way for achievement in big things is the preparing of one's self for doing the big things — by going into training and doing the little things well. It was this characteristic of Livingstone, the great explorer, that made him what he was, and that has marked the career of all good scouts.

Things Scouts Must Know

To be a good scout one should know something about the woods and the animals that inhabit them, and how to care for one's self when camping.

The habits of animals can be studied by stalking them and watching them in their native haunts.

The scout should never kill an animal or other living creature needlessly. There is more sport in stalking animals to photograph them, and in coming to know their habits than in hunting to kill.

Woodcraft

Woodcraft is one of the activities of the Boy Scouts of America and means the becoming acquainted with things that are out of doors. It includes the tracking of animals by the marks left by their hoofs, and by stealing out upon these animals, not to do them harm, but for the sake of studying their habits and getting acquainted with them.

In the woods

It also means to be able to distinguish the different birds — to know a song sparrow from an ordinary sparrow; to know a thrush from a lark; and to be able to distinguish the birds by their plumage and by their song. It means to understand the reptile and snake life, which sometimes is abundant in our forests, and to actually know that there are only three kinds of snakes that are dangerous — the rattlesnake, the moccasin, and the copperhead. All the other kinds are harmless, and part of woodcraft is to know the habits of these reptiles and to look upon them as friends.

It also means to know the fishes, to tell the pools where the muscalonge can be caught, know the ripples where the trout sport, know where the pickerel and the perch have their haunts, and not only to enjoy the sport of pursuing them, but the delight of eating them baked or cooked in the woodman's style. It means to be able to know the trees, and to be able to tell by the foliage and bark the difference between the oak and the maple, and the birch and the chestnut, as well as the other trees which grow so abundantly in our woods. It means to be in close touch with nature. To understand plant life in the different ferns and grasses; to know which flowers bloom in the spring, which in the summer, and which in the fall — in short, to get so intimately in touch with nature as to know her at her best and to love her in her many moods — to truly enjoy this great world which God has made.

It means to know the secrets of the streams and the trails in the forest. To know the stars by name and to be able to find one's way by them. It means to understand and appreciate the whispers of the sea as well as the hoarse dash of the ocean waves against the rocky coast. It means to appreciate the song of the surf as it dashes over the pebbles; and, in fact, to live and understand the great outdoor life which is all about us.

Campcraft

Camp life means to live under canvas, away from the piles of brick and stone that we generally call our cities. It means to be in the open air, to breathe pure oxygen, to sleep upon "a bed of boughs beside the trail," to hear the whisper of the trees from amidst the fragrance of the "couch of boughs," to look at the camp-fire and the stars when the sun has set, to ply the oar or wield the paddle in the moonlight; to dive in the cool waters of the lake or river at the dawn; to eat the plain, substantial food of the forests and the wilds, with the delicacy of the fish and fruit which they afford; and to come heart to heart with nature in constant communion with the woods, the mountains, and streams — all of this is camping, and all of this is good.

But the camp affords a better opportunity than this. It offers the finest method for a boy's education. Between the ages of twelve and eighteen years the interests of a boy are general and reach all the way from the catching of minnows and tadpoles to finding God in the stars. Each day brings him new discoveries, and each night sends him back to his camp bed, to sleep among the branches of the balsam or fir, with an unspeakable joy tugging at his heart.   A summer spent like this puts red blood in the boy's veins, a glow of health to his cheek, the hardness of steel to his muscles and sinews, and fits him for the struggle of the school or the shop that is going to test his endurance during the long winter months.

The life of a camp is profitable because of its varied activities. A boy learns to build his own bed out of fallen timber, to make his own mattress out of fir or balsam tips or by weaving it out of grass; to cook his own meals; to make his own fishing equipment; to catch his own fish; to build his own fire; to keep his camp clean, and in short to rely upon himself and to take care of himself.

In God's out of doors

He learns self-resourcefulness in this outdoor life faster than he would anywhere else; and somehow or other, every lake, and tree, and star, and pool of water come to be his personal friends, so that no matter where he is, he is never alone; and whether in solitude or with companions, is cheerful and sunny, and always ready to help others.

Some boys cannot go to camp for a summer, while others cannot even go to camp for one week or two weeks, but almost any boy, no matter in what city he lives or how big it may be, can go out into God's out of doors for a week-end hiking party or camp.

Prevention

In the past our scouts have done good scouting along lines of first aid to the injured.   To-day we have added a new field of activity.   The Watchword is "Be Careful—Safety First."

It is far better to prevent an accident than to apply first aid after it happens.

The scout of to-day knows that the prevention of accident.

and injuries by all possible means is a personal duty that he owes not only to himself but also to his fellowmen.

Self-preservation is the first law of nature. In the days of our old scouts this instinct enabled them to evade enemies and escape accidents. Still earlier some of our ancestors lived in caves, thus avoiding injury from man and beast. Transplanted into our modern cities, only the most sturdy and alert could survive. In those early days instinct sufficed to protect them. The changing conditions of civilization have dulled that instinct and have created dangers against which instinct cannot guard them.

A scout will prevent accidents because of his training in observation through scouting. A scout can apply his knowledge of prevention in the home, in the school, on the street. Not only does he apply his knowledge in this way, but he can apply it to society at large. Through knowledge acquired on his hikes and in his daily intercourse, he becomes a master of preventive principles as applied to his community, its traffic regulations, its building laws, its sanitary regulations, and its industries. He distinguishes between carefulness and cowardice, and he has the courage to refuse a dare that involves foolish risk.

Life Saving

The Boy Scouts of America are also taught to make themselves valuable to the community by saving life. Accidents occur every day. Some one falls and breaks a bone. Or there is an accident by rail or by water. Never a day passes in the history of the world but many are seriously injured by some unsuspected and unforeseen happening, and it is the part of the boy scout to live up to his motto, which is "BE PREPARED" so as to be able to relieve the unfortunate one who is hurt or wounded in any of these happenings.

For this reason the boy scout needs to know what we call "First Aid to the Injured." For this purpose he has to know something about the structure of the human body. He has to know the main bones, the joints, the muscles. He has to know how the blood circulates and whether the veins or the arteries carry the blood to or from the heart. He has to know about the method of breathing, and also the method of digesting food. He has to know something about the nervous system, and the five senses of touch, sight, taste, smell, and hearing. He also has to know something about the skin.

Understanding the construction of the body, he should know how to bandage a broken limb. He should know how to use a

tourniquet for the stopping of the flow of blood. He ought
to know what to do in case of a faint. He ought to know what
a compress is, and how stimulants are used.

There are various kinds of accidents of which a boy scout
ought to have sufficient knowledge to handle rightly. There
are those injuries in which the skin is not pierced or broken,
such as bruises, strains, sprains, dislocations, and fractures.
There are those injuries in which the skin is pierced or broken,
such as wounds and hemorrhage, nosebleed, abdominal wounds,
wounds in which foreign bodies remain.

There are injuries from local effects of heat and cold and

Boy Scouts to the rescue

electricity, such as burns, and scalds, and frost-bite. Then
there are injuries which produce unconsciousness, such as
shock, fainting, injury to the brain, sunstroke, heat-stroke,
freezing, suffocation, intoxication, besides the accident of
poisoning by drugs or in some other manner.

Then there are injuries which result from indoor and outdoor sport, as in the gymnasium, in a baseball or football
game, in Fourth of July celebrations, in boating, skating,
swimming, shooting, fishing, automobiling, and in camping
and outings.

Not only this, but there are hundreds of cases of drowning
every year, and the boy scout ought to know how to rescue

those who are in peril of their lives by water, how to produce artificial respiration, and how to act in every case of accident and emergency. To know what to do, and to "Be Prepared" to do it, is one of the privileges and duties and the glories of every boy scout.

Citizenship

The great aim of the Boy Scouts of America is to make every boy scout a better citizen. It aims to touch him physically—in the campcraft and woodcraft of the outdoor life in order that he may have strength in after days to give the best he has to the city and community in which he lives, as well as to the

Practical instruction   Helping the police

nation of which he is a part. It seeks to develop him by observation and the knowing of things far and near, so that later on when he enters business life he may be alert and keen and so be able to add to the wealth of the nation. It teaches him chivalry and unselfishness, duty, charity, thrift, and loyalty; so that no matter what should happen in the business or social or national life, he may always be a true gentleman, seeking to give sympathy, help, encouragement, and good cheer to those about him. It teaches him life saving, in order that he may be able in dire accidents and peril by land and sea to know just what to do to relieve others of suffering. It teaches him endurance, in order that he may guard his health by being temperate, eating pure food, keeping himself clean; so that being possessed of good health, he may be always ready to serve his country in the hour of her need. It teaches him patriotism by telling him about the country he lives in, her history, her army and navy, in order that he may become a good citizen and do those things which every citizen ought to do to make the community and land that he lives in the best community and land in the world.

Good citizenship means to the boy scout not merely the doing of things which he ought to do when he becomes a man, such as voting, keeping the law, and paying his taxes, but the looking for opportunities to do good turns by safeguarding the interests of the community and by the giving of himself in unselfish service to the town or city, and even the nation, of which he is a part. It means that he will seek public office when the public office needs him. It means that he will stand for the equal opportunity and justice which the Declaration of Independence and the Constitution guarantees. It means that in every duty of life he may be on the right side and loyal to the best interests of the State and Nation. By the "good turn" that he does daily as a boy scout, he is training himself for the unselfish service that our cities and land need so much.

A Boy Scout's Religion

Scouting presents greater opportunities for the devel pment of the boy religiously than does any other movement instituted solely for the boys. Its aim to develop the boy physically, mentally, and spiritually is being realized very widely.

The movement has been developed on such broad lines as to embrace all classes, all creeds, and at the same time, to allow the greatest possible independence to individual organizations, officers, and boys.

Scout Training Neither Military nor Anti-Military

The boy scout movement neither promotes nor discourages military training, its chief concern being the development of character and personal efficiency of teen-age boys. To accomplish this, the program necessarily includes special attention to the virtues of loyalty, reverence, courtesy, chivalry, bravery, obedience, order, resourcefulness, cleanliness, cheerfulness, kindness, temperance, neatness, moral courage, alertness, physical strength, and endurance.

To this end, special instruction is given in patriotism, signaling, cooking, camping, sanitation, first aid to the injured, how to care for oneself in the open, chivalry, woodcraft, personal hygiene, public hygiene, and the general principles conducive to good discipline. While some of these things are included in the ordinary preparation for the responsibilities of the life of the soldier, in the scout program they are all indispensable if a scout is to live up to the motto, "Be Prepared" and to fulfill his obligations as a citizen in times of peace, no matter how humble his position may be. This means personal efficiency and character development, and thus makes the boy scout movement in reality as strong a factor as any other one agency which the country now has for preparedness.

The uniform, the patrol, the troop, the special scout drills and activities are not for military tactics, nor can they be fairly considered as military training when these terms are correctly used. They are for the uniformity, the harmony, and rhythm of spirit which boys learn in scouting. It is in the wearing of the uniform, and the doing of things together as scouts that they absorb the force and truth of the Scout Law which states that "a scout is a friend to all and a brother to every other scout." The rifle, the sword, and other purely military accoutrement are not included in the equipment of troops of Boy Scouts of America.

A Scout is Chivalrous

Obviously a boy scout must be chivalrous. That is, he should be as manly as the knights or pioneers of old. He should be unselfish. He should show courage. He must do his duty. He should show benevolence and thrift. He should be loyal to his country. He should be obedient to his parents, and show respect to those who are his superiors. He should be very courteous to women. One of his obligations is to do a good turn every day to some one. He should be cheerful and seek self-improvement, and should make a career for himself.

All these things were characteristics of the old-time American scouts and of King Arthur's knights. Their honor was sacred. They were courteous and polite to women and children, protected the weak and aged, and helped others to live better. They trained themselves to be strong, so as to be able to protect their country against enemies. They kept themselves strong and healthy, constantly prepared. So the boy scout of to-day must be chivalrous, manly, and gentlemanly.

When he gets up in the morning he may tie a knot in his necktie, and leave the necktie outside his vest until he has done a good turn.   Another way to remind himself is to wear his scout badge reversed until he has done his good turn.   The good turn may not be a very big thing—help an old lady across the street; remove a banana skin from the pavement so that people may not fall; remove from streets or roads broken glass, dangerous

The daily good turn

to automobile or bicycle tires; give water to a thirsty horse; or deeds similar to these.

A Scout Knows How to Save Life

The scout also ought to know how to save life.   He ought to be able to make a stretcher; to throw a rope to a drowning person; to drag an unconscious person from a burning building, and to resuscitate a person overcome by gas fumes.   He ought also to know the method of stopping runaway horses, and he should have the presence of mind and the skill to calm a panic, and deal with street and other accidents.   Prevention is the scout's watchword if the scout is to "Be Prepared" to save life. A scout should acquaint himself with every device that will aid him in this service.

A Scout Keeps Himself Healthy and Strong

This means also that a boy scout must always be in the pink of condition.   A boy cannot do things like these unless he is healthy and strong. Therefore, he must be systematically taking exercise, playing games, running, and walking. It means that he must sleep enough hours to give him necessary strength, and if possible, sleep very much in the open, or at least with the windows of his bedroom open both summer and winter.

Scout requirements

It means also that he should take a cold bath often, rubbing dry with a rough towel. He should breathe through the nose and not through the mouth. He should at all times train himself to endure hardships.

A Scout Knows and Loves His Country

In addition to this a scout should be devoted to his country. He should know his country, how many states there are in it, what are its natural resources, scope, and boundaries. He ought to know something of its history, its early settlers, and of the great deeds that won his land; how they settled along the banks of the James River; how Philadelphia, New York, and other great cities were founded; how the Pilgrim Fathers established New England and laid the foundation for our national life; how the scouts of the Middle West saved all that great section of the country for the Republic. He ought to know how Texas became part of the United States, and how our national heroes stretched out their hands north and south, east and west, to make one great united country.

He ought to know the history of the important wars. He ought to know about our army and navy flags and the insignia of rank of our officers. He ought to know the kind of government he lives under, and what it means to live in a republic.

Electrician   Pathfinder

He ought to know what is expected of him as a citizen of his state and nation, and what to do to help the people among whom he lives.

Scout Characteristics

There are other things which a scout ought to know and which should be characteristic of him if he is going to be the kind of scout for which the Boy Scouts of America stands.

A Scout is Obedient

To be a good scout a boy must learn to obey the orders of his patrol leader, scoutmaster, and scout commissioner. He must learn to obey before he is able to command. He should so learn to discipline and control himself that he will have no thought but to obey the orders of his officers. He should keep such a strong grip on his own life that he will not allow himself to do anything which is ignoble, or which will harm his life or weaken his powers of endurance.

Obedience

A Scout is Courteous

A scout is always courteous. He is polite to women, children, old people, and the weak and helpless, and ought to have a command of polite language. He ought to show that he is a true gentleman by doing little things for others.

A Scout is Loyal

Loyalty is also a scout characteristic. A scout ought to be loyal to all to whom he has obligations. He ought to stand up courageously for the truth, for his parents and friends.

A Scout Has Respect for Himself and Others

Another scout virtue is self-respect. He ought to refuse to accept "tips" from any one. He ought to work for the money he gets.

For this same reason he should never look down upon any one who may be poorer than himself, or envy any one richer than himself. A scout's self-respect will cause him to value his own standing and make him sympathetic toward others who may be, on the one hand, worse off, or, on the other hand, better off as far as wealth is concerned. Scouts know neither a lower nor a higher class, for a scout is one who is a comrade to all and who is ready to share that which he has with others.

A Scout's Honor is to be Trusted

The most important scout characteristic is that of honor. Indeed, this is the basis of all scout virtues and is closely allied to that of self-respect. When a scout promises to do a thing on his honor, he is bound to do it. The honor of a scout will not permit of anything but the highest and the best and the manliest. The honor of a scout is a sacred thing, and cannot be lightly set aside or trampled on.

A Scout is Faithful

Faithfulness to duty is another one of the scout virtues. When it is a scout's duty to do something, he dare not shirk. A scout is faithful to his own interest and the interests of others. He is true to his country and his God.

A Scout is Cheerful

A scout is cheerful. As the scout law intimates, he must never go about with a sulky air. He must always be bright and smiling, and as the humorist says, "Must always see the doughnut and not the hole." A bright face and a cheery word spread like sunshine from one to another. It is the scout's duty to be a sunshine-maker in the world.

A Scout is Kind to Animals

Another scout trait is that of thoughtfulness, even to animals; not merely the thoughtfulness that eases a horse from the pain of a badly fitting harness, or gives food and drink to an animal that is in need, but also that which keeps a boy from throwing a stone at a cat or tying a tin can on a dog's tail. If a boy does not prove his thoughtfulness and friendship for animals, it is quite certain that he never will be really helpful to his comrades or to the men, women, and children who may need his care.

The Scout Good Turn

And then the final and chief test of the scout is the doing of a good turn to somebody every day, quietly and without boasting. This is the proof of the scout. It is practical religion, and a boy honors God best when he helps others most. A boy may wear all the scout uniforms made, all the scout badges ever manufactured, know all the woodcraft, campcraft, scoutcraft, and other activities of boy scouts, and yet never be a real boy scout. To be a real boy scout means the doing of

Scoutcraft 19

a good turn every day with the proper motive, and if this be done, the boy has a right to be classed with the great scouts that have been of such service to their country. To accomplish this a scout should observe the scout law.

How to Become A Scout

Any boy who has reached his twelfth birthday may become a scout by applying to the scoutmaster of the troop already started in his town. If he lives in a large city where there is a scout commissioner or scout executive, it would be better to apply to that officer. If there is no scout organization in his town, a troop should be organized. To do this, first get a copy of the official Handbook For Boys from a local book store or from National Headquarters, 200 Fifth Avenue, New York City. Read the book carefully and get other boys interested. It is desirable to have eight boys form a patrol.

Troops of boy scouts should be connected with some school, church, or other institution when practical. The head of the institution should certify to his approval of the organization of the troop of boy scouts upon the application blank which the institution forwards to National Headquarters when it requests a charter. The institution should, through its proper authorities, furnish a committee of at least three responsible persons who shall be known as a troop committee. This troop committee is responsible for the selection of a scoutmaster. The best way for boys to become scouts is for them to apply to their Sunday School teacher or superintendent, or some leader interested in boys' work in their home town, and have him make himself responsible for the organization of a troop as suggested. In all cases the consent of the parent or guardian should be given. If it is difficult to secure help in organizing a troop, National Headquarters will gladly give assistance.

Patrol and Troop

Boy scouts are organized in patrols and troops.

A patrol consists of eight boys, one of whom becomes patrol leader and another assistant patrol leader.

A troop consists of not more than four patrols, preferably three, as a scoutmaster can do better work with a small group of boys than with a large one.

Where Organized

Troops are usually organized in connection with a Sunday School, Boys' Club, Playground, Public School, Settlement

House, or some other institution engaged in work for boys. This insures a troop committee, responsible supervision, a suitable meeting place, and proper support and permanency of the troop. Under special circumstances and where it is impossible to make use of an existing institution, troops are sometimes organized independently among the boys of a neighborhood.

The Scoutmaster

Every troop of scouts has as a leader a man who is known as scoutmaster. He receives a commission annually from

Scoutmaster at work

the National Council of the Boy Scouts of America upon the recommendation of the troop committee. This commission certifies as to his fitness and gives him authority to act as scoutmaster in carrying out the boy scout program in accordance with the official handbooks.

He must be at least twenty-one years of age and is chosen because of good moral character and his interest in work with boys. He attends all of the meetings and outings of the troop and is responsible for the general program and supervision of the work of the troop.

Blanks may be secured from the local or National Council for the use of men recommended for commissions as scoutmasters.

Every scoutmaster should have the official Handbook for Boys and the official Handbook for Scoutmasters.

Assistant Scoutmaster

Each troop has one or more assistant scoutmasters who receive their commissions annually from the National Council of the Boy Scouts of America upon the recommendation of the scoutmaster and the troop committee.

Assistant scoutmasters must be at least eighteen years of age and are often selected and promoted because of their experience as members of troops, and proficiency in scouting. The assistant scoutmaster performs such duties as may be assigned by the scoutmaster. (See Scoutmasters' Handbook.)

Patrol Leader

The patrol leader is one of the members of a patrol and may be selected either by appointment by the scoutmaster, or elected by the patrol. He is responsible for the discipline of his patrol to the scoutmaster and his assistants. He coöperates in giving instruction to the patrol in the scout program and preparing scouts for the various tests. The patrol leader may have as assistant one of the other members of his patrol.

Scout Scribe

Every troop from time to time elects or details one of its members to act as scout scribe, or troop secretary. This honor should be given to a boy who is proficient in scouting and is ca-

SCOUT SCRIBE BADGES

Tenderfoot   Second Class   First Class

pable of keeping the necessary troop records under the supervision of the scoutmaster or one of his assistants. The scout scribe furnishes the local scout headquarters or scout papers, and the official magazine of the National Council, with items of interest about scouting activities of his troop from time to time. He makes out an annual report to be sent to the local and National Councils and performs such other duties as the scoutmaster may direct. (The design of the badge of the scout scribe is a tenderfoot, second class or first class badge, according to the scout's rank, with two pens crossed beneath it.)

Troop Committee

Each chartered troop of the Boy Scouts of America shall be under the supervision of a troop or boys' work committee, consisting of three or more male citizens of the United States, twenty-one years of age or over, selected by the institution with which the troop is connected or, in the case of an independent troop, of those who make application for the troop charter, one of whom shall be designated as chairman.

If for any reason it becomes necessary for the scoutmaster to discontinue to serve, the troop committee assumes control of the troop and all of its property, until a suitable successor receives his commission from the National Council.

Term of Service

The boy scout program is so big and broad and attractive as to make it possible for the boy to maintain his interest indefinitely. No boy becomes too old to take some active part in scouting. Indeed the slogan "Once a scout, always a scout" is becoming generally accepted.

Very often the older boy serves as an expert instructor or as an assistant scoutmaster. There are abundant opportunities for the older boy to definitely take part in scouting and be of real service.

The boy scout scheme makes it possible for every boy who once takes the Scout Oath and subscribes to the Scout Law to permanently retain affiliation with the movement in some form, or to sever his official relationship with honor and credit to himself and the boy scout movement.

Associate Scout

The time is past when a boy drops out of the movement by simply ceasing to attend meetings or failing to pay dues.

Active members of a troop of boy scouts ordinarily hold regular weekly meetings. This is the condition of membership which is insisted upon wherever possible. However, when in the judgment of the scoutmaster and the troop committee it is impossible for a boy to maintain active membership in any troop, arrangements may be made according to the facts in each case to enroll the boy as an associate member of the troop upon the following conditions:

1. The associate scout obligates himself to observe the Scout Oath and Law and do his "daily good turn" in the same way as an active member of the troop.

2. He obligates himself to attend during the year such troop meetings as are agreed upon at the time he is enrolled as an associate scout. In no case can this be less than one meeting a year and it may be one a month or every meeting during the vacation period.

3. He agrees to do all in his power to advance himself in scouting activities, according to the circumstances in his case. In case of removal to another community, arrangements may be made whereby an associate scout may have the coöperation of local scout authorities in passing second class, first class, and merit badge tests.

4. He agrees to hold himself as a scout in readiness in case of any disaster or calamity requiring the services of his troop, and in case of removal to another community to make known his presence and place of residence to the scout authorities so that he may be available there for services in any emergency.

5. An associate scout pays his registration fees in the same manner as an active member of the troop.

Pioneer Scout

In case it is not possible for a boy to affiliate with a troop and attend at least one meeting a year, he may upon application be enrolled direct with the National Headquarters as a pioneer scout. He is entitled to all the benefits and privileges granted to regular scouts.

Blanks may be secured upon request setting forth all of the conditions of enrollment.

Veteran Scout

After five years of service in the movement a first class scout is entitled to the designation of veteran scout, upon the following conditions:

1. He shall agree to live up to the scout obligations for life.

2. Keep the local scout authorities of the community in which he lives informed as to his availability for service to the community in case of any emergency.

3. He agrees to take an active part in the promotion of the cause of scouting as the circumstances and conditions in his case permit, no matter where he may be, and, if possible, by service as a scout instructor, assistant scoutmaster, scoutmaster, member of a troop committee or local council, or as a contributor to the boy scout movement.

A veteran scout in renewing his scout oath to do his duty to God and his country and to keep himself physically strong, mentally awake, morally straight, and prepared for any emergency, should bear in mind the advantages that camp life affords. In maintaining his personal efficiency, he should avail himself not only of opportunities for attending outdoor camps, but he should, by following a definitely planned course of physical training, keep himself fit and alert and thus be constantly prepared for service in any emergency. A special badge and a certificate will be awarded to veteran scouts upon request.

Certificate of Service

Should it become necessary for a scout to sever his relationship with a troop of scouts after one, two, three, four, five, or more years of service, he may be given a certificate of service upon the recommendation of the scoutmaster and the troop committee. In every such case it must be shown that the scout has maintained a creditable record, that his reasons for leaving the troop are satisfactory, and that he has agreed to maintain his scout obligation.

Certificates for three, four, or five years' service are awarded on some public occasion with the parents, friends, and members of the troop in attendance, when a statement is made as to the boy's record and the reason for his ceasing to be a scout. These certificates will not be granted for periods of less than one year each, and only at the time of the re-registration of the troop. A nominal fee will be charged for these certificates.

The certificates will be made more valuable and the method of presentation more formal and impressive according to the length of service for which they are granted. These certificates shall be available for associate as well as for active scouts.

Troop Registration

A minimum registration fee of $3.00 is required annually from each troop. If more than twelve boys are registered 25 cents must be paid for each boy. The entire amount is to be paid to the treasurer of the National Council through the Local Council if there be one. It is recommended that the troop registration be earned by the troop as a whole or by the boys individually. Many troops pay registration fees from their troop treasury.

Registration entitles each member of the troop to an individual pocket membership certificate and pays the expense for a year's subscription to BOYS' LIFE, the official magazine, which is sent to the scoutmaster, and for SCOUTING, the semi-monthly bulletin for the scoutmaster and each registered assistant scoutmaster.

Under no circumstances can a boy be enrolled as a member of a troop who is not at least 12 years of age, or wear the scout badge and participate in the troop activities unless he has paid his registration fee. No one is authorized to make any exception to this rule. In accordance with the action of the annual meeting of February 12, 1914, special authority is required to enroll more than 32 boys in one troop.

Additional Names

Blanks are provided for the registration of additional boys who join the troop during the period covered by the registration of the troop.

In all cases the membership of additional scouts will expire at the same time the troop registration expires. A graduated scale of fees to correspond with the unexpired period of the troop's registration has been devised for such additional enrolled scouts. If the unexpired period for which the troop is registered is more than nine months, the fee of the new scouts shall be 25 cents each; if the period is for more than six and less than ten months, the fee shall be 20 cents; if for a period of six months or less, 15 cents. Scouts re-registering pay the full fee of 25 cents irrespective of the date of payment.

Where there is a local council all registration and annual reports are transmitted through the office of the local council to the National Headquarters. In all other cases the scoutmaster transmits them direct to National Headquarters.

Troop Representation

In communities supervised by local councils, each chartered institution shall be entitled to elect one of its members, other than the scoutmaster, as a member of the local council; and in the case of an independent troop, one representative citizen of the United States identified with the work of that troop, other than the scoutmaster, may be elected by the Troop Committee to membership on the local council, provided, however, in the larger communities where the local council work is subdivided among district committees, the representatives of troops shall be appointed to the committee in charge of the district in which the troop holds its regular meetings and the district committee shall, in turn, elect delegates to the local council in accordance with the provisions of the constitution and by-laws of the local council.

Members of troop committees may upon application and with the approval of the scout authorities wear the scout uniform and pin.

Local Council

In communities where there are two or more troops, scout work may be promoted and supervised under the direction of a local council which is made up of ten or more men. These men are elected as representatives of the various interests of the community including religious, educational, business, and civic activities. When such local councils provide an adequate budget for the maintenance of the local headquarters, the conduct of a boy scout camp, and the employment of one or more men to devote their entire time to the promotion and supervision of the program of the Boy Scouts of America, they shall be known and des'gnated as councils of the first class. Pending the organization as councils of the first class, the Field Department may in its discretion grant provisional or temporary charters to villages, towns, or small cities. Such councils shall be known and designated as councils of the second class.

All local council charters shall expire at the end of each calendar year and may be renewed upon application accompanied by reports or other evidence showing satisfactory effort to meet the responsibilities of a local council as herein provided.

Each council has a president and one or more vice-presidents, a secretary, treasurer, an executive committee, a court of honor of three or five men, a scout commissioner, and in some cases a scout executive and field officers.

The local council represents the National Council in supervising the work in the community for which a charter is granted, and through its court of honor conducts all examinations for the degree of first class scout and passes upon the examination of scouts for merit badges. It also investigates all cases of life saving and presents necessary evidence to the National Court of Honor for the award of honor medals. The local council acts as a final court to pass upon the appeals from the opinions of scoutmasters and their assistants.

Each chartered local council is entitled to elect one of its members as a delegate to the National Council and an additional member for every 1,000 boys enrolled as scouts.

District Councils

The work of the local council in large communities is facilitated by the organization of district councils, given certain duties and responsibilities as provided in a constitution agreed upon by the local council having jurisdiction and the district council, and with the approval of the National Council.

Scout Commissioner and Scout Executive

The scout commissioner is the ranking commissioned officer in scouting for the community. He receives his commission from the National Council upon the nomination of the local council and serves without compensation in the same manner as the scoutmaster. The duties vary according to the size of the community, local conditions, and leadership available. In larger communities where the detail work requires systematic and regular attention beyond what is reasonably to be expected of a volunteer worker, a scout executive is employed and commissioned by the National Council.

In such cases the local council, by a resolution, definitely fixes the responsibility of the scout commissioner and the scout executive.

Deputy Scout Commissioner

In some communities it has been found desirable to have the work of the scout commissioner supplemented by one or more men, who serve as deputy commissioners. These officials receive their commissions from the National Council upon the nomination of the local council and are assigned duties as specified by the local council.

National Council

The National Council is made up of delegates from the various chartered local councils, and such other men as may be elected by the National Council or Executive Board provided, however, that persons thus elected shall at no time constitute a majority of the entire membership of the National Council. Membership in the National Council is limited to American citizens whose service in scouting is entirely voluntary. A membership fee of at least $5.00 is paid for each member of the National Council either personally or by the council he represents.

Persons engaged professionally in scout work in any form shall be ineligible to membership in the National Council.

Executive Board

The National Council at its annual meeting elects an executive board which with its executive officers is charged with the responsibility for all questions of business, administration and supervision.

Among its duties and functions are the following:

It grants charters to local councils, and credentials to all scout officials;

Copyrights all badges, insignia, and other scout designs;

Selects designs for uniforms and scout equipment, and arranges for their manufacture and distribution;

Provides the services of field officers to coöperate with local councils and scoutmasters in organizing their work and solving problems;

Prepares and publishes suitable text-books and other literature for the use of scouts and scout officials;

Provides a National Court of Honor by which consideration is given to all applications for merit badges and honor medals;

Makes possible practical results by arranging for coöperation with state and national civic authorities in carrying out programs for community service by boy scouts.

The executive board is charged with the responsibility of guarding the movement against those who would, because of its popularity, profit by exploitation at the expense of boy scouts.

In addition to the above functions the executive board seeks to serve boy scouts and scout officials through the following departments.

Supply Department

Under the supervision of a committee of experts, the executive board maintains a supply department through which all duly registered scouts may secure at the lowest possible cost consistent with good quality, all necessary scout supplies, official badges, and such other things as they may desire because of the scout program. All profits from this department are used for the furtherance of the scout movement. Therefore, all scouts and scout officials are urged to make use of this department whenever possible. A catalog of scout supplies is issued semi-annually and will be sent without charge to any one upon application for same.

A scout cannot receive official badges, uniforms, or other scout equipment restricted to the use of scouts, without the written approval of the scoutmaster. Where there is a local council organized with a charter from the National Council, the approval of the scout commissioner or scout executive must be secured.

Badges and scout equipment restricted solely to the use of scouts will not be supplied to any boys who are not in good standing according to the records at National Headquarters. Local dealers in scout equipment will with the approval of local scout authorities sell uniforms to scouts on the presentation of membership certificates.

Department of Education

The Department of Education is organized to have supervision of all work of an educational character involving the principles and methods of pedagogy arising from the development of the boy scout scheme. It will prepare- literature setting forth principles and methods of education as applied to the boy scout program for educational leaders, showing how the movement can be used to supplement the work of general education, and as a supplement to the limited opportunity for character development afforded by the schoolroom.

Field Department

This department is responsible for organization of local councils composed of representative men of affairs; for the settlement of all problems of a jurisdictional nature; and for the issuance of commissions to those qualified to serve as special field scout commissioners, acting scout commissioners until a local council is organized, etc.; for the cultivation of institutional coöperation and the aggressive development of scouting in new communities and sections. It either directs or coöperates in an advisory capacity in raising local council budgets; assists in the selection and placing of paid executives, camp directors, etc.; and otherwise coöperates through visits, conferences, addresses, and correspondence in handling of field problems.

Library Department

The library department is maintained under the supervision of a group of expert bookmen who are for the first time in history making available reliable advice as to worth-while books for boys, and furthermore, under the leadership of this department, arranging with publishers for a high grade of books for boys. The results of this department in the shape of definite lists carefully subdivided are made available without charge to libraries, local councils, troops, and parents of boys throughout the country.

This committee has also secured the publication of *Every Boy's Library* consisting of forty-five books, each of which sells for 60 cents per copy. (*See book list in appendix.*)

Semi-monthly Bulletin Scouting

For the information and help of scout officials and others interested in work for boys, a semi-monthly bulletin is published. This bulletin contains reports of various scout centers and helpful suggestions and advice. All registered scout officials receive it without further expense, and others may secure same upon the payment of one dollar annually.

Boys' Life, the Boy Scouts' Magazine

It is one of the important features of the National Council's work to provide for all scouts the official monthly magazine, BOYS' LIFE, to serve as an aid and stimulus to better scouting. The ideals of the movement it carries effectively, in part, through entertaining "stories." "What Every Scout Wants to Know"— official news from National Headquarters by the Chief Scout Executive; instructions that help Scouts to pass their tests and earn merit badges; friendly, inspiring "talks" each month by Dan Beard, National Scout Commissioner, and by "The Cave Scout"; articles telling how to make things; scout puzzles and contests; a letter exchange that creates international friendships; pictures of scout activities—all these features, which no other magazine has, make BOYS' LIFE different and distinctive. The circulation is over 100,000 copies a month—and is growing steadily.

BOYS' LIFE publishes yearly over 600 pages, containing stories, articles, and pictures that would fill *seven* of the usual boys' books. The price is $1.50, but every scout may now have the magazine for *90 cents a year when his whole troop subscribes together.* Sample copy and details of the "troop subscription" plan sent free. Separate subscriptions are $1.50. (*See announcement in advertising section.*)

The Scout Motto

Among the very first things a boy must know to become a scout are the scout law, salute, sign, oath, motto, and significance of the badge.

The motto of the boy scouts is *Be Prepared*, and the badge of the boy scouts is a copyrighted design with this motto, "Be Prepared," on a scroll at its base.

The motto, "Be Prepared," means that the scout is always in a state of readiness in mind and body to do his duty; to be prepared in mind, by having disciplined himself to be obedient, and also by having thought out beforehand any accident or situation that may occur, so that he may know the right thing to do at the right moment, and be willing to do it; to be prepared in body, by making himself strong and active and able to do the right thing at the right moment, and then to do it.

Significance of the Scout Badge

The scout badge is not specifically intended to represent either the fleur-de-lis or an arrowhead, although it resembles both. It is a modified form of the sign of the north on the mariner's compass, which is as old as the history of navigation. The Chinese claim its use among them as early as 2634 B. C. and we have definite information that it was used at sea by them as early as 300 A. D. Marco Polo brought the compass to Europe on his return from Cathay. The sign of the north on the compass gradually came to represent the north, and pioneers, trappers, woodsmen, and scouts, because of this, adopted it as their emblem. Through centuries of use it has undergone modification. Now we have taken its shape as that of our badge, which is further distinguished by a shield and the American Eagle superimposed.

This trefoil badge of the scouts is now used, with slight local variations, in almost every civilized country as the mark of brotherhood, for good citizenship, and friendliness.

The trefoil refers to the three points in the Scout Oath.

Its scroll is turned up at the ends like a scout's mouth, because he does his duty with a smile and willingly.

The knot is to remind the scout to do a good turn to some one daily. The knot is the simple or overhand knot.

The arrowhead part is worn by the tenderfoot. The scroll part only is worn by the second class scout. The badge worn by the first class scout is the whole badge.

The official badges of the Boy Scouts of America are issued

by the National Council and may be secured only from the National Headquarters. These badges are protected by the U. S. Patent Laws (letters patent numbers 41412 and 41532) and any one infringing these patents is liable to prosecution at law.

The Scout Oath

Before he becomes a scout a boy must promise:

On my honor I will do my best—

1. To do my duty to God and my country, and to obey the scout law;

2. To help other people at all times;

3. To keep myself physically strong, mentally awake, and morally straight.

When taking this oath the scout will stand holding up his right hand, palm to the front, thumb resting on the nail of the little finger and the other three fingers upright and together.

The Scout Sign

The three fingers held up, palm front, the thumb resting on the nail of the little finger is the scout sign, and reminds the scout of his three promises in the Scout Oath.

The Scout Salute

The scout salute is rendered by raising the right hand with the fingers held as in the scout sign, to the forehead, or to the brim of the hat, palm being turned to the left, the fingers being in front of the corner of the eye, and the forearm making an angle of forty-five degrees with the horizontal. The scout salute is always rendered with the right hand.

The Scout Handclasp

The boy scout handclasp is made with the right hand, the fingers in the same relative position as in making the scout sign. The three fingers extended represent the three parts of the scout oath; and the bent position of the thumb and the little finger represents the knot or tie that binds these parts together into a strong unity. One scout shakes hands with another by a good warm handclasp with the three middle fingers extended in a straight line along the other's wrist, and with the thumb and little finger clasped around the other's fingers.

The Scout Law

There have always been certain written and unwritten laws regulating the conduct and directing the activities of men.

We have such unwritten laws coming down from past ages. In Japan, the Japanese have their Bushido or laws of the old Samurai warriors. During the Middle Ages, the chivalry and rules of the Knights of King Arthur, the Knights Templar, and the Crusaders were in force. In aboriginal America, the Red Indians had their laws of honor; likewise the Zulus, Hindus, and the later European nations have their ancient codes. The following laws which relate to the Boy Scouts of America are the latest and most up to date. These laws a boy promises to obey when he takes his scout oath.

1. A scout is trustworthy.

A scout's honor is to be trusted. If he were to violate his honor by telling a lie, or by cheating, or by not doing exactly a given task, when trusted on his honor, he may be directed to hand over his scout badge.

2. A scout is loyal.

He is loyal to all to whom loyalty is due: his scout leader, his home, and parents and country.

3. A scout is helpful.

He must be prepared at any time to save life, help injured persons, and share the home duties. He must *do at least one good turn to somebody every day*.

4. A scout is friendly.

He is a friend to all and a brother to every other scout.

5. A scout is courteous.

He is polite to all, especially to women, children, old people, and the weak and helpless. *He must not take pay for being helpful or courteous*.

6. A scout is kind.

He is a friend to animals. He will not kill nor hurt any living creature needlessly, but will strive to save and protect all harmless life.

7. A scout is obedient.

He obeys his parents, scout master, patrol leader, and all other duly constituted authorities.

8. A scout is cheerful.

He smiles whenever he can. His obedience to orders is prompt and cheery. He never shirks nor grumbles at hardships.

9. A Scout is Thrifty.

He does not wantonly destroy property. He works faithfully, wastes nothing, and makes the best use of his opportunities. He saves his money so that he may pay his own way, be generous to those in need, and helpful to worthy objects. *He may work for pay, but must not receive tips for courtesies or good turns.*

10. A Scout is Brave.

He has the courage to face danger in spite of fear, and to stand up for the right against the coaxings of friends or the jeers or threats of enemies, and defeat does not down him.

11. A Scout is Clean.

He keeps clean in body and thought, stands for clean speech, clean sport, clean habits, and travels with a clean crowd.

12. A Scout is Reverent.

He is reverent toward God. He is faithful in his religious duties, and respects the convictions of others in matters of custom and religion.

The Three Classes of Scouts

There are three classes of scouts among the Boy Scouts of America: the tenderfoot, second class scout, and first class scout. Before a boy can be recognized as a tenderfoot he must pass the prescribed tests. A tenderfoot on meeting certain requirements may become a second class scout, and a second class scout upon meeting another set of requirements may become a first class scout. The first class scout may then qualify for the various merit badges which are offered in another part of this chapter for proficiency in scouting. The requirements of the tenderfoot, second class scout, and first class scout are as follows:

Tenderfoot

To become a scout a boy must be at least twelve years of age. Upon demonstrating to the satisfaction of the scoutmaster his ability to repeat the Scout Oath and Law in full and his thorough knowledge of their meaning, and upon passing the following tests, the boy formally subscribes to the oath and law and is registered as a tenderfoot scout, and is then entitled to wear the tenderfoot badge and the official scout uniform.

Tenderfoot

Scoutcraft

1. Know the Scout Laws, motto, sign, salute, and significance of the badge. (See pages 31, 32, 33.)
2. Know the composition and history of the national flag and the customary forms of respect due to it. (See pages 439-441.)
3. Tie the following knots: square or reef, sheet-bend, bowline, fisherman's, sheepshank, halter, clove hitch, timber hitch and two half hitches. (See pages 78-82.)

Second Class Scout

A tenderfoot scout may, upon passing the following tests to the satisfaction of the proper local scout authorities, be enrolled as a second class scout. He is then entitled to wear the second class badge of the Boy Scouts of America.

1. At least one month's service as a tenderfoot.
2. Elementary first aid and bandaging: know the general directions for first aid for injuries; know treatment for fainting, shock, fractures, bruises, sprains, injuries in which the skin is broken, burns and scalds; demonstrate how to carry injured, the use of the triangular and roller bandages and tourniquet. (See pages 335-382.)

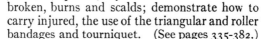
Second Class Scout

3. Elementary signaling: know the alphabet of the Semaphore or the General Service (International Morse) Code. (See pages 283-298.)
4. Track half a mile in twenty-five minutes; or, if in town, describe satisfactorily the contents of one store window out of four observed for one minute each.
5. Go a mile in twelve minutes at scout's pace—about fifty steps running and fifty walking, alternately.
6. Use properly knife or hatchet. (See pages 244-246.)
7. Prove ability to build a fire in the open, using not more than two matches.
8. Cook a quarter of a pound of meat and two potatoes in the open without any cooking utensils.
9. Earn and deposit at least one dollar in a public bank. (Liberty Loan subscriptions and war savings certificates are accepted.)
10. Know the sixteen principal points of the compass. (See pages 82-83.)

First Class Scout

After sixty days' service as a second class scout, a scout may, upon passing the following tests to the satisfaction of the local scout authorities, be enrolled as a first class scout and entitled to wear the first class badge of the Boy Scouts of America.

1. Swim fifty yards.

2. Earn and deposit at least two dollars in a public bank. (Liberty Loan subscriptions and war savings certificates are accepted.)

3. Send and receive a message by Semaphore, including conventional signs, thirty letters per minute, or by the General Service Code (International Morse), sixteen letters per minute, including conventional signs.

4. Make a round trip alone (or with another scout) to a point at least seven miles away (fourteen miles in all), going on foot, or rowing boat, and write a satisfactory account of the trip, and things observed.

5. Advanced first aid: know the methods for panic prevention; what to do in case of fire, ice, electric, and gas accidents; how to help in case of runaway horse, mad dog, or snake bite; treatment for dislocations, unconsciousness, poisoning, fainting, apoplexy, sunstroke, heat exhaustion, and freezing; know treatment for sunburn, ivy poisoning, bites and stings, nosebleed, earache, toothache, inflammation or grit in eye, cramp or stomach ache, and chills; demonstrate artificial respiration. (See pages 335-382.)

First-class Scout

6. Prepare and cook satisfactorily, in the open, using camp cooking utensils, two of the following articles as may be directed: Eggs, bacon, hunter's stew, fish, fowl, game, pancakes, hoe-cake, biscuit, hardtack or a "twist," baked on a stick; explain to another boy the methods followed. (See pages 236-240.)

7. Read a map correctly, and draw, from field notes made on the spot, an intelligible rough sketch map, indicating by their proper marks important buildings, roads, trolley lines, main landmarks, principal elevations, etc. Point out a compass direction without the help of the compass.

8. Use properly an ax for felling or trimming light timber; or produce an article of carpentry, cabinet-making, or metal work made by himself. Explain the method followed.

9. Judge distance, size, number, height, and weignt within 25 per cent.

10. Descrioe fully from observation ten species of trees or plants, including poison ivy, by their bark, leaves, flowers, fruit, or scent; or six species of wild birds by their plumage, notes, tracks, or habits; or six species of native wild animals by their form, color, call, tracks, or habits; find the North Star, and name and describe at least three constellations of stars.

11. Furnish satisfactory evidence that he has put into practice in his daily life the principles of the Scout Oath and Law.

12. Enlist a boy trained by himself in the requirements of a tenderfoot.

The Merit Badges

A boy who has passed all of the tenderfoot, second and first class scout requirements is now eligible to qualify for the various merit badges. Some are purposely restricted to boys living in rural communities, boys in school, and boys at work. These badges are intended to stimulate the scout's interest in the life about him, and are given for general knowledge. The wearing of these badges does not signify that a scout is qualified to make his living by the knowledge gained in securing the award.

Agriculture

To obtain a merit badge for Agriculture, a scout must:

1. Explain the nature of soil, its texture, its need of water, of air, and of plant and animal life; what the soil does for the plant, and how the soil may be improved.

2. Make a seed tester and test the germination of three chosen varieties of seeds, — 100 seeds of each variety.

3. Identify and describe ten common weeds of the community and tell how best to eliminate them.

4. Identify six common insect pests, tell what plants they usually infest, and how best to control them.

5. Have a practical knowledge, for his locality, of plowing, cultivating, harrowing, disking, draining, and harvesting, and the purposes of each. Describe also the farm implements used in each case.

6. Tell how plants are propagated, — by seeds, roots, cuttings, tubers, buds, and grafts. Explain where plants get their food and how they grow.

7. Explain how to read a weather map, know weather signals, and the making of local observations.

8. Name and distinguish ten common birds of his locality, and state their value to the farmer.

Angling

To obtain a merit badge for Angling, a scout must:

1. Catch and name seven different species of fishes **by the**

usual angling methods (fly-casting, bait-casting, trolling, and bait-fishing). At least one species must be taken by fly-casting and one by bait-casting. In single-handed fly-casting the rod must not exceed seven ounces in weight; in double-handed fly-casting one ounce in weight may be allowed for each foot in length; in bait-fishing and trolling the rod must not exceed ten feet in length nor twelve ounces in weight.

2. Show proficiency in accurate single-handed casting with the fly for distances of 30, 40, and 50 feet, and in bait-casting for distances of 40, 60, and 70 feet.

3. Make three artificial flies (either after three standard patterns, or in imitation of different natural flies) and take fish with at least two of them. Make a neat single gut leader at least four feet long, or a twisted or braided leader at least three feet long. Splice the broken joint of a rod neatly.

4. Give the open season for the game fishes in his vicinity, and explain how and why they are protected by the law.

Archery

To obtain a merit badge for Archery, a scout must:

1. Make a bow, arrow, and string:

(a) With which he shall shoot an extreme flight of 175 yards at an elevation of 45 degrees above the horizon;

(b) With which he shall at 60 yards score, on a regulation four-foot target, 120 points with 60 shots;

(c) With which he shall also score on such a four-foot target, at 40 yards, 200 points with 60 shots.

2. Know something of the history of Archery, and the principal archers of the past and the present and their records.

Architecture

To obtain a merit badge for Architecture, a scout must:

1. Present a satisfactory free-hand drawing.

2. Draw, without accurate measurements, the five orders of architecture, the drawings being of the character of sketches, but preserving the proportions.

3. Write an historical outline of the important periods of architectural development, giving the names of the important recognized architects identified with the development of each style.

4. Submit an original design for a two-story house, and tell what material is necessary for its construction, giving an outline of specifications, the design to consist of original working drawings at scale, drawn in ink on linen or paper suitable,for making prints.

Art

To obtain a merit badge for Art, a scout must:

1. Make a free-hand pencil sketch of an animal or bird showing in values the distribution of color.

2. Draw a cylindrical object and a rectangular object grouped together a little below the eye, and show light and shade.

3. Make a drawing of some example of historical ornament.

4. Make an original decorative arrangement in color, using any motif, and state for what use the design is intended.

5. State the essentials of the reproductive processes of etching, half-tone engraving, color printing, and lithography.

6. Paint a flower-spray or leaf-spray in color.

7. Present a camp scene either in water color or oil.

Astronomy

To obtain a merit badge for Astronomy, a scout must:

1. Have a general knowledge of the nature and movements of the stars and planets.

2. Point out and name twelve principal constellations; find the north by means of other stars than the Pole-star, in case of that star's being obscured by clouds.

3. Have a general knowledge of the positions and movements of the earth, sun, and moon, and of tides, eclipses, meteors, comets, and planets.

4. Plot on at least two nights per month for six months the positions of all naked-eye planets visible between sundown

and one hour thereafter. The plot of each planet shall contain at least three fixed stars, with their names or designations; colors of planets and stars are to be recorded as observed by him.

Athletics

To obtain a merit badge for Athletics, a scout must:

1. Write an acceptable article of not less than five hundred words on how to train for an athletic event.

2. Give the rules for two track and two field events, and define an amateur.

3. Prepare plans for the holding of an athletic meet, specifying duties of each required official.

4. Produce evidence of having satisfactorily served as an official in an athletic meet, or in a major athletic sport, such as football, baseball, or basketball.

5. Qualify in one event, according to his weight, in each of the following groups:

		Under 110 Lbs.	Under 125 Lbs.	Under 140 Lbs.	Over 140 Lbs.
1.	Running broad jump	12 ft.	13 ft.	14 ft.	15 ft.
	Running high jump	3 ft. 9 in.	4 ft.	4 ft. 3 in.	4 ft. 6 in.
	Standing broad jump	6 ft. 9 in.	7 ft. 3 in.	7 ft. 9 in.	8 ft. 3 in.
	Standing high jump	3 ft. 2 in.	3 ft. 4 in.	3 ft. 6 in.	3 ft. 8 in.
2.	50-yard dash	7⅘ sec.	7½ sec.	7 sec.	6¾ sec.
	100-yard dash		13 sec.	12¾ sec.	12½ sec.
	6-potato race	27 sec.	26 sec.	25 sec.	24 sec.
3.	20-yard swim	17¼ sec.	17¼ sec.	16¾ sec.	16 sec.
	40-yard swim	39 sec.	38 sec.	37 sec.	36 sec.
4.	Pull up	6 times	8 times	10 times	12 times
	8-lb. shot-put	24 ft.	28 ft.	32 ft.	36 ft.
	Push up from floor	10 times	12 times	14 times	16 times
	Rope climb 18 ft.	15 sec.	13 sec.	11 sec.	10 sec.

Automobiling

To obtain a merit badge for Automobiling, a scout must:

1. Demonstrate ability to start a motor, explaining what precautions should be taken.

2. Take off and put on pneumatic tires.

3. Know the principles of construction and the functions of clutch (two types), carbureter, valves, magneto, spark plug, differential, and two different types of transmission, explaining what special care each of these parts requires; and be able to explain three differences between a two- and a four-cycle motor.

4. Know how to put out burning gasoline or oil.

5. Be able to pass an examination equivalent to that required for a license to operate an automobile in the community in which he lives.

Aviation

To obtain a merit badge for Aviation, a scout must:

1. Have a knowledge of the theory of the aeroplane, helicopter, and ornithopter, and of the spherical and dirigible balloon.

2. Have made a working model of any type of heavier than air machine, that will fly at least twenty-five yards; and have built a box kite that will fly.

3. Have a knowledge of the types and makes of engines used for aeroplanes, the best known makes of aeroplanes, and feats performed or records made by famous aviators.

4. Have a knowledge of names of famous airships (dirigibles) and some of their records.

5. Understand the difference between aviation and aerostation, and know the types of apparati which come under these two heads.

Bee Keeping

To obtain a merit badge for Bee Keeping, a scout must:

1. Know how to examine a colony of bees, remove the combs, find the queen, and determine the amount of the brood, number of queen cells, and the amount of honey in the hive.

2. Distinguish between the drones, workers, eggs, larvæ, pupæ, honey, wax, pollen, and propolis; tell how the bees make the honey, and where the wax comes from; and explain the part played in the life of the colony by the queen, the drones, and the workers.

3. Have had experience in hiving at least one swarm. Explain the construction of the modern hive, especially in regard to the "Bee spaces."

4. Put foundations in sections and fill supers with sections; and also remove filled supers from the hive and prepare the honey for market.

5. Write an acceptable article of not more than two hundred words on the differences in honeys according to the flowers from which the nectar is obtained.

Bird Study

To obtain a merit badge for Bird Study, a scout must:

1. Produce a list of fifty species of wild birds which have been personally observed, and positively identified in the field.

2. Produce a list showing the greatest number of species that he has seen in the field in one week.

3. Produce a list, derived from personal observation, of twenty species of birds particularly noted for their value to agriculture in the destruction of insects.

4. Produce a list, derived from personal reading, of ten birds of prey particularly useful in the destruction of rats and mice.

5. Name ten species of birds particularly useful in protecting the trunks of trees from borers, bark-lice, and scale insects.

6. Describe at least two bird boxes and two food tables that have been erected by him, the species of birds that have been attracted by them, and how many of the birds have nested in these boxes.

7. State what he has done to protect birds from wicked and unjust slaughter; to promote long, close seasons for vanishing species, and to promote the creation of bird preserves and sanctuaries.

Blacksmithing

To obtain a merit badge for Blacksmithing, a scout must:

1. Make an open link of ⅜-inch stock.

2. Forge a chain hook out of ¾ x ½-inch soft steel, or ¾-inch round iron.

3. Make a bolt of ½-inch stock.

4. Bend and weld three links and form them into a chain, these links to be fastened to the hook of Requirement 2 by a ring, and links and ring to be made out of ⅜-inch round iron.

5. Make a straight lap weld of ¼ x 1-inch stock.

6. Make a cold chisel out of $\frac{5}{8}$-inch hexagonal tool steel.
7. Temper a rock drill.
8. Explain how to harden and temper a cold chisel.

Bugling

To obtain a merit badge for Bugling, a scout must:

1. Sound properly on the bugle the following calls: First Call, The Scouts' Call, Reveille, Mess, To the Color, Officers, Drill, Assembly, Recall, Fatigue, Church, Fire, Swimming, Retreat, Call to Quarters, Taps.

Business

To obtain a merit badge for Business, a scout must:

1. Write a satisfactory business and a personal letter.
2. Know simple bookkeeping, or shorthand and typewriting.
3. Keep a complete and actual account of personal receipts and expenditures for six months.
4. Be prepared to answer questions and problems in interest, percentage, and discount.
5. Present the certificate of his employers that for the period of six months preceding he has put into practice the Scout Oath and Law and shown efficiency in his application to business; that he has been prompt and regular in his attendance, and has shown due regard for his general appearance by keeping his hair combed, his hands, nails, and teeth clean, his shoes shined, and his clothes clean and orderly.

Camping

To obtain a merit badge for Camping, a scout must:

1. Have slept fifty nights in the open or under canvas, at different times.
2. Demonstrate how to put up a tent and ditch it.

3. Have made a bed of wild material, and a fire with rubbing-sticks or with flint and steel.
4. State how to choose a camp site and how to prepare it for rain; how to build a latrine (toilet); and how to dispose of the camp garbage and refuse.
5. Know how to construct a raft.

Carpentry

To obtain a merit badge for Carpentry, a scout must:

1. Know the proper way to drive, set, and clinch a nail, and draw a spike with a claw-hammer.
2. Know the use of the rule, square, level, plumbline, mitre, chalk-line, and bevel.
3. Lay out a rectangle by the use of 6, 8, 10, and prove it by its diagonals.
4. Know how to lay shingles.

5. Make an article of furniture for practical use in his home finished in workmanlike manner, all work to be done without assistance.

Chemistry

To obtain a merit badge for Chemistry, a scout must:

1. Pass a satisfactory test in elementary general chemistry.

2. Give correct tests for oxygen, hydrogen, nitrogen, chlorine, and carbon dioxide gases.
3. Tell which gases of Requirement 2 can be used to extinguish fire and explain how it can be accomplished.
4. Explain why baking soda is used to put out a small fire and why salt is used to throw in the stove when the chimney is on fire.
5. Explain the use of analytical weights in chemical analysis. Tell how a quantitative analysis differs from a qualitative analysis.
6. Give three commercial forms of carbon and tell how each is obtained. State what forms, if any, have been prepared artificially and how.
7. Explain the process of making lime and mortar from limestone.
8. Explain the process of making charcoal. Tell what gas is formed by burning of any form of carbon and what becomes of it.
9. Describe from observation a manufacturing plant which employs chemical process or processes.

Civics

To obtain a merit badge for Civics, a scout must:

1. State the principal citizenship requirements of a voter in his state, territory, or district.

2. Know the principal features of the naturalization laws of the United states.

3. Know how the President, Vice-President, senators, and congressmen of the United States are elected, and give their terms of office.

4. Know the number of judges of the Supreme Court of the United States, how appointed, and their terms of office.

5. Know the various administrative departments of the Government as represented in the President's Cabinet.

6. Know how the governor, lieutenant-governor, senators, representatives, or assemblymen of his state are elected, and give their terms of office; or, if living in a territory or the District of Columbia, know who the corresponding officers are in that territory or district, how elected, and their terms of office.

7. Know whether the judges of the principal courts in his state, territory, or district are appointed or elected, and the length of their terms.

8. Know how the principal officers in his town or city are elected, and for what terms.

9. Know the duties of the various city departments, such as fire, police, board of health, etc.

10. Draw a map giving location of the principal buildings and points of interest within a radius of two miles of his troop headquarters.

11. Give satisfactory evidence that he is familiar with the provisions and history of the Declaration of Independence and the Constitution of the United States.

Conservation

To obtain a merit badge for Conservation, a scout must:

1. Recognize in the forest all important commercial trees in his neighborhood; distinguish the lumber from each, and tell for what purpose each is best suited.

2. Know the principal game birds and animals in his neighborhood, the seasons

during which they are protected, the methods of protection, and the results.

3. Know the principal natural resources of his town and ᴏꜰ his state, and the principal laws of his state and local district for the preservation of the same.

4. Know the principal natural resources of the United States, and have some idea of the history of the development of their use to the present time.

5. Understand what soil conservation, water conservation, conservation of minerals (including mineral fuels), and forest conservation involve; and know what the Government is doing to promote them.

6. Present evidence that he has actually been of some help in making effective the laws of his state for the protection of forests, or birds and animal life.

Cooking

To obtain a merit badge for Cooking, a scout must:

1. Prove his ability to build a fireplace out of stone or sod or logs; build a fire in the fireplace, and cook the following dishes: camp stew, two vegetables, omelet, and rice pudding.

2. Demonstrate ability to mix dough, and bake bread in an oven; and also to make tea, coffee, and cocoa.

3. Carve properly and serve correctly to people at the table.

Craftsmanship

To obtain a merit badge for Craftsmanship, a scout must:

Qualify, unassisted, in the outlined requirements of one kind of craftwork.

Craftwork in Metal

1. Design and make some simple object in which the opera-tion of soldering is employed: such as box corners, a desk set, candlestick, ink-well.

2. Design and make some simple object in which the operation of riveting is employed: such as a candlestick, candle shade, Paul Revere lantern, stationery holder.

3. Design and make some simple object in which the operation of sawing or piercing is employed: such as a watch fob, escutch-eon plate, hinges, candle shade.

4. Design and shape some simple object by beating metal: such as a tray, bowl, spoon, ink-well.

Craftwork in Leather

1. Design and tool some simple object in leather: such as a mat, blotter-pad corners, bill-fold, magazine cover, belt.
2. Know the source and method of preparation of the best grades of leather for craftwork.

Basketry

1. Plan and weave a large reed or raffia basket or tray.
2. Weave a cane seat for a stool, or a rush seat for a chair, or cane a chair.

Pottery

1. Design and build by hand a pottery form: such as a vase, bowl, or ornamental tile to be fired and glazed.
2. Design and throw a pottery form on a potter's wheel to be fired and glazed.

Craftwork in Cement

1. Design and mould in a form a cement window-box or flower-pot, a garden jar, a garden seat, sun-dial, or hitching post.
2. Design and "build up" a cylindrical flower-pot, garden vase, or pedestal employing the process of turning or sweeping the form.

Bookbinding

1. Rebind in boards with leather or cloth some rare old book or a volume of a magazine.
2. Make a scrap-book bound in boards and cover with leather or cloth.

Woodcarving

1. Plan and carve an appropriate design in low relief on some simple object such as book ends, a tray, a pair of bellows, a chest, a screen, a clock case, a letter opener, or a box.
2. State the qualities of hardwood and softwood, and the best woods to use in woodcarving; name, describe, and explain how to sharpen the different kinds of woodcarving tools; and explain methods of handling the grain of the wood in designing.

Craftwork in Wood

1. Design and construct a small piece of furniture in which mortise and tenon or dowel joints are used, such as a tabouret, a small table, a chair, a footstool, a writing-desk, etc.

2. Make plans or intelligent rough sketch drawing of the piece selected.

Cycling

To obtain a merit badge for Cycling, a scout must:

1. Ride a bicycle fifty miles in ten hours.

2. Repair a puncture.

3. Take apart and clean a bicycle, and put it together again properly.

4. Know how to make reports, if sent out scouting on a road.

5. Read a map; and report correctly verbal messages.

Dairying

To obtain a merit badge for Dairying, a scout must:

1. Understand the management of dairy cattle.

2. Be able to milk.

3. Understand the sterilization of milk, and care of dairy utensils and appliances.

4. Test at least five cows for ten days each, with the Babcock test, and make proper reports.

Electricity

To obtain a merit badge for Electricity, a scout must:

1. Illustrate the experiment by which the laws of electrical attraction and repulsion are shown.

2. Understand the difference between a direct and an alternating current, and show uses to which each is adapted. Give a method of determining which kind flows in a given circuit.

3. Make a simple electro-magnet.

4. Have an elementary knowledge of the construction of simple battery cells, and of the working of electric bells and telephones.

5. Be able to replace fuses and to properly splice, solder, and tape rubber-covered wires.

6. Demonstrate how to rescue a person in contact with a live electrical wire, and have a knowledge of the method of resuscitation of a person insensible from shock.

Firemanship

To obtain a merit badge for Firemanship, a scout must:

1. Know how to turn in an alarm for fire.
2. Know how to enter burning buildings.
3. Know how to prevent panics and the spread of fire.
4. Understand the use of hose, — unrolling, joining-up, connecting to hydrant, use of nozzle, etc.
5. Understand the use of escapes, ladders, and chutes, and know the location of exits in buildings which he frequents.
6. Know how to improvise ropes and nets.
7. Explain what to do in case of panic, understand the fireman's lift and drag, and how to work in fumes.
8. Understand the use of fire extinguishers; how to rescue animals; how to save property; how to organize a bucket brigade; and how to aid the police in keeping back crowds.

First Aid

To obtain a merit badge for First Aid, a scout must:

1. Be able to tell what to do with an apparently drowned person, and demonstrate the Sylvester and Schaefer methods of artificial respiration.

2. Show how to apply bandages to the head, ankle, and hand.
3. Show how to apply a tourniquet to stop arterial hemorrhage at any point: (a) on the upper extremity below armpit; (b) on lower extremity below hip joint.
4. Demonstrate how to arrest venous hemorrhage on any part of the body.
5. Show how to apply a gauze dressing to a wound so that it will not be contaminated — that is, do it in an aseptic manner.
6. Show how to support by splints, etc., a broken arm or a broken leg so that the patient can bear transportation.

7. Be able to explain what to do for the bite of a mad dog, a venomous snake, a mosquito, and a scorpion sting.

8. Show how to rescue an individual from contact with an electric wire.

9. Produce satisfactory evidence that he has taken advantage of every opportunity to put into actual practice his knowledge of first-aid work during a period of at least six months since becoming a first class scout.

First Aid to Animals

To obtain a merit badge for First Aid to Animals, a scout must:

1. Have a general knowledge of domestic and farm animals.

2. Be able to treat a horse for colic.

3. Describe symptoms and give treatment for the following: wounds, fractures and sprains, exhaustion, choking, and lameness.

4. Know what to do for horses in harness when they fall on the street.

5. Know what to do when animals are being cruelly mistreated.

Forestry

To obtain a merit badge for Forestry, a scout must:

1. Be able to identify twenty-five kinds of trees when in leaf, or fifteen kinds of deciduous (broad leaf) trees in winter, and tell some of the uses of each.

2. Identify twelve kinds of shrubs.

3. Collect and identify samples of ten kinds of wood and be able to tell some of their uses.

4. Determine the height, and estimate the amount of timber, approximately, in five trees of different sizes.

5. State laws for transplanting, grafting, spraying, and protecting trees.

6. Tell what are the effects of fires on forests; what are the three general classes of fires, and how to fight each.

7. Tell how and when to collect tree seeds, how to extract seeds from cones, how to clean and store seeds, how and when to sow seeds, and how to care for seedlings and transplants, and to set them out.

Gardening

To obtain a merit badge for Gardening, a scout must:

1. Do two of the following things:

(a) Operate a garden plot of not less than 20 feet square and show a net profit of not less than $5 on the season's work.   Keep an accurate crop report.

(b) Grow $\frac{1}{20}$ acre of potatoes.   Select ten hills from which seed potatoes are to be taken.   Grade potatoes in three divisions — market, medium, and culls.   Manufacture the culls into potato starch for home use.   Keep an accurate crop report of the season's work.

(c) Keep both back and front yard in good condition for the summer vacation of three months, which will include care of garden, flowers, mowing of lawn, keeping the yard free from waste paper, rubbish, etc.   Keep an accurate record of the vacation's work.

(d) Build a back-yard trellis, and grow a covering of vines for it in a season's time of not more than four months.

2.   Write an account of not less than five hundred words stating how the work was performed.

Handicraft

To obtain a merit badge for Handicraft, a scout must:

1.   Paint a door.
2.   Whitewash a ceiling.
3.   Repair gas fittings, sash lines, window and door fastenings.
4.   Replace gas mantles, washers, fuse plugs, and electric light bulbs.

5.   Solder.
6.   Hang pictures and curtains.
7.   Repair blinds.
8.   Fix curtains, portière rods, or blind fixtures.
9.   Lay carpets and mend clothing and upholstery.
10.   Repair furniture and china.
11.   Sharpen knives.
12.   Repair gates.
13.   Fix screens on windows and doors.

Horsemanship

To obtain a merit badge for Horsemanship, a scout must:

1. Give the common name for the right and left sides of a horse, and state, using the common name, what side of a horse is habitually approached, and how to act while doing so.

2. State principal temperamental requirements of a good horse, also principal external points of a horse, and point out on a live horse thirty important points.

3. Know what defects and blemishes are. State the most common defects and blemishes, and how he would treat them.

4. Explain how he would examine a horse for soundness; and state the opinions of horsemen on the degrees of soundness.

5. Give several common diseases of the horse, the symptoms thereof, and the treatment.

6. State fully what he knows of the stable management and the care of a horse.

7. Point out ten important parts of the saddle, and show how he would put it on and remove it.

8. Point out ten important parts of the bridle, and show how he would fit, put it on, and take it off.

9. Illustrate on a horse the correct way of mounting and the correct position in a saddle.

10. Know the aids in riding and how they are used. Illustrate on a horse how he would move forward, increase or decrease the gait, halt, back, and change direction.

Interpreting

To obtain a merit badge for Interpreting, a scout must:

1. Carry on a simple conversation in a modern foreign language.

2. Write a simple letter in a modern foreign language on a subject given by the examiners.

3. Read and translate from sight a passage from a book or newspaper, in French, German, English, Spanish, Italian, or any language that is not of his own country.

Leather Working

To obtain a merit badge for Leather Working, a scout must:

1. Have a knowledge of tanning and curing.

2. Sole and heel a pair of boots, sewed or nailed, and generally repair boots and shoes.

3. Dress a saddle, and repair traces, stirrup leathers, etc., and know the various parts of harness.

Life Saving

To obtain a merit badge for Life Saving, a scout must:

1. Go down from the surface of the water at least seven feet deep and bring up an object twelve inches or more in diameter, weighing not less than ten pounds.

2. Swim twenty yards carrying a person of his own weight:
   (a) By a two-hand carry, using feet only for propulsion;
   (b) By a one-arm carry, using side stroke.

3. Dressed in trousers, coat, and shoes swim fifty yards, then undress before touching shore.

4. In deep water, demonstrate three approved methods of releasing death grip.

5. Demonstrate Schaefer (prone pressure) method of resuscitation.

Machinery

To obtain a merit badge for Machinery, a scout must:

1. Describe the construction of a lathe, planer, shaper, drill.

press, and steam boiler; also explain the purpose for which each is intended.

2. Name at least twelve of the principal hand tools used by machinists.

3. Construct a wood or metal model illustrating the principles of levers, gears, pulleys, or block and tackle.

Marksmanship

To obtain a merit badge for Marksmanship, a scout must:

1. Know the Boy Scout marksmanship code and agree to follow same. (See page 54.)

2. Make not less than 38 points standing, out of a possible

50 points in ten shots; and 42 points prone, out of a possible 50 points in ten shots; or a total score of 80 points out of a possible 100, at a distance of fifty feet from the end of the rifle to the target. (See note 2 for conditions.)

3. Must produce evidence that all practice and the test have been conducted under a range officer whose appointment has been approved by the National Court of Honor.

(1) The Boy Scout Marksman Code

I hereby promise upon my honor NEVER to

1. Thoughtlessly point my gun at any human being under any circumstances.
2. Handle a fire-arm without first examining to make certain it is empty.
3. Load a fire-arm while persons are in front of me.
4. Shoot at or kill a harmless animal or bird for the mere pleasure of killing.
5. Skylark with fire-arms in hand or while engaged in target practice.
6. Engage in aiming and snapping the hammer except with the fire-arm pointed toward the target.
7. Shoot in the open without first taking every precaution for the safety of others.
8. Be unsportsmanlike when engaged in contests of skill with fire-arms.
9. Lay aside a fire-arm without cleaning after being used.
10. Take anything for granted and always bear the above rules in mind.

(2) Conditions

RIFLE: Any single-shot, 22-calibre rifle with sightings other than telescopic in front of firing pin, weighing not over ten pounds, recommended

TARGET: Fifty-foot Junior Marksmanship target, two to five counts. These will be supplied through the courtesy of the National Rifle Association upon application to National Headquarters.

POSITION: Standing: All parts of the body to be free from artificial support.

Prone: Head toward target; forearm and rifle must be free from all artificial support. Use of strap allowed in the prone position only.

Masonry

To obtain a merit badge for Masonry, a scout must:

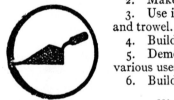

1. Lay a straight wall with a corner.
2. Make mortar and describe process.
3. Use intelligently a plumb-line, level, and trowel.
4. Build a stone oven.
5. Demonstrate a knowledge of the various uses for cement.
6. Build a dry wall.

Mining

To obtain a merit badge for Mining, a scout must:

1. Identify and describe twenty-five minerals.
2. Define vein, placer, lode, stratum, dip, strike, joint, fault; and identify ten different kinds of rocks.

3. State what metals are mined from placer. State in what general respects placer mining differs from lode or vein mining.

4. Describe how mines are ventilated. Give the conditions that differentiate coal mining from metal mining.

5. Describe systems for mine ventilation, safety devices, and rescue methods as taught by the American Red Cross Society.

Music

To obtain a merit badge for Music, a scout must:

1. Be able to play a standard musical instrument satisfactorily, as used in orchestra work.

2. Read at sight simple music required for the fourth grade in musical education.

3. Write a satisfactory essay of not less than five hundred words on the history of American Music.

Painting

To obtain a merit badge for Painting, a scout must:

1. Have a knowledge of how to combine pigments in order to produce paints in shades and tints of color.

2. Know how to add positive colors to a base of white lead or of white zinc.

3. Understand the mixing of oils, turpentine, etc., to the proper consistency.

4. Paint a porch floor or other surface evenly and without laps.

5. Know how and when to putty up nail holes and uneven surfaces.

6. Present for inspection a panel covered with three coats of paint, which panel must contain a border of molding, the body of the panel to be painted in one color and the molding in another.

Pathfinding

To obtain a merit badge for Pathfinding, a scout must:

1. In the country, know every lane, bypath, and short cut for a distance of at least two miles in every direction around the local scout headquarters; or in a city, have a general knowledge

of the district within a three-mile radius of the local scout headquarters, so as to be able to guide people at any time, by day or by night.

2. Know the population of the five principal neighboring towns, their general direction from his scout headquarters, and be able to give strangers correct directions how to reach them.

3. If in the country, know in a two-mile radius, the approximate number of horses, cattle, sheep, and pigs owned on the five neighboring farms; or, if in a town, know, in a half-mile radius, the location of livery stables, garages, and blacksmith shops.

4. Know the location of the nearest meat markets, bakeries, groceries, and drug stores.

5. Know the location of the nearest police station, hospital, doctor, fire alarm, fire hydrant, telegraph and telephone offices, and railroad stations.

6. Know something of the history of his place; and know the location of its principal public buildings, such as the town or city hall, post-office, schools and churches.

7. Present a large scale map showing as much as possible of the above required information.

Personal Health

To obtain a merit badge for Personal Health, a scout must:

1. Write a statement on the care of the teeth, and show that his teeth are in good condition as a result of proper care.

2. State a principle to govern in eating; and state in the order of their importance five rules to govern the care of his health.

3. Present satisfactory evidence that he has not been absent from school or work for a period of at least six months as a result of his failure to observe these rules.

4. Tell the difference in effect of a cold bath and a hot bath.

5. Describe the effects of alcohol and tobacco on the growing boy.

6. Tell how to care for the feet on a march.

7. Describe a good healthful game and state its merits.

8. Describe the effects of walking as an exercise.

9. Tell the dangers of specialization and overtraining in the various forms of athletics, and the advantages of an all-round development.

Photography

To obtain a merit badge for Photography, a scout must:

1. Have a knowledge of the use of lenses, of the construction of cameras, of the effect of light upon the sensitive film, and the action of developers.
2. Have a knowledge of several printing processes, and their relative advantages.
3. Take, develop, and print twelve separate subjects,—three interiors, three portraits, three landscapes, and three instantaneous "action photos."
4. Make a recognizable photograph of any wild bird larger than a robin; or a wild animal in its native haunts; or a fish in the water.

Physical Development

To obtain a merit badge for Physical Development, a scout must:

1. Produce satisfactory evidence of habitual good posture.
2. Have no remediable physical defects uncorrected.
3. Produce satisfactory evidence of daily practice of hygienic habits and a thorough knowledge of a standard book on hygiene.
4. Pass three of the tests, according to his weight, in the Athletic Schedule. See Athletics, p. 40.
5. Demonstrate proper form in running, high jump, hurdle, and shot-put.
6. Make up a daily drill of ten exercises for scouts, giving proper exercise for whole body; present evidence of having practised this daily for six months and having taught the same to two or more boys for a period of three months. (See chapter on Health and Endurance.)
7. Demonstrate reasonable efficiency in two outdoor games requiring physical development; give evidence of having taught at least ten scout games to a group of boys, and know ten more. (See Chapter IX.)

Pioneering

To obtain a merit badge for Pioneering, a scout must:

1. Tie twelve kinds of knots quickly.

2. Lash spars properly together for scaffolding.

3. Build a bridge or derrick (each) capable of supporting two hundred pounds in weight.

4. Make a camp kitchen.

5. Build a shack of one kind or another suitable for three occupants.

Plumbing

To obtain a merit badge for Plumbing, a scout must:

1. Submit a wiped joint in lead pipe, threaded joints connecting two pieces of iron pipe with a fitting, a repaired lead pipe, or a repaired iron pipe; and explain how to do all of the above.

2. Be able to repair a Fuller tap and a compression tap.

3. Understand the drainage system of a house, and explain the use of traps and vents.

4. Understand the ordinary hot and cold water system of a house, and explain how to make the system safe from freezing if the house has to be left without fires in the winter.

5. Know the regulations of the local health department with regard to plumbing.

Poultry Keeping

To obtain a merit badge for Poultry Keeping, a scout must:

1. Have a knowledge of incubators, foster-mothers, sanitary fowl houses, coops, and runs.

2. Understand rearing, feeding, killing, and dressing birds for market.

3. Be able to candle and pack eggs for market; describe the differences, in candling, which distinguish the bad eggs from the good; and tell how eggs are graded.

4. Raise a brood of not less than ten chickens.

5. Report his observation and study of the hen, turkey, duck, and goose.

Printing

To obtain a merit badge for Printing, a scout must:
1. Explain the point system, and identify ten sizes of types.
2. Set and correctly space type by hand from manuscript.

3. Set and print a display card or advertising handbill from original copy for use in connection with the local scout work.
4. Print one hundred copies of same on a 10 x 15, or smaller, job press, demonstrating correct methods of washing-up, inking, use of setting pins, use of make-ready, and accurate feeding.
5. Read and mark proof correctly.
6. Give the grade or kind of paper most suitable for various classes of printing.

Public Health

To obtain a merit badge for Public Health, a scout must:
1. State the chief causes and modes of transmission of each of the following diseases: tuberculosis, typhoid, malaria.
2. Draw a diagram showing how the house-fly carries disease.
3. Tell what should be done to a house which has been occupied by a person who has had a contagious disease.

4. Describe the method used in his community in disposing of garbage.
5. Tell how a city should protect its milk, meat, and exposed foods. State what are the laws in his community covering this subject, and to what extent they are being enforced.
6. Tell how to plan the sanitary care of a camp.
7. State the reason why school children should undergo a medical examination.
8. Tell how he may coöperate with the health authorities in preventing disease.
9. Produce satisfactory evidence that he has rendered service in some effort recommended by the public health authorities in the interest of Public Health.

Safety First

To obtain a merit badge for Safety First, a scout must:

1. State four or more dangerous conditions in the average home and indicate what steps should be taken to correct these conditions.

2. Produce satisfactory evidence that he is personally responsible for the application of at least two constructive safety first principles in his own home.

3. Name the most serious violation of public safety principles which has come under his observation and produce satisfactory evidence that he has done all within his power to correct the same.

4. State in writing at least six of the most important regulations covering street safety to meet the conditions of the neighborhood in which he lives.

5. State in writing at least six of the most important regulations covering street safety to meet the conditions of the school he last attended.

6. Submit in writing an outline of his own plan for a school fire drill and explain the method of properly carrying it into effect.

7. State in writing at least six violations of Safety First principles which are responsible for accidents in connection with railroads.

8. Stand a satisfactory examination showing a knowledge of the importance of the Safety First Movement and the most important principles it involves, and satisfactorily demonstrate his ability to assume leadership in case of a fire, panic, or other disaster.

Scholarship

To obtain a merit badge for Scholarship, a scout must:

1. Have been in attendance at one school, grammar, high, private, or night school, for a period of at least one year, since becoming a first class scout.

2. Present a certificate from the teacher or principal covering the same period and showing:

> (a) That his attendance has been satisfactory;

(b) That his deportment has been above the average;

(c) That during the schoo year he has secured a satisfactory average in all of his studies.

Sculpture

To obtain a merit badge for Sculpture, a scout must:

1. Make a shaded drawing in pencil or charcoal of a cylindrical object and a rectangular object grouped together a little below the eye.

2. Model in c ay or plasteline two or more examples of Greek or Renaissance ornament, from a cast or model.

3. Make a copy in clay or plasteline in full size, of a part of an antique statue, as a head, a hand, or a foot.

4. Make a statue "in the round" of a head, of life size, from a living model.

5. Make a study "in the round" of an animal or a group of animals.

Seamanship

To obtain a merit badge for Seamanship, a scout must;

1. Prove intimate working knowledge of all tenderfoot knots and rolling hitch, bowline on a bight and carrick bend.

2. Make the following splices—eye splice, long splice, and short splice.

3. Reeve off and understand the use of any simple tackle and fling a rope coil.

4. Use palm and needle to whip the end of rope and to make a herring-bone stitch, a flat seam, and a round seam in sail canvas.

5. Swim twenty yards with clothes and shoes on.

6. Handle a rowboat with a pair of oars; also act as toxswain, giving orders for getting under way and making landings properly. Scull a boat with one oar.

7. Have a working knowledge of:

    (a) the lead line and patent log;

    (b) anchors and use of ground tackle;

    (c) weather wisdom and tides;

    (d) charts and pilotage.

8. Box the compass by quarter-points and point out direction by the stars and sun.

9. Know the lights used on sail and power vessels and be familiar with the elementary rules of the road.

10. Handle a boat under sail on all points of sailing, getting under way, making landing at dock or alongside another vessel and reefing.

Signaling

To obtain a merit badge for Signaling, a scout must:

1. Send and receive a message in Semaphore code, not fewer than forty-eight letters per minute, or in the General Service (International Morse) Code, not fewer than twenty-four letters per minute.

2. Give and receive signals by sound, using the buzzer, sounder, whistle, or bugle.

3. Make a buzzer outfit, wireless outfit or a heliograph outfit.

Stalking

To obtain a merit badge for Stalking, a scout must:

1. Know and recognize the tracks of ten different animals or birds to be found in his vicinity. For boys living in the city the tracks of domestic animals or birds may be counted.

2. Track an animal for one-quarter mile over ordinary ground without snow. In special cases where large wild animals cannot be found, a trail made by "tracking irons," or by a boy on stilts, may be substituted.

3. Make clear, recognizable photographs of live wild animals or birds, and score twenty-five points on the following basis:

(a) Each different species of wild bird, photographed on the nest, or of young birds, to count two points; (b) Each species of adult wild bird, photographed away from the nest, to count three points; (c) Each species of small wild animal to count four points; (d) Each species of wild animal larger than a woodchuck to count five points.

Surveying

To obtain a merit badge for Surveying, a scout must:

1. Map correctly from the country itself the main features of half a mile of road, with 440 yards each side, to a scale of two feet to the mile, and afterward draw same map from memory.

2. Measure the width of a river.

3. Measure the height of a tree, telegraph pole, or a church steeple, describing the method adopted.

4. Be able to measure gradient.

5. Understand the use of the plane table.

Swimming

To obtain a merit badge for Swimming, a scout must:

1. Be able to swim one hundred yards.

2. Dive properly from the surface of the water.

3. Demonstrate breast, crawl, and side strokes.

4. Swim on the back fifty feet.

Taxidermy

To obtain a merit badge for Taxidermy, a scout must:

1. Have a knowledge of the game laws of the United States and the state in which he lives.

2. Preserve and mount the skin of a game bird, or animal, killed in season, and without violation of any law.

3. Mount for a rug the pelt of some fur animal.

Life Scout

The life scout badge is awarded to all first class scouts who have qualified for the merit badges of first aid, physical development or athletics, personal health, public health, and life saving or pioneering.

Star Scout

The star scout badge is awarded to the first class scout who has qualified for ten merit badges, including the five badges of the life scout.

Eagle Scout

The eagle scout badge is awarded to any first class scout qualifying for twenty-

one merit badges. These twenty-one badges shall include first aid, life saving, personal health, public health, cooking, camping, civics, bird study, pathfinding, pioneering, athletics or physical development, and any ten others.

National Court of Honor

The National Court of Honor consists of citizens of the United States, of sterling personal character and notable achievement in those lines of activity which are represented by the various merit badges awarded by the Boy Scouts of America, whose accomplishments will serve to inspire proper motives and ambition in the Boy Scouts.

These men are known as counsellors, are elected annually by the National Council, and include so far as practicable at least one person of exceptional ability or accomplishment in each subject and activity for which merit badges are awarded.

The members of the National Court of Honor serve as advisors to the Executive Board in all matters pertaining to the awarding of merit badges and honor medals.

The National Scout Commissioner acts as the chairman of the National Court of Honor. Seven or more members of the National Court of Honor are elected as an Executive Committee of this body designated to pass upon claims of honor medals. This committee meets quarterly. Special meetings may be called at other times when the application for consideration makes it desirable.

Honor Medals

The various badges previously referred to, awarded to boy scouts for passing the different standard tests, should not be confused with the honor medals, which are awarded by the National Court of Honor in recognition of unusual bravery and heroism displayed by scouts in the actual saving of life. An honor medal is a national honor and is awarded only by the National Council in the following manner: where there is a local council the applicant must be personally examined by a local court

of honor, and its recommendation, properly endorsed by the local council, forwarded on the blank form provided for this purpose to the National Court of Honor. Where possible, the detailed statements of three reliable witnesses should be secured and attached to this form.

Where there is no local council, the same committee which has been authorized to conduct examinations for merit badges should conduct this investigation and make recommendation to the National Court of Honor.

The honor medal is a cross upon which the tenderfoot emblem is superimposed and which is attached to the second class emblem pin by chains, making of the whole a first class scout badge mounted on a ribbon. At the top of the cross is the word "Honor" and at the bottom, the words "Boy Scouts of America." A scout to whom one of these medals is awarded is entitled to wear the same on the left breast. (See page 73.)

The bronze medal is mounted on a red ribbon and is awarded to a scout who has actuallv saved life where risk is involved.

The silver medal is mounted on blue ribbon and is awarded to a scout who saves life with considerable risk to himself.

The gold medal is mounted on white ribbon and is the highest possible award for heroism. It may be granted to a scout who has gravely endangered his own life in actually saving the life of another.

Blanks which will facilitate the presentation of claims for the consideration of the National Court of Honor may be obtained upon request from National Headquarters, 200 Fifth Avenue, New York City.

Manner of Conducting Scout Tests

Special care should be exercised to guard against too rapid advancement by scouts, so as to insure thoroughness in their work. This must be especially borne in mind with reference to tests for merit badges.

Boy Scout requirements

The members of the local courts of honor and expert examiners who may be duly appointed to conduct examinations should keep in mind that the lists of questions as set forth for the various tests are merely an outline of the scope of the examination to be given and do not restrict the examination to the lists. In no case, however, is the court of honor or other examiner authorized to omit any of the points covered by the list, or accept as an equivalent any examination which does not include each of the questions as set forth in this handbook. It is required that the applicant personally appear before the court of honor with at least three members present and satisfy them that he is entitled to receive the badge. Such procedure is of great value to the scout who through such a meeting learns of the interest of the community in his welfare.

It should further be remembered that the purpose of these examinations is not to secure mere technical compliance with the requirements, but rather to ascertain the scout's general knowledge of the subject covered as a result of his own application and study. *Practical knowledge* rather than *book knowledge* is desired.

The rule requiring a tenderfoot to remain such for at least thirty days is to be strictly followed, and it is also required that second class scouts remain such for at least sixty days.

Every examination given for advanced work should include questions of review covering previous tests taken by the applicant. He should also [be required to show that he knows and has put into practice the Scout Oath and Law.

Care should be exercised in all tests involving severe physical exertion, such as the fourteen-mile hike required of first class scouts; the merit badge tests in swimming, cycling, and seamanship. In case of doubt as to the scout's physical fitness to stand the test, a physician's certificate should be requested.

Tenderfoot

Tenderfoot scout tests are given by the scoutmaster of the troop in all communities, whether there is a local council or not. This does not, however, relieve the local council of the responsibility of maintaining standards.

Second Class

In communities where there is a local council, second class scout tests should be given by the scout commissioner personally, whenever practicable, or by a deputy designated by him. A scout must serve as a second class scout for two months before becoming a first class scout.

First Class

In communities where there is a local council, first class scout tests, whenever practicable, should be conducted by the court of honor, or under the personal supervision of the scout commissioner or by a deputy designated by him.

In all other communities where local councils have not been

organized the examination for second class and first class scout tests should be given by the scoutmaster of the troop with the coöperation of the troop committee, or by a special committee representing the court of honor which has been selected to conduct examinations for merit badges.

Merit Badges

Examinations for merit badges should be given by the court of honor of the local council.

In communities where a local council has not been organized, a local committee of representative men, including the superintendent or principal of schools, should be organized to conduct these tests.

Whenever the members of the local court of honor are called upon to conduct an examination in any subject with which they are not familiar, they should obtain the aid of an expert in such subject to conduct the examination. The qualifications of such

Every scout should appear before a regularly constituted Court of Honor before he can be granted a Merit Badge or Honor Medal

expert should be definitely agreed upon by the court of honor in advance of his selection. His certificate is to be accepted only as evidence covering the technical points involved in the examination. This does not relieve the members of the court of honor from responsibility of further testing the scout, and satisfying themselves as to his knowledge of the subject for which the merit badge is sought and his right to receive it in accordance with the official requirements.

The local court of honor, having satisfied itself that the applicant has met the requirements for a merit badge, must submit in writing to the Court of Honor of the National Council a certificate endorsed by the expert who conducted the examination, and certified to by the members of the local court of honor, showing that they had satisfactory proof that the scout has actually passed the test, that he has personally appeared before the court of honor, and is entitled to receive the badge. Blanks are provided by the National Council upon which all claims for merit badges should be made. By using these blanks and carefully following the directions thereon, delay and disappointment may be avoided. Blanks not properly filled in cannot be accepted by the National Court of Honor.

Patrol Signs

Each troop of boy scouts is named after the place to which it belongs. For example, it is Troop No. 1, 2, 3, 4, etc., of New York or Chicago. Each patrol of the troop is named after an animal or bird, but may be given another kind of name if there is a valid reason. In this way, the Twenty-seventh New York Troop, for instance, may have several patrols, which may be respectively the Ox, Wolf, Jackal, Raven, Buffalo, Fox, Panther, and Rattlesnake.

Each scout in a patrol has a number, the patrol leader being No. 1, the assistant patrol leader No. 2, and the other scouts the remaining consecutive numbers. Scouts in this way should work in pairs, Nos. 3 and 4 together; 5 and 6 together; 7 and 8 together.

Each scout in a patrol should be able to imitate the call of his patrol animal. That is, the scouts of the Wolf patrol should be able to imitate a wolf. In this way scouts of the same patrol can communicate with each other when in hiding, or in the dark of night. It is not honorable for a scout to use the call of any other patrol except his own.

The patrol leader calls up his patrol at will by sounding his whistle and by giving the call of the patrol.

When the scout makes signs anywhere for others to read he also draws the head of his animal. That is to say, if he were out scouting and wanted to show that a certain road should not be followed by others, he would draw the sign, "not to be fol-

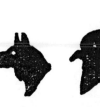

MONGOOSE
Squeak —"Cheep"
BROWN AND ORANGE

HAWK
Cry (same as Eagle)
—"Kreeee" PINK

WOLF
Howl —"How-oooo"
YELLOW AND BLACK

PEEWIT
Whistle — "Tewitt"
GREEN AND WHITE

HOUND
Bark — "Bawow-wow"
ORANGE

CAT
Cry — "Meeaow"
GRAY AND BROWN

JACKAL
Laughing Cry —"Wah-
wah-wah-wah-wah"
GRAY AND BLACK

RAVEN
Cry —"Kar-kaw"
BLACK

BUFFALO
Lowing (same as Bull) —
"Um-maouw"
RED AND WHITE

PEACOCK
Cry —"Bee-oik"
GREEN AND BLUE

BULL
Lowing —"Um-maouw"
RED

SEAL
Call —"Hark"
RED AND BLACK

OWL
Whistle —"Koot-koot-koo"
BLUE

TIGER
Purr—"Grrrao"
VIOLET

LION
Roar —"Eu-ugh"
YELLOW AND RED

KANGAROO
Call —"Coo-ee"
RED AND GRAY

HORSE
Whinney —"Hee-e-e-e".
BLACK AND WHITE

FOX
Bark —"Ha-ha"
YELLOW AND GREEN

BEAR
Growl —"Boorrr"
BROWN AND RED

STAG
Call —"Baow"
VIOLET AND BLACK

STORK
Cry —"Korrr"
BLUE AND WHITE

PANTHER
Tongue in side of mouth —
"Keeook"
YELLOW

CURLEW
Whistle —"Curley"
GREEN

HYENA
Laughing Cry —
"Ooowah-oowah-wah"
YELLOW AND BROWN

RAM
Bleat —"Ba-a-a"
BROWN

WOOD PIGEON
Call —"Book-hooroo"
BLUE AND GRAY

EAGLE
Very shrill cry —"Kreeee"
GREEN AND BLACK

HIPPO
Hiss —"Brrussssh"
PINK AND BLACK

RATTLESNAKE
Rattle a pebble in a small
potted meat tin
WHITE AND PINK

WILD BOAR
Grunt —"Broof-broof"
GRAY AND PINK

COBRA
Hiss —"Pssst"
ORANGE AND BLACK

CUCKOO
Call —"Cook-koo"
GRAY

OTTER
Cry —"Hoi-oi-oick"
BROWN AND WHITE

BEAVER
Slap made by clapping
hands
BLUE AND YELLOW

ALLIGATOR	PELICAN	FLYING EAGLE	RACCOON
GRAY AND GREEN	GRAY AND VIOLET	RED, WHITE AND BLUE	BLACK AND BROWN

BLACK BEAR	PINE TREE	CROW
KHAKI AND RED	BROWN AND GREEN	BLACK AND BLUE

lowed," across it and add the name of his patrol animal, in order to show which patrol discovered that the road was bad, and by adding his own number at the left of the head to show which scout had discovered it. Other patrol emblems and colors are as follows: Moose, colors white and gray; Antelope, colors khaki and green; Bat, colors black and khaki; Elephant, colors white and violet; Swallow, colors khaki and blue; Woodpecker, colors green and violet; Rhinoceros, colors khaki and orange; Bob-White, colors white and khaki.

Each patrol leader carries a small flag on the end of his staff or stave with the head of his patrol animal shown on both sides. Thus the Tigers of the Twenty-seventh New York Troop should have the flag shown below.

Badges of Rank

The following devices are used to distinguish the various ranks of scouts. For exact positions see diagram.

Tenderfoot: The tenderfoot badge should be worn on the left breast pocket of the uniform or by scouts in civilian dress on the coat lapel or left breast pocket.

First and Second Class Badges: The badges of the first and second class scouts are embroidered in yellow and are worn on the left sleeve midway between the elbow and wrist. The metal second and first class badges are to be worn only on the summer uniform and by scouts who do not have uniforms or by scouts in civilian dress on the coat lapel or left breast pocket. This badge cannot be worn on the uniform.

Scouts winning any of the badges are entitled to place after their names the insignia of the badges won. For instance, if he has successfully passed the signaling and seamanship tests, he signs his name in this manner—

Service Stripes: For each year of service as a boy scout he will be entitled to wear a stripe of dark green braid on the right sleeve only, parallel with and three inches from the edge of the cuff, three green stripes being changed for one red one. Five years of scouting would be indicated by one red stripe and two green stripes.

Patrol Leaders: The patrol leader's insignia consists of two dark green bars, one and one half inches long and three eighths of an inch wide. These should be worn one inch below the troop numerals on the left sleeve.

The assistant patrol leader's insignia consists of one dark green bar only.

Scout Scribe: The insignia of a scout scribe is a tenderfoot, second class, or first class badge, according to the scout's rank, with two pens crossed below the badge.

Patrol Colors: Patrol colors should only be worn on the right shoulder. They are five and one half inches long and three quarters of an inch wide.

Troop Bugler: The troop bugler's insignia consists of the badge of his proper rank, with a bugle below it.

Troop Numbers: Members of each troop should wear on the left sleeve a block of red felt one and one half inches below the seam and one and three quarters of an inch in depth, on which a white figure one and one quarter inches high is placed. This figure indicates the number of the troop in the local council.

Metal Numbers: Where it is desired to wear metal numerals instead of the cloth numerals, the metal numerals should be worn on the collar. Each local council shall decide which class of numerals will be worn in its district and all troops must adopt the same method.

Merit Badges: Merit badges can be worn on the right sleeve only, in rows of not more than three, parallel with the edge of

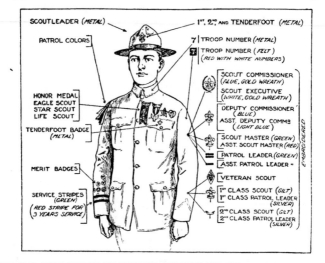

OFFICIAL DESIGNATION OF CORRECT POSITION FOR WEARING SCOUT BADGES

the cuff and two inches above the service stripes. It is suggested that the merit badges be sewed on a false half sleeve that may be fastened by hooks or snaps, so that it may be worn on the proper occasions, but detached on hikes and at times when wearing badges might seem undesirable.

Eagle, Star, and Life Scout Badges: These should be worn only on the left breast above the pocket in the order given from right to left.

Honor Medals: Honor medals should be worn only on the left breast above the pocket.

Scout Commissioner: The insignia of a scout commissioner is a first class badge reproduced in dark blue surrounded by a gold wreath.

Scout Commissioner

Scoutmaster

Scout Executive: The insignia of a registered scout executive is the same badge reproduced in white and surrounded by a gold wreath.

Deputy Scout Commissioner: The insignia of a deputy scout commissioner is the first class badge reproduced in dark blue.

Assistant Deputy Scout Commissioner: The insignia of an assistant deputy scout commissioner is a first class badge reproduced in light blue.

Scoutmaster: The insignia of a scoutmaster is the first class badge reproduced in green.

Assistant Scoutmaster: The insignia of an assistant scoutmaster is the first class badge reproduced in red.

The badge of the scout commissioner, scout executive, deputy scout commissioner, scoutmaster, and assistant scoutmaster should be worn three inches below the shoulder seam of the left sleeve. The use of these badges is strictly restricted to men holding commissions from the National Council.

Other Badges and Insignia: No other badges or insignia are to be worn on the scout uniform unless presented by the Nation, State, City, or some civic organization engaged in work for the general good, for services performed or proficiency attained in competitive tests. Scouts and scout officials should wear only their badges of highest rank. This does not apply to badges of distinction, however. Commissioned leaders should encourage the strict adherence to this regulation.

National Scout Commissioner: The badge of the National Scout Commissioner and Chairman of the Court of Honor consists

National Scout
Commissioner

of a gold laurel wreath, silver eagle, red, white,
and blue shield, scout badge in gold, and silver
powder-horn.

Uniform for Officials

The uniform for officials is similar to that for
boys except that the Norfolk jacket, long
trousers, and leather puttees may be worn for
officers above the rank of patrol leader when
desired.   Imitation of army uniform should be
avoided.

The Boy Scout Salute

That scouts may understand the significance of the salute,
something of its history and object is stated.

When a gentleman raises his hat to a lady he is but continuing a custom that had its beginning in the days of knighthood.   Failure to do so then signified distrust, to-day it signifies
impoliteness.

To acknowledge another's presence by some courtesy is one
of the natural, nobler instincts of man.

Sometimes a person is found who has the mistaken idea that
he sacrifices his independence and the American spirit of freedom by saluting: Of course such ideas do not exist in the mind
of a scout.   It is considered an application of every-day courtesy and common sense.

The salute should begin when at least six paces away from
the person saluted.   The head and eyes should always be turned
toward the person saluted as long as the hand is raised.

The Boy Scout Uniform

The scout uniform should be an outward expression of the
scout's inward feeling of friendliness to every other scout, no
matter to what class in society the other scout belongs.   It
represents the spirit of true democracy.   It definitely identifies
the boy as part of the great brotherhood of boys following the
scout program in his own country as well as in practically all of
the civilized nations of the world.

The uniform intensifies good comradeship, encourages loyalty
to the group, and stimulates a feeling of self-respect which results
in the group presenting a much smarter appearance than it
otherwise would.

While it is not necessary for a boy to have a uniform or

any other special equipment in order to carry out the boy scout program, it has been found that most boys are eager for the opportunity of having the scout uniform. It is comfortable, wears well, and is inexpensive. It is far better for a troop of scouts to do without a uniform, however, than to undertake to secure the same by soliciting contributions for that purpose. Indeed, it is advisable, whenever it can be done, for each scout to personally earn the money with which to secure his uniform. This is so even if the boy's parents can well afford to give him the money with which to buy it.

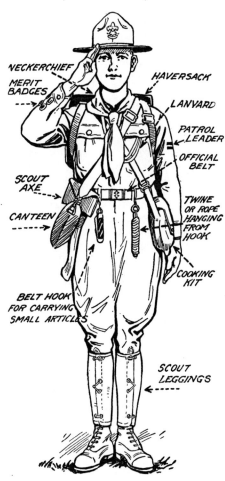

NECKERCHIEF

MERIT BADGES

HAVERSACK

LANYARD

PATROL LEADER

OFFICIAL BELT

SCOUT AXE

TWINE OR ROPE HANGING FROM HOOK

CANTEEN

COOKING KIT

BELT HOOK FOR CARRYING SMALL ARTICLES

SCOUT LEGGINGS

The scout salute and accoutrement

Many troops of scouts have started with little or no equipment and have gradually fully equipped themselves by the individual efforts of the boys.

The official uniform for boy scouts is made up of standard khaki material. This material was selected with the greatest of care. It was submitted to severe tests and chosen because of its wearing qualities.

The manufacturer of this uniform was chosen because of his ability to maintain this high standard of quality and furnish the uniform at a lower price than any other competitor.

The boy scout uniform consists of the following: Hat — olive drab, flat brim; Shirt—khaki, coat style, bellows pockets; Coat — khaki, four bellows pockets, standing collar, metal buttons with scout emblem; Shorts, or Breeches — standard khaki material; Belt — olive drab web; Haversack — worn as a knapsack; Shoulder Knots — 5½ inches, worn in colors of patrol on right shoulder; Leggings, Puttees, or Stockings — to match uniform.

Numerous imitation uniforms have been placed upon the market. Boy scouts should be very certain that they are not being defrauded when purchasing a uniform. The official uniform is stamped with the seal of the organization and all of the buttons bear the patented design of the scout badge.

Before purchasing any part of the uniform, write to National Headquarters for a copy of the latest supply catalog which will give you prices of all equipment.

KNOTS EVERY SCOUT SHOULD KNOW

By Samuel A. Moffat, Boy Scouts of America

Every scout knows what rope is. From the earliest moment of his play life he has used it in connection with most of his games. In camp life and on hikes he will be called upon to use it again and again. It is therefore not essential to describe here the formation of rope; its various sizes and strength. The important thing to know is how to use it to the best advantage. To do this an intelligent understanding of the different knots and how to tie them is essential. Every day sailors, explorers, mechanics, and mountain-climbers risk their lives on the knots that they tie. Thousands of lives have been sacrificed to ill-made knots. The scout, therefore, should be prepared in an emergency, or when necessity demands, to tie the right knot in the right way.

There are three qualities to a good knot: 1. Rapidity with which it can be tied. 2. Its ability to hold fast when pulled tight. 3. The readiness with which it can be undone.

The following knots, recommended to scouts, are the most serviceable because they meet the above requirements and will be of great help in scoutcraft. If the tenderfoot will follow closely the various steps indicated in the diagrams he will have little difficulty in reproducing them at pleasure.

In practising knot tying a short piece of hemp rope may be used. To protect the ends from fraying a scout should know how to "whip" them. The commonest method of "whipping" is as follows:

Lay the end of a piece of twine along the end of the **rope.**
Hold it to the rope with the thumb of your left hand **while**
you wind the standing part around it and the rope until **the**

end of the twine has been covered. Then with the other **end**
of the twine lay a loop back on the end of the rope and **continue**
winding the twine upon this second end until
all is taken up. The end is then pulled back
tight and cut off close to the rope.

For the sake of clearness a scout must
constantly keep in mind these three principal
parts of the rope:

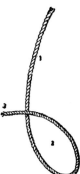

1. *The Standing Part* — The long unused
portion of the rope on which he works;

2. *The Bight* — The loop formed whenever
the rope is turned back upon itself; and,

3. *The End* — The part he uses in leading.
Before proceeding with the tenderfoot requirements, a scout should first learn the
two primary knots: the overhand and figure-
of-eight knots.

The Overhand Knot.
Start with the posi-
tion shown in the pre-
ceding diagram. Back
the end around the
standing part and up
through the bight and
draw tight.

*The Figure-of-Eight
Knot.* Make a bight
as before. Then lead
the end around back
of the standing part
and down through the
bight.

After these preliminary steps, the prospective tenderfoot
may proceed to learn the required knots.

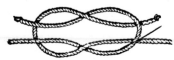

Square or Reef Knot. The commonest knot for tying two ropes together. Frequently used in first aid bandaging. Never slips or jams; easy to untie.

False Reef or Granny. If the ends are not crossed correctly when making the reef knot, the false reef or granny is the result. This knot is always bad.

Sheet Bend or Weaver's Knot. This knot is used in bending the sheet to the clew of a sail and in tying two rope-ends together.

Make a bight with one rope *A B*, then pass end *C* of other rope up through and around the entire bight and bend it under its own standing part.

The Bowline. A noose that neither jams nor slips. Used in lowering a person from a burning building, etc.

Form a small loop on the standing part, leaving the end long enough for the size of the noose required. Pass the end up through the bight, around the standing part and down through the bight again. To tighten, hold noose in position and pull standing part.

Halter, Slip, or Running Knot. A bight is first formed and an overhand knot made with the end around the standing part.

Sheepshank. Used for shortening ropes. Gather up the amount to be shortened, then make a half hitch round each of the bends as shown in the diagram.

Clove Hitch. Used to fasten one pole to another in fitting up scaffolding; this knot holds snugly; is not liable to slip laterally.

Hold the standing part in left hand, then pass the rope around the pole; cross the standing part, making a second turn around the pole, and pass the end under the last turn.

The Fisherman's Bend. Used aboard yachts for bending on the gaff topsail halliards. It consists of two turns around a spar or ring, then a half hitch around the standing part and through the turns on the spar, and another half hitch aoove it around the standing part.

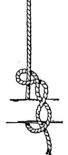

Timber Hitch. Used in hauling timber. Pass the end of the rope around the timber. Then lead it around its standing part and bring it back to make two or more turns on its own part. The strain will hold it securely.

Two Half Hitches. Useful because they are easily made and will not slip under any strain.

Their formation is sufficiently indicated by the diagram.

Blackwall Hitch. Used to secure a rope to a hook. The standing part when hauled tight holds the end firmly.

Becket Hitch. For joining a cord to a rope. May be easily made from diagram.

The Fisherman's Knot.
Used for tying silkworm
gut for fishing purposes.
It never slips; is easily
unloosed by pulling the
two short ends.

The two ropes are laid
alongside one another,
then with each end an
overhand knot is made
around the standing
part of the other. Pull
the standing parts to
tighten.

Carrick Bend. **Used**
in uniting hawsers for
towing. Is easily untied
by pushing the loops in-
ward.

Turn the end of one
rope *A* over its standing
part *B* to form a loop.
Pass the end of the other
rope across the bight
thus formed, back of the
standing part *B* over the
end *A*, then under the
bight at *C*, passing it
over its own standing
part and under the bight
again at *D*.

The Mariner's Compass

Boxing the compass consists in enumerating the points,
beginning with north and working around the circle as follows:

NORTH
North by east
North, North-east
North-east by north
NORTH–EAST
North-east by east
East, North-east
East by north

EAST
East by south
East, South-east
South-east by east
SOUTH–EAST
South-east by south
South, South-east
South by east

SOUTH
South by west
South, South-west
South-west by south
SOUTH–WEST
South-west by west
West, South-west
West by south

WEST
West by north
West, North-west
North-west by west
NORTH–WEST
North-west by north
North, North-west
North by west
NORTH

CHAPTER II

WOODCRAFT

Woodlore

How to Tell North, South, and Other Directions

*By Edward F. Bigelow, Editor, Guide to Nature, President
International Agassiz Society*

Some persons have so strongly developed a sense of direction
or orientation that at any time, in any place, and in any weather,
they are usually able to determine easily in which direction lies
the north, and consequently each of the other directions. I
have known some people who would approach positive accuracy
even if blindfolded, or at night in a dark cellar, or when in the
woods on a cloudy day or a dark night. Most of us do not possess this quality so perfectly developed, but it is a valuable and
important possession to every one that walks in the great outdoor world; it should be developed and cultivated.

The best method is to carry a small compass in the pocket or
on the watch chain. A magnetized needle is the simplest form
of compass, or an ordinary sewing needle that has been rubbed
on the end of a magnet. This may be carried in a small phial
and balanced on a splinter of wood and floated on a cup of water,
or on the surface of a quiet spring. The surface film will support it and it will swing into the plane of the magnetic south
which to most of us is in all probability the same as the geographi-
cal north and south.

Probably the next best way is to use an open-faced watch.
To use this method a shadow must be cast on the watch by a
match or a slender twig, but at certain times of the day, especially between eight and ten o'clock, this cannot be done with a
hunting case watch, as the open cover is in the way. Hold the
watch horizontally, with the face upward. Hold any slender
object upright at the edge of the watch opposite the end of
the hour hand. Turn around until the shadow falls on the
hour hand as shown in the illustration. In that position the

hour hand will point directly toward the sun. The south will then be halfway between the hour hand and the figure XII on the dial. At ten o'clock in the morning XI on the watch face will point to the south.

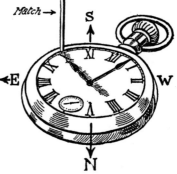

The same rule applies in the afternoon, only the point to indicate the south will then be backward on the watch, not forward; that is, at two o'clock the line southward will pass through I, at four o'clock it will pass through II, and so on. A little thought will show why this is so. The sun rises in the east, is directly south at noon, and sets in the west. That makes a semicircle, and includes approximately twelve hours. If you will in imagination travel to the point on the other side of the earth toward which your feet are directly pointing, you will see that this is there repeated, another semicircle. The sun goes around this entire circle. But in using the watch as an hourglass, each half-circle in the sky is represented by half of the circumference of your watch, or by six hours on the watch. Therefore, one hour in the sky is represented by half an hour on the watch. You find by experimenting with the shadow on the hour hand, on what part of the circle of your watch the sun is at that particular time. Then count forward or backward on the watch, two hours of sun time to one hour of watch time, counting backward or forward according as it may be forenoon or afternoon.

At exactly noon the slender shadow will extend directly along the hour hand at XII.

Let us say that the sun sets at six o'clock, and you point the hour hand at VI westward toward the sun. Then eastward is indicated by twelve o'clock, and south is III. It will therefore be seen that from XII to VI, six hours represents the twelve hours of daylight. Sunrise to sunset is represented from IX to III, while XII will be exactly south.

One could memorize the rule and so apply it, but the easier and more sensible method is to think of the sky as divided into twenty-four sections, twelve of which, or twelve hours of which, we own, while the other twelve belong to our friends on the other side of the earth.

To Know Directions by the Stars

Every one fond of rambling in fields and forests at night should learn how to ascertain the direction by the stars and should become familiar with the principal constellations. To be able to do this is a great joy. It gives one a sense of security. Polaris is readily found by following the "pointers" at the end of the Great Dipper. In the opposite direction these "pointers" point to a place halfway between the Sickle and the right-angled triangle in Leo. Every boy scout should be familiar with the Polar constellations, and keep them in mind as comparable to the face of a watch, with the exception that their direct movement is backward, or opposite to that of the hands of the watch. The Polar stars, to one familiar with them, are pretty good timekeepers.

To get approximately the time by night one must be familiar with the position of these constellations at that particular day of the year, because their position changes not only according to the hour of the night, but according to the day of the year. One month equals two hours in changes of position. If the stars are in a certain position, and you would like to see them as they will be two hours later, you can do that by waiting for two hours or by making another observation a month later. Waiting for one month will be followed by the same result as waiting for two hours.

On Starry Nights or Cloudy Days

Here the pocket compass is especially valuable and about the only dependable help, unless the sense of direction or orientation is almost abnormally developed. There are certain positions, however, of mosses and lichens that are fairly trustworthy in indicating direction, but the surroundings of the trees or the rocks upon which they grow must be considered. As a general rule mosses grow on the cool or shady northern side of a tree, but the cool or shady side of a tree is not always the northern side. This holds true on some hillsides, especially on the northern slope, where the tree has its dampest side near the ground and toward the south.

The flowers of some plants have a tendency to follow the sun, but they are not entirely trustworthy. A common belief is that sunflowers follow the sun from the east to the west, and consequently at night point toward the west, but this is largely imaginary, like many other "old sayings."

HOW TO BUILD A LOG CABIN

By Daniel Carter Beard

You must have logs with which to build and it may be necessary to cut down the trees yourself. Remember before beginning to chop to cut away all brush within reach of the axe so that you may swing it by the handle without striking anything. Very serious accidents often happen when the blade of the axe

strikes even a slight twig which deflects it or, in other words, causes it to glance and strike a leg in place of the tree trunk.

After cutting the brush away cut the kerf or notch on one side of the tree as shown in Fig. 1. Cut this notch big enough to do away with the danger of pinching your axe. If the kerf is too small and there is danger of its pinching, cut another notch above it and split out the space between.

Make your first notch halfway or more through the trunk of the tree, then cut the second notch on the opposite side of the tree a trifle higher than the first notch. When the wood separating the two notches becomes too small and weak to support the tree, the trunk will naturally slip and fall in the direction of the lower notch.

Figure 1

Do not stand behind a tree when felling it, because it is liable to kick, that is, shoot backward, and a kicking tree often results in fatal accidents. Don't try to fell a tree against the wind. If the wind is blowing briskly from the wrong direction, leave that tree alone until the wind dies down or blows from the right quarter. After a tree is felled and the branches are trimmed off it may be cut up into logs of any given length. While doing this stand on the log with your legs spread apart and chop between them, making the kerf as wide as the diameter of the log. You will find it much easier to cut a log in this manner than it is to try and roll a log over and cut one side and then the other.

When cut, the logs should be rolled on a skidway, the latter consisting of some small logs with the lower ends resting on the ground and the other ends resting on a log or bank. (See Fig. 2.)

Figure 2

Notching the Logs

To lock the logs together so that they will not roll apart when your house is built, it is necessary to flatten the ends or notch the logs near the ends. You may cut flat notches or round notches, or square and flatten the ends of the log like those in General Putnam's camp at Redding, Connecticut. The simplest notch is the rounded one shown by A—B, and C, Fig. 3. In some places people dovetail the ends of the logs together, but a rounded notch answers all purposes, and if the logs are straight it makes a snug cabin.

Figure 3

Chinking

A log cabin made of straight spruce logs may be chinked with sphagnum moss, the kind of moss you find in wet and marshy places, the kind the florists use to tie up roots and plants. Or the cabin may be calked with tow, as one calks a boat; but when you use pitch-pine logs, like those in my own cabin, or hardwood logs, they are seldom as straight as spruce and consequently the spaces between them are wider. They may be filled by quartering some logs, and using the quartered pieces to fill up the chinks, or the chinks may be filled with stones and chips held in place by mud or clay. Mix your clay as you would mortar and let it be about the same consistency or softness as putty, make it in balls and push the balls in between the chinks. The mud chinking will last for years. Some of the mud in the chinks in my cabin in Pike County, Pennsylvania, has been there now for ten or twelve years. It was chinked up before the Boy Scouts of America or England were born. It is the pioneer log house built for a summer home.

To Square the Corners of Your Cabin

Cut a stick and make it exactly 10 feet long and mark off the feet on it. With it measure from the corner 8 feet on your bottom log or sill log, and on the log which lies across the sill log measure from the same corner 6 feet. Adjust these two logs so that your 10-foot rod will touch the 8-foot point with one end and the 6-foot point with the other; then your foundation will be exactly square, that is, 90° or a right angle. If you doubt it, look into your geometry where it says that a square on the long side of a right-angled triangle is equal to the sum of the squares on the other two sides; thus we take the first 8 feet and square it, 8 x 8 = 64, then the 6 feet, 6 x 6 = 36, then the 10 feet, 10 x 10 = 100, and 64 plus 36 equals 100, hence we know that this is square.

After you have the first few logs in place you will discover that it takes some strength to hoist the others up. To simplify this, lay a few logs on the wall to act as skids and by the aid of ropes roll the other logs up these skids. Reverse each alternate log so that the big ends will not all be at one side of the wall.

The American log house differs from the Canadian log house principally in the shape of the roof; so says my book on "Shacks, Shelters, and Shanties" from which I am cribbing this material.

So that you will remember the gambrel roof, learn this rhyme.

"Gambrel! gambrel! Let me beg
You'll look at a horse's hinder leg;
First great angle above the hoof,
That's the gambrel, hence the gambrel roof."

When you wish to make an opening for a doorway or a window in a cabin, saw a section out of the top log, that is, the last log which crossed the proposed open space (See Fig. 4), then nail a couple of cleats, one on each side of the proposed opening to hold the logs in place, and go on with the building of your cabin. When the cabin walls are finished, it is an easy matter to saw out the doors and windows as indicated by the dotted lines in Fig. 4, after which nail a slab or board against the

AFTER DAN BEARD

Figure 4

ends of the logs in the opening to form the door jambs or window jambs, then the cleats may be removed and the nails in the jambs will hold the logs in the proper position.

The roof of a house is supposed to be built with small logs or poles. In making a roof, as in making walls, remember to reverse each alternate log or pole so that you have a thick end and a thin end all the way up. This will prevent one side of the roof being higher than the other side.

The house may now be roofed over with planks, or shingled with shakes, clapboards, splits, or bark, according to what is available in the section of the country in which you have built your cabin. Shakes are boards split from sections of logs by the use of a froe or even an axe.

The cabin may be a "mudsill," that is, have a pounded earthen floor, or it may be floored with puncheons. Puncheons are logs that are flattened by scoring and hewing off the rounded surface.

We have described a one-pen house. A two-pen or Southern saddlebag house is just what its name implies, two cabins set in line with each other about 10 feet apart and one roof extending over the two pens. The space between the two cabins in the South is called a gallery, in other places an areaway, and in the North a hallway. In this case the hall is open at both ends.

A saddlebag makes a most delightful summer camp. The doors to the cabin open on the gallery and are thus protected from the rain and wind.

There is scarcely a great man in early American history who did not know how to wield an axe and all were either born in a log cabin or lived considerable time in such a home. Although George Washington was skillful in using the axe, one of the greatest axemen among our great men was Abraham Lincoln.

It might even be said that American history was written with an axe.

MEASURING HEIGHTS AND DISTANCES

By Frederick K. Vreeland, Camp Fire Club of America

The Scout Staff and Pace

The two most important things for a scout to use in measuring are his scout staff, properly divided into feet and inches, and the length of his pace or step. Every scout should find out just what the length of his average step is. To do this, measure a certain distance, such as 100 feet, and walk over it again and again, counting the steps. Be careful not to lengthen or shorten the step, but walk perfectly naturally. Then note in your diary the number of steps or paces to 100 feet. Naturally 52.8 times this number will be a mile.

To measure the height of a tree or flag pole a scout staff is very useful. If A, B, Fig. 1, is a tree, measure off on the ground a distance twelve times the length of your staff, and mark the point C by driving a stake. Then measure off from C one staff length toward the base of the tree, and drive the staff in the ground at *b.* Place the eye close to the ground at C, having the staff

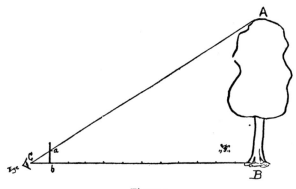

Figure 1

exactly in line with the tree, and note where the line to the top of the tree cuts the staff. We will call this *a.* The distance from *a* to *b*, measured on the staff in inches, will be equal to the height of the tree in feet.

If the ground is not level, or if the eye is not close to the ground, the distance from *a* to *b* should be measured to the point where a line to the base of the tree cuts the staff, and not all the way to the ground.

The reason of this is simple. The triangles A, B, C, and *a*, *b*, C have exactly the same shape, but one is bigger than the other. Since the distance B C is twelve times the distance *b*, C, the height of the tree A B must be twelve times the distance measured on the staff *a b*, hence every inch on the staff is equal to a foot on the tree.

Of course if it is not convenient to measure just twelve pole lengths from the tree, any other distance may be used, but in that case you will have to calculate the height from the rule

$$\frac{a\,b}{b\,C}=\frac{A\,B}{B\,C}$$

Every scout should know also the length of his reach, that is, the distance from his eye to an article, such as a stick or lead pencil, held at arm's length. This can be made useful in a number of ways. For example, instead of using the scout staff to measure the height of a tree you can use a sighting stick or ruler held upright in the hand. Hold the stick as shown in Fig. 2 so it covers the tree, with the top a of the stick

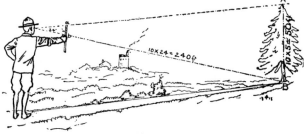

Figure 2

in line with the top A of the tree. Mark with your thumb the point b, in line with the base B of the tree, and measure its distance from the end of the stick. If the distance of the tree in feet is ten times the length of your reach in inches, then the height of the tree in feet will be ten times the height measured on the sighting stick in inches. For example, if the length of your reach is 24 inches and the distance of the tree is ten times 24 feet, or 240 feet, then if the height measured on your sighting stick is 5 inches, the height of the tree will be 10 x 5=50 feet.

The sighting stick may be used also for measuring distances by simply working backward, if you know the size of any object at the distant point. Suppose, for example, a scout wants to know how far away another scout is. Hold a sighting stick at arm's length and measure off the height of the scout on the stick. Then the distance is found by the rule:

$$distance=\frac{\textit{height of object} \times \textit{length of reach}}{\textit{height on stick}}$$

If the height on the stick be 1 inch, the distance in feet of a scout 5 feet tall will be five times the length of your reach in inches. If your reach is 24 inches the distance will be 120 feet. If the height on the sighting stick is only one-half an inch the distance will be twice this, or 240 feet, etc.

It is a good plan to carry a sighting stick divided to suit the length of your reach. To make such a stick stand exactly 100 feet from an average-sized scout and measure his height on the stick. Mark this point 100 feet. Divide the distance to the end of the stick in two and mark the division point 200 feet. Divide that again in two and mark it 400 feet. One-half of that, again, would be 800 feet, and so on until the marks are too close together to be practically useful. Other marks can be made in between if desired.

Fig. 3 shows the correct graduations for a scout with 24-inch reach. The other side of the stick should be divided into inches, like a foot rule.

To measure the distance of a point that you cannot reach, such as the opposite bank of a river, choose two landmarks upon the opposite bank, such as two trees A B, Fig. 4. Call the place where you are standing C. Hold a sighting stick horizontally at arm's length and sight across it. Put the end of the stick

1600
800
400
300
200
150
100
75
50

Fig. 3

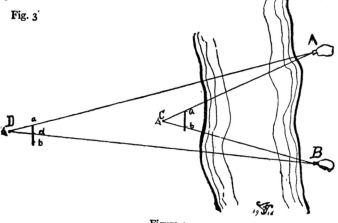

Figure 4

in line with the left-hand tree A and mark with your thumb a point in line with the right-hand tree. Mark this point *b* on the stick.

Now make another mark *d* on the stick just half as far from the end. Walk back, directly away from the river, to a distance which you think is a little greater than the width of the river and sight again across your stick. If your guess is correct, the distance between the two landmarks will be less than the distance *a d* on the stick. Then walk forward again, sighting over the stick as you walk, until the two landmarks A B line up exactly with the mark *d* and the end of the stick. Call the point where you are standing D. The distance from C to D will then be equal to the distance from C to the landmarks A B.

HOW TO FIND YOUR LATITUDE BY THE STARS

By Frederick K. Vreeland, Camp Fire Club of America

Every navigator of a ship on the high seas and every explorer in unknown and remote country finds it very important to measure his latitude, and when possible his longitude, in order to know just where he is on the earth's surface. Ordinarily this is done with an instrument called a sextant, which gives very accurate results; but any scout can measure his latitude closely enough for practice without any implements beyond a jackknife, a piece of string, and a foot rule.

First, he must understand just what latitude is and how it is measured.

Latitude is the distance of a place north or south of the equator measured in degrees on the curved surface of the earth. A degree of latitude is equal to 60 nautical miles or about 69 ordinary or statute miles.

Of course a traveler who wants to find his latitude cannot actually take a tape line and measure this distance, but he can find out what it is by observing the position of the sun or stars.

As the earth rotates on its axis the sun, stars, and planets all seem to revolve around the earth except one, and that is the North Star. That appears to stand always in the same place because it is almost exactly in line with the axis of the earth. If one stood at the North Pole the North Star would appear exactly overhead and all the other stars would appear to revolve in circles around it. But if we are not at the North Pole, the North Star appears lower in the sky. The farther the observer is from the North Pole, that is, the less his latitude is, the nearer the North Star will come to the horizon.

This can easily be seen from the diagram, Fig. 1, which represents the earth as it would appear if looked at from the sun. N is the north pole, S is the south pole, and E E is the equator. The North Star would be on the line S N but so far away that it is impossible to show it on the paper.

Now if you imagine yourself standing on the equator at E and looking north, the North Star would be exactly on the horizon. If you should then travel straight toward the North Pole, as you walked around the curved surface of the earth the North Star would appear to rise above the horizon, in precisely the same way that when you climb a round-topped hill a tree on the other side first appears just above the ground, and rises higher and higher as you climb. When you reached the North Pole the North Star would be directly overhead. The angle of the North Star above the horizon depends upon the distance you have traveled, that is, the latitude. Thus at any point A, the line of the horizon will be A H and the direction of the North Star A P. The latitude will be equal to the angle P A H. To find the latitude, therefore, we need only to measure the angle of the North Star above the horizon.

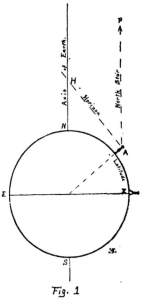

Fig. 1

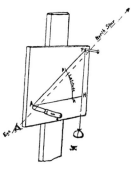

Fig 2.

To do this, choose a post or straight tree from which the North Star can be seen. Fasten a piece of board against the post, pointing edgewise to the North Star, as shown in Fig. 2. Drive a large wire nail in the corner of the board and hang a plumb line from the nail. With a ruler draw a line on the board exactly following the plumb line. Then put your eye close to the edge of the board and sight past the nail at the North Star. Move the eye until the North Star is directly below the nail. Then hold the point of your knife against the board below the eye and move it upward until you can just see the North Star between the knife blade and the nail. When this is done stick the knife carefully into the board. If properly adjusted the Star can be seen when the eye is in the right position, but if the eye is moved the least bit downward the knife blade cuts off the Star, and if it is moved upward the nail makes it disappear.

Now bring a light, and with a ruler draw a straight line A P from the edge of the knife blade to the nail. This line will indicate the direction of the North Star. With a carpenter's square or a card having a square corner, draw a line A H from the edge of the knife blade exactly at right angles to the mark drawn by the plumb line. The angle between this line and the line of the Star will be equal to the latitude of the place.

To measure this angle will of course be easy if you have a protractor, but if you have not it can be done with nothing but a foot rule, although a pair of compasses will help. With the point A as a center, draw an arc of a circle having a radius equal to $7\frac{8}{16}$ inches, cutting the lines A H and A P at points h and p. This represents on a small scale a section of the earth's surface, with h at the equator and p the point where you are standing. Then the distance from h to p *measured along the curve* will be equal to the latitude. Every eighth of an inch on this curve will equal a degree of latitude. Thus if the latitude is $41°$, as it is at National Headquarters, the curved arc $h\ p$ will be $\frac{41}{8} = 5\frac{1}{8}$ inches. The easiest way to measure the curve is to step it off with a pair of dividers, set with points $\frac{5}{8}$ inch apart. Each step will then be equal to 5 degrees. Or bend a narrow strip of paper to fit the curve, and measure the length of the strip.

In order to be exact we should remember that the North Star is not exactly in line with the North Pole, but is just about $1°$ away from it. Hence the North Star does not appear exactly stationary, but if your sights are carefully adjusted you will find that it appears to revolve in a very small circle. The direction of the North Star from the Pole is the same as the direction of the constellation Cassiopeia, which every real scout knows. When the constellation Cassiopeia is at the same height above the horizon as the Pole Star, the Pole Star is just as high as the true Pole, and an observation taken at that time will give the latitude exactly. If Cassiopeia is above the North Star the latter will appear too high and the latitude found may be too great by about 1°. If Cassiopeia is lower than the Pole Star the latitude found will be a little too small.

WHAT TO DO IF LOST

By C. L. Smith, Guide, Pittsburgh, Pennsylvania

One's actions if lost in the forests, mountains, or upon the plains should depend almost wholly upon circumstances and conditions. While it is a comparatively easy matter to lay down rules and give advice to scouts under ordinary circumstances, yet these same rules could not be made to apply to all cases.

Close observation is the best safeguard against getting lost. If you note carefully the direction taken when you leave camp and keep track of your course during your wandering, you will not need a compass; but if you have not done this, all the compasses you could carry would not help you except to travel in a general course. They cannot point out the direction of camp unless you know which side of camp you are on.

Getting lost and its attending miseries are generally caused by carelessness or lack of observation, and can only be avoided by paying very close attention to where one is going and by observing closely general landmarks such as streams and the direction of their course, dividing ridges between water courses that flow in opposite directions, and spurs. If you do this you will not need a compass, for you can always find your way back. Low rolling hills covered with forests and flat forest countries are the hardest to keep one's bearing in, on account of the similarity in the landscape.

It has been said that it comes sooner or later to every one who goes into the woods, to get lost. It may be so. I have spent forty years in the forests and mountains under almost every condition and have my first experience of the kind yet to come. One's ability to find his way depends to a great extent upon the organs of observation and sense of locality in the brain. In some these organs are strongly developed while in others they are deficient, though capable of cultivation. By constant cultivation from childhood these organs may be developed to such an extent that one unconsciously keeps track of his points of the compass.

Scouts as a rule do not go into the big woods, so there is slight danger of their straying very far out of the reach of help. If you leave camp and go up stream or down, you know which way to follow the stream back to camp. As all streams which are small run into larger ones, and all ridges, except watersheds or main divides, end sooner or later in the forks of streams, it is easy to go in a general direction downstream without having to follow the bed of the stream, which is generally rough going on account of brush and other obstructions; but if you are going upstream it is a different matter on account of side streams coming in. One should in this case stay close to the water in order to be sure to follow the main course.

Ì cannot recommend the practice of climbing to the highest point in view to get one's bearings, for the reason that it is a well-known fact that looking at a piece of country from an altitude changes its appearance, and if one is lost he may see the very country over which he has come and not recognize it; besides, this practice as a rule only takes one farther from camp and multiplies one's bewilderment. If you have companions in camp my advice is to stay right where you are and make yourself comfortable, build a shelter and a good fire, and conserve your strength. Your companions are sure to find you if you will call at intervals of a half-hour. Keep a good smoke going by day and a bright fire at night; keep cool and wait. There are many unfailing signs placed by nature to guide one in the woods, but it takes an accomplished woodsman to read them. One of these signs is the difference in the growth of vegetation growing on a north or shady side of a hill from that growing on the southern or sunny slope. Sometimes an expert may also be able to read nature's compass within a few points by the moss on the trees, if he has a general knowledge of the prevailing winds during the wet part of the season.

The trouble with the average person when lost is that he thinks he knows the direction of camp and is so sure of this that I have known intelligent men to dispute their compass and say it had gone wrong. Don't make this mistake. Set your compass, remove all iron or steel from its immediate vicinity, let the needle settle, and if you know the variations between the magnetic and true north you will be able to lay your course accurately.

Another wise thing to do is to follow your back track. This is easy if there is snow on the ground, but difficult where there is none, unless you have been careful to observe the country you have passed by turning frequently and looking back; for you must remember that on your back track you are seeing the country from an opposite angle and it will not look the same. By glancing back as you go out, you familiarize yourself with its appearance and can easily retrace your steps. If you are camping alone and get lost in a big forest and must rely on your own resources to get out, my advice is most emphatically to go downstream. I don't mean you should follow the bed of the stream, but its general course. It will surely bring you out somewhere, and if you know anything of the geography of the country you will be able to tell to a certainty where you will land, while if you go climbing for high points you may wander until you perish, as I have known men to do in the mountains of Oregon, when two days spent following a stream would have brought them to settlement. If you are lost with a companion you will nearly always find him as firm as yourself in his convictions in regard to the points of the compass, and unless you have a compass the best way to convince him is by pointing out nature's compass; that is, by showing him the difference in the vegetation on a north hillside from that growing on a southern exposure, the brush and plants being less dense where the sun has a fair chance.

A good scout is always prepared for almost every emergency while in the woods by having with him knife, axe, and matches, or flint and steel, and with his general knowledge of plants there is but little danger of his meeting with anything like fatal difficulties. There are so many edible plants and roots in the woods that he can always find something to keep starvation away for weeks. Then there are crawfish in plenty in nearly all of our streams, which can be caught with the hands by turning over stones along the shore. These make good food when roasted. The most important thing of all is not to get frightened or allow yourself to get excited, for no harm can come to you if you keep your head; once you lose it your real troubles begin. To illustrate what will most likely occur if you allow yourself to become panic-stricken I will tell the story of R. Henderson, policeman of the town of Michel, B. C., who went out grouse shooting on a mountain only a mile or two from town. This was a round-topped mountain covered with forest and the town could not be seen from its top. After killing three birds he started, as he thought, for town, but lost his bearings and went down the wrong side of the mountain. As soon as he discovered he was lost he became panic-stricken and wandered for three days in a piece of country from which three hours' travel downhill in any direction would have brought him to a settlement. Instead he tried to find a place from which he could see the town. A great deal of the time he was in plain view of his own ranch in the Elk River Valley only a few miles away and did not recognize it. I was trailing him all this time but could not overtake him. He heard me shooting but would neither stop nor come to me.

This action you will say is absurd, but let me tell you, I have known men to do worse while under the spell of a panic from being lost. Henderson was finally caught by Mr. John M. Phillips, of Pittsburgh, Pa. His clothes were torn, his shoes worn out, and he was still carrying the three grouse in his coat, having wandered all this time without food.

I would suggest in order to make the scout more observant and self-reliant that each scout be required to go at least three miles from camp in summer, alone, cook his three meals, build a shelter, and find his way back alone, finding as much of his food as possible in the forest.

How to Make Fire Without Matches

By Dr. Walter Hough, Smithsonian Institution, Washington, D. C.

Kinds of Wood

The best wood is dry and long seasoned till it begins to show signs of decay, as in a dead branch. It must not be gummy, or resinous or fibrous like walnut or pine, or acid like oak, ash, and chestnut. The test for all wood is that the dust ground off is real dust and not gritty. Try the dust in the fingers and if it feels sandy try some other wood. Elm, linden, poplar, soft maple, sycamore, and buckeye will often furnish good wood. The best wood is of the roots of the cottonwood of the west and of the willow.

Root wood is better than stem wood as a rule. The flowering stalks of the yucca are excellent for fire making.

Scouts should be on the lookout for wood and tinder. There is nothing so good as questioning nature yourself; you may thus become a discoverer.

The Tools

A flat piece of wood or a branch flattened on two sides and not over $\frac{3}{4}$ inch thick is selected for the hearth or lower piece. It may be of any length, but long enough to set the foot firmly on one end. The spindle should be whittled out tapering to both ends, not over $\frac{3}{4}$ inch in diameter at the middle, and 12 inches long. It will wear down and can be used as short as 4 inches. The ends should be rounded, not sharp.

The bow is 17 inches long, $\frac{5}{8}$ inch wide, $\frac{1}{2}$ inch thick, and has a curve $\frac{1}{2}$ inch high on the belly. It can thus be whittled out of a strip $1\frac{1}{8}$ inches wide. The ends are swelled a little and holes put through for the cord.

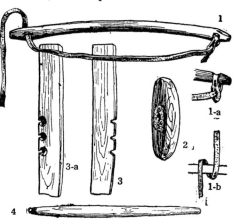

The thong may be of belt lacing 5-16 inch wide or of any good pliable leather. One end of the thong is slit, put through the hole, the other end put through the slit and drawn down. Merely run the thong through the other hole in the bow. The nut is a block 6 inches long, $1\frac{1}{4}$ inches square. Set in the middle a piece of soapstone and make a small smooth pit in the soapstone.

1. Drill bow; 1-a. Applying the thong; 1-b. position of cord on spindle
2. Hand rest for top of spindle
3. Hearth showing slots; 3-a. Hearth showing pits and slots
4. Spindle of correct form

As to the tinder, or first swaddling clothes of the fire, this is of many kinds and may be found anywhere by any scout who sees that soft, finely divided, inflammable material is needed. Cedar bark, dry grass, willow or other catkins, leaves, wood scrapings, a bird's nest, etc., etc.; whatever comes handy, rubbed and reduced to a fluffy mass. Have ready also a bunch of long-stemmed grass, a strip of bark, or anything that can be bent over the new fire.

Fire

Now to make fire: Scratch or nick a small place on the upper surface near the edge of the hearth and set it on firm ground or on flat rocks. If the ground is soft, imbed a rock under the hearth where the pressure comes. Take the spindle, upper end from you, in the left hand, bow in right hand, string to left. Lay the spindle diagonally on the cord and give the bow a half turn. Grasp both so, and set the end of the drill on the hearth near the edge. Make a few turns to start the socket, then cut a clean groove down the edge of the hearth well into the socket. Take the tools up again and run the drill easily at first, and when it

5. The fire drill set up ready for operation

bites a little put on more pressure. When the dust pushes out of the slot as a compact bunch you likely have fire. If so, fan it gently for a moment with the hand till the fire appears and transfer it to the finely divided mass of fuel which has been laid on a strip of bark or grass stems, fold over and wave with gentle circular motion in the air and it will burst into flame. Bows are of two kinds, elastic and rigid. If elastic the spindle can be set in on a stretched cord, but this sort of bow does not give good results. In the rigid bow the spindle is set in with a loose cord, the cord is then drawn tight and given a turn around under the hand against the bow to secure it. Then reach forward the thumb and pinch the cord down against the curved forefinger. By moving the thumb up and down, the cord is tightened or slackened as desired. A little practice will show the relation between the pressure on the top of the spindle and the tension of the cord. This has to be learned and thoroughly under control before fire can be successfully made. Keep the spindle straight up and keep the bow away from it. The spindle must not joggle or the hearth shake, or you will lose the fire. Both fire-making pieces may be of the same wood; indeed it is better that they should be the same. Some tribes, when their wood is not long enough to make a spindle, splice a bit of the good wood in at the point of another piece.

ARCHERY

By H. H. McChesney, Minneapolis, Minnesota

"The greatest sport in the world," enthusiasts call it, and certainly no one will deny that it is one of the oldest and most picturesque. Archery combines the skill of the craftsman and of the good shot, for most archers prefer to make their own equipment and depend upon ingenuity and accuracy for the graceful bows and straight, keen-pointed arrow. There is a certain pride of accomplishment in seeing the instruments one has made prove true and strong, that cannot be given by the use of the machine-made gun. Since the days of Robin Hood men have had a wholesome respect for the woodsman who could fashion his own bow, successfully carry through the difficult process of forming a straight, light arrow, with a well-fitted head and characteristic feathering, and with his own equipment shoot a deer or cut a cord at sixty yards. No scout's woodcraft education is complete unless he knows something of the science and art of archery.

Making the Bow

The tools used in bow-making are few and simple: one large plane, one small plane, a sharp knife, a small round file, a thin flat file with round edge, and a saw. A vise comes in handy, but is not absolutely necessary.

America furnishes many woods well adapted to bow-making. These, in their order of excellence, are probably as follows: Oregon yew, Osage orange, Southern red cedar, mulberry, black locust, sassafras, ironwood, slippery elm, apple tree, black walnut, hickory, white ash, and white oak. Perhaps the best for the scout are hickory, ironwood, and white ash.

Whatever wood is chosen, see to it that it has been thoroughly seasoned—at least a year, and it will be all the better if two or three years have passed since it was cut. Wood not well seasoned will make a bow of poor "cast."

The scout who lives in the country probably has access to a pile of specially straight grained and well-seasoned timber cut for wagon poles, whiffletrees, etc., but the city scout must be content with the lumber yard. In either case the process is the same. Select a piece that is of straight, even, close grain, free from knots, cracks or other defects. Be sure and see to it that when the wood is sawed into pieces $\frac{7}{8}$ by $\frac{3}{4}$ inch the grain will be flat, as in Fig. 1, page 104.

Now take your stick to the nearest sawmill and have it cut as follows: Length, $5\frac{1}{2}$ feet, $\frac{7}{8}$ inch wide and $\frac{3}{4}$ inch thick. (These dimensions are for hard woods, such as hickory, ironwood, etc. If you have selected Southern red cedar or some other soft wood, increase width and thickness 3-16 inch.)

When home is reached, take your stick to the work bench and
with the large plane smooth one of the broad sides, taking care
to cut no deeper than is necessary to remove the saw marks.
Find the center of the stick (it should be 33 inches from each
end) and mark with a straight line drawn squarely across the
wood.   At points 2 inches in either direction from the center
line draw two other lines, also cutting squarely across the stick.
At the ends of your stick make marks ½ inch apart and then connect these with the outside marks at the center by lines drawn
with a straight edge.   (A yardstick that has straight edges does
nicely.)
    With the large plane carefully plane the stick to the lines.   At

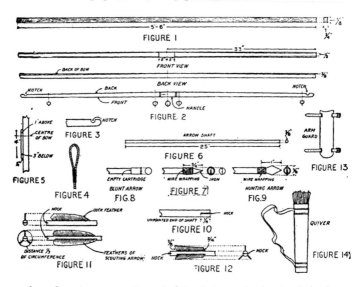

each end make a pencil mark ⅜ inch from the back of the bow,
i. e., the first planed surface.   Connect these end marks with
lines drawn with the straight edge to the center.   Use the large
plane again to cut away the surplus wood, taking great care not
to cut through the lines.
    Now with the small plane round the inside of the bow till a
section of it looks like Fig. 2.   This rounded part is always
held toward you when shooting.   At points 1 inch from the
ends cut the notches with the round file for the cord, slanting
from the back to the inside as in Fig. 3.   The bow may now be
laid aside for a time and work begun on the bowstring.

The Bowstring

This is best made of shoemaker's thread, Barbour's No. 12 preferred, waxed with beeswax. Run twelve strands of this thread between two nails driven 6 feet 2 inches apart. Detach one end, wax string slightly. Then twist the strands into a firm string, twisting *away* from yourself. Prepare two other strands in the same way, and to finish the string put all three together and twist in the opposite direction from the first. That is, twist *toward* you. When all three have been firmly twisted together, wax the whole string thoroughly, and a round, even, very strong bowstring is the result. Make eye splices at both ends of the string and wrap the loops thus formed with a cord made of eight strands of the shoemaker's thread twisted and waxed as in Fig. 4.

Now slip one loop of the string over one end of the bow and put the other in the nock at the other end and, placing the end with the loop in the nock against the inside of the right foot, grasp the center of the bow with the right hand and with the left hand slip the other loop into the nock at the upper end.

Now you can test the strength and bend of the bow. If one limb bends more than the other, slip off the string and with the small plane set very fine, plane down till both ends bend alike. If too strong, thin a little all along. When of the right strength and even bend, finish by scraping with glass and medium coarse sandpaper, and finally rub with very fine sandpaper.

Now make a piece of soft wood 4 inches long and about ¼ inch thick, rounded on ends and side. Glue this on the back of the bow so that one end is 1 inch above the exact center of the bow, as in Fig. 5. This makes one limb a little longer than the other, and the long one is always held up in shooting. Glue a piece of plush or velvet over the handle thus formed. Finish the ragged edges by gluing strips of thin leather ½ inch wide over them.

The bow is now ready for the final finish and polish. The best varnish for bow and arrow work is that sold on the market under the name of Chi-namel. It spreads easily, dries quickly, is very tough and elastic, and is also waterproof.

Put on two coats of varnish and rub down with powdered pumicestone and oil. Now whip the string for 2 inches above and 4 inches below the nocking point with strong linen thread, and the bow is complete. To whip the string begin at the correct distance above the center and wrap about ⅜ inch of the thread under. When the required length has been whipped, cut off the thread, leaving an end of about 6 inches. Double a piece of the thread, lay it along the string and wrap over it three or four turns, then slip the loose end through the loop in the doubled thread, pull through and cut off the waste. This makes a whipping with no knots to come untied.

The Arrow

Strange to say, it is much easier to make a good bow than a fair arrow. A good arrow is straight, stiff enough to stand the shock of the bow and not gad or flirt, has three feathers, a nock that is straight and true, and some kind of a head or point to keep it from splitting when it strikes the target or the ground.

Arrows may be made of pine, but are much better if made of hickory, ash, or white oak. If the scout happens to live where he has access to a woodworking establishment, the work of arrow-making is much simplified. Take the wood selected to the mill and tell the man in charge that you want it ripped and turned into dowels 5-16 inch in diameter if hard wood, $\frac{3}{8}$ inch if pine. If a doweling machine cannot be had, the wood must be ripped 5-16 inch square and planed round by first planing off the corners and making an octagon of the stick, then rounding it up. (Fig. 6.) Finish the shaft with sandpaper. Now the head must be fitted on. The best heads are hollow conical steel heads obtained at Headquarters. Cut one end of the shaft so that it is a tight fit, dip it in shellac or glue and drive home in the hollow of the point with a mallet or block of wood. The steel jackets of .30 calibre rifle bullets make excellent heads. Melt out the lead and ream off the flange, then treat as mentioned above for the regular heads.

If neither of these can be obtained, saw a slit $\frac{1}{2}$ inch deep in the end of the shaft, put in a piece of sheet iron $\frac{3}{4}$ inch long, cut the same width as the arrow, and wrap with fine wire. The iron can now be pointed with a file and a good head is the result (Fig. 7), though, of course, it will not stand as much as either of the other two. For blunt heads empty central fire .32 calibre cartridges do nicely. Simply fit over the end of the shaft and file off the flange (Fig. 8). To make a hunting head cut out of hoop iron or sheet steel, with a cold chisel or tin snips, a diamond shaped head 1 inch long and $\frac{5}{8}$ inch wide having a tang $\frac{1}{2}$ inch long. Put this in a slit sawed in the end of the shaft and wrap with fine wire. (Fig. 9.)

The shaft may now be cut to its proper length of 25 inches and the nock cut. Saw a slit $\frac{1}{4}$ inch deep in the unpointed end of the shaft. (Fig. 10.) Enlarge this with a knife and finally finish with the round-edged flat file. See to it that the nock is in the center of the shaft and that its edges are true and smooth.

Feathering the Arrow

The arrow is now ready for the most delicate operation of all —the feathering. Three feathers are used, all from the same side of the bird. The wing feathers of geese and turkeys are the best, but any feather that is broad enough and stiff enough will do. Strip off the broad side of the feather by beginning at the end and working toward the quill. Cut the long strip into pieces 2 inches long. At right angles to the nock, $1\frac{1}{4}$ inches from it, glue one of these strips, as shown in Fig. 11. This is called the "cock" feather and should be selected or stained a different color from the other two. It is always held to the left in shooting. Glue the other two feathers on the shaft so that they are one third the circumference of the shaft from it. (Fig. 11.) The best glue for arrowmaking is equal parts of best commercial glue and Russian isinglass boiled in half alcohol and half water. However, for most work LePage's liquid glue is all right. After the glue has dried thoroughly—an hour is ample time—the feathers should be trimmed evenly and neatly with a pair of sharp scissors. Cut them about $\frac{3}{8}$ inch wide at the end next the nock and taper to about 3-16 at the other end. (Fig. 12.) The feathers of the scouting arrow should not be cut, but left full width. (Fig. 11.)

Painting the arrow is the last step. (Fig. 11.) With a good waterproof paint and a fine brush, paint between the feathers, covering the ribs of the feathers, but taking care not to get any paint on the vanes. Carry this down 3 inches below the lower end of the feathers. This is known as the "shaftment." When the paint is dry put a coat of varnish over the entire arrow, shaftment and all. This will protect the arrow from the damp. At the lower end of the shaftment, paint one, two, or three rings of some color which harmonizes well with the color of the shaftment. This is the "crest," and no arrow is complete without it. It also serves as an owner's mark.

If the directions have been followed faithfully and the work done carefully, the scout will now have a bow and arrow but little inferior to those in the stores.

The Target

The standard target is 4 feet in diameter with a 9-inch yellow center, called the gold, and four outer rings, red, blue, black, and white, each $4\frac{3}{4}$ inches wide. A hit in the gold counts nine, in the outer rings seven, five, three, and one. The regulation target is made of straw covered with cloth and supported by a tripod similar to an artist's easel.

How to Shoot

The majority of archers recommend standing with heels five to eight inches apart on a line drawn from the gold, each foot at an angle of 45 degrees with the line, the left side toward the target.

When the bow is strung as described above, grasp it by the plush handle with the right hand and place the notch of the arrow on the right hand. Lay the shaft across the bow on the left side, just above the left hand, resting on the first knuckle. Catch the string so that it rests on the balls of the fingers of the right hand, with the arrow nock between the first and second fingers. Extend the left arm and tip the bow slightly to the right, as this keeps the arrow well in place and lets the string be drawn more easily. Draw the string

CORRECT FORM IN SHOOTING
The diagram at side is to show the centers of heels in line with target

steadily until the arrow-head is near the left hand and the right hand just below the chin. Loose the string and the arrow flies.

While drawing the string the archer takes aim. If the distance is more than forty yards the arrow will rise in a curve as it flies, higher than the top of the target. So if you wish to hit the gold you must first find what is called the point of aim. This point is higher than the target and varies with the distance to the target. It must be determined by experiment. As the arrow is below the level of the eyes, you cannot sight along it as you could along a gun. You should look over the arrow point to the point of aim and yet the eye should see indirectly the whole length of the arrow.

The farthest possible flight of any missile is obtained by throwing or shooting at an angle of 45 degrees above the horizon. To secure this angle the archer must aim halfway between the horizon and the zenith, or point directly overhead.

After the correct point of aim is secured the accuracy of the shot depends upon the steadiness and smoothness with which the string is drawn and loosed. The fingers should slip from the string gently without jerking or dragging it. The left arm must hold its position firmly until after the shot is made. Sixty yards or less is the best distance for target practice.

Accessories

An arm guard or bracer of hard, smooth leather strapped to the left forearm and wrist should be worn as a protection from the recoil of the bowstring. (Fig. 13.) The Indians make them of wood and grass also. The three fingers of the right hand should be protected by caps of smooth-fitting, flexible leather, with the ends open. An old glove may be used with the thumb and little finger cut away.

The bow and arrows should have waterproof cases, arranged to sling on the back. The arrows should project several inches when the quiver is open so that they may be drawn out easily. (Fig. 14.)

The history of archery is the history of the world up [to the close of the sixteenth century. The bow and arrow has played its part in the rise and fall of kingdoms. Archery is the "sport of kings" as well as "the king of sports."

Though there are many forms of bows and arrows scattered throughout the world, only two are worthy of special attention. One of these is the powerful Turkish bow, and its cousins, the Persian and Chinese bows, and the other, the old English longbow, whose ringing cord and well-sent "grey goose shafts" won many a battle for the island kingdom.

From the English longbow has come down to us our present pastime of archery. Beginning with the disuse of the weapon in war and the chase, archery has flourished as a pastime in England from the close of the sixteenth century until the present time. There were a few archers in the United States prior to the Civil War, but archery was practically introduced to the American public by the writings of Maurice Thompson, in 1878–79. Ere these articles, at first published in the leading magazines, could be printed in book form, the sport had become national. During the succeeding years it lost some of its popularity, but at present many flourishing clubs exist, especially in the east and in Chicago.

The finest archer the world has seen was Horace A. Ford, of England. Shooting the double York round (144 arrows at 100 yards, 96 arrows at 80 yards, and 48 arrows at 60 yards) he scored 1256 points. Though this score has been exceeded in private practice, it still stands an unmatched record of public skill, though made in 1856.

Our best American record at the double York round was made by H. B. Richardson, in 1910. He scored 1111.

The longbow has been successfully used in hunting, especially by the Thompson brothers, Z. E. Jackson, J. M. Challies, H. B. Richardson, and others.

The farthest distance covered by a modern archer is 462 yards. This tremendous distance was covered this summer by an English archer, using an old Turkish bow over two hundred years old, and a light arrow.

THE STARS

By Garrett P. Serviss

Every boy scout ought to know the North Star, which for ages has been a sign-post in the sky, guiding wanderers by both sea and land. You can never be lost if you know that star, for it holds its place unchanging. It is within but little more than a single degree (about twice the diameter of the full moon), from the true North Pole of the heavens, around which it describes in 24 hours a circle so small that the motion is unnoticed by the naked eye. It is a surer guide to the north than the compass needle, because the latter points many degrees west of north in the eastern United States, and many degrees east of north in the western states. Only along a crooked line running from South Carolina to Lake Superior does the compass needle point true north. East of that line its declination is westward, and west of that line, eastward, the declination increasing with distance from the line. The amount of declination at any particular place may be ascertained from the magnetic charts published by the Geological Survey. These have to be corrected from time to time, because the declination of the needle slowly changes. Still, the compass affords a fair general idea of direction, when accuracy is not required. In using a compass care should be taken to avoid the neighborhood of iron or steel, and of "magnetic rocks," which often exist unsuspected. They have been known to completely reverse the pointing of a needle. The North Star as a guide has none of these disadvantages. In the daytime take the direction of the sun at noon as a guide to the south; but in order that this should be accurate your watch must be set to local and not standard time, although the error arising from a difference of time of that kind is ordinarily not very large.

To recognize the North Star you should face north, in some locality where the points of the compass are known to you, and then lift your eyes to an elevation, for the middle latitudes of the United States a little less than halfway to the zenith, or point directly overhead. You will see a rather lonesome looking star there, of the second magnitude (which is next to the brightest star in brilliance), at the end of the handle of a dipper-shaped figure, composed mostly of small stars, the handle being bent the wrong way. That is the North Star.

In order to make sure of it consult the chart here given. Find first the Great Dipper, shown in the chart, and notice the two stars in the front of its bowl, which are called the "Pointers," because a line drawn through them runs very close to the North Star. The position of the Great Dipper in the northern sky will depend upon the time of year and the time of night, but

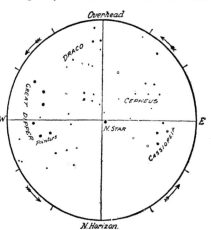

it is a conspicuous constellation, and you cannot fail to find and recognize it with a little attention. On the other side of the North Star, about as far away from that star as the Great Dipper is, you will see the constellation Cassiopeia, which you can recognize very easily on account of the W-shaped figure formed by its stars. Cassiopeia and the Great Dipper swing round the pole, always keeping opposite to each other, once every twenty-four hours. They also gradually advance around it in the same direction with a slower motion, due to the earth's revolution around the sun, but this second motion is not noticed in the course of a single night's observation.

All the stars shown in the chart are within about 40 degrees of the pole. Unless you are in the northern part of the United States, or in Canada, the Great Dipper will partly disappear below the northern horizon when it swings under the pole. You will observe that the true pole is a little aside from the North Star, in the direction of the handle of the Great Dipper. The Great Dipper is a part of the constellation called Ursa Major, or the Great Bear. The fainter stars in front of the Pointers are in the head of the imaginary "bear," while the handle forms his tail. The Little Dipper, having the North Star at the end of its handle, is likewise part of a constellation called Ursa Minor or the Lesser Bear, whose head is just beyond the bowl of the Little Dipper, for he hangs by his tail from the pole! Underneath the chart are directions by which you can teach yourself to find the hour of the night, in a general way, by noting the position of a straight line drawn from the Great Dipper to Cassiopeia. If you want to be sure that you have normal eyesight, try if you can see the little star close to the middle star in the handle of the Great Dipper. The pair are called Mizar and Alcor, or, as the Arabs say, "the horse and his rider."

You ought to know some of the other stars and constellations, also. It is impossible in a brief space to describe or figure them, but there are many books which will show you how to recognize them. You should know Sirius, the brightest star in the heavens, which shines in the southern part of our sky in mid-winter, and Arcturus. the bright reddish star which seems to follow, a long way off, the tail of the Great Bear. Try, also, to find Vega, a very diamond for brilliance, whose location you can determine by drawing a line from the North Star close past the lozenge-shaped head of Draco on the edge of the chart. Then learn to recognize the twelve constellations of the zodiac, which are called Aries, Taurus, Gemini, Cancer, Leo, Virgo, Libra, Scorpio, Sagittarius, Capricornus, Aquarius, and Pisces, and which lie along the circle of the ecliptic, through which the sun marches, or seems to march, once a year.

I give, just to show you how interesting these things are for an imaginative boy, sketches of two of the most famous constellations, one conspicuous in the winter, and the other in the summer. Orion, the first of these, is the most splendid constellation in the heavens. The ancients said it represented a mighty hunter. It has two great first-magnitude stars, Betelgeuse and Rigel, and several fine ones of the second magnitude, three of which form the "belt." Orion is on the meridian in winter, and glows very brilliantly over the snows.

Scorpio is one of the twelve constellations of the zodiac, and is on the meridian, low above the southern horizon in summer.

The shield of the lion's hide

BETELGEUSE

The Belt
The Sword→

...RIGEL

ORION

The stars in the "belt" serve as pointers to Sirius, the "Dog Star," the brightest in the sky, which is some 20 degrees southeast of Orion; and that above, and to the west of the "shield" is the red star Aldebaran in the V-shaped group of the Hyades, while a little further in the same direction is the glimmering cluster of the Pleiades. The Hyades mark the head of Taurus, the Bull, and the Pleiades hang on his shoulder.

Its chief star, Antares, is fiery red, and the telescope shows a minute, bright-green companion star half hidden in its dazzling rays.

If you will learn the stars you will be delighted to find how friendly and companionable they seem on lonely nights when you are far from home, in the midst perhaps of some half-cleared space in the woods, and you will find out for yourself many ways

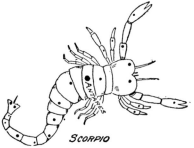

SCORPIO

in which they will serve as guides.   The Indians used them in that way before the white man came.

BIRD STUDY

By Clinton G. Abbott of the National Association of Audubon Societies

Any boy who cares enough for outdoors to be a scout is sure to want a good acquaintance with the birds.   Even dull people cannot help taking notice of our "little brothers of the air," on account of their beauty and their songs.   But most folks never take the trouble to try to learn the names of any except a few common birds.   Scouts whose eyes are sharp and ears are keen will find the study of birds a fascinating sport, which may prove to be the best fun that the woods provide.

The hunter's season is limited by law, but the bird lover may hunt the year round.   The discovery that photography can be successfully used for bird study has given the student a real weapon and added to this bloodless hunting as keen a zest and excitement as is to be found in any more deadly sport.   It destroys no life and gives results far superior to those of the gun.   To be a good shot with the camera requires more skill, coolness, patience, and brains than to shoot with a gun.   And to run to earth a bird who has long evaded you and add him, triumphantly identified, to your slowly growing list, is indeed a solid satisfaction.

Knowing the Birds

It is no easy matter, this trying to get to know the birds; but scouts are not looking for the easiest jobs, and it is great sport for them to follow some shy songster through the briery thicket until a really good look can be had, to sit stock still for half an hour to watch some unknown bird come home to her nest, or to wriggle on all fours through the grass to have a glimpse over the top of the knoll at the ducks in the pool beyond.

The only equipment necessary for bird study is an opera or field glass, a note-book, and a good bird reference book.*   As soon as you get a good look at a strange bird, notice its colors and markings, and then, if it moves, follow it up until you have seen practically all of its most prominent features.   It will be impossible to carry these facts in your head, and unless some definite memorandum is made at the time, you will probably

---

*"Land Birds and Water Birds."—*Chester A. Reed.*

Method of Using Field Observation Book

Location___*Bordentown, New Jersey*___

Date___*May 10th, 1913*___ Hour___*8.15 a. m.*___

Weather___*Clear*___ Wind___*Still*___

Redstart (Male)

be hopelessly perplexed when you go to consult the bird book later. As it is hard to jot down satisfactory notes in the field, while catching fleeting glances of some timid bird, a handy little booklet has been prepared in which observations can be recorded very rapidly. These can be procured for fifteen cents apiece from the National Association of Audubon Societies, 1974 Broadway, New York City.

Each booklet contains outline figures of the five leading types of birds: (1) small perching birds, (2) hawks, (3) snipes, (4) herons, (5) ducks. On the page opposite is a list of numbers corresponding to colors. You can quickly mark on the outline the proper numbers, and note with your pencil any marks on the bird. Then check the other data on the page, add any additional memoranda, and you have your "bird in the hand," ready to take back and look up at your leisure.

Careful Observation

Notice particularly the "range" of the birds in your reference book, and eliminate all those not stated as occurring in your

Method of Using Field Observation Book

SIZE:—
Smaller than wren
~~Between wren and sparrow~~ ✓

Between sparrow and robin
Between robin and crow
Larger than crow

SEEN:—
~~Near ground~~ or <u>high up</u> ✓
<u>In heavy woods</u> ✓

Bushy places
Orchard
Garden

Swamp
Open country
Near water

COLORS

✓1 <u>Black</u>	6 Chestnut	11 Gray
✓2 <u>White</u>	✓7 Yellow	12 Slate
3 Blue	✓8 <u>Orange</u>	13 Rusty
4 Red	9 Green	14 White washed
5 Brown	10 Olive green	with yellow

REMARKS:

(Such as wing bars, white in tail, eye ring, shape of bill, marks on head, notes or song, characteristic movements, details of nest.)

Flitting about the trees searching for insects. Often kept his tail spread out like a fan, and held the tips of his wings under his tail like a bantam rooster. His song sounded like see-see-see-see, all in one note.

territory. Notice, too, dates of the birds' coming and going, and do not expect to find species at any other time of year than within the dates mentioned. By thus narrowing down the possibilities the task is much simplified. As a final resort, the National Association of Audubon Societies stands ready to help all scouts who are positively "stumped," and if the descriptive slips are mailed with return envelopes to the secretary of the association, 1974 Broadway, New York City, an identification will be made, if the information furnished renders it in any way possible.

The next time you see a bird that you have once identified, you will probably remember its name, and in this way you will be surprised to find how rapidly your bird acquaintance will grow.

Bird Lists

A scout should make a list of all the birds he has positively identified. This is his "life list" and is added to year by year. In addition he will keep daily lists of the birds seen on special trips in the field. Two or more patrols can enjoy a friendly rivalry by covering different regions and seeing which can observe the largest variety of birds. Hundreds of well-known ornithologists often have the fun of this kind of competition, sending in their lists to a central bureau. As many as one hundred and twenty different kinds of birds have been counted in a single day by one energetic band of bird-lovers. Such a

Bob-white at feeding station

list is, however, attainable only under exceptionally favorable circumstances and by skilled observers who know their country thoroughly. For most scouts, thirty to forty species on a summer day, and fifty to sixty during the spring migration, would be regarded as a very good list.

Nesting Season

Undoubtedly the most interesting season to study birds is during the nesting period, which is at its height in June. It takes a pair of sharp eyes to find most birds' nests in the first place, and once found, there are dozens of interesting little incidents which it is a delight to watch. Only a foolish scout would rob himself of his chance to observe the secrets of nest life by stealing the contents, or would take any delight in piling up a collection of egg shells whose value at its best is almost nothing, and whose acquisition is necessarily accompanied by genuine heart pangs on the part of the rightful owners. It is more exciting to try to hide yourself near the nest so skilfully that the birds will carry on their domestic duties as though you were not near. A blind made of green cloth and set up near the nest like a little tent will often give opportunity for very close observation. It is surprising how near many birds will allow one to come in this way. Even though the blind looks very strange and out of place, the birds soon seem to get used to it, so long as it is motionless and the inmate cannot be seen. A simple type of blind can be constructed by sewing the edges of long pieces of green cloth together, drawing in the top with a cord, and then draping it over an open umbrella.

How to Photograph

From such a hiding place, photographs can often be secured of timid birds at their nests. In attempting to take photo-

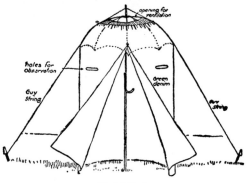

Bird blind

graphs it must be remembered that cameras of the pocket variety or fixed box type are almost useless. Most of them cannot be worked without special attachments at closer range than six feet, and even if the focus is correctly guessed, the image is apt to be very small. In this work it is far better to invest in a cheap camera (second-hand if need be) with which one can obtain a definite image on the ground glass where the plate or film is to be. Focus the camera on some spot where it is expected the bird will come; usually this is on the nest or young, sometimes it is the food, a favorite perch, or some form of decoy. The next requisite is patience. If the coveted opportunity arrives, set off the shutter by hand in the blind, or, where this is not possible, by means of a long thread, after carefully hiding the camera with boughs, leaves, sods, etc.

How to Know

An idea of the details of a bird's life which a scout may come to know, may be had from the following table:

1. Description. (Size, form, color, and markings.)
2. Haunts. (Upland, lowland, lakes, rivers, woods, fields, etc.)
3. Movements. (Slow or active, hops, walks, creeps, swims, tail wagged, etc.)
4. Appearance. (Alert, listless, crest erect, tail drooped, etc.)
5. Disposition. (Solitary, flocking, wary, unsuspicious, etc.)
6. Flight. (Slow, rapid, direct, undulating, soaring, sailing, flapping, etc.)
7. Song. (Pleasing, unattractive, long, short, loud, faint, sung from the ground, from a perch, in the air, etc. Season of song.)
8. Call notes. (Of surprise, alarm, protest, warning, signaling, etc.)
9. Season. (Spring, fall, summer, winter, with times of arrival and departure and variations in numbers.)
10. Food. (Berries, insects, seeds, etc.; how secured.)
11. Mating. (Habits during courtship.)
12. Nesting. (Choice of site, material, construction, eggs, incubation, etc.)
13. The young. (Food and care of, time in the nest, notes, actions, flight, etc.)

So varied is a bird's life that there is still plenty to be learned about even our common birds. It is quite possible for a scout to discover some facts that have never yet been published in books.

What One Boy Did

Red-breasted nuthatch

A boy once originated the idea of varying the usual "bird's nesting" craze into a systematic study of the breeding of our common birds. In one spring he found within the limits of a single village one hundred and seventy robins' nests. "One hundred were in suitable situations on private places, forty-one were in woods, swamps, and orchards, eight were placed under bridges (two being under the iron girders of the railroad bridge), four were in quarries, sixteen were in barns, sheds, under piazzas, etc., and one was on the ground at the foot of a bush."

In addition to searching out the birds in their natural haunts,

Downy woodpecker

there is a great fascination in trying to attract them to our homes. During winter evenings boy scouts can busy themselves making nesting boxes. Even an old cigar box or a tomato can with a hole in it the size of a quarter will satisfy a house wren. Other boxes which are suitable for bluebirds, chickadees, tree swallows, purple martins, and starlings will, if set up in March, often have tenants the very first season. In many cases it is feasible to have hinged doors or sides on the nesting boxes, so that they may occasionally be opened, and the progress of events within observed. It is needless to add, however, that great caution must be exercised to prevent desertion of the nest, or other disturbance of the birds' home life. Under favorable circumstances, even some of the shyer inhabitants of the woods, such as woodpeckers, owls, and ducks, can be induced to patronize artificial cavities, if they are made right and erected right.

Caring for Birds

Another way of attracting birds in summer is by providing drinking and bathing places. A little artificial pool, protected from cats, will be a source of joy to the birds, and of delight to the observer from morning to night. Apply to the

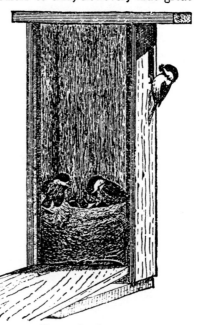
Observation box, open

National Association of Audubon Societies for information as to where ready-made nest boxes and fountains can be procured, also books on this subject, as well as on the subject of making friends of the birds through feeding.

House wren and tomato-can house

The Bird Lunch Counter

How best to feed the birds is almost an art in itself. A winter lunch counter spread with suet, nuts, hemp seed, meat, and crumbs will attract nuthatches, chickadees, downy and hairy woodpeckers, creepers, bluejays, etc. Canary seed, buckwheat, oats and hay-chaff scattered on the ground beneath will provide an irresistible banquet for other feathered boarders. A feeding place of this sort can be arranged for convenient observation from a window, and afford no end of diversion and instruction. But whether close to home or far afield, the great secret of success in such work is regularity. Begin to put the food out early in November, and let the birds get to know that they are always sure to find a supply of dainties in a certain spot, and the news will soon spread among them. In wintry weather especially, it is amazing what can be accomplished by feeding the birds regularly, and at least the following birds have been induced to feed from the human hand: chickadee, white-breasted nuthatch, red-breasted nuthatch, brown creeper, Carolina wren, cardinal, evening grosbeak, tufted titmouse, Canada jay, Florida jay, Oregon jay, and redpoll. Even in spring untiring patience has resulted in the gratification of this supreme ambition of the bird-lover, and bluebird, robin, catbird, chipping sparrow, ovenbird, brown thrasher, and yellow-throated vireo have been known to feed from the hand of a trusted friend, even with plenty of food all around. What scout can add to this list?

Birch-bark house

Protecting the Birds

Many a boy thinks that just because a bird is alive and moves it is a proper target for his air rifle or his sling shot.

Let us be thankful that there has now arisen a new class of boys, the scouts, who, like the knights of old, are champions of the defenceless, even the birds. Scouts are the birds' police, and woe betide the lad who is caught with a nest and eggs, or the

White-breasted nuthatch

limp corpse of some feathered songster that he has slaughtered. Scouts know that there is no value in birds that are shot, except a few scientific specimens collected by trained museum experts. Scouts will not commend a farmer for shooting a hawk or an owl as a harmful bird, even though it were seen to capture a young chicken. They will post themselves on the subject and find that most hawks and owls feed chiefly on field mice and large insects injurious to the farmer's crops, and that thus, in spite of an

occasional toll on the poultry, they are as a whole of tremendous value. The way the birds help mankind is little short of a marvel. A band of nuthatches worked all winter in a pear orchard near Rochester and rid the trees of a certain

insect that had entirely destroyed the crop of the previous summer. A pair of rose-breasted grosbeaks were seen to feed their nest of youngsters four hundred and twenty-six times a day, each time with a billful of potato-bugs or other insects. A professor in Washington counted two hundred and fifty tent caterpillars in the stomach of a dead yellow-billed cuckoo, and, what appeals to us even more,

Bluebird at entrance of nesting box

five hundred bloodthirsty mosquitoes inside of one night-hawk.

It must not be forgotten that large city parks are among the best places for observing birds. As an example of what can be accomplished, even with limited opportunities, there was a boy who happened to know where some owls roosted.

Now all owls swallow their prey whole, and in digesting this food they disgorge the skulls, bones, fur, and feathers in the form of hard, dry pellets. This boy used to go out on Saturday or Sunday afternoon and bring home his pockets full of pellets, and then in the evening he would break them apart. In this way he learned exactly what the owls had been eating (without killing them) and he even discovered the skulls of certain field mice that naturalists had never known existed in that region. He let the owl be his collector.

Patrol Work

It is a good idea to keep at patrol headquarters a large sheet on the wall, where a list of the year's bird observations can be tabulated. Each time a new bird is seen, its name is added, together with the initial of the observer, and after that its various occurrences are noted opposite its name. The tables show the appearance and relative abundance of birds in a given locality. A plan of tacking up a colored picture of each bird, as soon as it is thoroughly known, has been found very successful.

Such pictures can be obtained very cheaply from the Perry Pictures Co., Boston, Mass., or the National Association of Audubon Societies, 1974 Broadway, New York City. Groups of ten scouts or more can form official Junior Audubon Societies and receive bird pictures and leaflets, and also the splendid magazine *"Bird-Lore,"* full of suggestions. The National Association will be glad to send particulars.

MOLLUSCA — Shells and Shellfish

By Dr. William Healey Dall, of the United States Geological Survey

Among the shy and retiring animals which inhabit our woods and waters, or the borders of the sea, without making themselves conspicuous to man except when he seeks the larger ones for

FIG. 1
White-lipped snail
(*Polygyra albolabris*)

food, are the mollusca, usually confounded with crabs and crayfish under the popular name of "shellfish," except the few which have no external shell, which are generally called slugs. Hardly any part of the world (except deserts) is without them, but, shy as they are, it takes pretty sharp eyes to find them. Some come out of their hiding places only at night, and nearly all our American kinds live under cover of some sort.

The mollusks can be conveniently divided into three groups: those which inhabit fresh water, those which breathe air and live on dry land, and lastly those which are confined to the sea. The land shells, or snails, have generally thin shells of spiral form and live upon vegetable matter, many of them laying small eggs which look like minute pearls. Their hiding places are under leaves in shady or moist places, under the bark of dead trees or stumps, or under loose stone. They creep slowly and are most active after rain. Some of our larger kinds are an inch or two in diameter, (see Fig. 1, the white-lipped), but from this size there are others diminishing in size to the smallest, which are hardly larger than the head of a pin. In collecting them the little ones may be allowed to dry up.

Fig. 2

Whelk (*Buccinum undatum*)

The big ones must be killed in boiling water, when the animal can be pulled out with a hook made of a crooked pin, leaving the shell clean and perfect. The slugs are not attractive on account of the slime which they throw out, and can only be kept in spirits. Some of the species found in California are as large as a small cigar, but those of the states east of the Rocky Mountains are smaller and have mostly been introduced from Europe, where they do a lot of mischief by eating such garden plants as lettuce.

Fig. 3

Pond snail (*Lymnæa palustris*)

Many of the fresh-water snails are abundant in brooks and ponds, and their relations, the fresh-water mussels, are often very numerous in shallow rivers. They have a shell frequently beautifully pearly, white or purple, and sometimes have the brown outer skin prettily streaked with bright green.

The principal fresh-water snails are the pond snail (*Lymnæa:* see Fig. 3); the *Physa* (see Fig. 6), which is remarkable for having the coil turned to the left instead of the right; and the orb-snail (*Planorbis:* see Fig. 4), which has its coil flat. All of

Woodcraft 125

these lay minute eggs in a mass of transparent jelly, and are to be found on lily pads and other water plants, or crawling on the bottom, while the mussels bury themselves more or less in the mud or lie on the gravelly bottom of streams. There is also a very numerous tribe of small bivalve shells, varying from

half an inch to very minute in size, which are also mud lovers, and are known as *Sphærium* or *Pisidium*, having no "common" English names, since only those who hunt for them know of their existence.

On the seashore everybody knows the mussel (*Mytilus:* see Fig. 5), the soft clam, the round clam, and the oyster, as these are sought for food; but there is a multitude of smaller bivalves which are not so well known. The sea-snails best known on the coast north of Chesapeake Bay are the whelk (*Buccinum:*

Fig. 4
Orb-Shell (*Planor-bis trivolvis*)

see Fig. 2), the sand snail or *Natica*, which bores the round holes often found in clam shells on the beach, in order to suck the juices of its neighbors, and the various kinds of peri-winkles (rock snails or *Littorina*) found by the millions on the rocks between tides. These, as well as the limpets, small boat-shaped or slipper-shaped conical shells found in similar places, are vegetable feeders. Altogether, there are several hundred

Fig. 5
Black mussel (*Mytilus*)

kinds found on the seashore and the water near the shore, and a collection of them will not only contain many curious, pretty, and interesting things, but will have the advantage of requiring no pre-servative to keep them in good condition after

Fig. 6
Bubble snail (*Physa heterostro-pha*)

the animal has been taken out.

The squids, cuttle-fishes, octopus, and their allies are also mollusks, but not so accessible to the ordinary collector, and can only be kept in spirits.

Books which may help the collector to identify the shells he may find are:

For the land and fresh-water shells:

"Mollusks of the Chicago Area" and "The Lymnæidæ of North America,"
by F. C. Baker. Published by the Chicago Academy of Sciences.

For shells in general:

"The Shell Book." Published by Doubleday, Page & Co., Garden City,
N. Y.

On the Pacific Coast the "West Coast Shells," by Prof.
Josiah Keep of Mills College, will be found very useful.

REPTILES

By Dr. Leonhard Stejneger, Head Curator National Museum

By reptiles we understand properly a certain class of verte-
brate or backboned animals, which, on the whole, may be
described as possessing scales or horny shields, since most of
them may be distinguished by this outer covering, as the
mammals by their hair and the birds by their feathers. Such
animals as thousand-legs, scorpions, tarantulas, etc., though
often erroneously referred to as reptiles, do not concern us in
this connection. Among the living reptiles we distinguish
four separate groups, the crocodiles, the turtles, the lizards,
and the snakes.

The crocodiles resemble lizards in shape, but are very much
larger, and live only in the tropics and the adjacent regions of the
temperate zone. To this order belongs our North American
alligator, which inhabits the states bordering the Gulf of Mexico,
and the coast country along the Atlantic Ocean as far north
as North Carolina. They are hunted for their skin, which
furnishes an excellent leather for traveling-bags, purses, etc.,
and because of the incessant pursuit are now becoming quite
rare in many localities where formerly they were numerous.
The American crocodile, very much like the one occurring in
the river Nile, is also found at the extreme southern end of
Florida.

The turtles are easily recognized by the bony covering which
encases their body, and into which most species can withdraw
their heads and legs for protection. This bony box is usually
covered with horny plates, but in a large group, the so-called
soft-shell turtles, the outer covering is a soft skin, thus forming a

notable exception to the rule that reptiles are characterized by being covered with scales or plates. While most of the turtles live in fresh water or on land, a few species pass their lives in the open ocean, only coming ashore during the breeding season to deposit their eggs. Some of these marine turtles grow to an enormous size, sometimes reaching a weight of over eight hundred pounds. One of them is much sought for on account of the delicacy of its flesh; another because of the thickness and beauty of its horny plates which furnish the so-called tortoise-shell, an important article of commerce. Turtles appear to reach a very old age, specimens having been known to have lived several hundred years. The box tortoise of our woods, the musk turtles, the snapping turtles, are familiar examples of this order, while the terrapin, which lives in brackish ponds and swamps along our seacoasts, is famous as a table delicacy.

The lizards are four-legged reptiles, usually of small size, living on the ground or in the trees, but very rarely voluntarily entering water. The so-called water lizards are not lizards at all, but belong to the salamanders and are distinguished by having a naked body not covered with scales. Most of the true lizards are of very graceful form, exceedingly quick at running; others display the most gorgeous coloration which, in many of them, such as the chameleons, changes according to the light, or the temperature, or the mood of the animal. Not all of them have four legs, however, there being a strong tendency to develop legless species which then externally become so much like snakes that they are told apart with some difficulty. Thus our so-called glass-snake, common in the Southern States, is not a snake at all, but a lizard, as we may easily see by observing the ear openings on each side of the head, as no snake has ears. This beautiful animal is also known as the joint-snake, and both names have reference to the exceeding brittleness of its long tail, which often breaks in many pieces in the hands of the enemy trying to capture the lizard. That these pieces ever join and heal together is of course a silly fable. As a matter of fact, the body in a comparatively short time grows a new tail, which, however, is much shorter and stumpier than the old one. The new piece is often of a different color from the rest of the body and greatly

Harlequin snake

resembles a "horn," being conical and pointed, and has thus given rise to another equally silly fable, *viz:* that of the horn snake, or hoop snake, which is said to have a sting in its tail and to be deadly poisonous.   The lizards are all perfectly harmless, except the sluggish Gila monster (pronounced Heela, named from the Gila River in Arizona) which lives in the deserts of Arizona and Mexico, and whose bite may be fatal to man. The poison glands are situated at the point of the lower jaw, and the venom is taken up by the wound while the animal hangs on to its victim with the tenacity of a bulldog. All the other lizards are harmless in spite of the dreadful stories told about the deadly quality of some of the species in various parts of the country.

The snakes form the last group of the reptiles.   Universally legless, though some of the boas and pythons have distinct outer rudiments of hind limbs, they are not easily mistaken. And it is perhaps well so, for unless one is an expert at distinguishing between the poisonous and the harmless kind it is just as well to keep at a respectful distance from them. It is safest not to interfere with them, especially as those that are not poisonous are usually very use-

Rattlesnake

ful in destroying rats and mice and other vermin, except perhaps those living in trees and feeding on eggs and young birds, which certainly do not deserve our protection. Of course the rattle-snake is not to be mistaken. The horny appendix to its tail, with which it sounds the warning of its presence, is enough to distinguish it. It should here be explained that both lizards and snakes at various intervals shed the outer layer of their skin, the so-called epidermis.   This transparent layer, after a certain length of time, loosens and is usually stripped off whole by the animal crawling out of it and turning it inside out, as a tight glove is turned.   Now, at the end of a rattle-snake's tail there is a horny cap which is called the button, and being narrowed at the base and more strongly built than the

rest of the epidermis it is not shed with the rest of the skin, but
remains attached. Thus for each shedding a new joint or ring
is added to the rattle. How often the shedding takes place depends on various circumstances, and may occur an uncertain
number of times each year. Such a rattle, loose-jointed as it is,
is rather brittle, and the tip of the sounding instrument is easily
broken and lost. It will therefore be easily understood that the
common notion that a rattlesnake's age can be told by the number of the rings in its rattle is absolutely erroneous. Another
equally common and equally erroneous notion relates to the
tongue of the snake, which the ignorant often term its "sting,"
and which they believe to be the death-dealing instrument. Of
course, the soft, forked tongue which constantly darts out and
in of the snake's mouth is perfectly harmless. It serves rather
as a "feeler" than as a taste organ. The wound is inflicted by a
pair of large, curved teeth or fangs, in the upper jaw. These
fangs are hollow and connected by a duct with the gland on the
side of the head in which the poison is formed. Pressure on this
gland at the time of the strike — for our poisonous snakes

strike rather than bite —
squirts the poison into the
wound like a hypodermic syr-
inge. The fangs when shed or
damaged are replaced within a
short time with new ones, so
that a poisonous snake can
only be made harmless for a
short period by breaking them
off. Only in exceptional cases
need snake bites prove fatal.
It is estimated that in North
America only about two per-

Copperhead

sons in a hundred bitten are killed by the poison, though many
more die from carelessness or bad treatment, *the worst of which is
the filling up with whiskey, which aids the poison rather than coun-
teracts it.* The essential things in case of snake bite are: (1)
keeping one's wits; (2) tying a string, or the like, tightly around
the wounded limb between the wound and the heart, and loosening it about once in fifteen minutes so as to admit the poison
slowly into the circulation; (3) making the wound bleed freely
by enlarging it with a knife or otherwise; (4) if permanganate
of potash be handy it should at once be applied to the wound;
(5) treat the wound as antiseptically as it is possible with
the means at hand and hurry to a doctor. The danger de-

pends greatly on the amount of the poison injected, hence upon
the size of the snake.   It is for this reason that the big Florida
rattlesnakes which grow to six feet and over are more to be
feared than are other poisonous snakes.   Of these, we have in
our country, besides the rat-
tlesnakes, the water moc-
casin or cottonmouth, the
copperhead, and the coral
snake. The latter is a bright-
colored snake of red, yellow,

Water moccasin

and black rings found in the South, but it is usually small, and
not aggressive, so that but few cases of poisoning are known.
The other two are common enough, the former from Norfolk,
Va., south, the other all over the eastern country from Texas
to Massachusetts.   They are usually confounded, however,
with two perfectly harmless snakes, the cottonmouth with the
common water snake, the copperhead with the so-called spreading adder, but as their differences have to be learned from actual
inspection and are very hard to express in a description which
would help to identify living specimens, it is wisest to keep away
from all of them.

See "The Poisonous Snakes of North America," by Leonhard Stejneger.
Published by Government Printing Office, Washington.

Insects and Butterflies*

United States Bureau of Entomology

There is an advantage in the study of insects over most other
branches of nature, excepting perhaps plants, in that there is

Chrysalis

plenty of material.   You may have to
tramp miles to see a certain bird or
wild animal, but if you will sit down
on the first patch of grass you are sure
to see something going on in the insect world.

Butterflies

Nearly all insects go through several
different stages.   The young bird is
very much like its parent, so is the
young squirrel or a young snake or a

*Illustrations are copies from Comstock's "How to Know the Butterflies," through cour
tesy of D. Appleton & Company.

young fish or a young snail; but with most of the insects the young is very different from its parents. All butterflies and moths lay eggs, and these hatch into caterpillars, which when full grown transform to what are called pupæ or chrysalids — nearly motionless objects with all of the parts soldered together under an enveloping sheath. With some of the moths, the pupæ are surrounded by silk cocoons spun by the caterpillars just before finally transforming to pupæ. With all butterflies the chrysalids are naked, except with one species which occurs in Central America in which there is a common silk cocoon. With the moths, the larger part spin cocoons, but some of them, like the owlet moths whose larvæ are the cutworms, have naked pupæ, usually under the surface of the ground. It is not difficult to study the transformations of the butterflies and moths, and it is always very interesting to feed a caterpillar until it transforms, in order to see what kind of a butterfly or moth comes out of the chrysalis.

Take the monarch butterfly, for example. This is a large, reddish-brown butterfly, a strong flier, which is seen often flying about in the spring and again in the late summer and autumn. This is one of the most remarkable butterflies in America. It is found all over the United States. It is one of the strongest fliers that we know. It passes the winter in the Southern states as an adult butterfly, probably hidden away in cracks under

the bark of trees or elsewhere. When spring comes the butterflies come out and begin to fly toward the north. Wherever they find the milkweed plant they stop and lay some eggs on the leaves. The caterpillars issue from the eggs, feed on the milkweed, transform to chrysalids; then the butterflies issue and continue the northward flight, stopping to lay eggs farther north on other milkweeds. By the end of June or July some

Empty chrysalis and butterfly

of these Southern butterflies have found their way north into Canada and begin the return flight southward. Along in early August they will be seen at the summer resorts in the Catskill Mountains, and by the end of October they will have traveled far down into the Southern states, where they pass the winter.

The caterpillar of the monarch or milkweed butterfly is a very striking creature. It is nearly two inches long when full grown. Its head is yellow striped with black; its body is white with narrow black and yellow cross-stripes on each segment. On the back of the second segment of the thorax there is a pair of black, whiplash-like filaments, and on the eighth joint there is a similar shorter pair. When this caterpillar gets ready to transform to chrysalis, it hangs itself up by its tail end, the skin splits and gradually draws back, and the chrysalis itself is revealed — pale pea-green in color with golden spots. Any one by hunting over a patch of milkweed anywhere in the United States during the summer is quite apt to find these caterpillars feeding. It will be easy to watch them and to see them transform, and eventually to get the butterfly.

Larva getting ready to transform

The same thing may be done with any one of the six hundred and fifty-two different kinds of butterflies found in the United States.

Full grown larva

Moths

When it comes to moths, there is a much greater variety.

Instead of six hundred and fifty-two, there are fifty-nine hundred and seventy in Doctor Dyar's big catalogue. Perhaps the most interesting of these caterpillars are the big native silk-worms, like those of the cecropia moth, the luna moth, the polyphemus moth, or the promethia moth. These caterpillars are very large and are to be found feeding upon the leaves of different trees, and all spin strong silken cocoons. People have tried to reel these cocoons, thinking that they might be able to use the silk to make silk cloth as with the domestic silk-worm of commerce, but they have been unable to reel them properly. The polyphemus moth, for example, has been experimented with a great deal. It is found over a greater part of the United States, and its caterpillar feeds upon a great variety of trees and shrubs such as oak, butternut, hickory, basswood, elm, maple, birch, chestnut, sycamore, and many others. The caterpillar is light green and has raised lines of silvery white on the side. It grows to a very large size and spins a dense, hard cocoon, usually attached to leaves. There are two generations in the Southern states, and one in the Northern states. The moth which comes out of the cocoon has a wing spread of fully five inches. It is reddish-gray or some-

what buff in color with darker bands near the edge of the wings, which themselves are pinkish on the outside, and with a large clear spot near the centre of the fore wing and a regular eyespot (clear in part and blue in the rest) in the center of the hind wing.

One wishing to know about butterflies and moths should consult a book entitled, "How to Know the Butterflies," by Prof. J. H. Comstock of Cornell University and his wife, Mrs. Comstock, published by D. Appleton & Co., of New York, or, "The Butterfly Book," by Dr. W. J. Holland of Pittsburg, published by Doubleday, Page & Co., of New York, and "The Moth Book," also by Doctor Holland, and published by the same firm.

Caterpillar to chrysalis

Other Insects

There are many more different kinds of insects than there are of flowering plants, and if we were to add together all of the different kinds of birds, mammals, reptiles, fishes, crabs, mollusks, and all of the lower forms of animal life, they would not all together amount to so many different kinds as there are insects. This makes the classification of insects quite complicated. There are eighteen or nineteen main orders, and each one is subdivided almost indefinitely. There is not one of these that is not full of interest. The habits of ants, for example, living in communities by themselves, afford a tremendous opportunity for interesting observation. A good book about them has been recently written by Dr. W. M. Wheeler of Harvard, entitled, "Ants, Their Structure, Development, and Behavior," published by the Columbia University Press, New York.

Many insects live in the water, and to follow their life histories in small home-made aquaria is one of the most interesting occupations one could have, and there is a lot to be learned about these insects. Go to any stagnant pool and you will find it swarming with animal life: Larvæ or "wigglers" of mosquitoes, and a number of other aquatic insects will be found feeding upon these wigglers. Water bugs of different kinds will be found and the life histories of most of these were until quite recently almost unknown.

Beetles and Wasps

The order *Coleoptera*, comprising what we know as beetles, has thousands of species, each one with its own distinctive mode of life; some of them feeding upon other insects, others boring into wood, others feeding upon flowers, others upon leaves, and so on in endless variety.

The wasps also will bear study. Here, too, there is a great variety, some of them building the paper nests known to every one, others burrowing into the surface of the ground and storing up in these burrows grasshoppers and other insects for food for their young which are grub-like in form; others still burrowing into the twigs of bushes, and others making mud nests attached to the trunks of trees or to the clapboards of houses or outbuildings.

This is just a hint at the endless variety of habits of insects. The United States National Museum publishes a bulletin, by Mr. Nathan Banks, entitled, "Directions for Collecting and Preserving Insects," which gives a general outline of the classification, and should be possessed by every one who wishes to take up the study from the beginning.

FISHES

By Dr. Hugh M. Smith, United States Commissioner of Fisheries

There is no more fascinating and profitable study than the fish life of the lakes, ponds, rivers, brooks, bays, estuaries, and coasts of the United States; and no more important service can be rendered our American boys than to teach them to become familiar with our native food and game fishes, to realize their needs, and by example and precept to endeavor

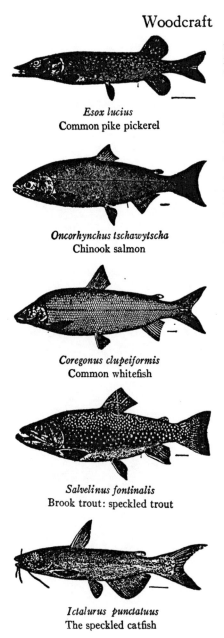

Esox lucius
Common pike pickerel

Oncorhynchus tschawytscha
Chinook salmon

Coregonus clupeiformis
Common whitefish

Salvelinus fontinalis
Brook trout: speckled trout

Ictalurus punctatuus
The speckled catfish

to secure for the fishes fair consideration and treatment.

Classes of Fish

Fishes may be roughly classified as (1) fresh water, (2) migratory between fresh and salt water, and (3) marine. Among the families of American fresh-water fishes that are conspicuous on account of their size, abundance, or economic importance, or all of these, there may be mentioned the sturgeons, the catfishes, the suckers, the minnows or carps, the pikes, the killifishes, the trouts, salmons, and whitefishes, the perches, and the basses, and sunfishes.

Migratory Fish

The migratory fishes fall into two groups, the anadromous and the catadromous. The anadromous fishes pass most of their lives in the sea, run upstream only for the purpose of spawning, and constitute the most valuable of our river fishes. In this group are the shads and the alewives or river herrings, the white perch, the striped bass or rock fish, some of the sturgeons, and the Atlantic salmon, all of which go back to sea after spawning, and the Pacific salmon (five species), all of which die after spawning. Of the catadromous fishes there is a single example in our waters — the common eel. It spends most of its life in the fresh waters and sometimes becomes permanently landlocked there, and runs down to the sea to spawn, laying its eggs off shore in deep water.

Marine Fish

The marine fishes that are found in the coastal waters of the United States number many hundred species, some of them of great value as food. Among the most important are cod, haddock, hake, halibut, flounder, herring, bluefish, mackerel, weakfish or squeteague, mullet, snapper, drum, and rock fishes.

Studying Fish

The study of living fishes is most entertaining and is rendered somewhat difficult by the medium in which they live, by their

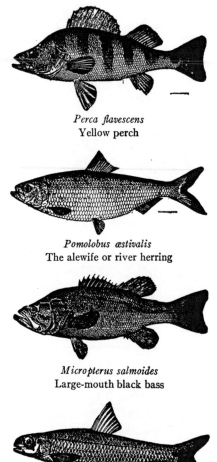

Perca flavescens
Yellow perch

Pomolobus æstivalis
The alewife or river herring

Micropterus salmoides
Large-mouth black bass

Notropis hudsonius
Minnow or shiner

Acipenser oxyrhynchus
The Atlantic sturgeon

shyness, and by the necessity of approaching closely in order to obtain any accurate view. The spawning, feeding, swimming, and other habits of very few of our fishes are so well known that further information thereon is not needed; and the boy scout's patience, skill, and powers of observation will be reflected in the records that may be, and should be, kept about the different fishes met with. Fishes may be studied from a bank, wharf, or boat, or by wading, and the view of the bottom and the fishes on or adjacent thereto may be greatly improved by the use of a "water bucket" — an ordinary wooden pail whose bottom is replaced by a piece of window glass. A more elaborate arrangement for observation is to provide at the bow of a row-boat a glass bottom box over which may be thrown a hood so that the student is invisible to the fishes.

Fundulus diaphanus
Killifish: top minnow

Identification of Specimens

While many of the fishes in a given section are easily recognizable, there are in every water fishes which, on account of their small size, rarity, retiring habits, or close similarity to other fishes, are unknown to the average boy. These latter fishes often afford the most interesting subjects for study; and in all parts of the country it is possible for energetic observers and collectors to add to the list of fishes already recorded from particular districts.

When fishes cannot be identified in the field, the larger ones may be sketched and notes taken on their color, while the smaller

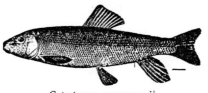

Catostomus commersonii
Common sucker: white sucker

ones may be preserved with salt, formalin, or any kind of spirits. Specimens and drawings may be forwarded for identification to the zoölogical department of the local state university, to the state fish commission, to the Bureau of Fisheries, Washington, D. C., or to the United States National Museum in the same city.

Angling

This most delightful of outdoor pastimes requires for its enjoyment no elaborate or expensive paraphernalia: a rod cut on the spot, a cork float, an ordinary hook baited with angle-worm, grasshopper, grub, may-fly, or any of a dozen other handy lures, will answer for most occasions. At the same time, the joys of fishing will often be increased if one possesses and learns how to use a light, jointed rod, with reel, fine line, and artificial baits. The necessary equipment for scientific angling is so light and compact that it should form a part of the outfit of every one who spends much time in the open air.

It should be the invariable practice of anglers to return to the water all uninjured fish that are not needed for food or study. "It is not all of fishing to fish," and no thoughtful boy who has the interest of the country at heart, and no lover of nature, will go fishing merely for the purpose of catching the longest possible string of fish, thus placing himself in the class of anglers properly known as "fish hogs."

Special Service by Boy Scouts

Valuable service may be rendered by boy scouts in all parts of the country by bringing to the attention of the proper state, county, or municipal authorities matters affecting the welfare of the fishes. Among the subjects that should be reported to fish commissioners, fish wardens, or local legal officers, are:

(1) All cases noticed where fish are being killed by dynamite, poisons, or other illegal and improper means.

(2) Threatened destruction of fish by the drying of streams or ponds.

(3) The existence of obstructions to the passage of fish on their way to their spawning grounds. All dams in streams in which are migratory fish should have fish-ways or fish-ladders.

AQUARIUM
By William Leland Stowell, M. D.

Every boy should have an aquarium. The aquarium will give ten times as much pleasure as annoyance, and the longer time you have one undisturbed the greater will be its revelations.

A simple tank can be made from a large water bottle or demijohn. File a line around the top and carefully break it off. For the back yard, cut a paint barrel in two or coat a tub inside with spar varnish. Anything that will hold a few gallons of water, two inches of clean sand, and some water plants will be a suitable home for fish and other creatures. A boy handy with tools can make a frame of wood or iron, and with plate glass and proper cement construct a large tank.

If you buy a tank, select one with straight sides, not a globe. Those made with metal frames and slate bottoms are best.

A balanced aquarium is one in which the growing plants give off oxygen for the animals to breathe. The animals "do a good turn daily" in giving off carbonic acid gas which the plants breathe or absorb. Thus the water is kept pure and need not be changed for years — only add enough fresh water to replace loss by evaporation.

Starting the Aquarium

The swamps and slow streams afford great numbers of plants. If you know the plants, get pond weeds, Canadian water weed, Ludwigia, willow moss, and tape grass. (Look in the dictionary for official names of the plants or get special books from the library.) Take some tape grass (Vallisneria) to your teacher or doctor and ask him to show you under the microscope how the sap flows and the green coloring matter is deposited; also take along fresh water fleas that you may see the blood circulate in them. The simplest form of vegetation, algæ, grows on the sides of the tank. This may be left on the side toward the window to act as a screen from the sun. Keep the side toward the room clean by a nail brush or little mop. Put in snails to keep algæ off the plants.* Watch the snails' eggs develop in clusters. Buy, if you cannot find, banded swamp snails (known as Japanese snails) that give birth to their young instead of laying eggs.

Any pond or stream will furnish fish that are beautiful, or interesting to watch, e. g. killies, sunfish, catfish, carp, shiners, blacknosed dace, minnows — the mud minnow that seems to stand on his tail — darters, etc.** If you get your supply from dealers, buy gold fish, of which there are several varieties,— fantailed, comets, fringe tails and telescope eyed. Mirror carp and golden orfe are lively, especially if you have several pairs. Paradise fish and Danios are as beautiful as butterflies.

Put in rock work to suit your taste. Include a piece of gypsum or plaster of paris so that the snails may have lime for their shells.

Have a pair of newts, if possible. Watch to see them get out of their skin when it grows too tight, like a boy pulling off a damp shirt to go swimming.

Put in a few fresh water clams and insects in variety, water boatmen, diving spiders, and whirligigs. A tank of beetles will be full of interest. Always add two or three tadpoles as

*See article on snails, page 123
**See fish on page 135.

scavengers, and watch their legs grow out as the tail grows short and they become frogs.   You can find or buy a variety of turtles which will soon be tame and eat from your fingers.   Do not keep turtles with fish.   They need to come out of the water to sun themselves.

On every hike or tramp carry a wide-mouthed bottle for specimens and a piece of rubber cloth in which to bring home water plants. Fish can be carried, wrapped in damp moss, for hours, and will be found well and lively when put in the aquarium. If carried in a pail or bottle, give plenty of air.

As an example of a balanced aquarium, note the contents of the tank as shown in the illustration.

Reading from left to right, note the fol-

A balanced aquarium

lowing; Plants: Anacharis or water weed; Cabomba or fan-wort: Sagittaria natans or floating arrow head; Sagittaria mulerttii or broad-leaved arrow head; and Sagittaria pusilla or slender arrow head.   Animals: Newt at top; Giant or Japanese snail; Planorbis or Ram's-horn snail; Fish — black telescope-eyed below, comet above, fantail below and fringe tail above. Other contents: Tuft stone in the center, supporting limb for newt or frog.

Fish Nests

Every one knows something of birds' nests and of the care and labor with which they are built. Birds, however, are not the only nest builders.   Have you ever noticed nests made by four-footed animals?   Perhaps the kind you might most often see are those well-constructed little nests made by the squirrel or by the harvest mouse.   And there are also the fishes and the insects.   Did you ever watch sticklebacks build their barrel-like nest, or the Paradise fish his floating nest, and the father fish take all the care of the young?   Did you ever see the newt roll her eggs in small leaves, or the caddis fly make a case of bits of stick, leaves, and sand?   For a real marvel watch a pair of diving spiders weave their balloon-like nest under water and actually carry air down to fill it, so that the young may be dry though submerged.

Fish require very little food other than the minute creatures that develop in the water.

The dealers supply proper foods for aquaria, or you can prepare your own. Fine vermicelli is good for gold fish; scraped lean beef is just what the sunfish and Paradise fish want. Ant eggs suit many fish, and powdered dog biscuit will fill many mouths. The yolk of hard-boiled eggs is the food for very young fish, called the fry.

It is evident that an article so brief as this is only suggestive. The libraries contain many books, three of which are recommended:

"Home Aquarium and How to Care for It," by Eugene Smith, 1902. Published by Dutton, New York. $1.20.

"Book of Aquaria," by Bateman and Bennett, 1890. Published by L. Upcott Gill, 170 Strand, W. C., London. $1.40.

"Gold Fish Breeds and Other Aquarium Fishes," by H. T. Wolf. Published by Innes & Sons, Philadelphia. $3.00.

ROCKS AND PEBBLES

United States Geological Survey

Geologists study the materials of the earth's crust, the processes continually changing its surface, and the forms and structures thus produced. In a day's tramp one may see much under each of these heads.

The earth's crust is made up chiefly of the hard rocks, which outcrop in many places, but are largely covered by thin, loose surface materials. Rocks may be igneous, which have cooled from a melted condition; or sedimentary, which are made of layers spread one upon another by water currents or waves, or by winds.

Igneous rocks, while still molten, have been forced into other rocks from below, or poured out on the surface from volcanoes. They are chiefly made of crystals of various minerals, such as quartz, felspar, mica, and pyroxene. Granite often contains large crystals of felspar or mica. Some igneous rocks, especially lavas, are glassy; others are so fine grained that the crystals cannot be seen.

In places one may find veins filling cracks in the rocks, and

Fold in stratified rock

Wearing the soft and hard beds by rain and wind

made of material deposited from solution in water. Many valuable minerals and ores occur in such veins, and fine specimens can sometimes be obtained from them.

Sedimentary rocks are formed of material usually derived from the breaking up and wearing away of older rocks. When first deposited, the materials are loose, but later, when covered by other beds, they become hardened into solid rock. If the

Quartz vein in rock

layers were of sand, the rock is sandstone; if of clay, it is shale. Rocks made of layers of pebbles are called conglomerate or pudding-stone; those of limy material, derived perhaps from shells, are limestone. Many sedimentary rocks contain fossils, which are the shells or bones of animals or the stems or leaves of plants living in former times, and buried by successive beds of sand or mud spread over them. Much of the land is covered by a thin surface deposit of clay, sand, or gravel, which is yet loose material and which shows the mode of formation of sedimentary rocks.

Some rocks have undergone, since their formation, great pressure or heat and have been much changed. They are called metamorphic rocks. Some are now made of crystals though at first they were not; in others the minerals have become arranged in layers closely resembling the beds of sedimentary rocks; still others, like slate, tend to split into thin plates.

The earth's surface is continually being changed; the outcropping hard rock is worn away by wind and rain, and is broken up by frost, by solution of some minerals, etc. The loose material formed is blown away or washed away by rain and deposited elsewhere by streams in gravel bars, sand beds, and mud flats. The streams cut away their beds, aided by the sand and pebbles washed along. Thus the hills are being worn down and the valleys deepened and widened, and the materials

Wave-cut cliff with beach and spit built by waves and currents

of the land are slowly being moved toward the sea, again to be deposited in beds.

Along the coast the waves, with the pebbles washed about, are wearing away the land and spreading out its materials in new beds elsewhere. The shore is being cut back in some places and built out in others. Rivers bring down sand and mud and build deltas or bars at their mouths.

Volcanoes pour out melted rock on the surface, and much fine material is blown out in eruptions. Swamps are filled

Woodcraft

145

by dead vegetable matter and by sand and mud washed in. These materials form new rocks and build up the surface. Thus the two processes, the wearing down in some places, and the building up in others, are tending to bring the surface to a uniform level. Another process, so slow that it can be observed only through long periods of time, tends to deform the earth's crust and to make the surface more irregular. In times past, layers of rock once horizontal have been bent and folded into great arches and troughs, and large areas of the earth's surface have been raised high above sea-level.

At almost any rock outcrop the result of

Rock ledge rounded smooth and scratched by ice

Sand-dune with wind-rippled surface

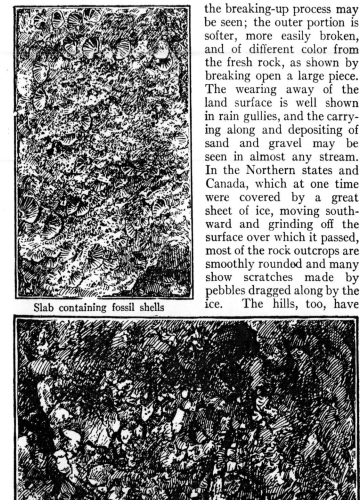

Slab containing fossil shells

the breaking-up process may be seen; the outer portion is softer, more easily broken, and of different color from the fresh rock, as shown by breaking open a large piece. The wearing away of the land surface is well shown in rain gullies, and the carrying along and depositing of sand and gravel may be seen in almost any stream. In the Northern states and Canada, which at one time were covered by a great sheet of ice, moving southward and grinding off the surface over which it passed, most of the rock outcrops are smoothly rounded and many show scratches made by pebbles dragged along by the ice. The hills, too, have

Conglomerate or pudding-stone

smoother and rounder outlines, as compared with those farther south where the land has been carved only by rains and streams. Along the coast the wearing away of the land by waves is shown at cliffs, found where the coast is high, and by the abundant pebbles on the beaches, which are built of material torn from the land by the waves. Sand bars and tidal flats show the deposition of material brought by streams and spread out by currents. Sand dunes and barrens illustrate the carrying and spreading out of fine material by the wind.

In many regions the beds of sedimentary rocks, which must have been nearly horizontal when formed, are now found sloping at various angles or standing on edge, the result of slow deforming of these beds at an earlier time. As some beds are more easily worn away than others, the hills and valleys in such regions owe their form and position largely to the different extent to which the harder and softer beds have been worn down by weather and by streams. The irregular line of many coasts is likewise due to the different hardness of the rocks along the shore.

It is by the study of the rocks and of the remains of life found in them, by observing the way in which the surface of the earth is being changed, and examining the results of those changes, and by concluding that similar results were produced in former times in the same way, that geologists are able to read much of the past history of the earth, uncounted years before there were men upon it.

PLANTS, FERNS, AND GRASSES

By Dr. L. C. Corbett, Horticulturist, United States Bureau of Plant Industry

The appearance of the blossoms and fruits of the fields and forests in any locality note the advent and progress of the seasons more accurately than does the calendar. Plants and seeds which have lain asleep during the winter are awakened, not by the birth of a month, but by the return of heat and moisture in proper proportions. This may be early one year and late another, but, no matter what the calendar says, the plants respond to the call and give evidence of spring, summer, or autumn as the case may be. The surface of the earth is not flat. We have valleys and we have mountains; we have torrid and we have temperate zones. The plant life of the world has been adjusted to these varied conditions, and as a result we have plants with certain characteristics growing in the tropics at sea-level, but a very different class of plants with different habits and characteristics inhabiting the elevated regions of this same zone. It must be remembered that even under the tropics some of the highest mountains carry a perpetual snow-cap. There is therefore all possible gradations of climate from sea-level to the top of such mountains, even at the equator, and plant life is as a result as varied as is climate. Each zone, whether determined by latitude or by altitude, possesses a distinctive flora.

But altitude and latitude are not the only factors which have been instrumental in determining the plants found in any particular locality. This old earth of ours has not always been as we see her to-day. The nature we know and observe is quite different from that which existed in earlier ages of the earth's history. The plants, the trees, and the flowers that existed upon the earth during the age when our coal was being deposited were very different from those we now have. There has been a change, but, strange as it may seem, there are in some places upon the earth to-day some of the same species of plants which were abundant during the coal-forming periods. These are among the oldest representatives of the plant world now extant. Then we are told that there was a period when the north temperate zone was covered with a great ice field which crowded down as far as southern Pennsylvania and central Ohio. This naturally brought about a profound change in the location and character of the plants of this region. There are in the Black Hills of Dakota species of plants which have no relatives anywhere in the prairie region, and no means is known by which these representatives of a Rocky Mountain family could find their way into the Black Hills, save that, previous to the ice age, this species was generally scattered over the territory, and that, during the ice age, the species was perpetuated in the hills, but was killed out between there and the Rocky Mountains where it is found in abundance. These are some of the natural reasons for the existence of varied plants in different localities. They are sufficient to explain the reason for the existence of local floras.

But nature has provided untold ways for the perpetuation as well as the dispersal of plants for the purpose of, so far as possible, enabling the plants of the world to take possession of all parts of the earth's surface. If this adjustment were complete, the plants would be practically alike all over the surface of the earth, but we have already explained why this cannot be and why we have a different flora in each zone, whether it be marked by lines of latitude or height of the

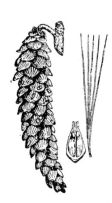

Poison Oak.—Distinguished by its berries and leaves

White Pine.—Common in the Northeastern states and adjacent portions of Canada. One half natural size

Butterfly Weed.—The bright, orange colored flowers are conspicuous in dry meadows from June to September

Poison Ivy.—Can be distinguished from the harmless woodbine by its three-lobed leaves

mountains. Plants are perpetuated by seeds, by bulbs, and by woody parts. Some seeds are highly perishable and must be sown as soon as ripe; others remain years without losing their power to produce plants. Some grow as soon as they come in contact with the soil; others must fall, be buried, and frozen before they will germinate. Some plants are perpetuated by bulbs, tubers, or roots in which a supply of food material is stored away to carry the plant over a period when its above-ground parts cannot thrive owing to frost or drought. Upon the return of favorable conditions, these resting parts throw out shoots and again make the round of growth, usually producing both seeds and underground parts for the preservation of the species. There are both wild and cultivated plants in nearly all sections which illustrate these methods of preservation. Besides plants which have bulbs, tubers, or perennial roots, we have the large, woody plants which live many years and so perpetuate themselves, not only as individuals the same as plants with perennial roots; but they, too, as a rule, produce seed for the multiplication of their kind.

The agencies which serve to spread plants about over the earth's surface are very varied and interesting. Nature has provided seeds with many appendages which assist in their dispersal. Some seeds have wings, and some parachutes to take advantage of the wind. Some seeds are provided with hooks and stickers by which they become attached to the fur of animals and are in this way enabled to steal a free ride. Other seeds are provided with edible coverings which attract birds, but the seeds themselves are hard and not digestible; the fruit is eaten and the seeds rejected and so plants are scattered. Besides these methods of perpetuation and dispersal, some plants are perpetuated as well as dispersed by vegetative reproduction, i. e., by cuttings as in the case of willows; by runners as in the case of the strawberry; and by stolons as with the black raspberry. (For further information on this point see Bailey's "Lessons with Plants.")

Some plant characteristics, however, of greatest interest to the scout may be enumerated. Plants not only mark zones, but they indicate soils with certain characteristics, and the crop wise say that the soil on which chestnut abounds is suitable for buckwheat or peaches. Plants also indicate the influence of local conditions such as lakes, ponds, or even variations in contour. A knowledge of the local flora of a region will at once tell one whether he is upon a northern or a southern hillside by the plants of the area. The creek bottom will abound with species not to be found on the hillsides, but species common to both plain and mountain will mark the progress of the season up the slope.

In the north temperate zone the moss if any will be found growing upon the north side of the tree trunk. Each hundred feet of elevation in a given latitude makes from one to two days difference in time of blooming of plants. The character of the vegetation of a region is an index to its climate. Certain plants are adapted to frigid regions, others to temperate, and still others to tropical areas. Some plants are adapted to humid sections while others are admirably adjusted to desert conditions. A knowledge of these differences in plants will be of the greatest value to the scout, and if this is supplemented by information about the value and uses of the various plant products many hardships can be avoided. Many plants produce valuable juices, gums, and resins, while others yield us valuable timber for building and cabinet uses.

While it is impossible to even suggest the great variety of plants found within the confines of the United States, the following books on botany will be found helpful in each of the different sections for which they are designed.

Bibliography

For the botany of the Northeastern United States use:

"New Manual of Botany," 7th ed. Asa Gray.
"Illustrated Flora of the United States and Canada." N. L. Britton and Hon. Addison Brown.

For the botany of the Southern United States use:

"Flora of the Southern United States." A. W. Chapman.
"Southern Wild Flowers and Trees." Alice Lounsberry.

For the botany of the Rocky Mountain region use:

"New Manual of Botany of the Central Rocky Mountains." John M. Coulter; Revised by Aven Nelson.
"Rocky Mountain Wild Flower Studies." Burton O. Longyear.
"The Trees of California." Willis Linn Jepson.

For general information regarding the shrubby plants of the United States use:

"Ornamental Shrubs of the United States." Austin C. Apgar.
"Our Northern Shrubs." Harriet Louise Keeler.

For the wild flowers outside of those already mentioned for the Southern United States and the Rocky Mountain region use:

"Our Garden Flowers." Harriet Louise Keeler.
"How to Know the Wild Flowers." Frances Theodora Parsons.
"Field Book of American Wild Flowers." F. Schuyler Mathews.

For the ferns and grasses it will be found worth while to consult:

"How to Know the Ferns." Frances Theodora Parsons.
"The Fern Collector's Guide." Willard Nelson Clute.
"New England Ferns and Their Common Allies." Helen Eastman.
"The Grasses, Sedges, and Rushes of the North United States." Edward Knobel.

For the study of the monarchs of our forests the following books will all be found exceedingly useful:

"Manual of the Trees of North America." Charles Sprague Sargent.
"Trees of the Northern United States." Austin C. Apgar.
"Handbook of the Trees of the Northern United States and Canada. Romeyn Beck Hough.
"North American Trees." N. L. Britton.
"Familiar Trees and Their Leaves." 1911. F. Schuyler Mathews.

Besides these, several states have issued through their state experiment stations bulletins dealing with the local plant inhabitants. In some instances these publications cover forest trees, grasses, and shrubs, either native or introduced. Several of the educational institutions, as well as the experiment stations, now regularly issue nature study leaflets or bulletins which treat of popular subjects of interest in connection with outdoor things. It would be well to write the state experiment station in your state for literature of this nature.

MUSHROOMS AND SOME OTHER COMMON FUNGI

By Vera K. Charles, Assistant Mycologist, Bureau of Plant Industry, United States Department of Agriculture

NOTE—The greatest care should be taken in using mushrooms as food, on account of the great difficulty in distinguishing the edible from the poisonous varieties. Expert guidance in the selection should always be insisted upon.

This group of plants contains thousands of species, intensely interesting on account of their bright colors, curious shapes, manner of growth and striking odors. One peculiarity which distinguishes fungi from other classes of plants is their inability to manufacture their own food material. They possess no chlorophyll, the green coloring matter which makes it possible for green plants to convert the carbon from the air and hydrogen and oxygen from the water into food (starch and sugar), but must feed upon material already prepared by higher plants.

They live either as parasites, obtaining their nourishment directly from a living plant (Fig. 1), or as saprophytes, growing on decaying vegetable matter.

Figure 1. Natural size

Fungi do not have seeds, but are reproduced by numerous microscopic bodies called spores. These spores are borne in various ways, on gills in the gill fungi, in pores or small tubes in the pore fungi, on spines in hedgehog fungi, and in other ways (Fig. 2). Fungi are widely distributed throughout the world, but their occurrence and abundance depends on weather conditions. They are found in a great variety of places, in pastures, lawns, or deep woods; on living trees, decaying wood, or along streams and sandy banks.

Many mushrooms, or toadstools as they are commonly called, are perfectly harmless while others are deadly poisonous. There is absolutely no test by which poisonous and edible species can be distinguished. Consequently it is never safe even to nibble a specimen until it has been named.

The parts common to most mushrooms and certain other fungi are the cap and stem. In some fungi there may be also a volva or veil or both. The volva is a membranous envelope which in the young state completely surrounds the plant. In certain mushrooms the gills are at first covered by a thin veil, which, as

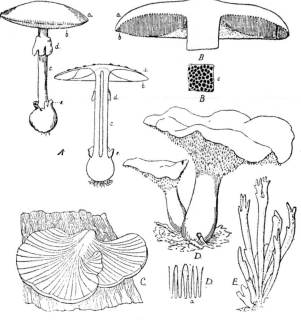

Fig. 2.

A.—A gill fungus; a. cap; b. gills; c. stem; d. ring; e. volva
B.—A pore fungus; a. cap; b. pores; c. surface view of pores
C.—Beefsteak fungus
D.—A hedgehog fungus; a. teeth
E.—A coral fungus

the plant develops, may entirely disappear or remain as a ring about the stem. The color of the gills is generally due to the color of the spores, which may be white, yellowish brown, pink, purplish, dark brown, or black. The color of the gills changes with age as the spores ripen.

Amanita

The most poisonous fungi belong to this genus, and, although it contains some edible forms, the surest way to avoid danger is to *let all Amanitas alone*. Species of this genus grow out of a cup (volva), a part of which often remains on the top of the cap or around its margin as scales, or as a broken cup at the base of the stem.

Death Cup

(Amanita phalloides)

(Poisonous.) Fig. 3

Cap white, lemon, or olive-colored to brownish, fleshy, sticky when moist, broadly oval, bell-shaped, c o n v e x; gills white; stem bulbous; volva large and free; ring large, unbroken, white. Cap 3 to 4 inches broad; stem 3 to 5 inches long. This is the most dangerous of all mushrooms and no antidote is known which will overcome its deadly effect.

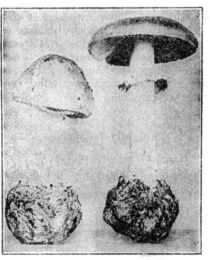

Figure 3.   Reduced one half

It is found growing in woods or on cultivated land from early spring until late autumn.

Fly Agaric

(Amanita muscaria)

(Poisonous.) Fig 4

Cap ranging in color from yellow to orange or blood-red, remnants of the volva remaining as scales; stem white, bulbous, usually marked by scaly ridges or incomplete rings. The fly agaric is very common and may be found from early summer until fall, growing singly or in small patches.

Figure 4.   Reduced one half

Parasol Mushroom

(Lepiota procera)

(Edible.) Fig. 5

Cap ovate, later expanded, with a central elevation; cuticle breaking up into brown scales; gills white; stem long, slender; ring large, readily movable when old. An attractive and graceful species, appearing during summer and early fall.

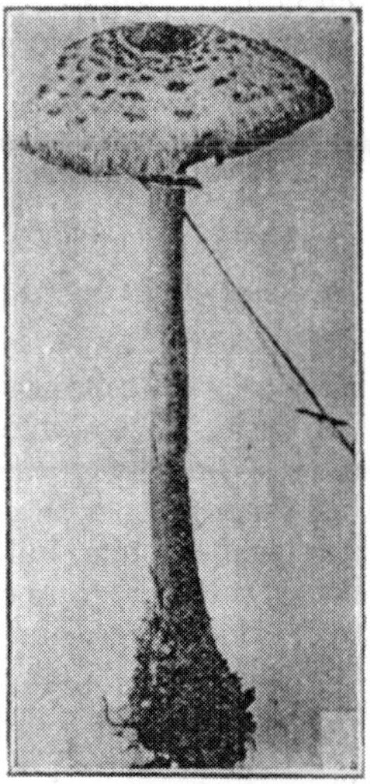

Figure 5. Reduced one half

Knightly Tricholoma

Tricholoma equestre

(Edible.) Fig. 6

Cap convex, becoming expanded, margin incurved at first and slightly wavy, pale yellow with a green or brownish tinge; gills *sulphur-yellow;* stem stout. Abundant under pine trees and generally covered with a mat of pine needles.

Fig. 6. One third nat. size

Oyster Mushroom

(Pleurotus ostreatus)

(Edible.) Fig. 7

Cap with or without a stem, shell-shaped, fleshy, white, cream, grayish or brownish ash-color; gills white; stem, if present, short. Generally growing in clusters on limbs or trunks of living or dead trees.

Figure 7. One third natural size

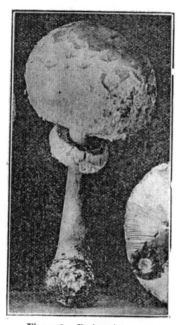

Figure 8.   Reduced one half

Green Gill

(Lepiota morgani)

(Poisonous) Fig. 8

Cap fleshy, rounded, white, with a yellowish or brownish cuticle, which breaks up into scales except in the center; gills white, slowly becoming green; ring large, movable. Often form large fairy rings.

Orange Cantharellus

(Cantharellus aurantiacus)

This mushroom may be distinguished from *Cantharellus cibarius* by the orange to brownish-orange cap and thinner gills. This plant has been known to produce illness and therefore should be avoided.

Chanterelle

(Cantharellus cibarius)

(Edible.)   Fig. 9

Cap fleshy, convex, or somewhat funnelshaped, egg-yellow; flesh white; gills running down the stem, thick; stem short, expanding into the cap of the same color.

Figure 9.   One third natural size

Lactarius

Plants belonging to this genus are easily recognized by the milky or colored juice contained in the gills and other parts of the plant.

Indigo Lactarius

(*Lactarius Indigo*)

Fig. 10

This is a very striking plant because of its rich indigo-blue color.
In age or when bruised the gills change
to greenish.

Pepper Cap

(*Lactarius piperatus*)

Cap fleshy, thick, white, smooth,
funnel-shaped when mature; gills
white, sometimes forked; stem short   Fig. 10.   One third nat. size
and solid. The milk in this species
is very abundant, white, and peppery, and does not change
color on exposure to the air. Eating it is not advisable.

Emetic Russula

(*Russula Emetica*)

(Poisonous)

Cap oval to bell-shaped, smooth, shiny, rosy to dark red when
old; gills white; stem stout, white.

Figure 11.   Reduced
one half

Fairy=ring Mushroom

(*Marasmius oreades*)

(Edible.)   Fig. 11

Cap 1 to 2 inches across, convex,
with a central elevation, tough, brownish buff, later cream-colored; gills white,
broad, not crowded; stem tough, solid.
An interesting characteristic of this genus
is the peculiarity which the plants possess of drying up and shriveling in dry
weather, but expanding and resuming
their original form when moistened.

Common or Cultivated Mushroom

(Agaricus campestris)

(Edible.) Fig. 12

Cap rounded, convex, nearly flat when expanded, generally smooth, silky, white or light brown; gills when very young white, soon pink, finally purple-brown, dark brown, or blackish; veil thin, white, frail; ring delicate, soon disappearing. This is the most common and best known of all the edible mushrooms. It is cultivated in caves, cellars, and specially constructed houses; it is also very abundant in pastures, grassy places, and richly manured ground. One must be sure that the gills are pink before eating it; otherwise, it might be mistaken for a poisonous *Amanita* which always has white gills.

Figure 12. Reduced one half

Figure 13. One third natural size

Coprinus

This genus is easily recognized by the black spores and close gills which, as the plants grow older, dissolve into an inky fluid.

Shaggy Mane

(Coprinus comatus)

(Edible.) Fig. 13

Cap bell-shaped, moist, cuticle breaking up into *shaggy scales;* gills at first white, finally black; ring thin, movable.

These two excellent, edible species occur quite commonly, singly or in clusters on rich ground or lawns, or in gardens.

Inky Cap
(*Coprinus atramentarius*)
(Edible.)

Cap egg-shaped, slightly expanding, silvery to dark gray or brownish, smooth, silky, or with small scales; gills broad, crowded, white, soon changing to pinkish gray, later black and inky; stem smooth, whitish, and hollow; ring near the base of the stem soon disappearing.

Polyporaceae

Members of this family are recognized by the numerous small tubes or pores instead of gills as in the common mushroom.

Boletus
Fig. 2

Species of this genus have a cap and stem like the common mushroom, but instead of gills have numerous small pores. Some of the species are edible, but the species are difficult for the beginner to determine. It is wiser, therefore, to let them alone. *Boletus* is an interesting genus on account of its bright colors and the phenomenon of changing color upon being bruised.

Beefsteak Fungus
(*Fistulina hepatica*)
(Edible.) Fig. 2

Specimens of this species are shelving and may be with or without a stem. The caps are liver-shaped with the margin more or less scalloped, and are blood-red on top; tubes short, yellow. This fungus is found growing from crevices of trees, especially chestnut.

Polyporus

Many fungi causing diseases in valuable and ornamental trees belong to this genus. Some are edible, but many are hard and woody. The species show great variation in form and texture. They are widely distributed and occur mostly on trees. One very common form is *Polyporus betulinus*, occurring on birch trees. This fungus is tough and fleshy, later corky, hoof-shaped, white when young, brownish when old. The lower surface with its whitish, crowded pores affords a good material on which to make outdoor sketches.

Polystictus

The species of this genus also have pores but the caps are thin and pliable. *Polystictus pergamenus* is whitish to brownish and the tubes violet or purplish. *Polystictus versicolor* is easily distinguished by the bands of different colors, mostly bay or black, which mark the cap. The tubes are white. Both species grow in dense clusters on dead stumps on many varieties of trees. A very striking form of this genus is *Polystictus cinnabarinus*, which can be easily recognized by its bright cinnabar color.

Hydnum
Fig. 2

This genus belongs to the family *Hydnaceae*, which has pointed teeth instead of gills or pores. The plants either have a stem or are bracket-shaped; they may be fleshy, corky, leathery, or woody.

Clavariaceae
Fig. 2

In the *Clavariaceae*, or coral fungi, the plants are erect, simple, club-shaped, or variously branched. Many species are very beautifully colored, lavender, orange, yellow, pink, or red-tipped. Many of the coral fungi are edible, but as various cases of poisoning have been known it is safer not to eat them.

Puffballs
Lycoperdaceae

Plants belonging to this family are somewhat irregularly ball-shaped, with or without a stem. When they are ripe the contents break up into a powdery mass which consists of spores. They are generally found growing on the ground but sometimes on wood. Fig. 14, *Lycoperdon pyriforme*,

Figure 14. Puffball

is a very common puffball, appearing in dense clusters on rotten stumps or logs. It is edible when young while the flesh is white, but must never be eaten after the flesh has begun to turn yellow.

Calvatia

This genus contains the largest and some of the most delicious puffballs, but as already stated, these forms must be eaten when fresh while the interior is perfectly white; otherwise they are indigestible.

Figure 15
Reduced one half

Stinkhorn Fungi

(*Phallaceae*)

Most of the fungi which belong to this family have a very disagreeable odor. The following species is very common and is easily recognized:

Stinkhorn Fungus

(*Ithyphallus impudicus*)

Fig. 15

This fungus is interesting on account of its peculiar form and manner of development. It generally grows about decayed stumps, first appearing as a gelatinous egg with thread-like strands at the base. The central portion of the egg is occupied by a tubular part which elongates and bursts through the outside cover.

Common Morel

(*Morchella esculenta*)

(Edible.) Fig. 16

This fungus belongs to a family in which the spores are produced in microscopic sacs. On blowing or shaking the full-grown plants, the spores may be seen as a fine powder. The morel has a stem and more

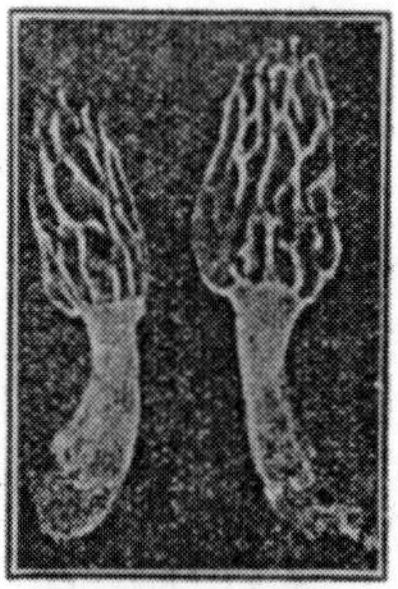

Figure 16
One third natural size

or less cone-shaped cap, which is dingy yellow or greenish, and deeply pitted. This fungus grows on the ground, or along banks, or in sandy places.

Cooking Mushrooms

There are a great many ways of cooking mushrooms, but for camp life the easiest way is to fry or cream them. They may be cleaned by washing and scraping, rolled in egg and bread-crumbs, and fried. Sliced bacon is often a pleasant addition. If stewed, butter, salt, and pepper may be added, or a cream dressing made and thickened a little bit with flour and milk.

Treatment for Poisoning

In all cases of mushroom poisoning a physician should be called immediately, but an emetic should be given before his arrival. His treatment will depend on what mushroom has caused the poisoning, and the symptoms and condition of the patient. The physician will come prepared to administer apomorphine and stimulants, such as atropine, digitalin, and strophanthin.

REFERENCE BOOKS USEFUL TO THE AMATEUR

ATKINSON, G. F.
1903.   Studies of American Fungi, Mushrooms, Edible, Poisonous, etc. Ed. 2, New York, 323 p., illus. pl. (partly col.)

CLEMENTS, F. E.
1910.   Minnesota Mushrooms. Minneapolis, 169 p., illus., 4 col. pl. (Minnesota Plant Studies, IV.)

HARD, M. E.
1908.   The Mushroom, Edible and Otherwise, Its Habitat and Time of Growth . . . Columbus, Ohio, 609 p., illus.

McILVAINE, CHARLES, and MACADAM, R. K.
1912.   Toadstools, Mushrooms, Fungi, Edible and Poisonous; One Thousand American Fungi, rev. ed., Indianapolis, 749 p., illus., pl. (partly col.)

MARSHALL, NINA L.
1905.   The Mushroom Book . . . New York, 170 p., illus., pl. (partly col.)

PATTERSON, FLORA W., and CHARLES, VERA K.
1915.   Mushrooms and Other Common Fungi . . . Washington, 64 pp., 38 pl., 1 text fig. (U. S. Department of Agriculture Bull. 175.)

NATIVE FOREST TREES

By George B. Sudworth, Dendrologist, U. S. Forest Service

Over 500 different trees grow naturally within the United States. There are also a good many foreign trees that have become naturalized here. The Ailanthus or tree of heaven and the white poplar are familiar examples. Some trees grow to be little higher than a man's head, while others attain over 300 feet in height. The largest number of different sorts of trees are found in the eastern part of our country. The western mountainous parts of the United States contain the next greatest number, while the plains region, lying between the eastern base of the Rocky Mountains and the Mississippi River, has fewest trees and these occur chiefly along the waterways which drain this great prairie region. The intervening treeless areas are covered with grass and often extend as far as the eye can reach. Long ago there may have been trees there, but too little rain, cold, fierce winds in winter and hot dry ones in summer now prevent their natural growth.

Like some animals, trees of certain kinds grow in great numbers by themselves, forming what foresters call pure forests. The pines and some oaks have this habit. They live so close together that few or no other trees are able to associate with them. Other sorts of trees are the hermits of the forest, one or two, or more, living here and there in a suitable spot. Another interesting fact about trees is that some of them may be distributed over hundreds of square miles of territory, the range of a few trees extending from the Atlantic almost to the Pacific Ocean, while others may pass their entire existence within one or two square miles.

Some trees such as the pines, spruces, balsam firs, hemlocks, etc., have long or short needle-shaped leaves, while still another class of trees, such as the cedars and junipers, have minute, scale-like leaves. All of these are "evergreens," and they lose an old set of leaves and gain a new one every year.

Another class of trees, such as the maples, oaks, elms, etc., have more or less broad, flat, veined leaves. These are known as broad-leafed trees. Most of them lose their leaves every autumn, and are called deciduous-leafed trees. But some of the broad-leafed trees, such as the holly, lemon, and orange trees, have "evergreen" leaves, and seem never to lose them. Watch them from early spring until midsummer, and you will discover that they lose the old set of leaves gradually as a new set is formed.

Trees, like animals, have their natural enemies. Insects and fungous diseases kill great numbers of them. But perhaps the greatest enemy of forest-forming trees is fire, which destroys millions of full-grown trees and little seedling trees that have just begun to grow. It is said that the Indians used to set fire to forests to drive out game animals so that they could be easily killed in large numbers. At one time, long ago, sheep herders and cattlemen used to burn the chaparral-covered western mountain slopes in order to make the shrubs produce new tender shoots for their flocks and also so that the animals could get about more easily. These fires killed millions of trees. So, too, without thinking, hunters, fishermen, and others tramping in the woods have carelessly left campfires or burning matches from which great forest fires have spread. Altogether, millions of dollars' worth of forest trees have been burned up by people who did not know how to enjoy and to use the forest without destroying it.

Wanton destruction of this sort is excusable in the case of Indians, because they were uncivilized and thought only of their own immediate needs. But in the case of white people such useless waste of what, in most cases, did not belong to them, is criminal—uncivilized. The forests that belong to our government belong to the people of the United States, and each one of us is not a good citizen if we do not help to prevent their being burned. If every one who uses the government's forests, or the woods that belong to private individuals, would always be careful with fire, there would be no forest fires.

Learning to know the different sorts of trees by their looks as we meet them in the crowded forest, in the fields, and by the roadside is intensely interesting. Acquiring this knowledge gives us something pleasurable to do when we take a long "hike" across country. Each species of tree has its distinguishing marks. We have only to find out by close study in the woods what these marks are. Did you ever stop to consider how easily you recognize your friends by sight? Something distinguishes each one from the others. Different sorts of trees look pretty much alike to many people; but by observing their different traits we can learn to know a large number of trees just as we have learned to know our friends. The natural history of trees can be learned only by keeping our eyes open, training ourselves to observe closely. We must learn to know just what sort of leaf, acorn, and bark a white oak tree has before we can have a distinct mental picture of

this tree.   We must also find out in the woods where the white
oak lives—on dry land or in wet ground, whether it lives alone
among other sorts of trees or makes a forest by itself, whether
it becomes a large tree when full-grown or is a small tree.   To-
day, we may find a white oak one foot in diameter.   To-morrow's
search may discover one twice as large.   Finally, we shall
know from our own observations how large the biggest white
oak trees are.   It is best to learn to know one tree at a time,
that is, the half day or day given to observing the different
characteristics of the white oak should not be crowded with
studying those of other trees.   Set yourself the task of learning, one at a time, to know at sight all of the trees that grow
in your neighboring woods, fields, and along the roads.   You
should also learn to know them, not only in the summertime,
but in the winter when they have no leaves, if they are of the
deciduous sort.

Lack of space permits calling attention here to only a few of
our common trees and brief reference only to some of the many
interesting facts about them.   The boy scouts who wish to
know more about trees should consult the works given at the
end of this chapter.

NEEDLE-LEAFED TREES

All of these trees bear cone fruits.   They include the pines, larches or tamaracks, spruces, hemlocks, balsam fir trees, cypresses,
sequoias, cedars, juniper, and yew trees.   The pine trees are recognized by their needle-like leaves being borne in little bundles of two, three, four, and five, and these are the commonest
pines.   (One pine is exceptional in having a round single leaf.)
All of the needle-leafed trees except the larch trees and the
bald cypress are "evergreens."   The larches and bald cypress
shed their leaves every autumn.   The spruce trees, hemlocks,
and balsam fir trees bear their needle-like leaves singly.   The
leaves of the spruce trees can be distinguished from those of
the hemlocks and balsam firs by their squarish or more or less
4-sided form, easily seen when a leaf is cut in two with a sharp
knife.   The leaves of the hemlocks are flat and have a distinct
little stem.   The balsam fir leaves are also flat, but they are
of the same width throughout.   The leaves of the bald cypress
tree are similar in general shape to those of the balsam firs,
but they are very soft.   The leaves of all of the other cone-
bearing trees, such as the redwoods (Sequoias), cedars, and
junipers are minute and scale-like and, therefore, very unlike

any of the other evergreen trees that bear cones. These tiny leaves clasp the twigs somewhat like little shingles, each one overlapping the one just above and completely covering the twigs.

The fruits or cones of all of these trees are distinct from each other in their appearance. The thick cone scales of the pine trees bear a prickle or are marked by a well-defined tip. The cones of all of the other needle-leafed trees have thin, pointless scales. A singular fact about the cones of the balsam fir trees is that when ripe they fall to pieces, thus scattering their seeds. The cones of all of the other needle-leafed trees remain intact when ripe, the warm sun opening their scales and allowing the seeds to escape. Pine trees require two seasons' growth for maturing their cones, while but one season's growth is necessary for the maturing of the cones of the other common needle-leafed trees.

PINE TREES

The pine trees are divided into two classes, white pines and the pitch pines. White pines are 5-leafed species and have light soft wood. Pitch pines are 2- and 3-leafed species and have heavy, hard, resinous wood. White pines produce the most valuable wood, because it can be used for the greatest number of different purposes, and is easily worked. Wood of the pitch pines, though harder to work, has many important commercial uses for which the white pine woods are not adapted, particularly those requiring strong, durable pine. The following are some of the common pines.

White Pine

(*Pinus strobus, Linn.*)

A 5-leafed species, growing in northeastern United States and adjacent portions of Canada and forming extensive pure forests. The most valuable of all of our white pines and the first to be cut for lumber. Great forests of it, once common, are now very largely cut off. From 100 to 150 feet in height and 2 to 4 feet in diameter.

White Pine
One half natural size

Sugar Pine
(Pinus lambertiana, Dougl.)

Sugar pine, a 5-leafed species, is one of the two largest pine trees in North America, growing only in California. It is from 160 to 200 feet in height and 4 to 8 feet in diameter. The cones are the longest of any other pine, being from a foot to nearly 2 feet in length. Sugar pine grows interspersed singly and in groups among other trees. Lumber of the sugar pine is of great value in the Pacific country for construction and interior finish.

One sixth
natural size

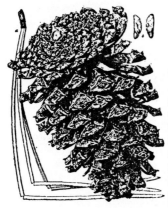

One fourth natural size

Western Yellow Pine
(Pinus ponderosa, Laws)

This and the sugar pine are the two largest pine trees in North America. It is a 3-leafed species growing in the mountains of western United States at elevations of from 1,800 to 9,700 feet, where it forms extensive forests. It attains a height of from 125 to over 200 feet and a diameter of from 3 to 8 feet, the largest trees being 400 or 500 years old. It produces large quantities of most useful lumber which is used for all sorts of buildings and construction work.

Piñon Pines
(Pinus edulis, Engelm. and Pinus monophylla, Torr. and Frem.)

These piñon or nut pines grow in the southern Rocky Mountain region and the southern California Sierras, where they form open forests that look like apple orchards, on the dry foot-

One half natural size

hills and high plateaus, at elevations between 5,000 and 9,000 feet above sea-level. They are mostly about 25 feet in height. Indians gather large quantities of the large nut-like seeds for food, while nowadays many of them are sold in different cities as sweetmeats. The trees are cut for fuel and sometimes for railway ties. The piñon (*Pinus edulis*) is a 2-leafed species, and the single-leaf pine, also called "piñon" (*Pinus monophylla*), has but a single leaf.

Lodgepole Pine

(*Pinus contorta*, Loud.)

Lodgepole pine, a 2-leafed species, grows chiefly in the high mountains of western United States, at elevations of 6,000 to 11,500 feet above sea-level. In the

north Pacific region, however, its range is from sea-level up to 6,000 feet. The name "lodgepole pine" was given to it because the Indians used the young slender trees for the poles of their lodges. The long, clean stems are 50 to 100 feet in height and 12 to 14 inches in diameter. Extensively used for rail- One third natural size way ties, timbering of mines, and by the settlers for fence and corral poles.

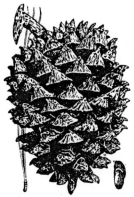

One fourth natural size

Digger Pine

(*Pinus sabiniana*, Dougl.)

Digger pine, a 3-leafed species, is a common and picturesque tree of the dry foothills in California, at elevations of 400 to 5,000 feet above sea-level. The foliage is a distinct grayish green. The name "digger pine" was given to it because the Digger Indians used the large nut-like seeds for food. The huge cones (6 to 10 inches long) hang on the branches for several years. California Indians extract the seeds from these cones by heating them in a slow fire until the scales become so spread apart that the seeds can be easily shaken out. A familiar sight is a number of squaws sitting around a smoky fire extracting the seeds of these pine cones. The wood is used almost entirely for fuel.

Scrub Pine

(*Pinus virginiana*, Mill.)

Scrub pine, so called because of its scrubby form, is a 2-leafed species common in the Middle Atlantic States, particularly in Maryland and Virginia, forming pure stands on poor soil from sea-level to elevations of 2,000 feet above the sea. Height, 25 to 30 feet and diameter, 8 to 12 inches. Bark, brown, thin, and scaly. Much used for cordwood.

One half natural size

Jack Pine

(*Pinus banksiana*, Lamb.)

Jack pine, another 2-leafed species, grows on very poor, sandy soil from Nova Scotia to Minnesota and north to Hudson Bay and northwestward nearly to British Columbia, the greater part of its distribution being in Canada. It is the only North American pine that extends from the Atlantic coast nearly across the continent. Usually a scrubby tree 40 to 70 feet in height and 8 to 12 inches in diameter. The small curved cones remain on the trees a great many years. They are also peculiar in their habit of remaining tightly closed for several seasons, the hot sun occasionally opening up a few of the scales and liberating the seeds from time to time.

One third
natural size

Forms pure forests and is mingled with other trees. Yields large quantities of knotty, low-grade lumber which is used mainly for secondary purposes.

Longleaf Pine

(*Pinus palustris*, Mill.)

A 3-leafed species, called longleaf pine on account of its very long leaves (8 to 18 inches). It is commercially the most valuable pine tree of the southern states, once forming great forests in the coast region from southern Virginia to Florida and to eastern Texas, but large areas of it have been cut off for lumber, which is highly prized for its durability, strength, and wearing qualities. It has long been used for the decks of ships, for bridge timbers, and for flooring. Houses built in the time of George Washington had floors of this pine. Some of these houses, still standing, show how durable the wood is. The tall, scaly-barked, clean-looking stems are 80 to 120 feet in height and 2 to 3 feet in diameter. Longleaf pine also yields most of the turpentine and resin ("naval stores") manufactured in this country, amounting in value to millions of dollars each year. These products are derived by distilling the crude "gum" or resin, which is obtained by "chipping" the trunks of the trees every two weeks from March to September, the resin being collected in a receptacle below the wound made in the

One fourth natural size

tree. Negro laborers gather the resin and transport it to the "still," as they call it, where it is distilled, which separates the "spirits" or oil of turpentine from the resin.

LARCH TREES

Larch trees, some of which are called "tamaracks," are easily recognized from other needle-leafed trees by their little brush-like clusters of leaves scattered all over the twigs, and also by their habit of shedding their leaves in the autumn.

One half natural size

Tamarack

(Larix americana, Michx.)

The tamarack has its leaves in clusters of 12 to 20, and is a straight, scaly-barked tree 50 to 80 feet in height and 20 to 24 inches in diameter. It grows in cold, mucky swamps in our northeastern states as far west as Minnesota, and in adjacent portions of Canada; it also extends through the Canadian provinces to Alaska. It forms a dense, pure forest. The hard, strong wood was once much used for railroad ties and the largest trees were cut for lumber.

Western Larch
(*Larix occidentalis*, Nutt.)

This is the largest and commercially most valuable of North American larches, its gray, thick-barked stems attaining a height of from 100 to 200 feet and a diameter of 3 to sometimes 8 feet. Its leaves are in clusters of from 14 to 30. The cones have bristle-pointed bracts extending beyond the ends of the cone scales. Western larch grows on high foothills and mountain slopes of British Columbia, Montana, Idaho, Washington, and Oregon at elevations of 2,000 to 6,000 feet, and forms forest by itself, or in some places is mingled with other trees. It yields excellent lumber and large construction timbers.

One half natural size

SPRUCE TREES

The spruce trees have tall, straight, tapering trunks. Their pointed, 4-sided leaves are borne singly and bristle about or closely cover the twigs and branches. The bark is always scaly.

Black Spruce
(*Picea mariana*, [Mill.] B. S .P.)

Black spruce, so called because of the dark green color of its foliage, inhabits cool, moist, or wet places in our northeastern

One half natural size

states and adjacent sections of Canada; it also extends west through Canada to Alaska. Common in cold bogs and on the margins of northern lakes, where it forms more or less pure stands. The small cones remain on the trees for several years, this being very characteristic of the species. It is usually 35 to 40 feet in height and 4 to 18 inches in diameter, exceptionally large trees being 50 to 80 feet high and 2 feet in diameter. The least valuable of our eastern spruces, because of its small size.

White Spruce

(*Picea canadensis*, [Mill.] B. S. P.)

Called white spruce because of the whitish
tinge of its leaves, which are sharp-pointed and
bristle around the twigs. Woodsmen sometimes
call it "cat spruce" on account of the disagreeable odor the crushed leaves give off. It is one of
the two largest and most valuable of our eastern
spruces, reaching a height of 50 to 100 feet and
a diameter of 1 to 3 feet, exceptional trees being 4 feet in diameter. It grows in our northeastern states and far northward in Canada,
extending west also in Canada to Alaska. The
cones of this tree fall from the twigs in the autumn, after they have become fully ripe, a
habit unlike that of the black spruce. It yields
excellent straight, fine-grained, finishing lumber, but much of
the wood is used for paper pulp.

One half
natural size

Engelmann Spruce

(*Picea engelmanni*, Engelm.)

This spruce, named in honor of an
eminent tree botanist, Dr. George En-
gelmann, who first described it, is a common forest-forming species in our Rocky
Mountain states, at elevations of 8,000
to 12,500 feet above the sea, and to
some extent
also in the
mountains of
Oregon, Wash-
ington, and
western Canada. It attains a height of
80 to 100 feet and a diameter of 18 to 36
inches. Its straight trunks are cut for
lumber, railway ties, and mine timbers.

One third natural size

Blue Spruce

(*Picea menziesii*, Engelm. = *P. pungens*, Engelm.)

Blue spruce, so called because of the
blue or silvery green color of its leaves,

One third natural size

is the best known of our spruces because it is so much planted as an ornamental evergreen. Its leaves are as sharp-pointed as a needle. It grows along streams in the middle and southern Rocky Mountain region at elevations between 6,500 and 10,000 feet above the sea, and is 60 to 130 feet in height and 18 to 48 inches in diameter. Trees grow mostly by themselves. The wood of this species is the least valuable of all spruces, because of its knotty, poor quality. Sometimes used for fuel, log houses and for railway ties.

Sitka or Tideland Spruce
(*Picea sitchensis*, [Bong.] F. & M.)

This spruce, the largest of all of our spruce trees, grows in moist places on the Pacific coast from Alaska to Northern California, and is a massive tree 80 to 125 feet in height and 40 to 70 inches in diameter, exceptionally large trees being from 160 to 180 feet in height and 8 to 12 feet in diameter. Its leaves are exceedingly sharp-pointed —almost like needles. It grows in pure forests or is mixed with other trees. The soft, light, whitish wood is of great value on the north Pacific coast, where it is extensively used for lumber, especially for fruit boxes. The Sitka spruce lives to an age of from 400 to 750 years or possibly more.

One third natural size

HEMLOCK TREES

Hemlock trees are distinguished by their small, flat, single leaves which are attached to the twigs by a thread-like stem. The cones of most species are very small. They are large, rough-barked trees, with soft, graceful looking foliage.

One third natural size

Hemlock
(*Tsuga canadensis*, [Linn.] Carr.)

This hemlock forms nearly pure forests, or is sometimes mingled with other trees. in rather

moist ground mainly in our northeastern states and adjacent
parts of Canada. It attains a height of 80 and sometimes 100
feet and a diameter of 2 to 4 feet. The hard bark is marked with
deep furrows and ridges, and has long been used for tanning
leather. At one time the trees were cut only for their bark, the
wood, of inferior quality, being left unused. With the scarcity
of timber trees in the East, lumbermen came to use the peeled
trunks for coarse construction lumber.

Western Hemlock
(*Tsuga heterophylla*, [Raf.] Sarg.)

Western hemlock, very similar in appearance to the eastern
species, is a valuable timber tree growing in the
Pacific coast region from Alaska to northern California and inland through British Columbia, northern Idaho, and Montana, and in the Cascade
Mountains of Oregon and Washington. It is from
125 to 160 feet in height and 2 to 5 feet in diameter.
Like its eastern relative, it forms pure stands or is
scattered singly or in groups among other trees in
moist situations from sea-level to 7,000 feet above
the sea. The wood is much superior to that of
the eastern hemlock, while the bark also contains
a larger percentage of tannin, making it useful for
tanning leather.

One half
natural size

FALSE HEMLOCKS

These trees are interrelated both to the balsam firs and to
the hemlocks. Their leaves are similar in shape to those of
the true hemlock. They resemble the balsam firs in having
resin blisters in the smooth bark of young trunks and in the
smooth bark of the upper stems of old trees. The cones have
3-pointed bracts extending conspicuously from among the
cone-scales.

Douglas Fir
(*Pseudotsuga taxifolia*, [Lam.] Britt.)

Douglas fir, so called after its discoverer, is one of the largest
of 3 or 4 big western timber trees. It grows from sea-level to
elevations in the mountains of 7,000 feet above the sea, in the
central and southern Rocky Mountains and also from central

One half natural size

California to British Columbia, where it is from 180 to 200 feet in height and 8 to 10 feet in diameter, much smaller trees growing in the Rockies. The magnificent forests it forms are so dense sometimes as to exclude the sunlight. Douglas fir is the most valuable lumber tree of the Pacific coast region, yielding millions of feet of clear, straight-grained pinelike lumber which is used for all sorts of building purposes. The largest trees are from 400 to 500 years old.

BALSAM-FIR TREES

Balsam-fir trees have straight, tapering trunks and sharp-pointed crowns. The leaves are flat, sharp-pointed on the upper branches and blunt on the lower branches, where they often grow on two sides of the twigs like the teeth of a comb. The erect cones of fir trees grow only at the top of the tree, and when ripe in autumn they fall to pieces, leaving their sharp-pointed central stem still attached to the branches. Perhaps the most distinctive mark of balsam-fir trees are the numerous blister-like excrescences in the smooth bark of young trees and of the upper stems of large trees. They contain a clear, resinous, honey-like fluid which has a turpentine-like odor. The name balsam fir was doubtless given to these trees because of these blisters.

Balsam Fir

(*Abies balsamea*, [Linn.] Mill.)

Balsam fir, the first species of its kind discovered in this country, forms nearly pure stands in moist places about lakes and ponds in our northeastern states and far north

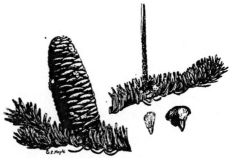

One third natural size

into Canada and west through Canada to British Columbia. It is a rather small scaly-barked tree 25 to 75 feet in height and 10 to 28 inches in diameter. Balsam-fir wood is light and soft, its most important uses being for paper pulp and lumber for packing boxes. The resin of the bark blisters is collected by puncturing the blisters and squeezing the contents into a large-mouthed bottle or gourd. The product, known in apothecary shops as "Canada balsam," is used for certain medicinal and mechanical purposes.

DECIDUOUS-LEAFED CYPRESS TREES

Unfortunately, several different groups of cone-bearing trees have come to be known as cypresses. But the trees here described belong to the botanist's genus Taxodium, and shed their leaves in the autumn. All other "cypresses" have ever-green leaves. Deciduous cypresses have spherical, ball-like cones, which fall to pieces when ripe, liberating the beech-nut-like seeds. These trees are exceptional because of the stump-like "knees" which grow above ground from their roots. Cypress trees live mostly in water or in very wet places, where beneath the trees numbers of "knees" can be seen projecting 2 or more feet above the water or ground. Trees in drier places do not produce "knees." It is believed, therefore, that the trees growing in water obtain air through these "knees."

Bald Cypress
(*Taxodium distichum*, [Linn.] Rich.)

Bald cypress, so-called probably because it loses its leaves in the autumn and has a bald appearance in winter, is a large, straight tree forming for-

ests in swampy or inundated ground in our southeastern states, being common in the South Atlantic and Gulf states. It is 80 to 150 feet in height and 2 to 5 feet in diameter. The base of the trunk is much enlarged.

One half natural size

The cinnamon-brown bark (becoming gray by exposure) is furrowed and ridged. The soft, yellowish-brown, durable wood is very valuable for lumber, which is used for many purposes.

SEQUOIA TREES

Sequoia trees are the largest in the world.   They are also remarkable because they live to be older than almost any other trees, their age often being from 1,000 to 5,000 years or more. They are world-renowned, having been visited by people from nearly every part of the world.

Bigtree or Giant Sequoia
(*Sequoia washingtoniana*, [Winsl.] Sudw.)

The bigtree is very massive in form, attaining a height of 150 to nearly 350 feet, and a diameter of 12 to 27 feet.   The cinnamon-brown bark is 12 to 18 inches thick and marked with deep furrows and high ridges.   Found in 26 groves and small forests scattered along the California Sierras at elevations of 5,000 to 8,500 feet above the sea.   The total area covered by these trees is about 50 square miles.   Some of the groves are composed entirely of bigtrees, while in others, pines and fir trees are mingled with the bigtrees.   The grandeur of these forest monarchs is unsurpassed.   All of the different groves have special names and many notably large trees are named in honor of such celebrated men as George Washington, Generals Sherman and Grant.   It was feared at one time that

One third natural size

these trees might become extinct, for a good many of them have been cut down for lumber; but the majority of the groves are now included within National Forests or National Parks, and will be preserved to future generations.

The freshly cut wood is a brilliant rose-purple red, but exposed to the air it becomes a dull purplish-red brown.   It is very light and soft, but remarkably durable when exposed to the weather.   Much used for shingles, clapboards, and interior finish of houses.

The giant sequoia lives to an age of from 4,000 to 5,000 years, but the largest trees now standing are probably not over 4,000 years old.

Redwood
(*Sequoia sempervirens*, [Lamb.] Endl.)

This also is a giant tree attaining 190 to sometimes 350 feet in height and 8 to 20 feet in diameter.   It forms pure stands in the Pacific coast region from the southwestern corner of Oregon to Monterey County, California, extending inland from the coast only from 10 to 30 miles. The trees grow from near the sea-level to about 2,500 feet above the sea. His-

torically, this sequoia is not as interesting as the bigtree. No fear is felt that it will become extinct, for it reproduces itself by sprouts from cut stumps, while a part of the virgin forest is now permanently protected. Extensive lumbering has consumed great areas of redwood forest, the larger part of the enormous quantities of "redwood" lumber and shingles marketed being cut from this tree. The wood is very similar to that of the bigtree.

One third natural size

Redwood attains an age of from 1,000 to 1,300 years.

CEDAR TREES

As in the case of the cypresses, several groups of cone-bearing evergreens are called cedars. The trees here described belong to the botanist's genus Thuja, and are often called arborvitæs. They have flat twigs with small, scale-like leaves and bear very small cones. The crushed twigs emit a pleasant cedar-like odor, which is peculiar also to the freshly cut, light, soft, brown wood.

White Cedar; Arborvitæ

(Thuja occidentalis, Linn.)

Known to lumbermen as "white cedar" and to nurserymen as "arborvitæ." It attains a height of 30 to 60 feet and a diameter of 1 to 3 feet. Dense forests occur in swampy ground and rocky, moist borders of streams in northeastern United States and north to Nova Scotia and New Brunswick. Old trees have the base of the trunk much enlarged. The pale reddish-brown bark is thin, and shallowly furrowed. The soft, yellowish brown, light wood is durable and much used for fence posts, shingles, and tubs.

Two fifths
natural size

Western Red Cedar
(*Thuja plicata*, Don.)

Lumbermen know this as "red cedar" on account of the reddish-brown color of its light, soft, odorous wood. A very large tree of from 150 to 200 feet in height with a diameter of  3 to 16 feet. The base of large trees is enormously swell-butted and fluted for 10 to 20 feet above the ground. This tree grows in moist ground from southern Alaska to northern California, and eastward through southeastern British Columbia and northern Washington to northern Idaho and Montana and to the Cascade Mountains of Washington and Oregon, at elevations from sea-level to 7,500 feet. It is mingled with other trees or occasionally forms small pure stands. The stringy fibrous cinnamon-brown bark, outwardly weathered to a grayish-brown, has shallow seams and narrow ridges. Indians peel strips of this bark, 20 or 30 feet in length, from young trees

One third natural size and use it in basket making. The wood is very durable, old logs that have lain half buried in wet places for over 50 years showing but little decay; very extensively used for shingles. A very long-lived tree, attaining an age of from 200 to possibly 800 years.

JUNIPER TREES

Juniper trees are all so similar in the general appearance of their scale-like foliage that it is difficult to recognize the different species. They are readily distinguished from all other evergreens by their berry-like fruits, known as "juniper berries." The latter are cones in structure, but their scales, distinct when the fruit is young, later become fleshy and so grown together that they resemble a berry and show only their tips near the top of the berry. Juniper seeds are very hard and bony, in this respect unlike the seeds of other cone-bearing trees. Most of the junipers have thinnish, fibrous, stringy, brownish bark, one only having thick checkered bark. They are short-trunked trees growing in dry soils and usually in open or dense stands. Juniper woods are soft, fine-grained, odorous, and durable, that of some species having remained sound for

40 or 50 years in the ground. It varies in color from a pale yellow-brown in some species to a clear rose-purple red in others.

Characteristics of the Commonest Junipers

Our commonest eastern juniper is the red cedar (*Juniperus virginiana*, Linn.), which has small blue-black berries and red wood, the latter being used for lead pencils, chests, and fence posts. Another very similar juniper is the mountain red cedar

One third natural size

(*Juniperus scopulorum*, Sarg.), of the Rocky Mountain region, this also having small blue-black berries and red wood, the botanical distinction between these two junipers being that the latter matures its fruit in two seasons, while the former requires but one season for maturing its berries. The mountain red cedar grows at elevations of 2,000 to 9,000 feet above the sea. Other junipers common in the central and southern Rocky Mountain region are the Utah juniper (*Juniperus utahensis*, [Engelm.] Lemm.), which has large blue-black berries, and the one-seed juniper (*Juniperus m o n o s p e r m a*, [Engelm.] Sarg.), which has small copper-colored, one-seeded berries. These grow at elevations of 5,000 to 8,000 feet above sea-level. But the most easily recognized of all junipers is the alligator juniper (*Juniperus pachyphloea*, Torr.), which has thick, sharply checkered bark, resembling the plates of an alligator's skin. It grows in the mountains at elevations of 4,500 to 8,400 feet above sea-level in southwestern Texas, Arizona, New Mexico, and Mexico. A common mountain juniper of Utah, Washington, Oregon, and California is the western juniper (*Juniperus occidentalis*, Hook.), found mostly at elevations of 5,000 to 10,000 feet above the sea. Its large, bluish-black berries have a tough skin and the foliage is conspicuously dotted with tiny specks of resin. California juniper (*Juniperus californica*, Carr.) is frequent on the hills and mountains of that state, at elevations of 2,000 to 4,000 feet above the sea. The large bluish-black, white-coated berries have an exceedingly thin papery skin covering a sweetish pulp.

WALNUT AND BUTTERNUT TREES

These are well known because of their
edible nuts and valuable, rich-brown durable
woods.   When crushed the young twigs and
green foliage give off a pungent aromatic
odor.   The pith of the twigs has a partition-
like structure (seen by slicing the twig
lengthways).   Leaves of the walnuts and
butternuts, called compound, are made up
of a long central stem with 5 to 11 pairs of
pointed leaflets.

Black walnut (*Juglans nigra*, Linn.), so
called because of its dark-brown wood,
grows in fertile bottomlands from Ontario to
Florida and west to Minnesota, Nebraska,
Kansas, and Texas; mingled with other
trees.   One hundred to 150 feet in height
and 4 to 6 feet in diameter; yields valuable
furniture wood.   The fruit is spherical with a thick dry flesh
covering the hard-shelled nut.

One ninth natural size

Butternut (*Juglans cinera*, Linn.), so called on account of the

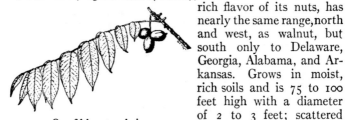

rich flavor of its nuts, has
nearly the same range, north
and west, as walnut, but
south only to Delaware,
Georgia, Alabama, and Ar-
kansas.   Grows in moist,
rich soils and is 75 to 100
feet high with a diameter
of 2 to 3 feet; scattered
among other trees.   Fruit

One fifth natural size

elongated, pointed, and with a thin sticky skin covering the
prickly hard-shelled nut.   Light, soft, pale-brown, coarse-
grained wood used for furniture.

Mexican walnut (*Juglans rupestris*, Engelm.), with spherical
nuts about ½ to ¾ inch in diameter, is 25 to 50 feet high, and 1 to
2 feet through and grows singly in the mountain canyons of
Texas, New Mexico, and Arizona, while the similar California
walnut (*Juglans californica*, Wats.) grows singly in the coast
mountains of California.   It is 30 to 60 feet high and 12 to 20
inches through, bearing nuts about an inch in diameter.   Wood of
the last two is similar to that of the black walnut, but rarely
used for any purpose.

HICKORY TREES

Hickory trees are well known because of the hard, strong, elastic, useful wood and edible nuts of some species. They have compound leaves, with from one to several pairs of pointed leaflets on a slender stem, which has a single leaflet at the end, the number of leaflets, therefore, always being odd. The fruit is characteristic in its thick or thinnish woody husk, which at maturity is split into sections, liberating the hard, smooth-shelled nut. Hickories grow only in eastern United States scattered among other forest trees. Wood of most hickories is used for all sorts of tool handles, agricultural implements, and spokes of wheels.

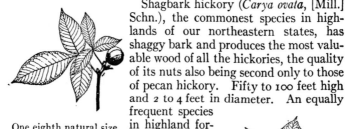

Shagbark hickory (*Carya ovata*, [Mill.] Schn.), the commonest species in highlands of our northeastern states, has shaggy bark and produces the most valuable wood of all the hickories, the quality of its nuts also being second only to those of pecan hickory. Fifty to 100 feet high and 2 to 4 feet in diameter. An equally frequent species in highland forests, mainly of

One eighth natural size

central southeastern United States, is the mocker nut (*Carya alba*, [Linn.] Koch.). It has a very hard, shallowly seamed bark, downy leaves, large gray winter buds, and grows to a height of 50 to 80 feet with a diameter of 18 to 30 inches, producing commercially valuable wood. An-

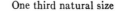
One third natural size

other well-known hickory with deeply furrowed, rough bark, is the pecan (*Carya pecan*, [Marsh.] Schn.), which is 90 to 150 feet high and 2 to 5 feet through, in rich bottomlands, and grows from southern Illinois and Indiana to Arkansas and Texas. Improved varieties of this hickory are extensively cultivated for their nuts, which are of very large size and with extremely thin shells.

One fifth natural size

POPLAR TREES

Poplar trees and willows belong to the same family. Their tiny cotton-covered seeds are easily carried long distances by the wind. For this reason poplar trees are widely distributed. The characteristic flattened leaf stems cause poplar leaves to flutter constantly even in a gentle breeze. They have bitter bark and light-colored, soft, brittle wood, which rots quickly when exposed to the weather. They are fast-growing but short-lived.

The commonest of these trees is the aspen (*Populus tremuloides*, Michx.), which often forms extensive pure stands from Labrador and our northeastern states to Alaska, and through our Rockies and the mountains of the Pacific slope states, often at 10,000 feet above the sea. It is the first tree to

One fourth natural size

cover mountain forest land denuded by fire. Fifty to 100 feet high and 10 to 30 inches through. Bark smooth, whitish, or pale yellow-green. Fire-killed trees, frequent in the western mountains, make the best of camp wood.

Another poplar, easily recognized by its smooth gray-green bark and toothed leaves, of our northeastern states and eastern Canada, is the large-tooth aspen (*Populus grandidentata*, Michx.). It is 40 to 60 feet high and 1 to 2 feet through.

One third natural size

Two common, large rough-barked poplars, are the cottonwood (*Populus deltoides*, Marsh.) which grows along streams in eastern United States, and black cottonwood (*Populus trichocarpa*, Torr. & Gr.), common in river bottoms in the northwestern states. They are large trees, 100 to 200 feet high and 3 to 8 feet through, and cut for lumber.

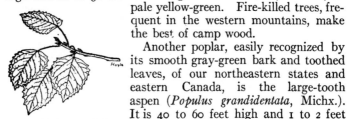

The Fremont cottonwood (*Populus fremontii*, Wats.) is a common tree along the

One third natural size

One third natural size

lower courses of streams in the Pacific slope country, while the Wislizenus cotton-wood (*Populus wislizeni*, Wats.) is a familiar tree of like habitat in the Rocky Mountain region. Both have triangular shaped leaves and thick furrowed bark, and are 60 to 100 feet high with a diameter of 3 to 6 feet.

One fourth natural size

BIRCH TREES

Birch trees are well known because of their white, yellow, or copper-colored papery bark, which, in most cases, is easily peeled off in thin sheets. Their cone-like fruits fall to pieces when ripe and the minute winged seeds are blown long distances by the wind. Some produce hard, fine-grained wood which is used for furniture and for imitations or substitutes, when stained, for mahogany. It is also much used for spools, spindles, shoe-pegs, and broom handles. Birches grow chiefly in moist soils and in cool situations, mingled with other trees. They are 40 to 100 feet high and 1 to 5 feet through.

The best known birch is the canoe or white birch (*Betula papyrifera*, Marsh.), so called because Indians make canoes of the white bark. It is a large tree growing from Labrador to Hudson Bay, and southward through our northeastern states to Pennsylvania, Michigan, Iowa, Tennessee, Montana, and Washington. Once exten-

One fourth natural size sively used by the northern Indians for making canoes, the bark of a single large trunk being so cleverly peeled off and turned inside out that it forms a very light boat.

Another common but small white-barked birch is gray birch (*Betula populifolia*, Marsh.), which often grows in thick stands from Nova Scotia and New Brunswick to Delaware and through New England and New York. It grows in poor soils and quickly covers abandoned fields, and forest land denuded by fire.

One third natural size

One third natural size

Red or river birch (*Betula nigra*, Linn.), so called because of its copper-colored papery bark, and because it grows mostly along streams, and in other moist situations. It is found from Massachusetts and New York to Florida and westward near the coast to Texas; extending to Kansas and Missouri, Nebraska, Minnesota, southern Michigan and Ohio. It is the only birch tree growing as far south as the Gulf states.

Two other interesting birch trees are the yellow birch (*Betula lutea*, Michx. f.), so called because of its pale silvery-yellow bark, and the sweet birch (*Betula lenta*, Linn.), so called because of the wintergreen flavor and odor of its inner bark. Both trees grow in our northeastern states and adjacent portions of Canada, and yield most of the reddish-brown birch lumber used for furniture. Both are exceptional because of the wintergreen flavor of their bark, that of the sweet birch being very strong.

One fourth natural size

One third natural size

ALDER TREES

Alder trees have flowers and cone-like fruits similar in appearance to those of the birches. The long tassel-like male flowers of the alders are quite the same, as they appear on the bare twigs in early spring, but their cone-like fruits differ from those of the birches in the fact that they do not fall to pieces, as do those of the birches, but can often be seen clinging to the twigs in winter. Bark of the alders is often smooth and gray and with large chalky-white blotches; only the trunks of large trees have scaly bark and then chiefly at the base of the trunk. Small or medium-size trees, rarely over 75 to 90 feet in height and 1 to 2 feet in diameter. They grow in small pure stands throughout the United States from sea-level to 8,000 feet above the sea, in wet places along streams and in

swampy ground. Their hard, beech-like wood is used for cheap furniture and for fuel.

One of the common large alders of the Pacific states is the red alder (*Alnus oregona*, Nutt.), which grows near the coast from Alaska through Washington and Oregon to California. The wood is sometimes used for furniture.

A small, familiar eastern alder is the seaside alder (*Alnus maritima*, [Marsh.] Muehl.), which grows along streams and about ponds in southern Delaware and Maryland; also on the Red River in Oklahoma. Its leaves are

One fourth natural size

bright green on the upper surface and covered with pale glandular specks on the under side. More or less commonly cultivated as an ornamental tree in the eastern states.

BEECH AND CHESTNUT TREES

The beech and chestnut are two very well-known trees of our eastern forests, the beech because of its familiar smooth, straight trunks, and the chestnut because of its widely popular fruit.

The beech (*Fagus ferruginea*, Ait.) attains a height of 70 to 120 feet and a diameter of 3 to 4 feet. Forest-grown specimens of it have long clean stems, while those grown in the open have short trunks and broad, beautifully shaped crowns. The small prickly burs contain two 3-cornered, brown-shelled sweet nuts, the favorite food of squirrels, chipmunks, and many birds. Forty years ago millions of passenger pigeons used to feed on these nuts. The

One third natural size

greed of man has exterminated these birds, so that now we do not hear their familiar note in the beech forests. Beech trees grow in almost pure stands or are mingled with sugar maple.

linden, ash, and red oak. Enormous quantities of beech wood have been cut for fuel in sections where this tree abounds. Because of its hard, strong texture and toughness it was also used for shoe lasts, plane-blocks, tool handles, and to some extent for furniture.

The chestnut tree (*Castanea dentata*, [Marsh.] Borkh.) needs

no introduction. Every one knows it by the big prickly burs and their delicious nuts, and by the long sharp-toothed leaves. It grows mingled with other high-ground trees from southern Maine to

One third natural size

Vermont and southern Ontario, to Delaware, and along the Allegheny Mountains to Kentucky, Tennessee, central Alabama and Mississippi. In the forest it is 75 to 100 feet high and 2 to 10 feet in diameter, while single trees in fields have short thick trunks and wide-branched crowns. The hard, coarse-grained wood makes handsome interior finish, and being very durable it is also much used for railway ties, fence posts, telegraph and telephone poles. Recently many chestnut trees have been damaged or killed by the chestnut bark disease (a parasitic fungus). Dead branches and tops of the tree indicate the presence of this deadly parasite, for which the only remedy is to cut and burn the affected parts.

OAK TREES

Oaks are the best known of our forest trees. They stand for strength and majesty among trees, and there are scarcely any parts of our country that do not have some of the fifty or more different oaks in the United States, the greatest number being found in the East. Some are low shrubs, but most of them are very large trees, which yield the most useful wood of all of our forest trees for very many different uses, including agricultural implements, interior finish, flooring, and furniture. Bark of some oaks is used for tanning of leather.

Two botanical divisions are made of oak trees on account of differences in the character of their wood, in the time for maturing their acorns, and in the shape of their leaves. White oaks form one division, because they have lighter colored, stronger, less porous wood, and mature their acorns in one season. Black oaks form the other class, which, in general, have wood of a reddish tinge and of more porous structure, and require two seasons for maturing their acorns. The fruits (acorns) of oaks are composed of a basal, scaly cup containing a smooth, thin-shelled nut, which, in the case of the white oaks, is whitish and sweet, while, in the case of the black oaks, it is yellowish and bitter (due to the presence of tannin). Some of the western Indians gather acorns for food. The kernels are dried and made into flour, which they wash in hot water to dissolve out the tannin. A sort of bread is then made from the pulp. No such use is made of acorns in the East. They yield the food of many birds and forest mammals, squirrels burying them in the autumn, as they do other nuts, and eating them in the winter. Boy scouts who have rambled in the western pine forests have perhaps seen a woodpecker inserting acorns in holes previously cut out in the thick bark of the western yellow pine. This woodpecker later returns and eats the acorn (also the worm, if there).

White oaks and black oaks are also distinguished by the shape of their leaves, those of the common white oaks having, as a rule, rounded lobes, while, in the case of the black oaks, the ends of the lobes have a sharp point or bristle. Some of the oaks have evergreen leaves but most of them shed their leaves in the autumn. The oaks are very long-lived, some reaching an age of 200 to 600 years.

WHITE OAK TREES
White Oak
(*Quercus alba*, Linn.)

One fourth natural size

The commonest and commercially most valuable of all eastern species, and forming nearly pure large forests on high ground from southern Maine to Quebec and Ontario, through Michigan, southern Minnesota, western Nebraska and Kansas and southward to Florida and Texas. From 75 to 100 feet high and 2 to 4 feet in diameter. Its thick, light grayish or almost white bark is distinctly furrowed and ridged.

Bur Oak

(*Quercus macrocarpa*, Michx.)

One fifth
natural size

Bur oak, so called on account of the bur-like fringe of its acorn cups, grows mostly in moist, rich bottomlands from New Brunswick and Nova Scotia west through Ontario and southeastern Manitoba, and from Maine, Vermont, Massachusetts, and Pennsylvania, westward to Montana, Nebraska, and Kansas, and into Tennessee, Oklahoma, and Texas. Its range extends farther west than that of any other eastern oak, reaching the eastern foothills of the Rockies in Montana. A very large, rough-barked tree, 80 to sometimes 160 feet high and 2 to 4 feet through. Wood, very heavy, strong, durable, similar in appearance to that of white oak, and used for the same purposes.

Chestnut Oak

(*Quercus prinus*, Linn.)

One fifth natural size

Called chestnut oak because its leaves resemble in shape those of the chestnut. It forms nearly pure stands or is mingled with other oaks in dry, gravelly, and stony soils on the upper slopes and tops of hills from southern Maine and eastern Massachusetts to Maryland and to northern Georgia and Alabama; extending west into New York and to central Kentucky and Tennessee. Very distinct in its bluntly and shallowly toothed leaves and large acorns, which have a long nut and extremely shallow cup. Fifty to 100 feet high and 2 to 6 feet in diameter. The thick, hard, grayish conspicuously furrowed bark of this oak is the most valuable of all eastern oaks for tanning leather.

Valley Oak

(*Quercus lobata*, Née.)

The most picturesque and graceful of the white oaks. Called valley oak because it grows so abundantly in valley lands of western California from sea-level to nearly 5,000 feet above the sea. Usually widely scattered, never forming close stands, but often constituting the only tree growth. It is a massive

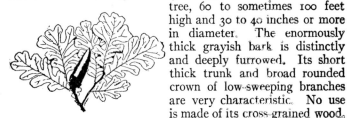

tree, 60 to sometimes 100 feet high and 30 to 40 inches or more in diameter. The enormously thick grayish bark is distinctly and deeply furrowed. Its short thick trunk and broad rounded crown of low-sweeping branches are very characteristic. No use is made of its cross-grained wood, except for fuel.

One fourth natural size

Blue Oak

(Quercus douglasii, Hook. & Arn.)

This is another familiar white oak of the dry California foothills. Its bluish-green leaves and sharply ridged, grayish-white bark make it conspicuous in the western hill country, where blue oak forms open pure stands. Thirty to 40 feet high and 10 to 15 inches in diameter, with a short, leaning or bent trunk and a broad, rounded, crooked-branched crown. The cross-grained, brittle wood is used only for fuel.

One third natural size

BLACK OAK TREES

Red Oak

(Quercus borealis, Michx. fils.)

Called red oak because of the reddish tinge of its wood. It is the largest and commercially the most valuable of this class. Eighty to 110 feet or more in height and 3 to 4 feet in diameter. It grows in rich, moist soil from Nova Scotia, New Brunswick, and Quebec to middle Tennessee and Virginia, and along the Appalachian Mountains to northern Georgia, also to Nebraska and Kansas. Small

One sixth natural size

groups or single trees are scattered among other trees. The hard, heavy, strong wood is much used for interior finishing lumber and for furniture, and as a substitute for white oak.

Black Oak
(*Quercus velutina*, Lam.)

One fifth natural size

Black oak, so called because of the rough blackish bark of large trees, is fully as large as the red oak and has nearly the same range and habitat, but it does not extend as far north into Canada. The brownish, red-tinged wood is heavy, hard, strong, and porous, the latter quality rendering it unfit for use except for coarse lumber and for fuel. The inner bark is bright orange-yellow and in the olden days this was used as a yellow dye.

Scarlet Oak
(*Quercus coccinea*, Moench.)

One sixth natural size

A common oak in dry, sandy, or gravelly land from Maine, Ontario, and Minnesota to Michigan, Illinois, North Carolina, and eastern Tennessee. Always scattered among other forest trees, and often with white oak, red oak, black oak, and hickories. Sixty to 75 feet or more in height, and 2 to 3 feet in diameter. The heavy, hard, coarse-grained, reddish-brown, porous wood has a strong odor and is used only for fuel.

California Black Oak
(*Quercus kelloggii*, Cooper.)

One fourth natural size

The Pacific slope country has one common species of the black oak class which resembles in its bark and leaves the eastern black oak. It grows from western Oregon to the southern boundary of California, and often forms patches, or occurs singly, interspersed in western yellow pine forests and sometimes among the giant sequoias, on dry, gravelly slopes and hills at elevations of 5,000 to 6,000 feet above the sea. Thirty to 75 feet in height and 2 to exceptionally 4 feet in diameter, the trunks usually being bent or leaning. Its porous, heavy, hard, brittle, pale reddish wood is used for fuel.

Turkey Oak
(*Quercus catesbaei*, Michx.)

One of the commonest black oaks on dry sandy ridges near

One sixth natural size

the coast from North Carolina to Florida and westward to Louisiana. Fifteen to 50 feet high and 6 to 30 inches in diameter. Forms open scattered stands among pines and where they have been cleared off, here being the most conspicuous oak tree of the region. Its large, lustrous, forked leaves are peculiarly distinctive. The heavy, very porous reddish-brown wood is used only for fuel.

Black Jack
(*Quercus marilandica*, Muenchh.)

Usually 15 to 30 feet high and 6 to 12 inches through, and forming extensive pure growths and scattered patches on dry, sandy, or heavy clay soils from New York through Ohio, Indiana, southern Michigan, southeastern Nebraska, and central Kansas to Florida and eastern Texas. Its stunted, gnarled trunks and thick, glossy leaves are very characteristic. The heavy, hard, dark-brown wood is used for fuel and charcoal.

One fifth natural size

One fourth natural size

Pin Oak
(*Quercus palustris*, Muenchh.)

The name pin oak is applied to this tree because during the first 30 or 40 years of its growth the twigs and branches bear short pin-like twigs. It grows on the borders of swamps, in partly overflowed river bottoms, and along streams scattered among other low-ground trees, from Massachusetts to southern Virginia, Missouri, Arkansas, and Oklahoma. Much planted as a street and lawn tree, because of its handsome form and resistance to breakage by storms. Sixty to sometimes 100 feet high and 3 to 5 feet through with 40 to 60 feet of clear trunk. During early growth the lower branches stand out at right angles from the trunk, but later they are curved downward. The very heavy, hard, strong wood is little used for commercial purposes, owing to its tendency to check and warp.

EVERGREEN OAK TREES

Only a few of our oaks are evergreen. From the small size of their leaves, some of which resemble the leaves of holly trees, they may, at first sight, appear to some people not to be oaks at all.

Live Oak
(*Quercus virginiana,* Mill.)

This is the most famous and widely known of all our evergreen oaks. It grows in the south Atlantic and Gulf states

One fourth
natural size

in rich, moist bottomlands and in barren sand from Virginia to Florida and west into Texas. Except in a very dense forest, where it is 50 to 75 feet high and 3 to 4 feet in diameter, live oak is mostly under 50 feet in height, with a short trunk 5 to 7 feet through and huge, horizontal branches, which form a broad, round-topped crown with a spread sometimes of 100 to 150 feet. Occasionally it grows in almost pure stands, or is mingled with other trees. Its hard, strong, tough wood is heavier than that of any other North American oak. Because of its great strength and toughness the wood was extensively used in the colonial days of this country for shipbuilding, and it is still sometimes used for certain parts of ships.

California Live Oak
(*Quercus agrifolia,* Née.)

Common in the coast region from northern California to lower California. It is a short, broad-crowned, crooked-

stemmed tree 25 to 50 feet high and 1 to 2
feet in diameter. The bark of young trees and
of the large limbs of old trees is smooth and
grayish-brown, with numerous whitish areas,
old trees having thick, hard, dark-brown,
roughly furrowed bark. In general appearance
this oak looks like an old apple tree. The
hard, very fine-grained, reddish-brown, heavy
wood is used only for fuel.

One fifth
natural size

Tan Oak
(*Quercus densiflora*, Hook. & Arn.)

The tan oak, so called from the fact that the bark is used
for tanning leather, grows abundantly from southwestern Oregon

One fifth natural size

through California from sea-level to elevations of 5,000 feet above the sea. It
has smooth, thick bark and is 50 to 80 feet
high and 1 to 4 feet in diameter, large
trees growing at lower elevation. Forms
nearly pure small stands but grows chiefly
in mixture with other trees, in valleys and
on mountain slopes in rich, moist, sandy,
and gravelly soils. Botanically the most
peculiar of all the oaks, because it is a connecting link between the oaks and the
chestnuts. Unlike the oaks, the clusters of
male flowers are borne on erect stems, as
in the case of chestnuts, while male flowers of oaks are tassel-
like pendent bodies. On account of the extensive use of its bark
for tanning leather, it is the most valuable oak of the Pacific
region. The light-brown wood, faintly tinged with red, is very
fine-grained and hard, and suitable for agricultural implements
and finishing lumber, but generally used chiefly for fuel.

ELM TREES

Elm trees grow only in the eastern half of this country
and Canada. They are distinguished from other trees by
their rounded, thin, flat seeds, and by their unequal-sided
leaves. Rough-barked trees. The best known and commonest of these trees is the slippery elm and the white or American elm.

Slippery Elm
(Ulmus pubescens, Mill.)

Called slippery because its inner bark is very mucilaginous when soaked in water or chewed. Nearly every country boy knows the tree from this characteristic. It grows scattered among the other highland forest trees from the St. Lawrence River through Ontario to North Dakota, eastern Nebraska, and to western Florida, central Alabama, Mississippi, and eastern Texas. Fifty to 70 feet high and 1½ to 2 feet through. Easily recognized by its large, exceedingly rough leaves and by the slippery inner bark, which can be tested any season of the year. Dried bark has a peculiar odor. Slippery elm wood is straight-grained and easily split, the wood of other elms being cross-grained and difficult to split. Very durable when exposed to the weather; and in the early days it was often split into fence-rails and fence-posts; used for agricultural implements.

One fourth natural size

White or American Elm
(Ulmus americana, Linn.)

The largest and commonest of our elm trees, reaching a height of 100 to 120 feet with a long, clear trunk 4 to 10 feet in diameter. Old trees have the trunks greatly enlarged at the base, while their broad, round-topped crowns of pendulous branches may sometimes have a spread of over 100 feet. It grows in low, often inundated ground, and frequently along rivers mingled with other lowland trees. Its range extends from Newfoundland to the eastern base of the Rockies and south to Florida, and west into the Dakotas, western Nebraska, Kansas, Oklahoma, and Texas.

One fourth natural size

The picturesque, graceful form of this elm makes it very popular for shade and ornament, being one of the commonest street and lawn trees used in eastern United States. The hard, strong, cross-grained wood is much used for wagon wheels, cooperage, furniture, and fuel.

MAGNOLIA AND TULIP TREES

The magnolia trees and the tulip-tree belong to the same family (*Magnoliaceae*). Their inner bark and twigs have a strongly aromatic or peppery odor and flavor when freshly bruised or broken. They bear large showy flowers.

Evergreen Magnolia

(*Magnolia grandiflora*, Linn.; *M. foetida*, [Linn.] Sarg.)

The best known of all magnolias because of its large, shiny, evergreen leaves, which make the trees conspicuous in the coast forests from North Carolina to Florida, and in the Gulf region to eastern Texas. Seventy-five to 80 feet high and with straight, smooth-barked trunks 3 to 4 feet in diameter. Mingled with other forest trees in moist, rich soils along rivers and

One fourth natural size

about swamps. Its brilliant evergreen foliage and large white blooms make it popular as an ornamental tree as far north as Pennsylvania. The pale, yellowish wood is occasionally used for fuel.

Tulip-tree or Yellow Poplar

(*Liriodendron tulipifera*, Linn.)

Lumbermen call this tree "yellow poplar" in allusion to the yellowish-brown heartwood. The tree's large tulip-like flowers suggested the name tulip-tree. One of the largest of eastern forest trees, growing to a height of 150 to nearly 200 feet with a long, straight, clean trunk, 6 to sometimes 10 feet in diameter. It grows in rich, moist soils, scattered or in small groups, among other trees from Rhode Island to Ver-

One fourth natural size

mont and west through southern Michigan and south to Florida, southern Alabama, Mississippi, and Arkansas. The shape of its leaves is unlike that of any other North American tree. The light, soft wood varies in color from a pale yellow-brown to a grayish brown, and is commercially one of the most valuable woods of our eastern forests. Now used mostly for interior finish and carriage work. Formerly it was extensively used for all sorts of construction, and the Indians made canoes from large trunks.

Sassafras

(*Sassafras officinale*, Nees & Eberm.)

Of all of our eastern trees none perhaps is so well known as sassafras and doubtless because of the agreeable flavor of its

One eighth
natural size

foliage and bark. "Sassafras tea" (made from the root bark) is a by-word in every country home. All of the other trees that belong to the family *Lauraceae*, of which the sassafras is a member, have similarly characteristic odors and flavor, the camphor-tree, and the bay-tree being well-known examples. Sassafras grows from eastern Massachusetts through southern Vermont, southern Ontario, and Michigan, southern Iowa, eastern Kansas and Oklahoma, and south to Florida and Texas. Often shrubby, but it may grow to be 60 to 90 feet high and 2 to 7 feet in diameter. The very light, yellow-brown wood has great durability; little used except for fuel. Oil of sassafras, distilled from the bark, is used as a flavor by confectioners.

Sweet Gum; Red Gum

(*Liquidambar styraciflua*, Linn.)

Lumbermen now call this tree red gum, on account of its reddish-brown wood, but before the wood was found to be commercially useful, the tree was called sweet gum because it yields a balsamic gum (dried juice) used by country children as a chewing gum. Easily recognized by its star-shaped leaves and ball-like, long-stemmed heads of fruit, which contain brown winged seeds. Sixty to 130 feet high

One sixth natural size

and 2 to 5 feet through. Grows from Connecticut to Missouri and Arkansas, and south to Florida and Texas, and also into Mexico. One of the commonest of forest trees in the South Atlantic States and lower Mississippi River basin, here often forming extensive pure stands in overflowed river bottoms and around swamps. The hard, fine-grained, reddish-brown wood is extensively used for furniture, interior finish, wooden plates, fruit baskets, and boxes. Wood of the basal part of the trunk is sometimes beautifully mottled.

SYCAMORE TREES

Sycamores are recognizable at once by their smooth, greenish-gray bark, the outer layer of which, on all but old trunks, is shed every year, the curled pieces of bark falling away as a result of the annual diameter growth. Sycamores also have characteristic ball-like heads of fruit, suspended from a long stem, while the base of the leaf stems forms a little cup which fits over a bud. Most other leaf stems are attached below the buds. The cross-grained, pale brown, reddish-tinged wood of all the sycamores is very similar, being conspicuously marked by wide pith-rays. Three different sycamore trees grow in this country, one in the eastern states, one in New Mexico and Arizona, and one in California.

Sycamore
(*Platanus occidentalis*, Linn.)

The largest of our native sycamores, attaining a height of 80 to 160 feet or more, and a diameter of 8 to 11 feet. It is a

One fifth natural size

swamp-loving tree, growing along streams and in low bottom-lands from Maine and Minnesota to Texas and Florida. Sometimes, in nearly pure stands, but often scattered among other low-ground trees. The long-stemmed "balls" (of seeds) are always single. Trunks of large trees are often hollow, the shell being not over 5 or 6 inches thick. Early settlers used these trunks for smoke-houses and rain-troughs. Sycamore wood is used for interior finish, furniture, packing boxes, and is a favorite wood for butchers' blocks.

California Sycamore
(*Platanus racemosa*, Nutt.)

Forty to 60 feet high and 18 to 30 inches through.   In poor soil along streams and in moist gulches, forming thin fringes and small groups, or mingled with alders and other trees.   Several trunks grow from the same root.   From 2 to 7 fruit heads are borne on a single stem.   Wood used only for fuel.

MAPLE TREES

One sixth natural size

Maples are well known because of their useful, hard, often beautifully curled and mottled ("bird's-eye") wood, and the delicious syrup and sugar two or three of them yield.   The largest and most important ones grow in eastern United States and Canada.   Their twigs, leaves and seeds grow in pairs, the seeds having wings.

Sugar Maple
(*Acer saccharum*, Marsh.)

Called sugar maple because it was doubtless the first one found to produce sugar, for which, with its wood, it is the most important species.   Eighty to 110 feet or more in height; 2 to 4 feet through.   It grows from southern Newfoundland and the northern border of the Great Lakes to the Lake of the Woods and M i n n e s o t a, southward through our northeastern states to Nebraska, Kansas, and Georgia.   Forms nearly pure

One sixth natural size

forests, in which are mingled beech, linden, and red oak, etc. The hard wood, sometimes curly, wavy, or with "bird's-eye" markings, is the best of all the maples for flooring and furniture. This tree yields most of the genuine "maple sugar" and "maple syrup" of markets.   These are products of the sap which "runs" only in early spring and only when there is a succession of bright, sunny days followed by sharp frosts at night.

Scarlet Maple; Red Maple
(*Acer rubrum*, Linn.)

Called scarlet maple on account of its brilliant scarlet-colored flowers.   Seventy to 100 feet high and 2 to 4 feet through.

One fifth natural size

growing in swampy places, around ponds, along streams, and in adjacent overflowed bottomlands, forming nearly pure stands. It ranges from New Brunswick, Quebec, Ontario, and the Lake of the Woods to Florida and eastern Texas. The wood, less excellent than sugar maple, is used as a substitute for that of sugar maple for flooring, furniture, and woodenware. The tree yields maple sugar and syrup of good quality, but it is not often "tapped" for these products.

Broad-leafed Maple

(*Acer macrophyllum*, Pursh.)

The largest maple in the Pacific coast region, being 60 to 100 feet high and 1 to 3 feet in diameter. It grows along streams, in alluvial bottomlands, and in mountain valleys from the coast of Alaska, British Columbia, western Washington, and Oregon to California. Pure stands of the largest trees occur in rich bottoms; sometimes with other lowland trees. Wood hard, fine-grained, light-brown with a tinge of red; is used for the same purposes as the eastern sugar maple.

One sixth natural size

DOGWOOD TREES

The dogwoods are a group of small trees that would be popularly little known except for the two species which have big, showy, flower-like white scales, often believed to be true flowers. The showy scales surround the true flowers which are inconspicuous. Dogwoods bloom in early spring when those with showy scales are very conspicuous among other leafless trees. One of these trees is common in eastern forests and the other in Pacific forests. Both have brilliant, coral-red, berry-like fruits, ripe in autumn. Both the twigs and the leaves grow in pairs. The wood of these trees is hard, fine-grained, and strong, that of the eastern species being considerably heavier than the wood of the western tree.

Flowering Dogwood
(*Cornus florida*, Linn.)

One fourth
natural size

A small tree, with red-brown checkered bark, and 15 to 30 feet high and 6 to 10 inches through—occasionally larger, growing in moist woodlands from eastern Massachusetts to Florida and west to Ontario, Michigan, Missouri, and Texas. The brown, red-tinged wood is used quite extensively for small turned ware.

Western Dogwood
(*Cornus nuttallii*, Aud.)

Usually 30 to 50 feet high, or occasionally taller, and 10 to 20 inches in diameter. Small trees have smooth, brownish-gray bark with a reddish tint, the largest trees having scaly bark. Like the flowering dogwood, it grows in the shade of other trees in moist soils from the southern coast of British Columbia through Washington, Oregon, and California. The pale, reddish-brown wood is suitable for turned ware and small cabinetwork, but it is little used for these purposes.

One fourth natural size

Persimmon Tree
(*Diospyros virginiana*, Linn.)

The persimmon tree belongs to the same family (Ebenaceæ) as the black-wooded ebonies of tropical countries, some of which are closely related to our persimmon. Thirty to 100 feet high and 1 to 2 feet in diameter, with thick, brownish, deeply checkered bark. It grows from Connecticut to Florida and from southern Ohio to Alabama and westward to Iowa, Missouri and Kansas, Oklahoma and Texas. Well known because of its edible fruit, especially in the southern states. The mature, orange-colored fruit is very astringent, except in the far South, but it has a sweetish luscious flavor after it has been thoroughly frozen. Large old trees have an irregularly disposed, deep-

One sixth
natural size

brown or nearly black heartwood, the sapwood being whitish. The wood is heavy, hard, and strong, and used for turned articles, shoe-lasts, plane-blocks, and weaving shuttles, for which it is preferred to all other woods.

ASH TREES

The ash trees are well known on account of their useful woods. They have tall, straight trunks and most of them sharply furrowed and ridged bark. They are also characterized by the opposite arrangement of their twigs and leaves, which are compound (several pairs of leaflets on a central stem ending with an odd one). Their slender seeds, borne in dense clusters, have a thin, flat wing at one end. Most of the ashes produce light-colored, hard, elastic, straight-grained wood, which splits easily, and is commercially very valuable.

White Ash
(*Fraxinus americana*, Linn.)

One sixth natural size

Called white ash because of the light clear color of its wood, which, with one exception, is superior in quality to that of the other species. Eighty to 100 feet or more in height, and 2 to sometimes 6 feet in diameter. It grows in rich, moist soils from Nova Scotia and Newfoundland to Florida and west to Ontario, Minnesota, Nebraska, Kansas, Oklahoma, and Texas. Sometimes forming a considerable part of the forest, but more often scattered among other trees. The wood is used for agricultural implements, carriages, oars, tool handles, cabinet-work, and interior finish. Frequently planted as a shade tree.

Black Ash
(*Fraxinus nigra* Marsh.)

Seventy to 90 feet high with long clear trunks 18 to 20 inches in diameter. Unlike other common ashes it has thin, loosely scaly, grayish bark. It grows in low, rich bottomlands subject to overflow, where it may form the greater part of the stand,

from Newfoundland to Manitoba and southward to Delaware, Virginia, southern Illinois, Missouri, and Arkansas. The wood of large trees is much used for interior finish and furniture because of its rich brown color. The tough, coarse-grained wood of small trees (mostly whitish sapwood) is easily separated into strips (by "wracking") and is used for barrel hoops and baskets.

One sixth natural size

Oregon Ash

(*Fraxinus oregona,* Nutt.)

A common ash tree of the Pacific States and the most valuable broad-leafed timber tree of that region. It grows mostly in small, pure patches, interspersed among other forest trees, along streams, and in rich bottoms from the shores of Puget Sound south through Washington, Oregon, and California. Sixty to 75 feet high and 16 to 30 inches in diameter with long, clean trunk. The pale brown wood is fine-grained, heavy, and similar in quality to the white ash, and used for the same purposes.

One sixth natural size

"Manual of the Trees of North America." By C. S. Sargent. Houghton Mifflin & Co., Boston and New York

"North American Trees." By N. L. Britton. Henry Holt & Co., New York.

"Forest Trees of the Pacific Slope," by Geo. B. Sudworth. Bulletin of the U. S. Forest Service. Price 60 cents. For sale by Superintendent of Documents, Government Printing Office, Washington, D. C.

"U. S. Forest Service Bulletins" (as far as issued) describing and illustrating forest trees of Rocky Mountain states; free on application. By Geo. B Sudworth.

CHAPTER III

WILD LIFE AND CONSERVATION

Wild Animals Every Scout Should Know

By William T. Hornaday

In selecting the animals to be introduced here, we have chosen the species most worth knowing, and have omitted many of the common ones that already are well and widely known. For further information consult "The American Natural History," by W. T. Hornaday (Scribners), which can be found in nearly every public library. The fraction indicates the size of the drawing as compared with the animal itself.

THE CAT FAMILY

The Jaguar

This fierce and powerful yellow-and-black cat is the largest spotted feline animal of the Western Hemisphere. It is larger

Jaguar $\frac{1}{27}$

than the largest leopard, built like a bulldog, and is an animal of very great strength. Its principal markings are black rosettes on a tawny yellow ground. It has powerful forelegs, neck, and jaws, and can easily kill a small horse. Its home is the northern half of South America, Central America, and Mexico; and in 1914 a female Jaguar with three cubs was killed in the Grand Canyon National Forest, Arizona. Shoulder height 30 in.

The Puma, Cougar, or Mountain Lion

The Puma often was called in Colonial times the "Panther," or "Painter." Its range extends from southern British Columbia to Patagonia. It reaches its maximum size and weight in

Colorado, where the largest specimens attain a length of eight feet from end of nose to tip of tail. No skin fairly measured and *not stretched* should be longer than eight feet. The Puma is a

Puma, Cougar, or Mountain Lion $\frac{1}{24}$

thin-bodied, lightly built gray or tawny cat, with a small head and a beautiful face. It is not courageous, and we know of only one aggressive case, wherein one actually attacked a boy without provocation, and killed him. "Buffalo" Jones has roped more than twenty full-grown Pumas in pine trees, without an accident of any kind. Pumas are very destructive to deer, elk calves, colts, young cattle, and sheep, and are regularly hunted and killed in the West by the hunters of the United States Government, as "pests."

The Ocelot, or Tiger Cat

Ocelot $\frac{1}{17}$

The Ocelot, or Tiger Cat, when fully grown, is often mistaken for a young Jaguar, and offered for sale on that basis. The former is worth $30, the latter $100. The Ocelot is about as large as a red fox, and its color markings consist of spots supplemented by a few short horizontal bars on the neck and sides. It inhabits the warm forests of Mexico, Central and South America.

The Canada Lynx

A Lynx is commonly spoken of as a "Wild Cat" or "Bob Cat"; and there are a number of species in North America. The Canada Lynx is the largest and handsomest. Its color is pepper-and-salt-gray, usually without spots; it has a long pencil of black hair on the tip of each ear, and its legs and paws are very heavily furred. A large specimen shot in March, 1916, near

Plattsburg, New York, was 24 inches high, 34 inches long, and weighed 35 pounds. As its name implies, the great northern territory known collectively as Canada is the home of this animal, but it also inhabits the northern United States, clear across the continent. Lynxes feed upon rabbits, ground game of every kind, small deer, and even have been known to pull down and kill mountain sheep.

Canada Lynx $\frac{1}{18}$

The Red or Bay Lynx

The Red or Bay Lynx is the more or less spotted species that inhabits the more heavily timbered regions of the United States, and is the species most frequently seen. It is found in the great plains as well as in the forest regions, often traveling through sage-brush flats, miles from the nearest timber. All Lynxes are destructive to poultry, lambs, and other small animals of value, and they are officially killed as predatory animals. About same size as Canada Lynx.

THE DOG FAMILY
The Gray Wolf

In spite of guns, dogs, traps, and poison, the Gray or Timber Wolf continues to live and thrive in the western mountains and plains, and destroys annually great quantities of colts, cattle, and

Gray Wolf $\frac{1}{19}$

sheep. The disappearance of game has had the effect of fastening these cunning and deadly marauders upon the best property of the stock-growers. Practically every state of the great plains and westward thereof pays a bounty on wolves, and now the United States Government is taking a hand, through professional hunters of "predatory animals" employed by the Forest Service and the Biological Survey of the Department of Agriculture. Shoulder height, 26 in.

The Coyote

Everything that has been said above may be repeated for the Coyote, but in a minor key, because the Coyote is of smaller size than the gray wolf, less power-ful, less courageous. It is a petty thief rather than a bold and danger-ous marauder, but it ventures much closer to the home ranch than the gray wolf cares to do. In spite of bounties and engines of destruction the Coyote simply will not give up, and so the war upon him must be unceasing. Shoulder height, 20 in.

Coyote $\frac{1}{12}$

The Red Fox

If any man thinks for one mo-ment that wild animals do not think, and cannot "reason" from cause to effect, let him look just once upon the Red Fox, living and thriving in the very lap of civilization and overpopulation, and from the cradle to the grave surrounded by deadly enemies. But, thanks to his keen wits and his perfect woodcraft, the Red Fox not only lives, but thrives, all over the northern United States except in the hog-and-corn area, where his cover has been almost totally destroyed. In 1911 a single firm of fur dealers in London sold 58,900 skins of Red Foxes. The Black Fox is a black color phase of the Red Fox, and the Cross Fox comes between the two.

Red Fox $\frac{1}{13}$

The Gray Fox

This is the Fox of our Southern States. Pepper-and-salt is the color of his coat, his vest is bright brown, and his trousers are black. When hard pressed by dogs, or other un-fair methods of hunting, a Gray Fox

Gray Fox $\frac{1}{13}$

can climb a small tree, straight up to twenty feet or so. This is the only Fox species personally known to me that can climb, and do it well. Shoulder height, 26 in.

THE MARTEN FAMILY OF SMALL FUR BEARERS

Into this Family has been thrown, helter-skelter, a lot of odd animals that failed to get into any other. The collection includes the Otter, Mink, Weasel, Marten, Wolverine, Skunk, and Badger.

The Otter

This animal is, for us, well-nigh an animal of the past, but for all that the Lampsons of London sold 17,399 skins in 1911. All save a very few came from Canada and Alaska. In the United

Otter $\frac{1}{14}$

States a live wild Otter is a great rarity, but a few are taken each year. There are Otters in the South, as well as in the North, but their fur is poor. I know of no other land animal that can swim and dive half as skilfully as the Otter. Unfortunately this animal does not fare well in captivity, on public exhibition, and therefore it is rarely seen. The head and body length is 27 inches and the tail 16 inches.

The Mink

The Mink and the Weasel are the worst wild-animal murderers that we know. Both kill birds for the love of slaughter, long after their appetites have been satisfied. A Mink will gladly kill a whole flock of gulls or ducks in one night. A Weasel once killed 24 ring-necked pheasants in one night, and its own life went into that tale of slaughter. The Mink is not so rare as the

Mink $\frac{1}{13}$

otter, and the way it persists in civilization, and even in the suburbs of cities, is wonderful. In wearing qualities, its fur is about the finest in the world. Color, rich, dark brown. Length of head and body, 19 inches, tail 7 inches. Even yet the supply of Mink fur is important. In temper this little animal is savage and courageous.

The Wolverine

Books might be written about the cunning and the meanness of this animal. Some of the stories of its diabolical cunning

and initiative seem almost incredible. It robs traps, breaks open caches and cabins, steals steel traps, and destroys food that it cannot carry away. In proportion to its size, its molar teeth are enormous, and its appetite matches its teeth. Although once fairly abundant in our western mountains, now it is exceedingly rare in the

Wolverine $\frac{1}{14}$

United States. It is still fairly abundant in Canada, the Northwest, and Alaska. Length 32 + 10 inches.

The Common Skunk

Despite the smelly reputation of this well-known animal, its fur is now dear to the American woman, and is growing dearer every minute. In 1911 the Lampsons sold *1,310,185* skins; and it was not a particularly good year for Skunks,

either! A wonderful thing about this animal is the fact that the furriers can eliminate the odor from its fur, and render it eligible to good society. Skunk farming for fur has been tried, and some success has been achieved, but usually it has been a

Common Skunk $\frac{1}{12}$

losing experiment. The reasons for failure are numerous and excellent; but excuses do not pay dividends. Yes; occasionally Skunks *do* have hydrophobia, and bite people with fatal effect. In the South the little Striped Skunks prevail.

The Badger

Now you may travel the West over without once seeing a Badger; but for all that, a few remain. Why is a Badger? I do not know, unless it is to eat up the devastating prairie-dogs, and contribute modestly to the annual fur supply. Going or coming, a Badger is an uncomfortable animal. Its temper is anarchistic; it is always unhappy and never satisfied. Its home range is our western mountains, from Mexico to Alaska. Once it inhabited also the western edge of the great plains. It is a burrowing animal, and I have seen it living in desert regions where its ability to exist was a mystery.

THE BEAR FAMILY

North America is particularly rich in Bears. There are many well-defined species, and they fall into four very distinct groups. The most that we can offer is a typical species from each group.

The Polar Bear

The Polar Bear is the great, white, seagoing bear of the Arctic regions, inhabiting the ice fields and seashores around

the North Pole, as far down as the center of Hudson's Bay. It lives chiefly upon seals and walruses, which it captures at the edges of the ice-floes. In the early days of Arctic exploration, when rifles were not what they now are, the Polar Bear was a bold and aggressive

Polar Bear $\frac{1}{38}$

animal. Now, the "Tiger of the Ice" has learned to respect modern firearms, and the moment he sees a man, he runs. The pursuit of this species for its skin has greatly diminished the total output of Polar Bear cubs for exhibition purposes.

The Alaskan Brown Bear

The illustration shown herewith correctly represents a typical species and individual of this group. Incredible as it may seem, it is only since 1884 that the great Alaskan Brown Bears, some of them the largest carnivorous animals now living, have been discovered and revealed as a new feature of our big game fauna. There are at least five species, and they inhabit the coast belt of Alaska and its islands from Admiralty Island

Alaskan Brown Bear $\frac{1}{24}$

to Prince William Sound, the Kenai Peninsula, Kadiak Island, the Alaska Peninsula, and the western mainland of Alaska clear up to the Kobuk River, 300 miles northeast of Nome. In summer these enormous bears, some of which weigh nearly or quite 1,200 pounds, feed bountifully on salmon, which they catch in the small streams of their home country with the hooks that Nature gave them. Shoulder height, 54 in.

The Grizzly Bear

I know of only one state in our country in which Grizzly Bears yet remain in sufficient numbers so that it is possible to go out hunting and *find* one. That is in the state of Wyoming. A few Grizzlies exist in a few other states, but they are exceedingly rare, and very hard to find when wanted. Until very recently no one insisted upon the necessity of regulating the killing of bears on a basis of continuing sport. The best Grizzly Bear hunting now to be found is in British Columbia and Alberta. This species now deserves a certain measure of protection from exterminating slaughter. No man should ever be permitted to kill *more than one Grizzly per year;* and *no trapping* of Grizzlies ever should be permitted. As yet British Columbia refuses to put a bag limit on bears, and many a man kills a mother bear and her two cubs without the slightest compunction, to win the plaudits of an unthinking multitude. We are now face to face with this question: Shall we permit the Grizzly Bear to become extinct in the hunting grounds of the United States? My vote on this question is NO!

The Black Bear

The Black Bear group contains four or five black species, all of them so well known that we will describe none of them. The Black Bear species are well-nigh indestructible. The success with which they live and breed in spite of persecution is wonderful. Practically every state which contains large areas of wild forest possesses Black Bears. The various species range from Alaska to the United States of Colombia in South America, and perhaps even farther south. The Cinnamon Bears are "color phases," belonging in the Black Bear group.

The Inland White Bear
(*Ursus kermodei*)

The Inland White Bear of northern British Columbia is a perfectly white bear that structurally belongs in the Black Bear group. It was discovered and described in 1905, and a striking group of five mounted specimens may now be seen in the Provincial Museum at Victoria, B. C. This is a small Bear, and its home is Gribble Island and the Nass and Skeena River regions of northern British Columbia. It is of a clear, creamy-white color, absolutely devoid of brown or black markings. Up to date about twenty-five specimens have been taken, but up to 1916 not one has been taken alive.

Inland White Bear ¹⁄₇

The Common Raccoon

The Common Raccoon of the United States is allotted a place near the bears because it is a plantigrade (flat-footed) animal of carnivorous habits. It is a cheerfully persistent animal, and firmly refuses to be exterminated. Unfortunately, however, the very great new demand for its humble "fur," and its rise in price, marks the beginning of the end of *Procyon lotor*. We will regret its final disappearance, because it is such a cheerful citizen, and takes so

Raccoon $\frac{1}{10}$

kindly to well-regulated captivity. No, there is practically no sale, at present, for live specimens, because the annual catch already is more than the "zoos" and zoölogical parks can assimilate on an exhibition basis.

THE SQUIRRELS, RABBITS, AND PORCUPINES

If there are any animals more than any others that deserve the sympathy and protection of the Boy Scouts of America, it is the Gray Squirrels, Fox Squirrels, and Chipmunks. Of all the companionable and desirable wild animals, they are the ones that hang on whence all but them have fled.

The Gray Squirrel

The Gray Squirrel is a prince of good fellows. Treat him fairly, protect him from gunners and cats, and he will be your fast friend for all his merry life. Feed him when he is hungry,

Gray Squirrel $\frac{1}{6}$

and he will not touch your wild birds nor anything else that you especially value. Yes, when penned up in a small city park and *not adequately fed*, when hunger gnaws at his small vitals, he will rob birds' nests, eat young birds or anything else that he can eat to keep from starving. At such times, *feed him!* Can it be possible that for his few ounces of smelly and bad-tasting flesh a real boy would rather shoot a Gray Squirrel than to have its living companionship? Perish the thought!

Save the squirrels—all except the red squirrel, which is an inveterate destroyer and an intolerable pest. Hunting Gray or Fox Squirrels is not real "sport"—not even for boys ten years old! I found that out when I was ten years old, without being taught the ethics of real sport. I saw that in squirrel "hunting" the poor little fellow in the tree had absolutely *no chance!* It is not a square deal. Ask your state legislatures to pass laws prohibiting the hunting of Gray, Black, and Fox Squirrels *at any and all times* except to catch them alive for restocking woods that contain none. If squirrels have no tree-holes in which to shelter and rear their young, put up suitable boxes, the same as the bird-lovers are doing so well. Shoulder height, 4 in.

The Chipmunks

The Chipmunks are Rock Squirrels, and neither the tree-tops nor the deep earth suit them. If the abominable hunting cats will leave them alone (which they will not until the hunting cats are killed!) they will live with civilized man wherever he makes his home and grows crops. Small as he is, there is inspiration in every Chipmunk. He radiates cheerfulness, contentment, courage, and resourcefulness. He always tries to live up to the scout rule: Be Prepared. Our country is a large place, and there is room for the Chipmunk. There are a great many species of Squirrels, Chipmunks, and Ground Squirrels. It is good sport to chase them through the books and pictures, and have a speaking acquaintance with a lot of them. The Chipmunks are scattered all the way from Maine to California. The eastern Chipmunk is best known, because it was the first one seen; and so far it refuses to be exterminated. I wish that we had 100 for every one that now remains. In winter they hibernate, because they cannot keep office hours in the open when the snow covers the lap of Nature. *Don't* let any one shoot or trap *your* Chipmunks! Save them for companionship and entertainment.

The Spermophiles

The Spermophiles are deep-burrowing Ground Squirrels; and some of the species (in the Northwest, for example) do much harm. The foolish destruction of hawks and owls has permitted the increase of the Franklin and Richardson and other Spermophiles until in some regions they are now very destructive to crops, and are being killed by wholesale

Thirteen-Lined Spermophile ⅓

methods. It is a bad thing to disturb the balance of Nature. The Thirteen-Lined Spermophile is common in the states westward of the Mississippi, and is so gaudily painted, in stripes and rows of dots, that it is readily recognized. So far as I know, it is nowhere so numerous as to be classed as a pest.

The Woodchuck

Temperamentally the Woodchuck is in the same class with the badger and snapping-turtle—unattractive, cross-grained,

Woodchuck $\frac{1}{12}$

and anarchistic. When you see a grizzled dark-brown animal like a huge, fat ground-squirrel run across the road in the early morning, or appear at the mouth of a burrow under a stump in a meadow or wood lot, that will be a Woodchuck, own cousin to the prairie-dog. He is surly and unsocial, and he can destroy a garden more completely than any deer that ever lived, because he has the tools with which to do it. The animal is a pest, with no redeeming qualities—so far as I can discover.

The Canada Porcupine

The Canada Porcupine is one of the largest of the multitude of gnawing animals of North America. In some provinces of Canada it is protected by law, because it is the only animal of the North Woods that a lost man can kill with a club. No, the Porcupine cannot "shoot its quills"; but when it strikes a man or a dog with a very swift sidewise blow of its tail, and leaves a lot of quills in the party of the second part, the victim may easily make the mistake of thinking that the quills have been thrown at him. The Porcupine has no sense of humor and he takes life very seriously. He is slow-moving; his barkless trail widely proclaims his presence, and he is easily found and killed.

Canada Porcupine $\frac{1}{16}$

There are none in the South, but in the North and in Canada we have the species named above; and in the West the Western Yellow Haired Porcupine. Except in a zoölogical park, the room of a Porcupine is always more prized than his company.

The Gray Rabbit

The Gray Rabbit is a wonderfully intelligent animal. When beset by danger his little brain acts like lightning, in sudden and brilliant flashes. Just why the rabbits of civilization have not been exterminated is not easy to explain. Like the gray squirrel, all the rabbits quickly recognize protection and respond to it. I never saw a dog chasing a rabbit without heartily wishing success to the rabbit. To me, rabbit hunting always seemed like mighty poor sport. In winter starving rabbits often eat the bark of young fruit trees; but it is not because the bark tastes good. Now that the fur of the humble Rabbit is masquerading in the fur departments under several different names, the rabbits of the United States are likely to become as rare as the otter or the beaver.

The Jack Rabbits

Jack Rabbit ⅛

The Jack Rabbits of the plains, the West, and the Southwest are still in the class of wild animal pests. Extensive damage is done by them annually in California, Idaho, Oregon, and Washington, but we do not hear so much as formerly from the Southwest. During the year 1914 the poisoning operations conducted by the Government in theNorthwest accounted for over 50,000 Jacks in one locality.

The American Beaver

' The American Beaver is making a gallant struggle to save himself from extermination, and he refuses to give up. Give him three feet of protected water and half a chance for food, and he will do the rest. Ten years ago Harry V. Radford restored the beaver to the Adirondacks; and now Adirondack beavers are becoming a nuisance to the proletariat—in spots, only. In Algonquin Park, Canada, the Canadian Government is taking each year the skins of about 1,000 surplus beaver—a perfectly legitimate industry. Any state that wants one of the wisest, most interesting, and most industrious workers in all the wild-animal world can easily colonize beavers in an extensive forest wherein the worker would not be grudged his food, wood, and sticks for his house and his dams. Books have been written about the Beaver and his wise doings; and the subject was worth them. The Canadian Government, at Algonquin Park, sells live beaver at $25 each.

Beaver ¼

The Muskrat

In its general appearance and habits the Muskrat is a small and humble understudy of the beaver; but we hasten to add that it belongs to the family of mice and rats, it does not have a trowel-flat tail, and it does not build dams. When living in ponds or marshes it builds excellent dome-shaped houses of

Muskrat ⅕

coarse grass or rushes, but in streams it burrows in the banks. It is not a woodcutter and barklover, like the beaver; it feeds on softer food. In parks it is very destructive to earth dams and canal embankments. Its fur is dark brown, and its tail is flattened, hairless, and carried on its edge. The use and value of the fur of this animal has been very great. When its fur is plucked, dyed, and manufactured it is known—according to the whim of the local trade—as "electric seal," "mink," "sable," "Hudson seal," "Red River seal," etc., etc. Even as late as 1912 the Lampsons of London sold 2,937,150 muskrat skins.

THE DEER FAMILY

Americans have good reason to be pleased with their allotment of the Deer of the world, because North America's share of species far surpasses the showing of all other continents, including Asia. We have the Giant Moose (two species), the picturesque Caribou (ten species), the lordly Elk, the strictly American Group of White-tails and Black-tails, and the little-known Brockets of Mexico and Central America. We may notice here only the most important and representative species.

The Alaskan Moose

The famous seven-league boots must have been given permanently to this animal, for verily "he doth bestride the world like a Colossus!" Fancy a huge brown bulk reared aloft on colossal legs to a shoulder height of *seven* feet; a high shoulder hump, hair like coarse thatch, no tail to speak of, an enormous head with a vast overhanging nose. Add to all that a forehead surmounted by 90 pounds of flat antlers of bone from 12 to 22 inches wide, cupped or not cupped, spreading from 60 to 76 inches, and garnished with 30 or 40 points. Such is the Alaskan Moose, the largest member of the Deer Family.

Alaskan Moose $\frac{1}{24}$

The Moose inhabits Maine, Minnesota, the Yellowstone Park, Wyoming, Idaho, Montana, New Brunswick, Quebec, Ontario, Manitoba, Alberta, Yukon, and Alaska. It stops at the Barren Grounds, but it is *the* big game of several portions of Alaska, particularly the Kenai Peninsula. It is quite certain that on account of its great size and the general desire to kill it, this picturesque and remarkable beast will some day become totally extinct everywhere save in the rigidly protected game sanctuaries where no shooting ever is permitted.

The Caribou

The Caribou Group covers in its distribution fully one half the mainland of North America and the great Arctic Islands. It begins with the *Greenland Caribou* of Greenland (small, long thin antlers of few points); then quickly jumps to the *Peary Caribou*, of Ellesmere Land, a very small, almost white species, with a deer-like head and small, thin antlers. Next westward comes the *Barren Ground Caribou*, of the Canadian Barren Grounds, also with long, rather naked antlers, and after that the *Grant Caribou* of the Alaska Peninsula, the largest member of the Barren Ground Group, and the one with the largest and most pointed antlers. The Woodland Caribou Group is headed by the great *Osborn Caribou* of the Cassiar

Mountains, followed by the true *Woodland Caribou* of middle Canada, the *Newfoundland* species, very light in color, and the *Black-Faced Caribou* of British Columbia. The species that enters the United States in Maine and Idaho is the true Woodland.

All the Caribou of America resemble the Reindeer of Europe and Asia. Their broadly spreading feet are like snowshoes specially designed for snowy travel. The hair of the Caribou is probably the warmest hair covering worn by a wild animal. The flesh of the Caribou is excellent food, and the Barren

Black-Faced Caribou $\frac{1}{16}$

Ground species, which still exists literally in millions, is the chief support of the Indians and Eskimos of the Canadian Barren Grounds.

THE ROUND-HORNED DEER GROUP

The American Elk or Wapiti

In every kingdom there are plenty of men larger in height and bulk than their king; and the largest man is not necessarily the one best fitted to wear the crown. The Moose is much larger than the Elk; but for all that the Elk is the king of the Deer of the world. Marvelous to relate, in the Altai Mountains of Central Asia there is an Altai Wapiti that is so much like our American Elk in size, form, and color that it is difficult to describe a real difference between the two! We believe that our Elk have descended from that Asiatic form, by the migration of

Asiatic Elk into North America by a frozen bridge at Bering Strait. Unquestionably a number of species of American animals have been derived from the Old World.

A full-grown male Elk stands 61 inches high at the shoulders and weighs 800 pounds. Its handsome form and magnificent antlers compel admiration, and its great bulk of excellent venison represents a valuable food item. Originally occupying about one third of the continent of North America, the *wild* Elk is now gone from our country save for the 50,000 in the Yellowstone Park herds, the 7,000 Elk of the Olympic Mountains,

Elk or Wapiti $\frac{1}{19}$

Washington; 2,000 on Vancouver Island, and about 3,000 elsewhere, chiefly in Canada. Outside of Wyoming, Elk hunting is almost an extinct sport.

At present great efforts are being made to ship Elk, in crates, from the Yellowstone Park into various states for the purpose of stocking new state game preserves. Elk hunting still goes on in northwestern Wyoming. Elk breed very readily in captivity, and there are a great many small captive herds.

The White-Tailed Deer or Virginia Deer

The people of America never should forget the part played by the White-Tailed Deer in the settlement and pioneer development of our country, in feeding hungry pioneers when no other meat was available. In those days this Deer was more than a game animal. It was an economic factor. Owing to the fact that this Deer is very hardy, prolific, and skilful

White-Tailed Deer $\frac{1}{19}$ in skulking and hiding, it will be the last big game animal that will furnish sport in North America. It will survive long after all other North American Deer have been exterminated.

This Deer is smaller than the Mule Deer, but larger than the Columbian Black-Tail and the Prong-Horned Antelope. Large bucks weigh all the way (according to locality) from 150 to 300 pounds. East of the Mississippi River there is Deer hunting in 20 states. In 1910 about 60,150 were killed in those states. Wherever female Deer are killed according to law, the Deer are being exterminated. No gentleman will kill a female Deer or a fawn, law or no law. Each high-class state has a "buck law," providing that in Deer hunting only bucks may be killed with horns at least three inches high above the hair. This law saves human life.

DEER TAILS
1. White-Tailed Deer
2. Mule Deer
3. Columbian Black-Tailed Deer

The Mule Deer, or "Black-Tail"

The Mule Deer, or "Black-Tail" of the Rocky Mountain States, is a fine, showy animal, proud-spirited, high-headed, and statue-like. It is about one fourth

larger than the White-Tailed Deer, and its home is the whole Rocky Mountain region from British Columbia and Alberta to northern Mexico. Its antlers are much larger, heavier and more erect than those of the White-Tail, and are distinguished by two Y's on each antler. The tail of the Mule Deer is not black. It is *white*, with a black tip.

The Mule Deer has an amount of curiosity that is fatal to it. When disturbed by a hunter it runs a short distance, then stops to look back; whereas the White-Tail runs and dodges with great speed, and pauses not. The Mule Deer is rapidly vanishing, and will soon disappear from all hunting grounds.

Mule Deer $\frac{1}{18}$

The Columbian Black=Tailed Deer

The Columbian Black-Tailed Deer, of the Pacific Coast, is a third type of which every scout should know something, because it is so widely *unknown*. It is decidedly smaller than the white-tailed species, and its short tail is blackish-brown above and white below. When its antlers are perfect each one shows a double Y, the same as those of the Mule Deer. This species is now nowhere abundant, but a few years ago thousands were slaughtered in Washington and Oregon for their poor little skins. Very few sportsmen are acquainted with it.

THE BISON, MUSK-OX, SHEEP, AND GOATS

The American Bison or Buffalo

In recognition of the great value of the Buffalo in the development of the West, and as a small atonement for a great and shameful slaughter, the United States Government has, with the help of the New York Zoölogical and the American Bison societies, established six national herds. They are thus situated: Yellowstone Park; Wichita Bison Range, southwest Oklahoma;

American Bison or Buffalo $\frac{1}{12}$

the Montana National Bison Range, Dixon, Montana; the Wind Cave Bison Range, South Dakota; Niobrara Range, Nebraska; Sully Hills, North Dakota. Canada has a herd of about 1,700 head at Wainwright, Alberta.

There are about 3,200 Bison in captivity, about 75 wild ones in the Yellowstone Park, and about 300 wild Wood Bison southwest of Great Slave Lake. So far as extermination is concerned, the future of the American Bison is secure; but the *wild* animal, subject to hunting, is gone forever. Fortunately this animal really enjoys captivity, and it breeds regularly and persistently.

The Musk=Ox

The Musk-Ox is in every way a remarkable creature. In the first place it is amazing to find that such an animal can survive the polar winter and the polar night, and come out in

Musk-Ox $\frac{1}{22}$

the spring feeling fine and fit. Just how any grazing animal can find its food in winter darkness with the cold at 60 or 70 degrees below zero is an unsolved mystery. The Musk-Ox herds successfully ward off the big arctic wolves by forming a defense circle whenever attacked, the adult bulls and cows standing in a close circle, heads out, and calves within. That serried ring of very sharp, down-curving horns—just right to puncture the vitals of a wolf—is impregnable to all foes save men with guns. The *White-Fronted Musk-Ox* inhabits Greenland and the great Arctic Islands of North America. The *Barren Ground* species is found on the Barren Grounds of northern Canada, northeast of Great Slave Lake. In spite of the violent change of climate, the Musk-Ox herd of the New York Zoölogical Park has lived for several years very comfortably in New York City.

The Mountain Sheep or Big-Horn

The Mountain Sheep or Big-Horn is the finest hoofed game animal of North America. It is bold, hardy, keen-eyed and

Rocky Mountain Sheep: Big-Horn ⅛

wary, difficult to approach, and when found is always surrounded by fine mountain scenery. A large ram stands 42 inches at the shoulders and weighs 350 pounds. The largest horns of this species (*Ovis canadensis*) are $17\frac{3}{4}$ inches in circumference at the base, and came from southwestern Alberta. This fine animal is found from the Pinacate Mountains, Northwest Mexico, to northern British Columbia. It does not thrive in captivity on the Atlantic Coast, and young specimens cannot mature there.

The beautiful *White Mountain Sheep*, smaller than the above, is found in many portions of Alaska and Yukon Territory.

The Rocky Mountain Goat, or White Goat

The Rocky Mountain Goat, or White Goat, is one of the most interesting of all our large animals. It has no near relations in America. In bulk and height it is a little smaller than a big-horn mountain sheep, with a shoulder height of 41 inches, and it weighs about 300 pounds. In form it is stockily built, its horns are short and small, but

Rocky Mountain Goat 1/12

sharp as daggers. Its color is almost snow white, and in winter its hair is long and shaggy. It inhabits the mountain summits above timberline from Montana to Cook Inlet, Alaska, and it is the best rock climber in America. When frightened or driven it will not leap off a precipice to certain death. It stands and fights. In New York it lives well, and breeds in captivity.

The Prong=Horned Antelope

Zoölogically the Prong-Horn is an animal of particular interest. It has no near relatives! It is the only hollow-horned animal which annually—or at any time—actually *sheds* the outer horn, leaving (for a time) only the bony horn-core! The

horn-core stands so high that even after the outer shell of horn has been dropped (in December) the animal still *appears* to have horns. This condition has led to many hot arguments, and even wagers.

The Prong-Horn originally was a plains animal, but with persecution it began to live in rough bad-lands and hills. When the Yellowstone Park was settled, as a park, it was found to contain on the open plains near Gardiner a large band, which has been preserved until now it contains

Prong-Horned Antelope ²⁄₂₅

about 500 head. Many of the states west of the plains have even now a few bands of Antelope, but owing to illegal killing, wolves and other causes, they are nearly everywhere steadily diminishing. Although some efforts are being made to preserve this unique animal in fenced ranges, it is so delicate and so easily upset that it wilts at the sight of adversity, and dies. It is almost impossible to breed it in captivity. Antelope hunting is forbidden in every Antelope state except Nevada. Canada now is making three large prairie preserves, especially for the preservation of this species, and these most praiseworthy efforts certainly deserve success. A recent census of the antelope of New Mexico revealed (1915) 1,740 head in that state.

The Opossum

The Opossum is the only American member of the wonderful Order of Pouched Animals (Marsupials), most of which are found in Australia.   With her lips the mother places the newly born young in her

pouch, when they are of marvelously small size, and there they remain, attached to the nipples of the mother, for weeks. Anatomically, the Opossum is one of

Opossum $\frac{1}{18}$

the most interesting small animals of all North America, but to many persons an Opossum is nothing more than an animal with a skin worth only 50 cents.   A wonderful feature of the Opossum is its prehensile tail, and its most remarkable mental trait is the readiness with which it feigns death in the hope of escaping real death.

CONSERVATION OF WILD LIFE AND FORESTS
By Dr. William T. Hornaday

The natural tendency of civilization is to destroy the products and the choicest handiwork of nature.   Civilized man exterminates whole species of wild birds, beasts, and fishes as no savages have dreamed of doing.   If left alone, the short-sighted, selfish, and cruel members of the American nation would quickly exterminate all our valuable forms of wild life, and our valuable timber and forests.

The ruthless destruction of the past must not be permitted to continue.   It is both wasteful, wicked, and suicidal.   Hereafter, in the United States and its territorial possessions, not one tree should be cut down, not one bird, mammal, or fish should be killed, without a reason so good that it fully justifies the act.

The Army of Destruction

The number of persons who are now determinedly bent on destroying the wild life and forests of North America for their own selfish purposes is enormous.   The number of men and boys who annually go out with deadly fire-arms to hunt the pitiful remnant of "game" in the United States must be between

3,000,000 and 4,000,000! Think of that army! And in that army there are hundreds of thousands of men and boys who will shoot and eat our most valuable song-birds, woodpeckers, grouse, and shore-birds, wherever they can do so without detection. There are also thousands of persons who are so heedless and so wicked that they do not mind setting fire to forests whenever their carelessness escapes detection and there is no fear of punishment.

The Army of Defence

Opposed to the great Army of Destruction is the numerically small Army of Defence, which for fifteen years has been struggling to keep down the records of slaughter, and protect the remnant of our wild life and forests. In this the national government and the state governments are assisting by every means they can command. A great many good men and women are struggling hard and expending money to preserve for the children and young people of the future the remnant of the wild life that once made our country so interesting and so beautiful. To them the protection of wild life and forests is a matter of duty, a "white man's burden" that cannot be ignored by conscientious people. Of course the mean and the sordid care nothing about it.

The Duty of the Boy Scouts

It is now quite time that the Boy Scouts of America should manfully take up and carry their share of this burden. But for the unselfish efforts of the men and women who worked hard in the past to protect your interests, there would to-day be not one wild bird left alive in the United States for any of you to study and enjoy!

The Boy Scouts of To-day have a solemn duty in the protection of the remaining beasts and birds for the Boy Scouts of To-morrow!

Merely to study the birds, and delightfully study their habits, is not enough. The demand of the situation is for hard labor and the sweat of toil in stopping slaughter. Far too long have the people of all North America enjoyed recklessly liberal killing privileges which they never should have had! All over the United States our birds and mammals are being *exterminated according to law*. All our birds, quadrupeds, and game fishes must have better protection; and it is time for the Boy Scouts of America to take up this cause as one demanding constant effort

Bird-Houses Every Scout Can Build

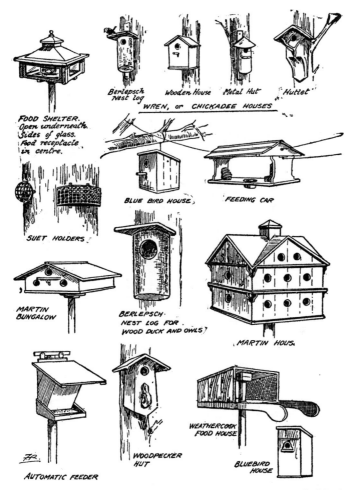

Bird houses.   Drawn from the originals in the New York Zoological Park

and constant sacrifice. It is a cause that now seriously affects the market-basket and the dinner-pail.

Kindness to Domestic Animals

To a body like the Boy Scouts of America it is necessary to mention this subject only by title. Every scout is a boy of honor, and therefore no scout ever would accord to a helpless animal any treatment that would be painful, neglectful, or in any manner unjust. A boy of honor cannot treat even a worm un-

From a picture printed in *The Outlook*
"The first Moro boys ever known to be kind to poor, helpless animals"

justly. He will remember that the cat, the dog, horse, and ox are helpless prisoners in his hands, dependent upon his mercy and thoughtfulness. It is only the meanest of men who treat their prisoners or their faithful servants with cruelty or neglect. "The bravest are the tenderest." The real heroes of life always are those who protect and care for those who cannot protect themselves.

Protection of Forests from Fires

This is another subject that need be mentioned only by title. Every American scout knows either by observation or by hearsay, the meaning of a bad forest fire; the marvelous quickness with which such fires get beyond human control; the danger to human life; the awful slaughter of timber resources; the destruction of wild life; and the long disfigurement of the face of Nature. To start a forest fire wantonly is a crime, severely punishable by law; to permit one to start by slothfulness or lack of care is criminal carelessness, and is enough to strip any scout of all his merit badges at one stroke.

But every scout knows all this, and may at once be ranked as

a defender of the forests. So much has this been recognized that the closest coöperation has come to exist between National and State Conservation Organizations and the Boy Scouts of America.

Medal for Distinguished Services to Wild Life

The Permanent Wild Life Protection Fund through Dr. William T. Hornaday, Trustee, and also Director of the New York  Zoölogical Park, awards a gold medal to any member of the Boy Scout organization who shall during a given year demonstrate to the National Court of Honor that he has rendered distinguished service in the conservation of wild life.

Distinguished services to wild life may be rendered in the following ways:

1. By actively supporting laws and law officers for the protection of birds, quadrupeds, and fishes. Report immediately to game wardens or policemen all violations of wild life protective laws, make formal complaints against violators, and give testimony at the trials.   In this every father or big brother should back up the scouts.

2. By securing the support of members of legislatures and Congress, for bills intended to enact better protective laws. Boy scouts can wield immense influence in this direction if they will! Combined effort is the key to success.

3. By securing the support of schools, or forming clubs, for the protection and increase of wild life.

4. By preventing, or punishing, nest robbing and song-bird killing by boys who have not been taught to protect wild life.

5. By addressing schools in behalf of wild life protection, and writing school essays on the rights of birds, the value of birds to man, the duty of boys to protect them, and the methods to be adopted.

6. By securing five-year close seasons for species of birds or quadrupeds that are locally becoming extinct.

7. By encouraging farmers to "post" their farms against all shooting.

8. By helping post notices of new protective laws.

CHAPTER IV

CAMPCRAFT*

Hiking and Over=night Camp

By H. W. Gibson

Several things should be remembered when going on a hike: First, avoid long distances. A foot-weary, muscle-tired and temper-tried, hungry group of boys is surely not desirable. There are a lot of false notions about courage and bravery and grit that read well in print, but fail miserably in practice, and long hikes for boys is one of the most glaring of these notions. Second, have a leader who will set a good, easy pace, say two or three miles an hour, prevent the boys from excessive water drinking, and assign the duties of pitching camp, etc. Third, observe these two rules given by an old woodsman: (1) Never walk over anything you can walk around; (2) never step on anything that you can step over. Every time you step on anything you lift the weight of your body. Why lift extra weight when tramping? Fourth, carry with you only the things absolutely needed, rolled in blankets, poncho army style.

Before starting on a hike, study carefully the road maps, and take them with you on the walk for frequent reference. The best maps are those of the United States Geological Survey, costing ten cents each. The map is published in atlas sheets, each sheet representing a small, quadrangular district. Send to the superintendent of documents at Washington, D. C., for a list.

For tramping the boy needs the right kind of a shoe, or the trip will be a miserable failure. A light-soled or a light-built shoe is not suited for mountain work or even for an ordinary hike. The feet will blister and become "road-weary." The shoe must be neither too big, too small, nor too heavy, and be amply broad to give the toes plenty of room. The shoe should be water-tight. A medium weight, high-topped lace shoe is about right. Bathing the feet at the springs and streams along the road will be refreshing, if not indulged in too frequently.

---

*In treating of camping there has been an intentional omission of the long-term camp. This is treated extensively in the books of reference given in the bibliography.

See Chapter on "Health and Endurance" for care of the feet and proper way of walking.

It is well to carry a spare shirt hanging down the back with the sleeves tied around the neck.   Change when the shirt you are wearing becomes too wet with perspiration.

The most practical and inexpensive pack is the one made for the Boy Scouts of America.   (Price $1.25.)   It is about 13 x 13 inches square, and 3 inches thick, made of water-proof canvas with shoulder-straps and with double pouches, and will easily hold everything needed for a tramping trip.

A few simple remedies for bruises, cuts, etc., should be taken along by the leader. You may not need them and some may poke fun at them, but, as the old lady said, "You can't always sometimes tell."   The amount and kind of provisions must be determined by the locality and habitation.

Both for camp and general troop use, the Hospital Corps Pouch recommended by the American Red Cross Society has been found to meet the principal needs.   It contains aromatic spirits of ammonia, carbolized vaseline, two one-yard bandages of steri-lized gauze, three one-inch roller bandages, three two and one-half inch, two triangular bandages, one U. S. tourniquet, one individual First Aid Outfit, two wire gauze splints, shears, tweezers, and safety pins.   The price is $3.00, with express charges extra.   This and other First Aid Outfits may be obtained from the National Headquarters of the Boy Scouts of America.

The Lean-to

Reach the place where you are going to spend the night in plenty of time to build your lean-to, and make your bed for

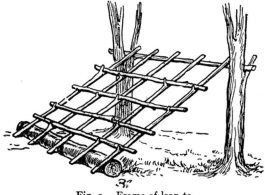

Fig. 1.   Frame of lean-to

the night. Select your camping spot with reference to water, wood, drainage, and material for your lean-to. Choose a dry, level place, the ground just sloping enough to insure the water running away from your lean-to in case of rain. In building your lean-to look for a couple of good trees standing from eight to ten feet apart with branches from six to eight feet above the ground. By studying the illustration (No. 1) you will be able to build a very service-able shack, affording protection from the dews and rain. While two or more boys are building the shack, another should be gathering firewood and preparing the meal, while

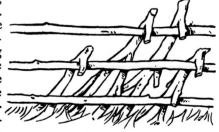

Fig. 2. Method of thatching

another should be cutting and bringing in as many soft, thick tips of trees as possible, for the roof of the shack and the beds.

How to thatch the lean-to is shown in illustration No. 2.

If the camp site is to be used for several days, two lean-tos may be built facing each other, about six feet apart. This will make a very comfortable camp, as a small fire can be built between the two, thus giving warmth and light.

Warning: Scouts never cut or deface live timber without ex-pert advice, and then only with the owner's permission under adult supervision.

The Bed

On the floor of your lean-to lay a thick layer of the fans or branches of a balsam or hemlock, with the convex side up, and the butts of the stems toward the foot of the bed. Now thatch this over with more fans by thrusting the butt ends through the first layer at a slight angle toward the head of the bed, so that the soft tips will curve toward the foot of the bed, and be sure to make the head of your bed away from the opening of the lean-to and the foot toward the opening. Over this bed spread your rubber blankets or ponchos with rubber side down, your sleeping blanket on top, and you will be surprised how soft, springy, and fragrant a bed you have, upon which to rest your " weary frame," and sing with the poet:

"Then the pine boughs croon me a lullaby,   To my face on the balsam where I lie
And trickle the white moonbeams   While the owl hoots at my dreams."
—*J. George Frederick.*

Hot Stone Wrinkle

If the night bids fair to be cold, place a number of stones about six or eight inches in diameter near the fire, so that they will get hot. These can then be placed at the feet, back, etc., as needed, and will be found good "bed warmers." When a stone loses its heat, it is replaced near the fire and a hot one taken. If too hot, wrap the stone in a shirt or sweater or wait for it to cool off.

Boys desire adventure. This desire may be gratified by the establishment of night watchers in relays of two boys each, every two hours. Their imaginations will be stirred by the resistless attraction of the camp-fire and the sound of the creatures that creep at night.

Observation Practice

Many boys have excellent eyes, but see not, and good ears, but hear not, all because they have not been trained to observe or to hear quickly. A good method of teaching observation while on a hike or tramp is to have each boy jot down in a small note-book or diary of the trip, the different kinds of trees, birds, animals, tracks, nature of roads, fences, peculiar rock formation, smells of plants, etc., and thus be able to tell what he saw or heard to the boys upon his return to the permanent camp or to his home.

Camera Snap Shots

One of the party should take a small, folding camera. Photographs of the trip are always of great pleasure and memory-revivers. A practical and convenient method of carrying small folding cameras represents an ordinary belt to which a strap with a buckle has been attached, which is run through the loops at the back of the camera case. The camera may be pushed around the belt to the point where it will be least in the way.

Camp Lamp

A very convenient lamp to use on a hike is the Baldwin Camp Lamp made by John Simmons Co., 13 Franklin Street, New York City. It weighs only five ounces when full; is charged with carbide, and is but $4\frac{3}{4}$ inches high. It projects a strong light 150 feet through the woods. A stiff wind will not blow it out. It can be worn comfortably in your hat or belt. (See the Scout Supply Catalog.)

Handy Articles

A boy of ingenuity can make a number of convenient things. A good drinking cup may be made from a piece of bark cut in parallelogram shape, twisted into pyramid form and fastened with a split stick. A flat piece of bark may serve as a plate. A pot lifter may be made from a green stick about 18 inches long, allowing a few inches of a stout branch to remain. By reversing the same kind of stick, and driving a small nail near the other end, or cutting a notch in it, it may be used to suspend a kettle over a fire. A novel candle-stick is made by opening the blade of a knife and jabbing it into a tree; upon the other upturned blade put a candle. A green stick having a split which will hold a piece of bread or meat makes an excellent broiler. Don't pierce the bread or meat. Driving a good-sized stake into the ground at an angle of 45 degrees and cutting a notch on which may be suspended a kettle over a fire will provide a way of boiling water quickly.

Building the Fireplace

Take two or three stones and build a fireplace, a stick first shaved and then whittled for shavings, a lighted match, a little blaze, some bark and dry twigs added, a few small sticks, place the griddle over the fire, and you are ready to cook the most appetizing griddle-cakes. After the cakes are cooked, fry slices of bacon upon the griddle; in the surplus fat fry slices of bread, then some thinly sliced raw potatoes done to a delicious brown. Here is a breakfast capable of making the mouth of a camper water.

Another way: Place the green logs side by side, closer together at one end than the other. Build the fire between. On the logs over the fire you can rest a frying-pan, kettle, etc. To start the fire have some light, dry wood split up fine. When sticks begin to blaze, add a few more of larger size and continue until you have a good fire. To prevent the re-kindling of the fire after it is apparently out, pour water over it, and soak the earth for the space of two or three feet around it. This is very important, for many forest fires have started through failure to observe this caution.

COOKING RECEIPTS

Cooking for Hikes and Over=Night Camps

The following tested receipts are given for those who go on hikes and over-night camps:

Griddle=Cakes

Beat one egg, tablespoonful of sugar, one cup diluted condensed milk or new milk. Mix enough self-raising flour to make a thick cream batter. Grease the griddle with rind or slices of bacon for each batch of cakes. Be sure to have the griddle hot.

Bacon

Slice bacon quite thin; remove the rind, which makes slices curl up. Fry on griddle or put on a sharp end of a stick and hold over the hot coals, or better yet remove the griddle, and put on a clean, flat rock in its place. When hot lay the slices of bacon on the rock and broil. Keep turning so as to brown on both sides.

Canned Salmon on Toast

Dip slices of stale bread into smoking hot lard. They will brown at once. Drain them. Heat a pint of salmon, picked into flakes, season with salt and pepper and turn in a tablespoonful of melted butter. Heat in a pan. Stir in one egg, beaten light, with three tablespoonfuls evaporated milk not thinned. Pour the mixture on the fried bread.

Roast Potatoes

Wash and dry potatoes thoroughly, bury them deep in a good bed of coals, cover them with hot coals until well done. It will take about forty minutes for them to bake. Then pass a sharpened hard-wood sliver through them from end to end, and let the steam escape and use immediately, as a roast potato soon becomes soggy and bitter.

Baked Fresh Fish

Clean well. Small fish should be fried whole with the back bone severed to prevent curling up; large fish should be cut into pieces, and ribs loosened from back bone so as to lie flat in pan. Rub the pieces in corn meal or powdered crumbs, thinly and evenly (that browns them), fry in plenty of hot fat to a golden brown, sprinkling lightly with salt just as the color turns. If fish has not been wiped dry it will absorb too much grease. If the frying fat is not very hot when fish are put in, they will be soggy with it.

Hunter's Stew

To make a hunter's stew, chop the meat into small chunks about an inch or one and one-half inches square. Then scrape and chop up any vegetables that are easily obtained,— potatoes, turnips, carrots, onions, etc.; and put them into the mess kit, adding clean water, or soup, till the mess kit is half full. Mix some flour, salt, and pepper together and rub the meat well into the mixture, then place this in the mess kit or kettle, seeing that there is just sufficient water to cover the food— and no more. The stew should be ready after simmering for about an hour and a quarter.

Eggs

Boiled: Have water to boiling point. Place eggs in carefully. Boil steadily for three minutes if you wish them soft. If wanted hard boiled, put them in cold water, bring to a boil, and keep it up for twenty minutes. The yolk will then be mealy and wholesome.

Fried: Melt some butter or fat in frying-pan; when it hisses drop in eggs carefully. Fry them three minutes.

Scrambled: First stir the eggs up and after putting some butter in the frying-pan, stir the eggs in it after adding a little condensed milk.

Poached: First put in the frying-pan sufficient diluted condensed milk which has been thinned with enough water to float the eggs in, and let them simmer three or four minutes. Serve the eggs on slices of buttered toast, pouring on enough of the milk to moisten the toast.

Coffee

For every cup of water allow a tablespoonful of ground coffee, then add one extra. Have water come to boiling point first, add coffee, hold it just below boiling point for five minutes, and settle with one fourth of a cup of cold water. Serve. Some prefer to put the coffee in a small muslin bag loosely tied.

Cocoa

Allow a teaspoonful of cocoa for every cup of boiling water. Mix the powdered cocoa with water or boiled milk, with sugar to taste. Boil two or three minutes.

Cocoa, chocolate, and malted milk are recommended in place of coffee in all boy scout camps.

Hoecake

Make a thick batter by mixing warm (not scalding) water or milk with one pint of cornmeal, and mix in with this a small teaspoonful of salt and a tablespoonful of melted lard. To cook hoecake properly, the frying-pan should be perfectly clean and smooth inside. If it is not, too much grease will be required in cooking. Scrape it after each panful is cooked, and then only occasional greasing will be required. Greasing is best done with a clean rag containing butter. Spread a thin batter in the pan with a spoon so that the cake will be very thin; disturb it as little as possible and when the cake is firm on one side turn it and cook on the other.

Biscuit

In general, biscuit or other small cakes should be baked quickly by a rapid or ardent heat; large loaves require a slower, more even heat, so that the outside will not harden until the inside is nearly done. For a dozen biscuits use: —

$1\frac{1}{2}$ pints flour.

$1\frac{1}{2}$ heaping teaspoonfuls baking powder. '

$\frac{1}{2}$ heaping teaspoonful salt.

1 heaping tablespoon cold grease.

$\frac{1}{2}$ pint cold water.

The amount of water varies according to the quality of flour. Too much water makes the dough sticky and prolongs the baking. Baking powders vary in strength; the directions on the can should be followed in each case.

Mix thoroughly with a big spoon or wooden paddle, first the baking powder with the flour and then the salt. Rub into this the cold grease (which may be lard, cold pork fat or drippings) until there are no lumps left and no grease adhering to bottom of the pan. This is a little tedious, but it doesn't pay to shirk it; complete stirring is necessary for success. Then stir in the water and work it with the spoon until the result is rather a stiff dough. Squeeze or mold the dough as little as possible; because the gas that makes the biscuit light is already forming and should not be pressed out. Do not use the fingers in molding; it makes biscuit "sad." Flop the mass of dough to one side of the pan, dust flour on bottom of the pan, flop dough back over it, and dust flour on top of the loaf. Now rub some flour over the bread board, flour the hands, and gently lift the loaf on the board. Flour the bottle or bit of peeled sapling which is to be used as a rolling pin, and also the edges of the can or can cover to be used as biscuit cutter. Gently roll the loaf to three quarters of an inch in thickness. Stamp out the biscuits and lay them in the pan. Roll out the culls or leftover pieces of dough and make biscuits of them, too. Bake until the front row turns brown; reverse the pan and continue until the rear row is similarly done. Ten to fifteen minutes is required in a closed oven, and somewhat longer over the camp-fire or camp earth or stone oven.

"Twist" Baked on a Stick

Work the dough, prepared as for biscuit, into a ribbon two inches wide. Get a club of sweet green wood (birch, sassafras, poplar, or maple) about two feet long and three inches thick, peel the large end, and sharpen the other and stick it into the ground, leaning toward fire. When the sap simmers wind the dough spirally around the peeled end. Turn occasionally while baking. Several sticks can be baking at once. Bread enough for one man's meal can be quickly baked in this way on a peeled stick as thick as a broomstick, holding it over fire and turning it from time to time.

Take bread and crackers with you from camp. Pack butter in small jar; cocoa, sugar, and chocolate in small cans or heavy paper; also salt and pepper. Wrap bread in a moist cloth to prevent drying up; bacon and dried or chipped beef in wax paper. Pickles can be purchased put up in small bottles. Use the empty bottle as candle-stick.

Sample Menu for an Over-night Camp and a Day Hike or Tramp

Breakfast

	Griddle-Cakes	
	Fried Bacon and Potatoes	
Bread	Cocoa, Chocolate, Milk or Coffee	Preserves

Dinner

	Creamed Salmon on Toast	
Baked Potatoes	Bread	Pickles
	Fruit	

Supper

	Fried Eggs	
Creamed or Chipped Beef		Cheese
	Bread Cocoa, Coffee	

Ration List for Six Boys, Three Meals

2 pounds bacon (sliced thin)
1 pound butter
1 dozen eggs
½ pound cocoa
½ pound coffee
½ pound chocolate
1 pound sugar
3 cans salmon
24 potatoes
2 cans condensed milk
1 small package of self-raising flour
Salt and pepper

Utensils

Small griddle
Small stew pan
Large spoon
Plate and cup
Matches and candle

Dish Washing

First fill the frying-pan with water, place over the fire, and let it boil. Pour out water and you will find the pan has practically cleaned itself. Clean the griddle with sand and water. Greasy knives and forks may be cleaned by jabbing them into the ground. After all grease is gotten rid of, wash in hot water and dry with cloth. Don't use the cloth first and get it greasy.

Leadership

The most important thing about a camping party is that it should always have the best of leadership. No group of boys should go camping by themselves. The first thing a patrol of scouts should do when it has determined to camp is to insist upon the scout master accompanying the members of the patrol. The reason for this is that there is less likely to be accidents of the kind that will break up your camp and drive you home to the town or city. When the scout master is one of the party, all the boys can go in swimming when the proper time comes for such exercise, and the scout master can stay upon the bank, or sit in the boat for the purpose of preventing accidents by drowning. There are also a hundred and one things which will occur in camp when the need of a man's help will show itself. A scout ought to insist on his scout master going to camp. The scout master and patrol leader should be present, in order to settle the many questions which must of necessity arise, so that there may be no need of differences or quarrels over disputed points, which would be sure to spoil the outing.

Scout Camp Program

In a scout camp there will be a regular daily program, something similar to the following:

6:30 A.M.	Turn out, bathe, etc.
7:00 A.M.	Breakfast
8:00 A.M.	Air bedding in sun, if possible, and clean camp ground
9.00 A.M.	Scouting games and practice
12.00 M.	Dinner
1:00 P.M.	Talk by leader
2:00 P.M.	Water games, swimming, etc.
6:00 P.M.	Supper
7:30 P.M.	Evening council around camp-fire
8:45 P.M.	Lights out.

Order of Business

1. Opening council
2. Roll-call
3. Record of last council
4. Reports of scouts
5. Left-over business
6. Complaints
7. Honors
8. New scouts
9. New business
10. Challenges
11. Social doings, songs, dances, stories
12. Closing council (devotional services when desired).

Water Supply

Dr. Charles E. A. Winslow, the noted biologist, is authority for the following statement: "The source of danger in water is always human or animal pollution. Occasionally we find water which is bad to drink on account of passage through the ground or on account of passage through lead pipes, but the danger is never from ordinary decomposing vegetable matter. If you have to choose between a bright clear stream which may be polluted at some point above, and a pond full of dead leaves and peaty matter, but which you can inspect all around and find free from contamination, choose the pond. Even in the woods it is not easy to find surface waters that are surely protected, and streams particularly are dangerous sources of water supply. We have not got rid of the idea that running water purifies itself. It is standing water which purifies itself, if anything does, for in stagnation there is much more chance for the disease germs to die out. Better than either a pond or stream, unless you can carry out a rather careful exploration of their surroundings, is ground water from a well or spring;

though that again is not necessarily safe. If the well is in good, sandy soil, with no cracks or fissures, even water that has been polluted may be well purified and safe to drink. In a clayey or rocky region, on the other hand, contaminating material may travel for a considerable distance under the ground. Even if the well is protected below, a very important point to look after is the pollution from the surface. I believe more cases of typhoid fever from wells are due to surface pollution than to the character of the water itself. There is danger which can, of course, be done away with by protection of the well from surface drainage, by seeing that the surface wash is not allowed to drain toward it, and that it is protected by a tight covering from the entrance of its own waste water. If good water cannot be secured in any of these ways, it must in some way be purified. . . . Boiling will surely destroy all disease germs."

The Indians had a way of purifying water from a pond or swamp by digging a hole about one foot across and down about six inches below the water level, a few feet from the pond. After it was filled with water, they bailed it out quickly, repeating the bailing process about three times. After the third bailing the hole would fill with filtered water. Try it.

Sanitation

A most important matter when in camp and away from modern conveniences is that of sanitation. This includes not only care as to personal cleanliness, but also as to the water supply and the proper disposal of all refuse through burial or burning. Carelessness in these matters has been the cause of serious illness to entire camps and brought about many deaths. In many instances the loss of life in the armies has been greater through disease in the camp than on the battlefields. To " Be Prepared " we must give attention to preventative measures.

Typhoid fever is one of the greatest dangers in camping and is caused by unclean habits, polluted water, and contaminated milk and food. The armies of the world have given this disease the most careful study with the result that flies have been found to be its greatest spreaders. Not only should all sources of water supply be carefully examined, an analysis obtained if possible before use, but great care should also be taken when in the vicinity of such a supply not to pollute it in any way. In districts where typhoid is at all prevalent it is advisable for each scout to be immunized before going to camp.

A scout's honor will not permit him to disobey in the slightest particular the sanitary rules of his camp. He will do his part well. He will do everything in his power to make his camp clean, sanitary, and healthful from every standpoint.

Safe Use of Knife and Axe

The knife and the axe are about the most useful implements of a backwoodsman. In fact a good camper, hunter, or mountaineer would be lost without them. The manner in which a camper handles his knife or axe is a sure sign whether he knows anything about woodcraft or not. It is only the unskilled and untrained who brandish an open knife or carelessly handle unsheathed axes; experienced men are always extremely careful in their use. These two tools should be carried not as playthings but for serious work whenever they are required. It is important that the following advice about the proper use of the knife and axe be noted, if a scout is to be prepared to prevent serious injury.

Scouts pride themselves because of their knowledge of handling an axe and a knife so as to prevent accidents, and such knowledge will commend them at once to woodsmen and campers.

1. They should be properly taken care of and never used upon objects or for purposes that will dull or break them.

2. They should be handled in such a way as not to injure the user or any person nearby.

3. They should never be used to strip the bark off birch, beech, or madrone tree or to disfigure other people's property by cutting initials thereon.

When Using the Knife

1. Whittle away from you, *not* toward you, to prevent injury.

2. Don't drive a knife into a stick by hammering on the back of it, and don't use the handle as a hammer.

3. Beware of wood with nails in it.

4. Keep the knife blade out of the fire.

5. Keep the blades clean; boil or scald the blades before cutting food.

6. Don't use the blade as a screw-driver, or to pry things open with.

7. Don't carry an open knife in your hand.

8. Don't lay it on the ground when not using it, or keep it in a wet place.

9. Know how to sharpen the blades properly.

A knife, if kept in good condition, is the most valuable and important personal tool.

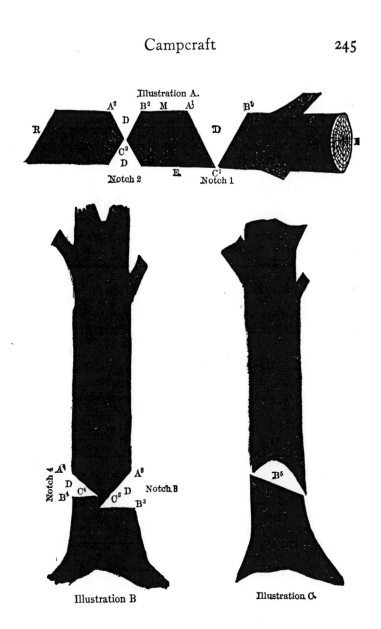

Illustration A.

Illustration B

Illustration C.

When Using the Axe

1. Never chop in such a position that the axe will cut you if it slips.
2. Never chop through wood on a hard surface.
3. Never chop pine or hemlock knots with a sharp axe.
4. If you carry an axe on your shoulder, always have the edge outward from your neck. Otherwise you might stumble and be killed.
5. Always muzzle the axe in traveling.

How to Cut a Log and Fell a Tree

The wood fibres running lengthwise form what is known as the grain of the wood, and this must be taken into consideration in splitting or cutting. Thus the line from R to K in illustration A is the grain and the direction of least resistance, while from M to E is across the grain and the direction of the greatest resistance. This being the case, the angle $A_1 - C_1$, which is a little less than 45 degrees, is the direction of least possible resistance when cutting across the grain of the log, and should be applied in all cross cuts, from the smallest branch to the largest log.

Notch No. 1 in the figure shows how to chop through a log that cannot be moved. It is made by alternating cuts from A_1 to C_1 and B_1 to C_1 until the notch is cut through, unless the latter is so wide that the chips at D do not fly out of their own accord, when an extra cut must be made parallel to $B_1 - C_1$ or to $A_1 - C_1$, midway between A_1 and B_1, as the notch deepens. This extra cut should not go deeper than the point where the chips release themselves from A_1 to B_1.

Notch No. 2 is used when the log can be rolled over, by cutting to the center of the log in the same manner as in the first case, then turning the log and chopping from the other side, keeping in mind the one great principle in wood chopping, that a true woodsman never cuts from more than two sides.

Notches No. 3 and 4 illustrate the proper method of felling trees. To cause a tree to fall in a desired direction, cut a notch $A_3 - C_3 - B_3$ low down on the side on which it is to fall, by repeated cuts, first from A_3 to C_3, and then from B_3 to C_3, with your cut $B_3 - C_3$ on a downward angle (as in B_5 in figure C, which shows the notch as the axe enters) until well past the heart-wood of the tree, when notch No. 4 is cut in like manner on the opposite side, and well above notch No. 3, until the tree falls.

Never chop from more than two sides, no matter how tempting it may be to give the standing part a few cuts between the notches. It would be far from good woodcraft, and might affect dangerously the fall of the tree. When the latter is down, trim the branches from the top, and the limbs will not interfere with your work.

An expert axman can chop with either the right hand or the left hand. When he is chopping left handed, the right hand is at the haft and the left hand slides and *vice versa*.

General Hints

Two flannel shirts are better than two overcoats.

Don't wring out flannels or woolens. Wash in cold water, very soapy, hang them up dripping wet, and they will not shrink.

If you keep your head from getting hot and your feet dry there will be little danger of sickness.

If your head gets too hot put green leaves inside of your hat.

If your throat is parched, and you cannot get water, put a pebble in your mouth. This will start the saliva and quench the thirst.

Water Hints

If you work your hands like paddles and kick your feet, you can stay above water for some time even with your clothes on. It requires a little courage

Ready for the hike

and enough strength not to lose your head.

Many boy swimmers make the mistake of going into the water too soon after eating. The stomach and digestive organs are busy preparing the food for the blood and body. Suddenly they are called upon to care for the work of the swimmer. The change is too quick for the organs, the process of digestion stops, congestion is apt to follow, and then paralyzing cramps.

Indian Bathing Precaution

The Indians have a method of protecting themselves from cramps. Coming to a bathing pool, an Indian swimmer, after stripping off, and before entering the water, vigorously rubs the pit of the stomach with the dry palm of his hands. This rubbing probably takes a minute, then he dashes cold water all over his stomach and continues the rubbing for another minute, and after that he is ready for his plunge. If the water in which you are going to swim is cold, try this method before plunging into the water.

Good Bathing Rule

The rule in most camps regarding entering the water is as follows: "No one of the party shall enter the water for swimming or bathing except at the time and place designated, and in the presence of a leader." Laxity in the observance of this rule will result disastrously.

Clouds

Every cloud is a weather sign. Low clouds, swiftly moving, indicate coolness and rain; hard-edged clouds, wind; rolled or jagged clouds, strong wind; "mackerel" sky, twelve hours dry.
Look out for rain when

A slack rope tightens.
Smoke beats downward.
Sun is red in the morning
There is a pale yellow or greenish sunset.

Rains

Rain with east wind is lengthy.
A sudden shower is soon over.
A slow rain lasts long.
Rain before seven, clear before eleven.
A circle round the moon means "storm."

"The evening red, the morning gray
Sets the traveler on his way;
The evening gray, the morning red
Brings down showers upon his head."

"When the grass is dry at night
Look for rain before the light."

"When the grass is dry at morning light
Look for rain before the night."

Clear

"When the dew is on the grass
Rain will never come to pass."

A heavy morning fog generally indicates a clear day.

East wind brings rain.
West wind brings clear, bright, and cool weather.
North wind brings cold.
South wind brings heat.

Direction of the Wind

The way to find which way the wind is blowing is to throw up little bits of dry grass, or to hold up a handful of light dust and let it fall, or to suck your thumb, wet it all around and let the wind blow over it, and the cold side of it will then tell you which way the wind is blowing.

Weather Flags

The United States Weather Bureau publishes a "Classification of Clouds" ir colors, which may be had for the asking. If you are near one of the weather signal stations, daily bulletins will be sent to camp upon request; also the weather map.

A set of flag signals run up each day will create interest. The flags are easily made or may be purchased.

Keep a daily record of temperature. A boy in charge of the "weather bureau" will find it to be full of interest as well as offering an opportunity to render the camp a real service. He will make a weather vane, post a daily bulletin, keep a record of temperature, measure velocity of wind, and rainfall.

How to Get Your Bearings

If you have lost your bearings, and it is a cloudy day, put the point of your knife blade on your thumb nail, and turn the blade around until the full shadow of the blade is on the nail. This will tell you where the sun is, and decide in which direction the camp is.

Face the sun in the morning, spread out your arms straight from body. Before you is the east; behind you is the west; to your right is the south; the left hand is the north.

Grass turns with the sun. Remember this when finding your way at night.

Building a Camp=fire

There are ways and ways of building a camp-fire. An old Indian saying runs, "White man heap fool, make um big fire — can't git near! Injun make um little fire — git close! Ugh! good!"

Make it a service privilege for a tent of boys to gather wood and build the fire. This should be done during the afternoon.

FOREST FIRES!

The great annual destruction of forests by fire is an injury to all persons and industries. The welfare of every community is dependent upon a cheap and plentiful supply of timber, and a forest cover is the most effective means of preventing floods and maintaining a regular flow of streams used for irrigation and other useful purposes.

To prevent forest fires Congress passed the law approved May 5, 1900, which—

Forbids setting fire to the woods, and

Forbids leaving any fires unextinguished

This law, for offences against which officers of the FOREST SERVICE can arrest without warrant, provides as maximum punishment—

A fine of $5,000, or imprisonment for two years, or both, if a fire is set maliciously, and

A fine of $1,000, or imprisonment for one year, or both, if fire results from carelessness

It also provides that the money from such fines shall be paid to the school fund of the county in which the offence is committed.

THE EXERCISE OF CARE WITH SMALL FIRES IS THE BEST PREVENTIVE OF LARGE ONES. Therefore all persons are requested —

1. Not to drop matches or burning tobacco where there is inflammable material.

2. Not to build larger camp=fires than are necessary.

3. Not to build fires in leaves, rotten wood, or other places where they are likely to spread.

4. In windy weather and in dangerous places, to dig holes or clear the ground to confine camp=fires.

5. To extinguish all fires completely before leaving them, even for a short absence.

6. Not to build fires against large or hollow logs, where it is difficult to extinguish them.

7. Not to build fires to clear land without informing the nearest officer of the FOREST SERVICE, so that he may assist in controlling them.

This notice is posted for your benefit and the good of every resident of the region. You are requested to co=operate in preventing its removal or defacement, which acts are punishable by law.

Secretary of Agriculture.

The above is a copy of one of a series of notices posted in forests by the U. S. Department of Agriculture directing attention to U. S. Laws on this important subject.

Two things are essential in the building of a fire — kindling and air. A fire must be built systematically. First, get dry, small, dead branches, twigs, fir branches, and other inflammable material. Place these on the ground. Be sure that air can draw under it and upward through it. Next place some heavier sticks and so on until you have built the camp-fire the required size. An interesting account of "How to Build a Fire by Rubbing Sticks," by Dr. Walter Hough, will be found in Chapter II. In many camps it is considered an honor to light the fire.

Never build a large camp-fire too near the tent or inflammable pine trees. Better build it in the open.

Be sure and use every precaution to prevent the spreading of fire. This may be done by building a circle of stones around the fire, or by digging up the earth, or by wetting a space around the fire. Always have the buckets of water near at hand. To prevent the re-kindling of the fire after it is apparently out, pour water over it and soak the earth for a space of two or three feet around it. This is very important, for many forest fires have started through failure to observe this caution.

Things to remember: First, *it is criminal to leave a burning fire;* second, *always put out the fire with water or earth.*

"A fire is never out," says Chief Forester H. S. Graves, "until the last spark is extinguished. Often a log or snag will smolder unnoticed after the flames have apparently been conquered only to break out afresh with a rising wind."

Be sure to get a copy of the laws of your state regarding forest fires, and if a permit is necessary to build a fire, secure it before building the fire.

Kephart, in his book on "Camping and Woodcraft" (p. 28), says: "When there is nothing dry to strike it on, jerk the head of the match forward through the teeth. Or, face the wind. Cup your hands back toward the wind, remove the right hand just long enough to strike the match on something very close by, then instantly resume former position. Flame of match will run up stick instead of blowing away from it.

The Camp-fire

"I cannot conceive of a camp that does not have a big fire. Our city houses do not have it, not even a fireplace. The fireplace is one of the greatest schools the imagination has ever had or can ever have. It is moral, and it always has a tremendous stimulus to the imagination, and that is why stories and fire go together. You cannot tell a good story unless you

tell it before a fire. You cannot have a complete fire unless you
have a good story-teller along!

"There is an impalpable, invisible, softly stepping delight
in the camp-fire which escapes analysis. Enumerate all its
charms and still there is something missing in your catalogue.

Around the camp-fire

"Any one who has witnessed a real camp-fire and participated
in its fun as well as seriousness will never forget it. The huge
fire shooting up its tongue of flame into the darkness of the
night, the perfect shower of golden rain, the company of happy
boys, and the great, dark background of piny woods, the weird
light over all, the singing, the yells, the stories, the fun, and
the serious word at the close, is a happy experience long to be
remembered."

Camp-fire Stunts

The camp-fire is a golden opportunity for the telling of
stories — good stories told well. Indian legends, war stories,
ghost stories, detective stories, stories of heroism, the history
of life, a talk about the stars. Don't draw out the telling of
a story. Make the story life-like.

College songs always appeal to boys. Let some leader start

up a song in a natural way, and soon you will have a chorus of unexpected melody and harmony. As the fire dies down, let the songs be of a more quiet type, like "My Old Kentucky Home," and ballads of similar nature. (See *Boy Scout Song Book*.)

When the embers are glowing is the time for toasting marshmallows. Get a long stick sharpened to a point, fasten a marshmallow on the end, hold it over the embers, not in the blaze, until the marsh-mallow expands. Oh, the deliciousness of it! Ever tasted one? Before roasting corn on the cob, tie the end of the husk firmly with string or cord; soak in water for about an hour; then put into the hot embers. The water prevents the corn from burning and the firmly tied husks enable the corn to be steamed and the real corn flavor is thus retained. In about twenty minutes the corn may be taken from the fire and eaten. Have a bowl of melted butter and salt at hand. Also a pastry brush to spread the melted butter upon the corn. Try it.

Story Telling

For an example of a good story to be told around the campfire this excellent tale by Prof. F. M. Burr is printed by permission:

How Men Found the Great Spirit

In the olden time, when the woods covered all the earth except the deserts and the river bottoms, and men lived on the fruits and berries they found and the wild animals which they could shoot or snare, when they dressed in skins and lived in caves, there was little time for thought. But as men grew stronger and more cunning and learned how to live together, they had more time to think and more mind to think with.

Men had learned many things. They had learned that cold weather followed hot; and spring, winter; and that the sun got up in the morning and went to bed at night. They said that the great water was kindly when the sun shone, but when the sun hid its face and the wind blew upon it, it grew black and angry and upset their canoes. They found that knocking flints together or rubbing dry sticks would light the dry moss and that the flames which would bring back summer in the midst of winter and day in the midst of night were hungry and must be fed, and when they escaped devoured the woods and only the water could stop them.

These and many other things men learned, but no one knew why it all was or how it came to be. Man began to wonder, and that was the beginning of the path which led to the Great Spirit.

In the ages when men began to wonder there was born a boy whose name was Wo, which meant in the language of his time, "Whence." As he lay in his mother's arms she loved him and wondered: "His body is of my body, but from whence comes the life — the spirit which is like mine and yet not like it?" And his father seeing the wonder in the mother's eyes, said, "Whence came he from?" And there was no one to answer.

and so they called him Wo to remind them that they knew not from whence he came.

As Wo grew up, he was stronger and swifter of foot than any of his tribe. He became a mighty hunter. He knew the ways of all the wild things and could read the signs of the seasons. As he grew older they made him a chief and listened while he spoke at the council board, but Wo was not satisfied. His name was a question and questioning filled his mind.

"Whence did he come? Whither was he going? Why did the sun rise and set? Why did life burst into leaf and flower with the coming of spring? Why did the child become a man and the man grow old and die?"

The mystery grew upon him as he pondered. In the morning he stood on a mountain top, and stretching out his hands cried, " Whence?" At night he cried to the moon, " Whither? " He listened to the soughing of the trees and the song of the brook and tried to learn their language. He peered eagerly into the eyes of little children and tried to read the mystery of life. He listened at the still lips of the dead, waiting for them to tell him whither they had gone.

He went out among his fellows silent and absorbed, always looking for the unseen and listening for the unspoken. He sat so long silent at the council board that the elders questioned him. To their questioning he replied like one awakening from a dream:

"Our fathers since the beginning have trailed the beasts of the woods. There is none so cunning as the fox, but we can trail him to his lair. Though we are weaker than the great bear and buffalo, yet by our wisdom we overcome them. The deer is more swift of foot, but by craft we overtake him. We cannot fly like a bird, but we snare the winged one with a hair. We have made ourselves many cunning inventions by which the beasts, the trees, the wind, the water, and the fire become our servants.

"Then we speak great swelling words: 'How great and wise we are! There is none like us in the air, in the wood, or in the water!'

"But the words are false. Our pride is like that of a partridge drumming on his log in the wood before the fox leaps upon him. Our sight is like that of the mole burrowing under the ground. Our wisdom is like a drop of dew upon the grass. Our ignorance is like the great water which no eye can measure.

"Our life is like a bird coming out of the dark, fluttering for a heart-beat in the teepee and then going forth into the dark again. No one can tell whence it comes or whither it goes. I have asked the wise men and they cannot answer. I have listened to the voice of the trees and wind and water, but I do not know their tongue; I have questioned the sun and the moon and the stars, but they are silent.

"But to-day in the silence before the darkness gives place to light, I seemed to hear a still small voice within my breast, saying to me, 'Wo, the questioner, rise up like the stag from his lair; away, alone to the mountain of the sun. There thou shalt find that which thou seekest.' I go, but if I fall by the trail another will take it up. If I find the answer I will return."

Waiting for none, Wo left the council of his tribe and went his way toward the mountain of the sun. For six days he made his way through the trackless woods, guided by the sun by day and the stars by night. On the seventh day he came to the great mountain — the mountain of the sun, on whose top, according to the tradition of his tribe, the sun rested each night. All day long he climbed, saying to himself, "I will sleep to-night in the teepee of the sun, and he will tell me whence I come and whither I go."

But as he climbed the sun seemed to climb higher and higher; and, as he neared the top, a cold cloud settled like a night bird on the mountain.

Chilled and faint with hunger and fatigue, Wo struggled on. Just at sunset he reached the top of the mountain, but it was not the mountain of the sun, for many days' journey to the west the sun was sinking in the Great Water. A bitter cry broke from Wo's parched lips. His long trail was useless. There was no answer to his questions. The sun journeyed farther and faster than men dreamed, and of wood and waste and water there was no end. Overcome with misery and weakness he fell upon a bed of moss with his back toward the sunset and the unknown.

And Wo slept, although it was unlike any sleep he had ever known before, and as he slept he dreamed. He was alone upon the mountain waiting for the answer. A cloud covered the mountain, but all was silent. A mighty wind rent the cloud and rushed roaring through the crags, but there was no voice in the wind. Thunder pealed, lightning flashed, but he whom Wo sought was not there.

In the hush that followed up the storm Wo heard a voice, low and quiet, but in it all the sounds of earth and sky seemed to mingle — the song of the bird, the whispering of the trees, and the murmuring of the brook.

"Wo, I am he whom thou seekest; I am the Great Spirit. I am the All Father. Ever since I made man of the dust of the earth, and so child of the earth and brother to all living, and breathed into his nostrils the breath of life, thus making him my son, I have waited for a seeker who should find me. In the fulness of time thou hast come, Wo the questioner, to the answerer.

"Thy body is of the earth and to earth returns; thy spirit is mine; it is given thee for a space to make according to thy will; then it returns to me better or worse for thy making.

"Thou hast found me because thy heart was pure, and thy search for me tireless. Go back to thy tribe and be to them the voice of the Great Spirit. From henceforth I will speak to thee, and the seekers that come after thee in a thousand voices and appear in a thousand shapes. I will speak in the voices of the woods and streams and of those you love. I will appear to you in the sun by day and the stars by night. When thy people and mine are in need and wish for the will of the Great Spirit, then shall my spirit brood over thine and the words that thou shalt speak shall be my words."

And Wo awoke, facing the east and the rising sun. His body was warmed by its rays. A great gladness filled his soul. He had sought and found and prayer came to him like the song to the bird.

"O Great Spirit, father of my spirit, the sun is thy messenger, but thou art brighter than the sun. Drive thou the darkness before me. Be thou the light of my spirit." As Wo went down the mountain and took the journey back to the home of his people, his face shone, and the light never seemed to leave it, so that men called him "He of the shining face."

When Wo came back to his tribe all who saw his face knew that he had found the answer, and they gathered again about the council fire to hear. As Wo stood up and looked into the eager faces in the circle of the fire, he remembered that the Great Spirit had given him no message and for a moment he was dumb. Then the words of the Great Spirit came to him again. "When thy people and mine shall need to know my will, my spirit shall brood over thine and the words that thou shalt speak shall be my words." Looking into the eager faces of longing and questioning, his spirit moved within him and he spoke:

"I went, I sought, I found the Great Spirit who dwells in the earth as your spirits dwell in your bodies. It is from Him the spirit comes. We are His children. He cares for us more than a mother for the child on her breast, or the father for the son that is his pride. His love is like the air we breathe: it is about us: it is within us.

"The sun is the sign of His brightness, the sky of His greatness and mother-love and father-love, and the love of man and woman are the signs of His love. We are but His children; we cannot enter into the council of the Great Chief until we have been proved, but this is His will, that we love one another as He loves us; that we bury forever the hatchet of hate, that no man shall take what is not his own and the strong shall help the weak."

The chiefs did not wholly understand the words of Wo, but they took a hatchet and buried it by the fire saying, "Thus bury we hate between man and his brother," and they took an acorn and put it in the earth saying, "Thus plant we the love of the strong and the weak." And it became the custom of the tribe that the great council in the spring should bury the hatchet and plant the acorn. Every morning the tribe gathered to greet the rising sun, and with right hand raised and left upon their hearts prayed: "Great Spirit, hear us; guide us to-day; make our wills Thy will, our ways Thy way."

And the tribe grew stronger and greater and wiser than all the other tribes — but that is another story.

TENT MAKING MADE EASY*

By H. J. Holden

The accompanying sketches show a few of the many different tents which may be made from any available piece of cloth or canvas. The material need not be cut, nor its usefulness for other purposes impaired, except that rings or tapes are attached at various points as indicated. For each tent the sketches show a front elevation, with a ground plan, or a side view; also a view of the material laid flat, with dotted lines to indicate where creases or folds will occur. Models may be made from stiff paper and will prove as interesting to the kindergartener in geometry as to the old campaigner in camping. In most of the tents a ring for suspension is fastened at the centre of one side. This may be supported by a pole or hung by means of a rope from any convenient fastening; both methods are shown in the sketches. Guy ropes are required for a few of the different models, but most of them are pegged down to the ground.

After making paper models, find a stack cover, a tarpaulin, a tent fly, an awning, or buy some wide cotton cloth, say 90-inch. All the shapes may be repeatedly made from the same piece of material, if the rings for changes are left attached. In Nos. 3, 4, 6, 7, 8, 9, 11, a portion of the canvas is not used and may be turned under to serve as sod-cloth, or rolled up out of the way.

*Reprinted from *Recreation*, April, 1911, by permission of the Editor.

If your material is a large piece, more pegs and guy lines will be required than is indicated in the sketches. The suspension ring, 1½ inches or 2 inches in diameter, should be well fastened, with sufficient reinforcement to prevent tearing out; 1-inch rings fastened with liberal lengths of tape are large enough for the pegs and guy lines. Also reinforce along the lines of the strain from peg to pole.

Fig. 1.—A square of material hung by one corner, from any convenient support, in a manner to make a comfortable shelter; it will shed rain and reflect heat. This square makes a good fly or a good ground cloth for any of the tents.

Fig. 2.— A rectangle equal to two squares. A shelter roomy and warm, with part of one side open toward the fire.

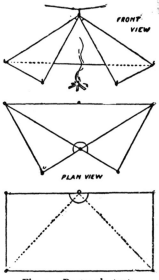

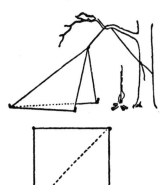

Fig. 1. Tent from a square of canvas. A 7 x 7 sheet is ample for a one-man shelter; 9 x 9 will house two

Fig. 2. Rectangle tent

Fig. 3.— Here the rectangle is folded to make a "lean-to" shelter, with the roof front suspended from a rope or from a horizontal pole by means of cords. The two corners not in use are folded under, making a partial ground cloth. A square, open front is presented toward the camp-fire.

Fig. 4.— Same in plan as No. 3, but has a triangular front and only one point of suspension.

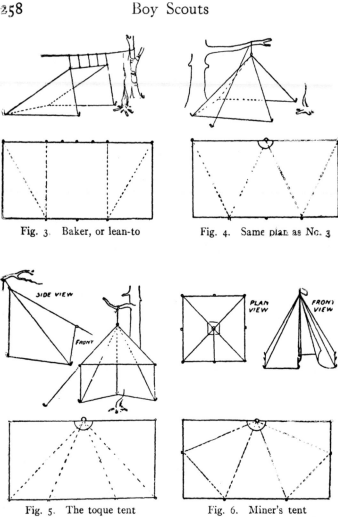

Fig. 3. Baker, or lean-to

Fig. 4. Same plan as No. 3

Fig. 5. The toque tent

Fig. 6. Miner's tent

Fig. 5.— Uses all the cloth, has a triangular ground plan, a square front opening, plenty of head room at the back and requires two or more guy lines. This shelter resembles a "toque."

Fig. 6.— Square or "miner's" tent. Two corners are turned under. This tent is enclosed on all sides, with a door in front.

Fig. 7.— Conical tent or "wigwam," entirely enclosed, with door in front. Two corners of the canvas are turned under.

Fig. 8.— Has a wall on one side and is called a "canoe tent" in some catalogues. It requires two or more guy lines and is shown with a pole support. The front has a triangular opening.

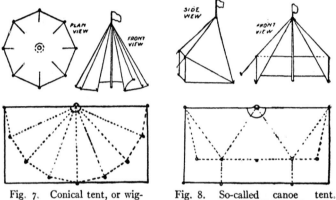

Fig. 7. Conical tent, or wig-wam

Fig. 8.   So-called canoe tent. Requires three guy lines, and can be supported by a rope instead of a pole

Fig. 9.— A combination of No. 8, with No. 1 in use as an awning or fly. This sketch shows both tent and fly suspended by means of a rope. The "awning" may be swung around to any angle.

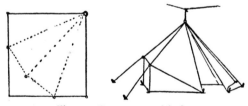

Fig. 9.   Canoe tent with fly

Fig. 10.— Combination of Nos. 1 and 2; they may be fastened together by a coarse seam or tied with tapes. The ground plan is an equal-sided triangle, with a door opening on one side, as shown. There is no waste cloth.

Fig. 11.— No. 10 changed to a conical shape and suspended as a canopy. The circular shape is secured by the use of small-size gas pipe or limber poles bent into a large hoop. Of course guy lines may be used, but would probably be in the way. Notice that a little more material for making a wall would transform the canopy into a "Sibley" tent.

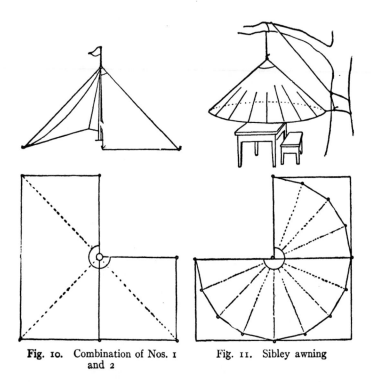

Fig. 10.   Combination of Nos. 1 and 2   Fig. 11.   Sibley awning

There are other shapes and combinations, but perhaps these sketches are enough in the line of suggestion.

The diagram Fig. 12 shows a method for laying out, on your cloth, the location of all the rings to make the tents and shelters. No dimensions are given and none is required. The diagram is good for any size. Most of the fastenings are found on radial lines, which are spaced to divide a semi-circle into eight equal angles, $22\frac{1}{2}$ degrees each; these intersect other construction lines and locate the necessary loops and rings. Figures are given at each ring which refer back to the sketch numbers.

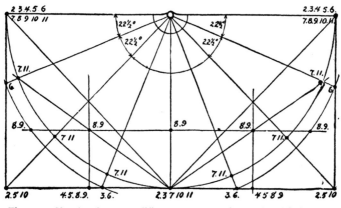

Fig. 12. Showing how ten different tents can be made with but one piece of canvas

Suppose the material at hand is the widest unbleached cotton cloth, 90 inches wide, 5 yards long, or $7\frac{1}{2}$ feet by 15 feet. The accompanying table will give the dimensions for the various shapes from Fig. 1 to Fig. 11.

If in doubt about the location of rings on your canvas, suspend the tent by the center ring and fasten the loops temporarily by means of safety pins, draw the tent into shape and shift the fastenings as required. The guy lines should have hooks or

TABLE OF DIMENSIONS, 90-IN. MATERIAL

Size	Area, Sq. Ft.	Height, Ft.	Remarks
1........$7\frac{1}{2}$ ft. triangle	25	$6\frac{1}{4}$	One side open
2........$6\frac{1}{2}$ x 15 ft.	65	$6\frac{1}{4}$	" " "
3........6 x $7\frac{1}{2}$ ft.	45	$4\frac{1}{2}$	" " "
4........$7\frac{1}{2}$ x 8 ft.	60	$5\frac{1}{2}$	" " "
5........$7\frac{1}{2}$ ft. triangle	25	$7\frac{1}{2}$	" " "
6........$6\frac{1}{4}$ x $6\frac{1}{4}$ ft.	39	7	Enclosed
7........$7\frac{1}{2}$ ft. diam.	44	$6\frac{1}{2}$	"
8........5 x $7\frac{1}{2}$ ft.	$37\frac{1}{2}$	$6\frac{1}{2}$	$2\frac{1}{2}$ ft. wall
9........$7\frac{1}{2}$ x 8 ft.	60	$6\frac{1}{2}$	No. 8, with fly
10........15 ft. triangle	97	$6\frac{1}{4}$	Enclosed
11........$11\frac{1}{4}$ ft. circle	108	5	Canopy, no sides

snaps at one end for ready attachment and removal; the othei
end should be provided with the usual slides for "take up."
The edge of the cloth where the large ring for suspension is
fastened should be bound with tape or have a double hem, for
it is the edge of the door in most of the tents shown.

Waterproofing a Tent

Dissolve half a pound of alum in two quarts of boiling water,
then add two gallons of pure cold water. In this solution place
the material and let it remain for a day. Dissolve a quarter
of a pound of sugar of lead in two quarts boiling water, then
add two gallons of cold water. Take the material from the
alum solution, wring it lightly, place in the second solution,
and leave for five or six hours; then wring out again lightly and
allow it to dry.

If you want to avoid trouble with a leaky tent, the following
solution is a "sure cure." Take a gallon or two gallons of
turpentine and one or two cakes of paraffin, drug-store size.
Chip the paraffin fairly fine; dump it into the turpentine. Place
the turpentine in a pail and set same in a larger pail or a tub of
hot water. The hot water will heat the turpentine, and the
turpentine will melt the paraffin. Stir thoroughly, and renew
your supply of hot water if necessary. Then pile your tent
into a tub and pour in the turpentine and paraffin mixture.
Work the tent all over thoroughly with your hands, so that every
fibre gets well saturated. You must work fast, however, as
the paraffin begins to thicken as it cools; and work out of doors,
in a breeze if possible, as the fumes of the turpentine will surely
make you sick if you try it indoors. When you have the tent
thoroughly saturated, hang it up to dry. It is not necessary
to wring the tent out when you hang it up. Just let it drip.
If you use too much paraffin the tent may look a little dirty
after it dries, but it will be all right after you have used it once
or twice.

AN OPEN OUTING TENT
By Warren H. Miller, Editor "Field and Stream"

To make an open outing tent, get thirteen yards of 8-oz.
duck canvas, which can be bought at any department store
or dry goods store for seventeen or eighteen cents a yard.
This makes your total expense $2.21 for your tent. Lay out
the strip of canvas on the floor, and cut one end square; measure
up 8 inches along the edge and draw a line to the other corner.
From this corner lay off 7 ft. 8 in. along the edge, and on the

opposite side lay off 5 ft. 9 in. beginning at the end of your 8-in. measurement. Now take a ruler and draw another diagonal across the canvas at the ends of these measurements and you have the first gore of your tent. Cut it across, turn the gore over, lay it down on the strip so as to measure off an-

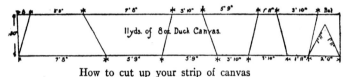

How to cut up your strip of canvas

other one exactly like it. This is the corresponding gore for the other side of the tent. To make the second pair of gores, lay off 5 ft. 9 in. along one side of the remaining strip of canvas beginning at the pointed end, and 3 ft. 10 in. on the other side. Join these points with a diagonal and you have a second gore,

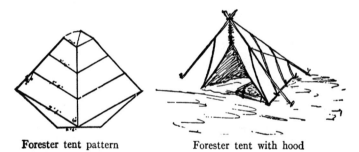

Forester tent pattern   Forester tent with hood

a duplicate of which is then cut by using it as a pattern, reversing and laying it down on the strip of canvas. To make the third gore, lay off 3 ft. 10 in., on one edge of your strip beginning at the point, and 1 ft. 11 in. on the other side. Draw a diagonal across and you have the third gore.

You have now used up all but two yards of your canvas, plus a little left-over piece of about 2 feet long. Out of this little left-over piece make a triangle 1 ft. 11 in. on the side, which will form the back triangle of your tent. Now pin your three gores together to make the side of your tent, just as in the illustrations, and pin the two sides together along the ridge. Then sew this tent up. Sew in the little back triangle and hem all around the edges. Leave a hole at the peak of the little triangle through which the ridge pole must go.

To set it up, cut three small saplings, one of which should be twelve feet long and the other two, ten feet long.　Tie these two together at the ends making what sailors call a "shears." Take the twelve-foot pole and run it down the ridge inside the tent, and out through the hole in the back.　Now raise the ridge pole with one end stuck in the ground and the front end resting on the two shear poles and tie all three of them together. At the end of each seam along the hem you must work in a little eyelet hole for a short piece of twine to tie to the tent pegs. Stretch out the back triangle, pegging it down at the two corners

Forester tent with hood

on the ground, and then peg out each hole along the foot until the entire tent stretches out taut as in our illustrations.　Three feet from the peak along the front edge you must have another eyelet hole with a little piece of twine, and you tie this out to the shear pole on each side which gives the tent the peculiar gambrel roof which it has, and which has the advantage of giving you lots more room inside than the straight tent would.　You now have what is known as the "open" forester tent.

If a thunder storm comes up with a driving rain it will surely rain in at the front unless you turn the tent around by moving the poles one at a time.　If you don't want to do this you can make a hood for the front out of the two yards of canvas you have left.　Simply draw a diagonal from one corner to the other of this two-yard piece of duck, and cut it down the diagonal, making two thin triangles which are sewed to the front edges of the open forester tent, making a hood of the shape shown in our picture. This prevents the rain beating in the opening of your tent but still lets the heat of your fire strike in and at the same time it keeps the heat in the tent as it will not flow out along the ridge pole as it does in the open type.

This tent weighs six pounds and packs into a little package fourteen inches long by seven inches wide by six inches thick, and can be carried as a shoulder strap, or put in a back pack or any way you wish to take it. It will sleep three boys, or two men and a boy, very comfortably indeed. While it really does not need to be water-proofed, as it immediately shrinks tight after the first rain, you can water-proof it if you wish by making a solution of ten ounces of quicklime with four ounces of alum in ten quarts of water. Stir occasionally until the lime has slackened. Put the tent in another pail and pour the solution over it, letting it stand twelve hours. Take out and hang it on the clothes-line to dry. It will then be entirely water-proof.

To make a good night fire in front of the tent, drive two stout stakes three feet long in the ground about three feet from the mouth of the tent; pile four logs one on top of the other against these stakes, or take a large flat stone and rest it against it. Make the two log andirons for each side of the fire and build your fire in the space between them. It will give you a fine cheerful fire and all the heat will be reflected by the back logs into the tent, making it warm and cheerful. Inside you can put your browse bags stuffed with balsam browse; or pile up a mountain of dry leaves over which you can stretch your blankets. Pile all the duffle way back in the peak against the little back triangle where it will surely keep dry and will form a sort of back for your pillows. You will find the forester tent lighter and warmer than the ordinary lean-to, as it reflects the heat better. After a couple of weeks in it you will come home with your lungs so full of ozone that it will be impossible to sleep in an ordinary room without feeling smothered.

CANOEING, ROWING, AND SAILING
By Arthur A. Carey, Chairman National Committee on Sea Scouting.

The birch-bark canoe is the boat of the North American Indians, and our modern canvas canoes are made, with some variations, on the Indian model. With the possible exception of the Venetian gondola, the motion of a canoe is more graceful than that of any other boat propelled by hand; it should be continuous and gliding, and so silent that it may be brought up in the night to an animal or an enemy, Indian fashion, without making any sound, and so take them by surprise.

Many accidents happen in canoes — not because they are unsafe when properly handled, but because they are unsafe when improperly handled — and many people do not take

Canoeing stroke (a)

the trouble even to find out the proper way of managing a canoe. Many canoes have seats almost on a level with the gunwale, whereas, properly speaking, the only place to sit in a canoe is on the bottom; for a seat raises the body too high above the center of gravity and makes the canoe unsteady and likely to upset. It is, however, difficult to paddle while sitting in the bottom of a canoe, and the best position for paddling is that of kneeling and at the same time resting back against one of the thwarts. The size of the single-blade paddle should be in proportion to the size of the boy who uses it — long enough to reach from the ground to the tip of his nose. The bow paddle may be a little shorter. The canoeman should learn to paddle equally well on either side of a canoe. When paddling on the left side the top of the paddle should be held by the right hand, and the left hand should be placed a few inches above the beginning of the blade. The old Indian stroke, which is the most approved modern method for all-round canoeing, whether racing or cruising, is made with the arms almost straight — but not stiff — the arm at the top of the paddle bending only slightly at the elbow. This stroke is really a swing from the shoulder, in which there is little or no push or pull with the arm. When

Canoeing stroke (b)

paddling on the left side of the canoe the right shoulder swings forward, and the whole force of the body is used to push the blade of the paddle through the water, the left hand acting as a fulcrum. While the right shoulder is swung forward, the right hand is at the same time twisted at the wrist so that the thumb goes down, this motion of the wrist has the effect of turning the paddle around in the left hand — the left wrist being allowed to bend freely — so that, at the end of the stroke, the blade slides out of the water almost horizontally. If you should twist the paddle in the opposite direction it would force the head of the canoe around so that it would travel in a circle. At the recovery of the stroke the right shoulder swings back and the paddle is brought forward in a horizontal position, with the blade almost parallel to the water. It is swung forward until the paddle is at right angles across the canoe, then the blade is dipped edgewise with a slicing motion and a new stroke begins. In paddling on the right side of the canoe the position of the two hands and the motion of the two shoulders are reversed.

Something should also be said about double paddles — that is, paddles with two blades — one at each end — as their use is becoming more general every year. With the double paddle a novice can handle a canoe head on to a stiff wind, a feat which

Canoeing stroke (c)

requires skill and experience with a single blade. The doubles give greater safety and more speed and they develop chest, arm, and shoulder muscles not brought into play with a single blade. The double paddle is not to be recommended to the exclusion of the single blade, but there are many times when there is an advantage in its use.

In getting in or out of a canoe, it is especially necessary to step in the very center of the boat; and be careful never to lean on any object — such as the edge of a wharf — outside of the boat, for this disturbs your balance and may capsize the canoe. Especially in getting out, put down your paddle first, and then, grasping the gunwale firmly in each hand, rise by putting your weight equally on both sides of the canoe.   If your canoe should drift away sideways from the landing-place, when you are trying to land, place the blade of your paddle flat upon the water in the direction of the wharf and gently draw the canoe up to the landing-place with a slight sculling motion.

When it is necessary to cross the waves in rough water, always try to cross them "quartering," *i. e.*, at an oblique angle, but not at right angles.   Crossing big waves at right angles or head on, is difficult and apt to strain a canoe, and getting lengthwise, or broadside to, between the waves, is dangerous. Always have more weight aft than in the bow; but when there is only one person in the canoe, it may be convenient to place a weight forward as a balance; but it should always be lighter

Canoe with sail

than the weight aft.   A skilful canoeman will paddle a light canoe even in a strong wind by kneeling at a point about one third of the length from the stern.

For the purpose of sailing in a canoe the Lateen rig is the safest, most easily handled, and the best all-round sailing outfit. For a seventeen-foot canoe a sail having forty square feet of surface is to be recommended, and, in all except very high winds, this can be handled by one man.

The Lateen sail is made in the form of an equilateral triangle, and two sides are fastened to spars which are connected at one end by a hinge or jaw. The mast — which should be set well forward — should be so long that, when the sail is spread and the slanting upper spar is swung from the top of the mast, the lower spar will swing level about six to eight inches above the gunwale and hang clear above all parts of the boat in going about. The sail is hoisted by a halyard attached at, or a little above, the center of the upper spar, then drawn through a block attached to the brace which holds the mast in position, and thus to the cleats — within easy reach of the sailor. The sheet line is fastened to the lower spar, about two feet from the outer end; and should be held in the hand at all times. Both halyard and sheet should at all times be kept clear, so as to run easily, and the halyards made fast to a cleat by turns that can easily be slipped.

The leeboard is a necessary attachment to the sailing outfit. It is made with two blades — about three feet long and ten inches wide would furnish a good-sized surface in the water — one dropping on each side of the canoe and firmly supported by a bar fastened to the gunwale. The blades should be so rigged that, when striking an object in the water, they will quickly release, causing no strain on the canoe. The leeboard, like a center board, is of course intended to keep the canoe from sliding off when trying to beat up into the wind. When running free before the wind the board should be raised. The general rules for sailing larger craft apply to the canoe.

The paddle is used as a rudder and may be held by the sailor, but a better plan is to have two paddles, one over each side, made fast to the gunwale or the brace. The sailor can then grasp either one as he goes about and there is no danger of losing the paddles overboard. In sailing, the sailor sits on the bottom, on the opposite side from the sail, except in a high wind, when he sits on the gunwale where he can the better balance the sail with his weight. The combination of sail, leeboards, and the balancing weight of the sailor, will render the canoe stiff and safe, with proper care, in any wind less than a gale. A crew may consist of two or three in a seventeen-foot canoe.

The spars and mast of a sailing outfit should be of spruce or some other light but strong wood, while cedar or some non-splitting wood is best for the leeboards. Young canoeists will enjoy making their own sailing outfits; or a complete Lateen rig as made by various canoe manufacturers can be purchased either directly from them or through almost any dealer.

In case of an upset the greatest mistake is to leave the boat. A capsized canoe will support at least four persons as long as

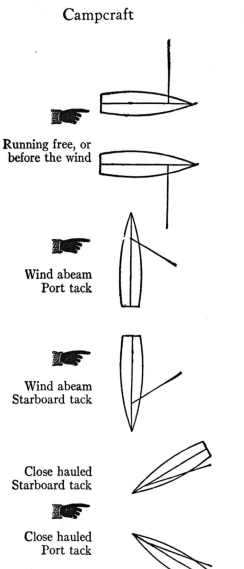

Running free, or
before the wind

Wind abeam
Port tack

Wind abeam
Starboard tack

Close hauled
Starboard tack

Close hauled
Port tack

This diagram illustrates some of the angles formed by boom and keel line of the boat in different positions. Hand indicates direction of wind.

they have strength to cling to it. A single man or boy, in case of upsetting beyond swimming distance to land, should stretch himself flat upon the bottom of the canoe, with arms and legs spread down over the tumblehome toward the submerged gunwales. He can thus lie in safety for hours till help arrives. When two persons are upset, they should range themselves one on each side of the overturned boat; and, with one hand grasping each other's wrists across the boat, use the other hand to cling to the keel or the gunwale. If the canoe should swamp, fill with water, and begin to sink, it should be turned over in the water. It is the air remaining under the inverted hull that gives the craft sufficient buoyancy to support weight.

Never overload a canoe. In one of the ordinary size — about seventeen feet in length — three persons should be the maximum number at any time, and remember never to change seats in a canoe when out of your depth.

Row=boats

There is a certain caution in the use of boats which you will always find among sailors and fishermen and all persons who are using them constantly. Such a person instinctively steps into the middle of the boat when getting in, and always sits in the middle of the thwart or seat. This is a matter of instinct with seafaring people, and so is the habit of never fooling in a boat. Only landlubbers will try to stand up in a small boat while in motion; and, as for the man who rocks a boat "for fun," he is like the man "who didn't know the gun was loaded."

Rowing

Row-boats are propelled either by rowing or by sculling; and rowing is either "pulling" or "backing water." The usual way of rowing is to "pull" and to do so, you sit with your back to the bow and propel the boat by pulling the handles toward your body and so pressing the blades of the oars against the water toward the stern, while pushing with your feet against a brace. In backing water you reverse the action of the oars, pushing the handles away from your body and pressing the blades of the oars against the water toward the bow.

Turning

To turn your boat to the right, when pulling, you row only with the left oar; or, if you wish to make a sharp turn "pull" with the left oar and "back water" with the right. To turn your boat to the left the action of the oars is reversed.

Feathering

To prevent the momentum of the boat from being checked by the wind blowing on the blades of the oars, the blades must be turned into a horizontal position as they leave the water. In "pulling" this is done by turning the hands backward at the wrist, and in backing water it is done by turning the hands forward at the wrist.

Sculling

To scull is to propel a boat by a single oar at the stern. The boat must be provided with rowlock or a semicircular scoop in the stern, and the boat is propelled by working the oar at the stern, obliquely from side to side. This is a convenient way of doing when you are working among boats in the water, and have to go short distances without the necessity of speed.

Steering

When rowing a boat without the use of a rudder, instead of constantly turning the head around to see where you are going, it is convenient to fix upon some object in the landscape on an imaginary line with the middle of the stern and the middle of the bow; you can then keep your boat approximately in the right position, without the trouble of turning your head, by keeping the object selected on a line with the middle of the stern board.

Coming Alongside

When coming alongside of a boat or wharf always approach on the leeward side or that opposite from which the wind is blowing, and come up so that the boat will be headed into the wind and waves. Stop rowing at a convenient distance from the landing-place and come up with gentle headway; then take in the oar nearest the landing, and, if necessary, back water with the other oar. If two or more are rowing at the same time, the person rowing in the bow will boat his oars, stand up, face forward and fend off with his boat-hook.

Keeping Stroke

When two or more are rowing together the length and speed of the stroke are set by the man sitting nearest the stern.

Rough Weather

Always try to row as nearly as possible into the waves at right angles. In this way you are likely to ship less water and to avoid capsizing.

Going Ashore

When going ashore always leave your oars lying flat on the thwarts on either side of your boat.

The Salute

To salute a passing vessel or boat, hold the oars up at right angles with the water, with the blades parallel to the keel of the boat (called tossing), and let the coxswain salute with his hand.

Every row-boat should be provided with a painter, at least 24 feet long, spliced to a ring or through a hole in the stern; an extra line at least three times the length of the boat; and a rough sponge and a tin dipper to be used in bailing out the water. Always bail out the water after a rain and keep your boat clean and tidy.

Sailing in Small Boats

The most convenient kind of a boat to learn to sail in is a cat-boat, which is a boat with a single fore and aft sail held in place by a boom at the bottom and a gaff at the top.

To understand the principle of sailing we must realize that a sail-boat, without the use of a rudder, acts in the water and wind very much the way a weather vane acts in the air. The bow of the boat naturally turns toward the wind, thus relieving the sail of all pressure and keeping it shaking. But if, by keeping the main sheet (the rope fastened to the main-boom) in your hand you hold the sail in a fixed position, and, at the same time, draw the tiller away from the sail, it will gradually fill with air, beginning at the hoist or mast end of the sail, and impel the boat in the direction in which you are steering. Given a certain direction in which you want to travel, the problem is, by letting out or hauling in your main-sheet, to keep the sail as nearly as possible at right angles with the direction of the wind. We must remember, also, that, while the sail must be kept full, it should not be kept more than full, that is, its position must be such that, by the least push of the tiller toward the sail, the sail will begin to shake at the hoist. It is even desirable in a strong wind, and especially for beginners, to always let the sail, close to the mast, shake a little without losing too much pressure. When you are sailing with the wind coming over the boat from its port side you are sailing on the port tack, and, when you are sailing with the wind coming across the boat on its starboard side, you are sailing on the starboard tack. The port side of the boat is the left hand side as you face the bow while standing on board, and the starboard side is the right hand side. An easy way of remembering this is by recalling the sentence, "Jack left port."

Direction of Wind

Of course, you will see that, if you should forget which way the wind is blowing, you could not possibly know the right position for your sail; and this is one of the first requirements for a beginner. It is quite easy to become confused with regard to the direction of the wind, and therefore every boat should be provided with a small flag or fly at its mast-head and you should keep watching it at every turn of the boat until the habit has become instinctive. It is convenient to remember that the fly should always point as nearly as possible to the end of the gaff, except when you are sailing free or before the wind.

Close to Wind

Sailing with the boat pointing as nearly as possible against the wind is called sailing by the wind, or close-hauled; when you have turned your bow to the right or left so that the wind strikes both boat and sail at right angles you are sailing with the wind abeam; as you let out your sheet so that the boom makes a larger angle with an imaginary line running from the mast to the middle of the stern you are sailing off the wind; and, when your sail stands at right angles to this same line, you are sailing free or before the wind.

Before the Wind

Sailing free, or before the wind, is the extreme opposite of sailing close hauled or by the wind, and the wind is blowing behind your back instead of approaching the sail from the direction of the mast. If you are sailing free on the port tack, with the boom at right angles to the mast on the starboard side, and you should steer your boat sufficiently to starboard, the wind would strike the sail at its outer edge or leech and throw the sail and boom violently over to the port side of the mast. This is called gybing and is a very dangerous thing; it should be carefully guarded against whenever sailing before the wind.

Reefing

If you find that the wind is too strong for your boat, and that you are carrying too much sail, you can let her come up into the wind and take in one or two reefs. This is done by letting out both the throat and peak halliards enough to give sufficient slack of sail, then by hauling the sail out toward the end of the boom, and afterward by rolling the sail up and tying the points under and around it, but not around the boom. Always use a square or reef knot in tying your reef points.

In case of a squall or a strong puff of wind, remember that you can always ease the pressure on your sail by turning the bow into the wind, and if for any reason you wish to shorten suddenly you can drop your peak by loosening the peak halliards.

Ready About

Before "going about," or turning your bow so that the wind will strike the other side of the sail at its mast end, the man at the helm should always give warning by singing out the words, "ready about," and then "hard-a-lee." "Going about" is just the opposite of gybing.

Right of Way

When two sailing-vessels are approaching one another, so as to involve risk of collision, one of them shall keep out of the way of the other as follows, namely:

(a) A vessel which is running free shall keep out of the way of a vessel which is close-hauled.

(b) A vessel which is close-hauled on the port tack shall keep out of the way of a vessel which is close-hauled on the starboard tack.

(c) When both are running free, with the wind on different sides, the vessel which has the wind on the port side shall keep out of the way of the other.

(d) When both are running free, with the wind on the same side, the vessel which is to the windward shall keep out of the way of the vessel which is to the leeward.

(e) A vessel which has the wind aft shall keep out of the way of the other vessel.

When a steam-vessel and a sailing-vessel are proceeding in such directions as to involve risk of collision, the steam-vessel shall keep out of the way of the sailing-vessel.*

Flying of Flag

While the "fly" or "pennant" is carried at the top of the mast, the flag is carried at the peak or upper corner of the sail at the end of the gaff. The salute consists of "dipping" or slightly lowering the flag and raising it again into position.

*Note — The above rules are quoted directly from the U. S. Government Steamboat Inspection Service "Pilot Rules," but it is always well for small boat skippers to go around the stern of a vessel and not cross her bows.

CHAPTER V

SIGNS, SYMBOLS, AND SIGNALING

Trail Marks
Daniel Carter Beard, National Scout Commissioner.

When America was first discovered there was a blanket of forest extending from the Atlantic Ocean to the Mississippi River, with the exception of a few prairies in Indiana and Illinois. This whole section of the country was one dense, dark, gloomy forest. It was traversed by traces which we now call trails. These traces were first made by the big game animals, then followed by the Indians, then by the pioneer trappers and explorers, then by the settlers with their pack-horses; after them came the wagons, and now the same trails are traveled by us all in the cars of the railway companies.

You can readily see that in a forest a man would use some method of marking a trace or trail, not only that he could find his way back, but that another fellow might follow him. This the woodsmen did by blazing the trees, that is, by chopping a piece of bark from a tree every once in a while as they traveled, so as to mark a path.

There are two kinds of blazed trails. The spot trail has the blaze made on the face of the tree so that you may see the blaze on the next tree in advance along the trail which he is following. Then there is the other method of blazing a tree on the side so that you may strike it easily with an axe or hatchet as you walk by. In the far North I have seen these blazed trails 15 feet above the ground; that is because the snows are from 6 to 12 feet on a level in the winter and that is when the Indians use this blazed trail. The surveyors blaze a trail along the line of a survey, cutting a piece of bark on that side of the tree along which the line passes, and when the line hits the center of the tree they mark it with three or more cuts and it is known as a line tree

A forester in making a new trail blazes the trees as already described, but if he finds that he has made a false trail he re-traces his steps to the right one, then starts afresh and marks the first two, three, or four trees with two notches so as to let you know that these are the right trees, then if you wander away on the false trail, you backtrail to the notches and start again in the right direction.

In the towns, villages, and country, the boy scouts mark the trails by chalk marks. Not only can they mark a trail thus but they can convey information to those following them. Bad dog (Fig. 1). Danger is shown by a rectangle with a round dot in the center (Fig. 2).

When you are walking through the woods note everything. For instance, a pebble in your path shows the damp side up. It only takes a little common sense for you to reason that something has been along there before you and knocked that pebble over with its foot, otherwise the moist side would not be on top. If in a muddy place you find the track of a boy and the mud which is splattered nearby is still wet, you know that that boy has been there recently. If the mud is dry then some time has elapsed since the boy passed that way. If the grass and leaves of a small bush are brushed the wrong way showing the under side of leaves or grasses you will know that something has been along there before you.

Really, boys, trailing is applying Sherlock Holmes' methods to the woods; it is using observation, noting what you see around you, and then reasoning out the cause. The more you know about nature the easier it is to decipher a trail. For instance, if you see by the leaves or grass that some animal has passed, and note high up on a tree some animal's hair, even a chump would know that that animal was a large animal and had hair on it. But it takes a woodsman to know what sort of an animal it was, because only woodsmen are familiar with the hair of the wild animals; it might have been a moose, it might have been a deer, or it might have been a bear. If the hair on a tree is low down on the trunk, the first guess would be that it was from a small animal. It may have been a rabbit, raccoon, mink, dog, or cat. The more you know about a mink, the more you know about muskrats, wild cats, and bears, the better able you will be to read these signs. There is no royal road to trailing. You must visit the woods, hit the trails, follow them out, and reason them out to become an expert trailer.

Take the Whiffle Poof and experiment with trailing. Next you can try following your dog or anybody's dog. If you can follow a dog you can follow a wolf. If you can follow a wolf you can follow a fox, although a fox as a rule will try to lead you astray. If you can follow a cow, you can follow a moose.

If you can follow a sheep, you can follow a deer, that is, all other things being equal. I do not intend to say that if you can follow a sheep's tracks in the snow or on a dusty road that you can follow a deer's tracks in the summer woods; but experiment on domestic animals and graduate on wild animals.

In winter time nothing can move on the ground without leaving a tell-tale trail in the snow. That is the time you can find more joy in working out the problem than at any other time of the year.

While writing this I took a trip to Pike County, Pennsylvania. The snow was waist deep in the woods, but packed so tightly that animals as large as a lynx could walk over it without sinking, leaving their tracks very distinctly upon the surface. My camp is 116 miles from headquarters at 200 Fifth Avenue, New York City, yet in driving down from my log house to the railroad station, a distance of four and a half miles, I saw one live deer, the fresh tracks of four others, the tracks of one Canadian lynx, two mink, one raccoon, one porcupine, numerous Molly Cotton-tails' tracks, four or five different tracks of the big white hare, innumerable fox tracks, ruffed grouse tracks, and hundreds of tracks of different field mice which could not be identified from our position in the sleigh. I tell this to show the reader how many tracks may be found within a short distance of one of the largest cities in the world.

Some of the mice and rats not only leave a trail of their feet but also a trail of their tails. Brother Fox will trot along the road and suddenly his trail will cease. Apparently he has taken wings and flown away, but he has really jumped, doubled up his track, and commenced again. He might not know that you are following his track, but he always suspects that some one is. He comes to the muskrat house, he wants to examine it. He goes around it in two or three circles, first to be sure that there are no trenches or 42 centimeter guns hidden around or behind the muskrat house. Brother Fox is always suspicious and makes a fine trail to follow. Heretofore we have shown you diagrams of these tracks, more or less accurate, but the real animals make real tracks which are always accurate. Go to nature and study them.

Signs of Alarm, Danger, and Trouble

It is of vital importance to the whole outdoor world that a uniform system of signals should be adopted and understood to mean trouble or disaster and a call for help. Owing to the

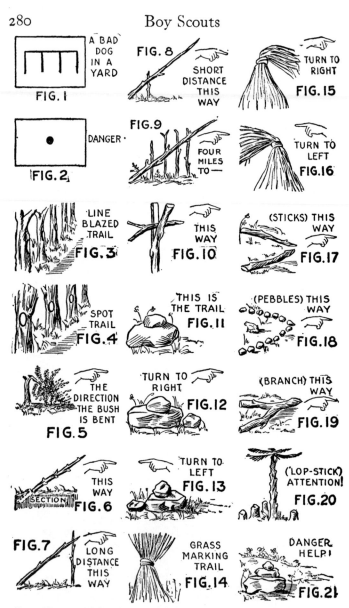

FIG. 1 — A BAD DOG IN A YARD

FIG. 2 — DANGER

FIG. 3 — LINE BLAZED TRAIL

FIG. 4 — SPOT TRAIL

FIG. 5 — THE DIRECTION THE BUSH IS BENT

FIG. 6 — THIS WAY

FIG. 7 — LONG DISTANCE THIS WAY

FIG. 8 — SHORT DISTANCE THIS WAY

FIG. 9 — FOUR MILES TO—

FIG. 10 — THIS WAY

FIG. 11 — THIS IS THE TRAIL

FIG. 12 — TURN TO RIGHT

FIG. 13 — TURN TO LEFT

FIG. 14 — GRASS MARKING TRAIL

FIG. 15 — TURN TO RIGHT

FIG. 16 — TURN TO LEFT

FIG. 17 — (STICKS) THIS WAY

FIG. 18 — (PEBBLES) THIS WAY

FIG. 19 — (BRANCH) THIS WAY

FIG. 20 — ('LOP-STICK) ATTENTION!

FIG. 21 — DANGER HELP!

Note: Figures 3, 4 and 5 represent methods used on the frontier where wood is nearly valueless. They should not be used by scouts generally, as they injure the trees.

fact that some writers have, through misapprehension or typographical error, given two shots as a call for help, it has put a dangerous confusion of ideas in many amateurs' minds. It should be recognized among all outdoor people, including hunters, explorers, military men, and boy scouts that THREE of anything stands for something serious, for a call for help, for a sign of danger. THREE might be called the Paul Revere among the signs, spreading and giving the alarm. Two shots from a gun, for instance, may simply mean that a man has fired the right and left barrel of a shotgun, but three shots in succession would attract any hunter's or sportman's attention, and if the three shots were again repeated in the same manner he would know that some one was in trouble.

There are also statements in print that three stones one on top of the other, three tufts of grass, and three blazes on a tree, are signs of danger or alarm, which is true enough, but confusion is made when three smokes are given as a sign for good news and two smokes for "I am lost, help!" Three of everything does, and must, have the same general meaning, a cry for succor, help, or alarm—the white man's custom of firing three shots as a call for help, the Apache's custom of three smokes as a sign of alarm, the mountaineer's custom of three stones one on top of another, also the three blazes on a tree, three tufts of grass, three short blasts on a steamboat whistle, full speed astern—all indicate trouble; consequently in this system of signs I have taken the liberty to ignore any apparent exceptions to the rule.

Whistle Signals

1. One long blast means "Silence," "Attention," "Look out for my next signal." Also used in approaching a station.

2. Two short blasts mean "All right."

3. A succession of long, slow blasts means "Go out " "Get farther away," or "Advance," "Extend," "Scatter."

4. A succession of short, sharp blasts means "Rally," "Come together," "Close in."

5. Three short blasts followed by one long one from the scoutmaster calls up the patrol leaders—i. e., "Leaders, come here."

6. Three long blasts mean "Danger," "Alarm," "Look out."

7. A succession of alternating long and sharp blasts means "Mess call," "Grub."

Any whistle signal should be instantly obeyed at the double—as fast as you can—no matter what other job you may be doing at the time.

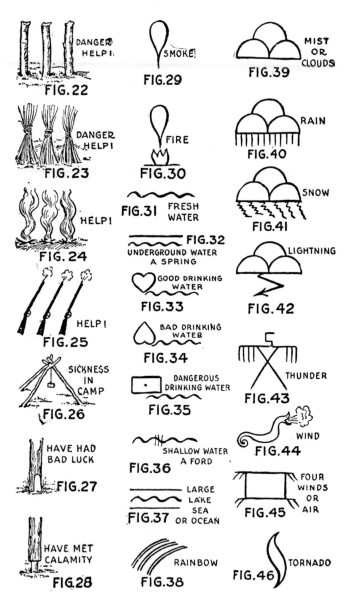

FIG. 22 — DANGER HELP!

FIG. 23 — DANGER HELP!

FIG. 24 — HELP!

FIG. 25 — HELP!

FIG. 26 — SICKNESS IN CAMP

FIG. 27 — HAVE HAD BAD LUCK

FIG. 28 — HAVE MET CALAMITY

FIG. 29 — SMOKE!

FIG. 30 — FIRE

FIG. 31 — FRESH WATER

FIG. 32 — UNDERGROUND WATER A SPRING

FIG. 33 — GOOD DRINKING WATER

FIG. 34 — BAD DRINKING WATER

FIG. 35 — DANGEROUS DRINKING WATER

FIG. 36 — SHALLOW WATER A FORD

FIG. 37 — LARGE LAKE SEA OR OCEAN

FIG. 38 — RAINBOW

FIG. 39 — MIST OR CLOUDS

FIG. 40 — RAIN

FIG. 41 — SNOW

FIG. 42 — LIGHTNING

FIG. 43 — THUNDER

FIG. 44 — WIND

FIG. 45 — FOUR WINDS OR AIR

FIG. 46 — TORNADO

GESTURE SIGNALS

Something is lost and a scout is sent back for it. He picks up a handful of dust or other material and throws it in the air. This means "I have found it."

Found   More or Faster   Lie down or Dismount   Go back   Halt

What do you see?   I see   Nothing to fear   Advance

Doubled fist of right hand moved vigorously up and down above the head is the command to move faster. Two hands extended in front of the body, arms bent, elbows at side of body, hands motioned downward by moving the forearm from the elbow is the command to lie down or dismount. Hand whirled around above the head in a horizontal position is the command to go back. Hand held up, palm out, is the command to halt. Palm of hand toward the front of the face, all fingers spread, hand moved from right to left a few inches in front of the eyes is the question; "What do you see?" Stick, staff, gun, or fishrod held horizontally by the two hands above the head tells the observer that what they are looking for is in sight. Both hands extended above the head with the palms to the front means that you have nothing to fear. Doubled fist, arm extended above the head, then brought down to a level with the shoulder, fist extended full length of the arm in front is the command to advance.

SIGNALING

Codes Used in Scouting

The second class tests require a scout to know the Semaphore or the General Service Code. It is suggested that scouts learn both codes.

The scout is required to have a knowledge of the theory of signaling, of the alphabet, numerals, and conventional signals. It is allowable for the examiner to call the letters for the candidate. The scout demonstrates in some simple manner. The scout chooses the code.

A first class scout should be able to send and receive a message at the rate of 16 letters per minute if he uses the General Service Code or 30 letters per minute if he uses the Semaphore Code. He should know the alphabet, numerals, and conventional signals so thoroughly that he can be depended upon in an emergency to send or receive a message either by Semaphore or the General Service Code. The scout chooses the code.

The General Service Code, known also as the International Morse and the Continental Code, is used in commercial wireless transmissions, between the Army and Navy, and for general signaling.

Scouts should thoroughly master tnese two standard codes before taking up any others, as no special system of signaling will be accepted as a substitute for them in passing the tests.

GENERAL SERVICE CODE

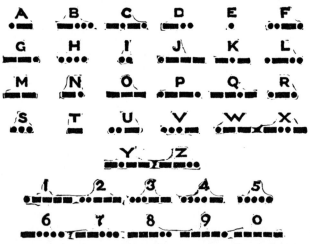

The General Service Code is the most generally applicable and the most widely used code. The equipment is also within reach of all scouts so far as expense is concerned. It can be used with hand flags by day, and with torches, lanterns, and flashlights by night. It is used with the heliograph—an instrument for

flashing the sun's rays at desired intervals and with searchlights.
It can be given by whistle, drum or bugle, and it is universally
used for wireless telegraphy, and, except in this country, on the
telegraph lines.   It is the code used in the Ardois system explained on page 294.   For these reasons it is by far the most important for the scout to know.

Single Flag or Wigwag Signaling

For the flag used with the General Service Code there is one
position and there are three motions.   The position is with the
flag held vertically, the signalman facing directly toward the
station with which it is desired to communicate.   The first
motion (the dot) is to the right of the sender, and will embrace
an arc of 90 degrees, starting with the vertical and returning to
it, and will be made in a plane at right angles to the line connect-

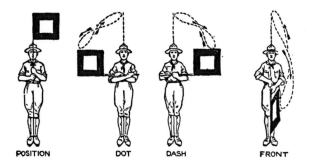

POSITION   DOT   DASH   FRONT

ing the two stations.   The second motion (the dash) is a similar
motion to the left of the sender.   The third motion (front) is
downward directly in front of the sender and instantly returned
upward to the first position.   One front indicates the end of a
word, two fronts, the end of a sentence, three fronts, the end
of a message.

In sending the message by hand flag, place yourself in such a
position that the observer can see the flag clearly.   Avoid standing in shadow or in such a position that the flag will appear the
same color as the background.

The inexperienced sender is often unable to make his signals
understood by the receiving station, due to the fouling of the

flag on the staff. This occurs when the sender tries to swing the flag down and back in the same line. The correct motion is to make the end of the staff describe a loop or figure eight, so that the flag on the up-stroke follows a path about four inches toward the wind from its path on the down-stroke.

When the wind is blowing from either side sending is of course difficult, but the experienced signaler makes the most of even this condition by facing slightly into or away from the breeze in a manner that will enable him to give the receiving station the greatest possible sight of the full fly of the sending flag. The flag at all times should be swung in a quiet, easy manner, avoiding jerk and whipping. Too much speed to start with will soon tire the signaler and result in poor signals.

Make signals with regularity; do not send one word rapidly, the next slowly; adopt such a rate of speed as can be read by the distant signaler without causing him to "break" frequently. Remember that it is easier to send than to receive, and the natural tendency is to send too fast. Make a distinct pause between letters. The motion, in using the flag, should be such as to display in the lateral waves the whole surface of the flag toward the point of observation.

When possible there should be three scouts in each signal party; one holding the flag to do the sending; one with field glasses to receive, and one with pad and pencil to record the message. In sending, the recording scout or scribe should call off the words, one by one, to the sender. In receiving, the scout with the glasses should call off each letter and front motion as it is received, and these should be taken down by the recording scout.

The scout should know the alphabet so thoroughly that he does not have to think of the code.

Rapidity is secondary to accuracy. Every letter should be made distinct and with an easy rhythm.

Get so far away that it is not possible to call back and forth, or run easily. Send real messages of ten words or more.

Never pass between scout signaling and station while he is signaling. Don't talk to scout reading.

To select a visual station, choose a point perfectly in view of the communicating station; fix the exact position in which the flagman is to stand, so arranged, if possible, that when viewed from the communicating station he will have behind him a background of the same color for every position in which the signals may be shown.

To determine the color of the background, first ascertain

whether the communicating station is higher, lower, or level with your own. If it be higher, the background for your signals, viewed thence, will be the color of the field, woods, etc., behind and lower than your flagman. If it be lower, your background will be the color of the ground, etc., behind and lying higher than your flagman. If the stations are of equal elevation, then the background for your signals will be that directly behind the flagman.

The color of the flag must contrast as strongly as possible with that of the background. With green or dark or with earth-covered background, the white flag should be used. The distant station is the best judge of background, and should it indicate the color of flag wanted, that flag should be used.

If a signal station asks another to move its station either to its right or left, so that its signal will be more distinct, each station will see that a signalman holds a flag or lighted torch above his head. The station asking for the change will lower its flag immediately upon the distant station arriving at a position with a good background.

When several messages are to be sent in succession "End of message" signal will be made after the signature of each, to be followed by the abbreviation "ahr," meaning "another," after which commence with the next message.

No message will be considered sent until its receipt has been acknowledged by the receiving station.

When a station has sent all messages on hand, the signal "Cease signaling" should invariably be made. When nothing more is to be sent from either station, both will make "Cease signaling."

Visual Signaling in General

The General Service Code is used also with the following methods of signaling:

(a) By torch, hand lantern, or beam of searchlight (without shutter).

(b) By heliograph, flash lantern, or searchlight (with shutter).

(c) By Ardois.

The conventional signals on following page are the authorized standards of the United States Signal Service.

The beam of the searchlight, though ordinarily used with a shutter like the heliograph, may be used for long-distance signaling, when no shutter is suitable or available, in a similar manner to the flag or torch, the first position being a vertical one. A movement of the beam 90° to the right of the sender indicates a dot, a similar movement to the left indicates a dash; the beam is lowered vertically for front.

To use the torch or hand lantern, a footlight must be employed

Exceptions.
Ardois

End of word	Interval	
End of sentence	Double interval	
End of message	Triple interval	
Signal separating preamble from address; address from text; text from signature	▬ • • • ▬	(Double interval (Signature preceded also (by "Sig. Interval.")
Acknowledgment (R)	• ▬ •	
Error	• • • • • • • •	A
Negative (K)	▬ • ▬	
Preparatory (L)	• ▬ • •	
Annuling (N)	▬ •	
Affirmative (P)	• ▬ ▬ •	
Interrogatory	• • ▬ ▬ • •	O
Repeat after (word)	Interrogatory, A, (word)	
Repeat last message	Interrogatory three times	
Send faster	Q R Q	
Send slower	Q R S	
Cease sending	Q R T	
Wait a moment	• ▬ • • •	None
Execute	I X, I X	
Move to your right	M R	
Move to your left	M L	
Move up	M U	
Move down	M D	
Finished (end of work)	• • • ▬ • ▬	None

"Intervals" are expressed as follows in the various systems:

	Interval	Double Interval	Triple Interval
Radio Flashing or Occulting light Sound	—space	• • • • • •	• ▬ • ▬ •
Wigwag	Front	(Twice)	(3 times)
Semaphore	Flags crossed or machine closed	2 chops	3 chops withdraw flags or close machine and indicator arm
Ardois	• ▬ • ▬	(Twice)	(3 times)

as a point of reference to the motion. The lantern is most conveniently swung out upward to the right of the footlight for a dot, to the left for a dash, and raised vertically for front.

To call when using the searchlight without shutter throw the beam in a vertical position and move it through an arc 18° in a plane at right angles to the line connecting the two stations until acknowledged; a similar procedure is employed with the torch or hand lantern.

SPECIAL METHODS OF SIGNALING

Signaling by Two-Arm Semaphore
Stationary Semaphore

Signals may be transmitted by the two-arm semaphore. With the machine, a third arm or "indicator" is displayed on the right of the sender, the left as viewed by the receiver. At night a red light screened to the rear indicates the direction of sending.

The machine will be mounted at some available point so situated that it may be seen through the greatest arc of the horizon. By means of electric lights installed on the vanes, the machine is made available for night as well as for day signaling. The vanes of the semaphore machine shall be painted yellow.

Signaling by the two-arm semaphore is the most rapid method of sending spelled-out messages. It is, however, very liable to error if the motions are slurred over or run together in an attempt to make speed. Both arms should move rapidly and simultaneously, but there should be a perceptible pause at the end of each letter before making the movements for the next letter. Rapidity is secondary to accuracy.

Conventional Signals

With the machine the interval "end of word" is the machine closed, but with the indicator showing; end of the sentence is the "chop-chop" signal, both arms being placed at the right horizontal and then moved up and down in a cutting motion, the indicator being displayed; the end of message is indicated by the closing of both arms and indicator.

To call a station, wave the arms toward the vertical, making the call at frequent intervals. The station called answers by making its own call. With the machine this call is left with the display fixed until the message has been received and understood. When the sender makes "end of message," the receiver, if message is understood, extends the arms horizontally and waves them until the sender does the same.

Signaling by Hand Flags with Two=Arm Semaphore Code

Hand flags on account of their small range are of limited application, and are chiefly serviceable for use within organizations, within fixed positions, or for incidental signaling. The range with flags of the usual size is of course dependent upon light and background, but is seldom more than one mile with the naked eye. This system of signaling has been highly developed and on account of its rapidity and simplicity should be familiar to all scouts. It is limited to visual signaling work and not adapted to general signaling as is the General Service Code. It will be found useful under many circumstances and is adapted to special work when rapid communication for short distances is needed. This method is also used to advantage for interior signaling.

The Semaphore hand flags for service use are 18 inches square divided diagonally into two parts, one of red and the other white; the staffs are 24 inches long.

Hand flags are used in the same manner as the Semaphore machine, except that in making the interval the flags are crossed downward in front of the body (just above the knees); end of message is three successive "chop-chop" signals, and withdrawing the flag from view. In calling a station face it squarely and make its call. If there is no immediate reply wave the flags over the head to attract attention, making the call at frequent intervals. When the sender makes "end of message" the receiver, if message is understood, extends the flags horizontally and waves them until the sender does the same, when both leave their stations. Care must be taken with hand flags to hold the staffs so as to form a prolongation of the arms.

Hints

A to D: Left arm at "Interval," right arm progresses upward.

E to G: Right arm at "Interval," left arm progresses downward.

A to G: Complete series one arm at "Interval."

K to N: Right arm inclined 45° downward, left arm progresses downward.

P to S: Right arm horizontal, left arm progresses downward.

H, I, and O: Left arm crosses the body.

W, X, and Z: Right arm crosses the body.

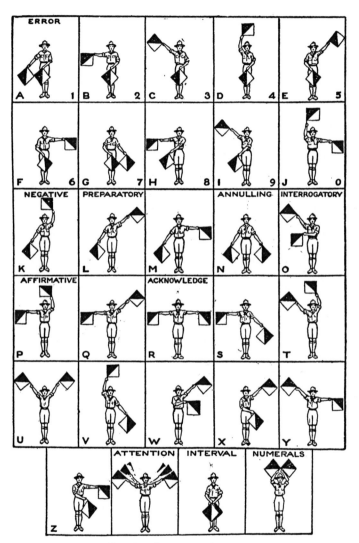

Two Arm Semaphore Code

Opposite letters: A and G, B and F, C and E, H and Z, I and X, J and P, K and V, O and W, M and S, and Q and Y.

"Numerals" precede every combination of numbers. After interval is made letters recur without further indication.

[FLAG SIGNALS BY PERMANENT HOIST
International Flag Code

The term "flag signals" or "flag code signals" as used upon the sea, applies to signals made by hoists of flags, and should not be confused with the use of the expression to indicate what is known as wigwag signals.

The International Code of Signals consists of 26 flags—one for each letter of the alphabet—and a code pennant. The flags are used in connection with the International Code Book of Signals. Explanation for the proper use of this code is given in the Code Book. Sets of International Code Flags, the International Code of Signals, and the Code List of American Vessels will be issued by the Signal Corps in cases only where the application therefor is approved by proper authority. Consult your Public Library for information.

SIGNALING WITH HELIOGRAPH,' FLASH LANTERN, OR SEARCHLIGHT (WITH SHUTTER)
General Service Code

The first position is to turn a steady flash on the receiving station. The signals are made by short and long flashes. Use a short flash for dot and a long, steady flash for dash. The elements of a letter should be slightly longer than in sound signals.

To call a station make its call letter until acknowledged.

If the call letter of a station be unknown, signal A until acknowledged. Each station will then turn a steady flash and adjust. When the adjustment is satisfactory to the called station, it will cut off its flash, and the calling station will proceed with its message.

If the receiver sees that the sender's mirror or light needs adjustment, he will turn on a steady flash until answered by a steady flash. When the adjustment is satisfactory the receiver will cut off his flash and the sender will resume his message.

To break the sending station for other purposes, turn on a steady flash.

NOTE: When it is desired to use one of the conventional signals in the interrogative sense, it must be followed by the signal of interrogation. Thus Q R Q alone means "Send faster," but when followed by the interrogation means "Shall I send faster?"

The Ardois System

The Ardois system is a display of four lights, usually electric, swinging from a staff, mast, or yard. These lights are manipulated by a keyboard placed at the station and marked with the appropriate signal letters or signs. The red lamp indicates a dot and the white lamp a dash. Four lamps are placed on a vertical staff and electrically illuminated to indicate dots and dashes which represent the letters of the alphabet. For instance, red-white, or dot-dash, represents the letter A, and white-red-red-red, or dash-dot-dot-dot, represents the letter B.

The lights are placed vertically and read from the top downward.

When the lamps are placed horizontally, they are read from the sender's right to his left, and consequently from the receiver's left to his right.

For numerals in the Ardois system secondary meanings (as numerals) have been assigned to the last ten letters, Q being 1, R being 2, and so on, Z being 0. When communicating with vessels the numerals of the International Morse Code must be spelled out in full.

When the letters of the alphabet are to be used to indicate the meaning set opposite them in the following tabulation, the upper light of the display is pulsated. This is effected by means of a special pulsating key.

In signaling by the Ardois system the Cornet W W W W is a general call to attention. A station desiring to exchange signals will display the call letters of the station wanted, which will be answered by a similar display from the station called, or from each station successively called.

If the call letters of a station be unknown, display the Cornet.

If it becomes necessary to put a signal message into cipher, the marking of the Ardois keyboard is on no account to be changed to accomplish this object.

COL I	COL II	COL III	COL IV	COL V	COL VI	COL VII	COL VIII
CHARACTER	INTERNATIONAL OR CONTINENTAL MORSE — WIG-WAG Sound, Flash, Sight, Wireless	AMERICAN MORSE — Land Telegraph Code	ARDOIS SYSTEM OF LIGHTS — Same as Col II, ● Red = Dot, ○ White = Dash	TWO ARM SEMAPHORE — MACHINE	TWO ARM SEMAPHORE — HAND FLAGS	INTERNATIONAL CODE OF SIGNAL FLAGS (MARINE) — White, Black, Red, Blue, Yellow	SECONDARY MEANING — Refer to Column indicated
A	·—	·—					NUMERAL 1 / ERROR / Cols V, VI
B	—···	—···					NUMERAL 2 / Col VI
C	—·—·	·· ··					NUMERAL 3 / Col VI
D	—··	—··					NUMERAL 4 / Col VI
E	·	·					NUMERAL 5 / Col VI
F	··—·	·—·					NUMERAL 6 / Col VI
G	——·	——·					NUMERAL 7 / Col VI
H	····	····					NUMERAL 8 / Col VI
I	··	··					NUMERAL 9 / Col VI
J	·———	—·—·					NUMERAL 0 / Col VI
K	—·—	—·—					NEGATIVE / Cols V VI
L	·—··	—					PREPARATORY / Cols V VI
M	——	——					

Comparative chart

Signaling systems

Numerals always preceded by "numerals follow" sign. When communicating with vessels numerals are always spelled out. Secondary meanings are the same for Col. V as for Col. VI.

THINGS TO REMEMBER WHEN SIGNALING
General Service Code

Each signal station will have its call, consisting of one or two letters, as Philadelphia, P; and each operator or signalist will also have his personal signal of one or two letters, as Jones, "Jo." These being once adopted will not be changed without due authority.

To acknowledge the receipt of a message, signal "R front" with flag, torch, hand lantern, and beam of searchlight (when similarly used) or "R" with flash signals, followed by the call letter of his station and the personal signal of the receiver.

In receiving messages nothing should be taken for granted, and nothing considered as seen until it has been positively and clearly in view. Do not anticipate what will follow from signals already given. Watch the communicating station until the last signals are made, and be very certain that the signal for the end of the message has been given. In reading messages, letters should be read as a whole and not by dot and dash, which is like counting on the fingers.

In receiving a message the scout at the telescope should call out each letter as received, and not wait for the completion of a word.

In reading it is important that the scout keep his attention fixed on the distant stations. There should be at least two scouts at each station, one to read or send and one to record or call off.

One of the best ways to practise signaling for second-class scouts is to have the troop count fours, then the odd numbers step two or three paces to the front, and all face halt right to follow the best-versed scout who acts as guide and is placed three paces in front.

The patrol can now wave the alphabet in unison as called for letter by letter, or in rotation; this makes a very pretty sight for exhibition if well done. With a larger number distance can be taken to the front No. 1—2—3—4 men stepping off together at two-pace intervals.

Try night signaling, using an old broom or bunch of oiled rags for a torch, or an ordinary hand lantern. In either case a foot light must be employed as a point of reference to the motions.

To use a stationary light, a lantern or Baldwin Lamp, the hat or a piece of paper may be passed back and forth in front of the light. A shutter of two or more pieces worked with a spring or rubber band to close it, and a button or key lever to open it, is much better and is readily constructed. Use a short flash for a dot and always a steady flash for a dash.

Try distance signaling—see how far apart signals can be read. Too often work is done indoors where the boys call back and forth.

For further information see Signal Book, United States Army, 1916, which can be obtained from the Superintendent of Documents, Government Printing Office, Washington, D. C. Price 20 cents.

ATTENTION

ATTENTION TO ORDERS.

FORWARD. MARCH.

HALT

DOUBLE TIME. MARCH.

TO THE REAR. MARCH

Wireless Telegraphy

The General Service Code is the universal standard for wireless telegraphy.

Many scout troops have developed this to a high degree.

The following conventional signals are used by radio stations:

Distress signal (ship stations only) ● ● ● ▬ ▬ ▬ ● ● ●

Attention (or call) The call is composed of the attention signal ▬ ● ▬ ● ▬ followed by the call letters of the station called, repeated three times (if unknown use C Q in place of call letters of station called), followed by D E and then the call letters of the calling station, repeated three times.

Invitation to transmit (go ahead) ▬ ● ▬

Signal separating preamble from address, address from text and text from signature ▬ ● ● ▬

End of message ● ▬ ● ▬ ●

End of work ● ● ● ▬ ● ▬ followed by the call letter of sending station and ▬ ● ▬

Received (acknowledgment of receipt of message) R followed by the call letter of the receiving station and personal signal of the receiving operator.

Here is another message ▬ ● ▬ ● ▬ (attention call)

Understood (or I understand) ● ● ● ▬ ● followed by the call letters of station.

Not understood (or repeat) ● ● ▬ ▬ ● ● (Interrogatory) and the last word received.

Error ● ● ● ● ● ● ● ●

Wait ● ▬ ● ● ●

Official (government) message O F M

(First word of preamble of all radiograms) R A D I O

Abbreviation	Question	Answer
Q R J	How many words have you to send?	I have —— words to send.
Q R K	How do you receive me?	I am receiving well.
Q R Q	Shall I send faster?	Send faster.
Q R S	Shall I send slower?	Send slower.
Q R T	Shall I stop sending?	Stop sending.
Q R U	Have you anything for me?	I have nothing for you.
X X	Interference	
C Q	General inquiry call (when call of station is unknown)	

The following is an example of the transmission of messages:

▬ ● ▬ ● ▬		Brown 175 King Street	Address
R A D I O		Circle City	
Circle City	Office of destination	▬ ● ● ●	Break
D E		Arrive to-morrow	Text
Fairbanks	Office of origin	▬ ● ● ●	Break
2	Number of message	Jones	Signature
L	Operator's sign	● ▬ ● ▬ ●	
8	Check	K M O	
Twelfth 4 P. M.	Date and hour of filing	▬ ● ▬	
▬ ● ● ● ▬	Break or double dash		

WIRELESS TELEGRAPHY APPARATUS

The Boy Scout Wireless Club
Y. M. C. A., Newark, N. J.

The following directions are given for a wireless apparatus for stationary use in the home or at the meeting place of each patrol.

We will consider the receiving apparatus first:

The first thing to do is to build an aerial. First find out how long your location will allow you to build it, and how high. It ought to be at least 50 to 60 feet high, and about 70 to 100 feet long. The main point in building an aerial is to have it

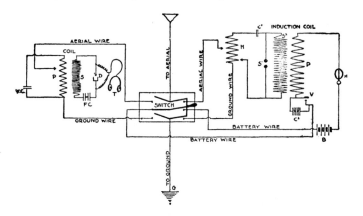

well insulated from the ground, and all connections in **wire** perfectly solid. It is advisable to solder every connection **and** to make your aerial strong as it has a great deal to do with the working qualities of the station.

After this is completed, the inside work on instruments should begin.

1. A pair of watch-case receivers having a resistance of 1000 ohms each, manufactured by a reliable firm.

2. A loose coupler tuning coil of about 800 meters.

3. A crystal or mineral detector of which there are several on the market.

4. A variable condenser of about 5–10 plates.

5. A fixed condenser so arranged that its capacity can be changed if desired.

With these instruments the receiving set is complete, so **we** **next** take up the sending apparatus.

1. A two-inch induction coil.
2. A heavy spark gap (zinc preferable).
3. One wireless key with heavy contacts.
4. A plate condenser which can be easily made by any scout. **Good glass is the main point.**
5. A triple pole, double throw erial switch. (Can be made by scouts.)

Now you have everything necessary to go ahead and assemble your station. The next thing is to connect them up.

Above is a diagram which will make a good station for a scout although it is not the only way to connect up the apparatus, as the scout will find out by experience. This station, if the aero is of the proper height, is capable of sending messages from 8 to 10 miles. Every scout desiring to operate a sending station should inquire and make himself familiar with the requirements of the Act of Congress, 1912, and other regulations requiring license for this purpose, and remember particularly that the wave-length for amateurs must **not** exceed 200 meters.

The Receiving Set

Perhaps the most fundamentally important part of a wireless telegraph station is the aerial. Its construction varies with each station, but a few general suggestions may be of use.

The builder should aim to get as high and as long an aerial as possible, height being the more important factor. In a stationary set the aerial may be fastened to a tree or pole or high building while in a field set a tree or an easily portable pole must be used.

The aerial itself should be made of copper wire and should be hung between spreaders as long as convenient, and insulated from them by two porcelain insulators in series at each end.

The experimenter should see that his leading-in wire is placed conveniently and comes in contact with the walls, etc., as little as possible. All points of contact must be well insulated with glass, porcelain, or hard rubber.

The tuning coil is very simple in construction. A cardboard tube about three inches in diameter is mounted between two square heads. This tube is wound with No. 24 insulated copper wire and very well shellacked to avoid loosening of the wire.

Two pieces of one-quarter inch square brass rod, to be fastened between the heads, are secured, and a slider, as shown in drawing, is made. The rods are fastened on the heads and the insulation in the path of the slides is then well scraped off. Binding posts are then fastened to rods and coil ends.

The detector, although the most important of the instruments, is perhaps the simplest. It is constructed of a hardwood base with a small brass plate fastened on by means of a binding post. On the other end of the base is fastened a double binding post which holds a brass spring, as in the drawing. On the end of this spring is fastened a copper point made by winding a

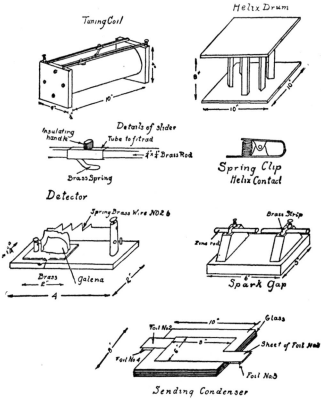

Details of instruments for field use

few inches of No. 36 or 40 wire on it and allowing about three sixteenths of an inch to project. This completes the detector, but for use in this instrument, lead sulphide or Galena crystals must be secured.

The condenser is made of two pieces of tin-foil, four by ten, and three pieces of waxed paper a little larger than the foil.

A piece of wire is twisted into the end of each piece of foil, and then one sheet of foil is laid on a sheet of paper. This is then covered by another sheet of paper upon which is laid the second sheet of foil. On top of this is laid the third sheet of paper, and the whole is folded into a convenient bundle. The sheets of foil must be well insulated from each other and the wires must project from the condenser.

The ground connection is made by soldering a wire to a cold-water pipe. In the case of a portable set the ground may be made by driving a metal rod into the ground or sinking metal netting into a body of water.

The telephone receivers cannot well be made and must therefore be bought. The type of 'phones used will therefore depend entirely on the builder's purse. The entire set can also be bought in many different forms at reasonable prices, and these will generally give better results than home-made apparatus.

The Sending Set

The same aerial and ground are used for sending as were used for receiving, and for the experimenter it will be far cheaper to buy a spark coil for his sending set than to attempt to make one.

For a field set there will be very little need of a sending helix, as close tuning will be hardly possible; but for the stationary set this is very useful.

The helix is made by building a drum with square heads fastened together by six or eight uprights, arranged on the circumference of a circle. On this then are wound ten or twelve turns of No. 10 or 12 brass or copper wire. Binding posts are fastened to the ends of the wire and variable contact made on the turns by means of metal spring clips.

The spark gap is made of a hardwood base with two uprights to which are fastened strips of brass. Under these strips are placed two pieces of battery zincs so as to make the gap between their ends variable. Binding posts are fastened to the strips for contact.

The sending condenser is the same as the receiving in construction, but different in material. The dielectric is glass, while the conducting surfaces are tin-foil, arranged in a pile of alternate sheets of glass and foil. The foil is shaped as in drawing and alternate sheets have their lugs projecting on opposite sides, all lugs on same side being connected together. For a one-inch coil but a few of these plates are needed, but for higher power a greater number are necessary.

All that now remains is the setting up of the instruments. They are arranged as in the drawing, a double-point, double-throw switch being used to switch from sending to receiving. Referring to the double-throw switch between the aerial and receiving and sending circuits, a modification may be made by which the aerial is connected to ground direct

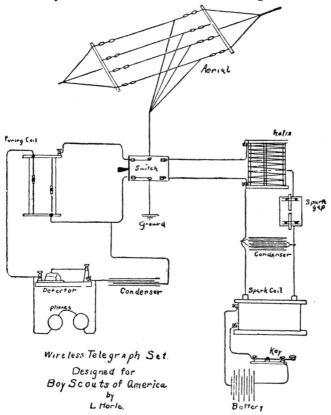

Wireless Telegraph Set.
Designed for
Boy Scouts of America
by
L. Horle.

during thunder storms or excessive static so as to protect the apparatus from lightning.

After having connected up the receiving instruments, the receiver is placed at the ear, and the point of the detector placed on the various parts of the mineral until the signals are heard clearly. Then the tuning coil is adjusted until the signals are loudest.

The sending apparatus is set up, the key and batteries having been bought or made, and used to call some other station. The clip is put on various turns of the helix until the other station signals that the signals are loudest. The station is then ready for actual operation.

Costs and Materials

As to costs, the following outline has been compiled for all the materials as used in the radio set described on pages 241-244, and as shown in the accompanying illustration of the fully constructed set.

A definite make of receivers is mentioned because so many amateurs are unsuccessful in radio work because they purchase poor receivers. This brand of 'phones are far superior to many of the same price, and the equal of almost any other.

Materials Cost List

1 ℔. No. 20 copper (DCC) wire. (Tuning coil)	$ .46
12 porcelain cleat insulators. (Aerial)	.18
1 ℔. No. 14 aluminum wire. (Aerial)	.48
1 double binding post. (Detector)	.12
10 single binding posts	1.00
Old brass	.15
2 ft. ¼-inch square brass rod. (Tuning coil)	.20
Tin-foil. (Condenser)	.10
Total (for material).....................................	$2.69
1 pair Brandes telephone receivers	5.00
Cost of complete receiving set	$7.69

CHAPTER VI

HEALTH AND ENDURANCE

George J. Fisher, M. D.
Secretary, Physical Department International Committee Young Men's Christian Association

Fitness

Two things greatly affect the conditions under which a boy lives in these days. One is that he lives indoors for the greater part of the time, and the other is that he must attend school, which is pretty largely a matter of sitting still. Two things, therefore, are needs of every boy: outdoor experience and physical activity.

To secure endurance, physical power, physical courage, and skill, the first thing needful is to take stock of one's physical make-up, put the body in the best possible condition for doing its work and then keep it in good order.

Proper Carriage

Walk with head up and chest raised is a good slogan for a boy scout who desires an erect figure. One can scarcely think of a round-shouldered scout. Yet there are such among the boys who desire to be scouts.

There is no particular exercise that a boy can take to cure round shoulders. The thing to remember is that all exercise that is taken should be done in the erect position, then the muscles will hold the body there.

An erect body means a deeper chest, room for the important organs to work, and thus affords them the best chance to act.

A few setting-up exercises each day in the erect position before breakfast will help greatly to get this result.

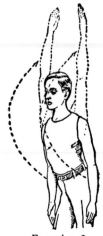

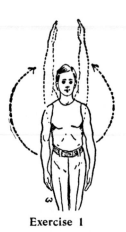

Exercise 1

Position: Heels together, arms down and at sides, palms in.
Movement: Swing arms sideways, upward to vertical, and return.

Exercise 2

Same as Exercise 1, except that arms are swung forward, upward to vertical.

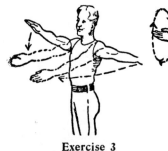

Exercise 3

Position: Arms extended to side horizontal.
Movement: Swing forward and return.
(Emphasis upon backward movement.)

Exercise 4

Position: Arms at side, horizontal, back slightly arched.
Movement: Circle arms backward.

Setting-up Exercises

Exercise 5

Position: Forearms flexed at side of chest.
Movement: Thrust arms forward and return.

Exercise 6

Position: Arms at front, horizontal, forearms flexed, fingers on shoulders.
Movement: Swing backward to side, horizontal in position.

Exercise 7

Position: Same as Exercise 6.
Movement: Swing downward, forward, bringing arms beyond sides of body. Rise on toes with end of backward swing.

Exercise 8a

Position: Arms at vertical, thumbs locked, head fixed between arms.

Exercise 8b

Movement: Bend forward as far as possible, without bending knees, and return.

Setting-up Exercises

Exercise 9a

Position: Arms at vertical.
Repeat exercise 8b

Exercise 9b

Movement: Arm circles, downward, inward, across chest. Reverse the movement.

Exercise 10

Position: Hands on hips.
Movement: Forward bend.

Exercise 11

Position: Same as Exercise 10.
Movement: Backward bend.

Exercise 12

Position: Same as Exercise 10.
Movement: Sideward bend, right and left.

Setting-up Exercises

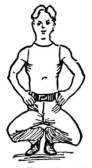

Exercise 13

Position: Same as Exercise 10.
Movement: Rotate body at waist.

Exercise 14

Position: Same as Exercise 10.
Movement: Raise high on toes. (Hold shoulders back firmly.)

Exercise 15

Position: Same as Exercise 10.
Movement: Full knee bend.

Setting-up Exercises

Growth

The chief business of a boy is to grow. He may have other affairs, but this is his chief concern. He should, therefore, have a few simple rules for living and make them a part of his daily life.

Outdoor Exercises

Each day should have its outdoor exercises. Walking is a splendid form of exercise. Walk to school or business; don't ride unless absolutely necessary because of unusual distance. Walk with a good, swinging stride with chest well up and spine fairly straight. Slow running across country is great; it lacks strain and yet affords splendid stimulation to heart and lungs. Cross-country running and hiking should be favorite sport for scout patrols and troops. A boy ought to have at least two hours of sport daily in some good, vigorous game, such as baseball or tennis, and, if he can possibly afford it, at least two periods a week, of an hour each, in a gymnasium, where he can receive guidance in body building. Boys under sixteen should avoid exercise of strain, such as weight lifting, or sprint running over one hundred yards, or long-distance racing. They should have careful guidance in all gymnastic work. Work on apparatus may prove harmful unless of the right sort. The horse and parallel bars should be used largely to jump over rather than perform upon. Exercises demanding a sustained support of the body with the arms are not helpful, but may be harmful. The chief activity should be of the legs, to strengthen heart and lungs. A boy should be careful not to overdo. In his excitement to win in a contest he is likely to do this unless cautioned. A boy should never try to reduce his weight. Now that there are weight classes in sports for boys there is a temptation to do this and it may prove very serious. Severe training for athletics should be avoided. Boys at this age should not play vigorous indoor games like basket ball for longer than two ten-minute halves, and should not play at all where the air is foul. All training should be in moderation.

Physical Examinations

Every boy ought to have, as he takes up his boy scout work, a thorough physical examination. Some physician who is interested in boys will be willing to act as examiner for a patrol or troop. A boy should know the condition of his heart and lungs before entering any contest. If he has any defects in his breathing apparatus — nose, throat, or lungs, these should be attended to or they will seriously interfere with his endurance tests.

Baths

Besides exercises a boy should have simple, workable rules for living. A boy ought to take a good soap bath at least twice a week and always after he has played a hard game or performed work of a nature that has caused him to perspire freely.

Each morning a quick sponge bath, immediately after the setting-up exercises, should be the first order of the day, in water as cool as he can stand it, followed by a good rub with a coarse towel. If there is a feeling of warmth after the bath, it is helpful, if not, the water should be slightly warm, or only a portion of the body should be bathed at a time.

Pain

One thing that should be regarded seriously is pain in any form in any part of the body. If there is a dull headache frequently, find out what causes it. Pain in the knee, the arch of the foot, or at any point, should be taken seriously. Pain means something wrong. It may be brave to bear it, but it is not wise. It may mean something serious. Remember that pain felt in one part of the body may be the result of something wrong in another part. See a wise doctor about it.

Eating

And now in reference to what one shall eat. The average boy ought to have and usually does have an appetite like an ostrich. Three points to remember are: don't eat too much, most healthy boys do; don't eat meat more than once a day; and, third, don't eat anything that you always taste for several hours after you have eaten it, even though you like it.

The fact that you taste it is an indication that your stomach is having a wrestling match with the food. Some people can't digest onions, others thrive upon them. Some can't eat cucumbers, others can do so readily. The one must give them up; the other can continue to eat them. Each person has some peculiarity of diet, and must observe it to be happy. Many a race has been lost through failure to obey this rule. A simple diet is best. Most boys eat too much of a mixed nature. They mix pickles, soda water, frankfurters, and chocolate without fear or favor. No wonder there is so much stomach ache. In boys' camps the chief trouble is indigestion caused by this riot of eating. Such boys are laying up for themselves for the future some beautiful headaches and bilious attacks, which, when they become chronic later, will cry out against them and seriously impair their value. Don't eat when very tired; lie down awhile and get rested. Don't eat heavily before exercising, or, better, put it the other way around, don't exercise immediately after eating. Never eat when excited or angry, and very lightly when worried or when expecting to study hard. We should learn to eat slowly and chew the food thoroughly, remembering that all food before it can be taken up in the blood must be as thin as pea soup. Chewing well will help digestive organs greatly. Always wash the hands before eating. Be careful about eating food that has been exposed to the dust unless it has been washed. Drink freely of clean water between meals. Never use a public drinking cup without thoroughly rinsing it. Don't touch your lips to the rim of the cup.

Boys who cook their own meals when in camp should be careful to have their food well done. Half-baked and soggy food proves indigestible.

Coffee and Tea

Should a boy drink coffee or tea? This is a question often asked by boys. Coffee and tea are the greatest stimulants known. But does a strong boy need a stimulant? What is a stimulant and what does it do? A stimulant is a whip, making the body do more at a given time than it ordinarily would. It doesn't add any fibre to the tissues, doesn't add any strength, isn't a food, but merely gets more out of the tissues or nervous system than they would ordinarily yield. Of course there is a reaction, because the tissues have had nothing to feed on. Herbert Fisher says that Peary's men, who drank lots of tea on their voyage north, during the most trying time of their trip, showed it in their haggard faces and loss of tissue. Their own tissues had turned cannibal and fed on their own material. Stimulants are not foods. They add no strength to the body. They exact of the body what ought not to be exacted of it. There is always a reaction and one is always worse off as a result. Growing boys especially should have nothing to do with tea, coffee, or any stimulant.

Alcohol and Tobacco

Alcohol is not a stimulant, but is really a narcotic that is very depressing. It dulls rather than stimulates. The same is true of nicotine in tobacco. No growing boy should use either. The first athletes to drop out of a race are usually drinkers, and all trainers know that smoking is bad for the wind.

Constipation

Those boys who find their digestion sluggish and are troubled with constipation may find the following plan helpful in over-coming the condition:

Drink a cool, copious draught of water upon arising. Then take some body-bending exercises. Follow this with the sponge bath. Then, if possible, take a walk around the block before breakfast. After school play some favorite game for at least an hour. In the absence of this, take a good hike of three or four miles or a longer bicycle ride. At least twice a week, if possible, enter a gymnasium class and make special emphasis of body-bending exercises.

Have a regular time for going to stool. A good plan is to go just before retiring and immediately upon arising. Go even though you feel no desire to do so. A regular habit may be established by this method. Always respond quickly to any call of nature. Toasted bread and graham bread and the coarser foods and fruit will be found helpful.

The Teeth

Closely related to the matter of eating is the proper care of the teeth.

Perhaps — without care — the mouth is the filthiest cavity of the body. We spend a great deal of energy trying to keep food clean and water pure, but what is the use if we place them in a dirty cavity as they enter the body? Full 90 per cent. of the children examined in our schools have decayed and dirty teeth. These decayed teeth provide cavities in which food particles decay and germs grow, and through which poisons are absorbed. These conditions need not exist. Now just a few suggestions about the care of the teeth. Every boy should own his own tooth brush. The teeth should be scrubbed at least twice a day. At night they should receive most careful cleansing, using a good tooth paste or powder. Then again in the morning they should be rinsed, at which time simply clean water is sufficient. Time should be taken in the cleansing of the teeth. The gums should be included in the scrubbing, as this acts as a good stimulant to the circulation of the blood to the teeth. Not only should the teeth be brushed with a backward and forward stroke, as we ordinarily do, but also upward and downward the length of the teeth. In addition to the scrubbing, particles of food which are lodged between the teeth should be removed after meals, or at least after the last meal of the day. This is most safely done by the use of a thread of a fair degree of thickness. Dentists and druggists furnish this thread in spools. Hard toothpicks often cause bleeding and detach fillings. A dentist should be visited once every six months so as to detect decay immediately. Never have a tooth drawn unless absolutely necessary.

Care of the Eyes

Most troubles with the eyes come from eye strain. Styes and red lids are usually due to this cause. See how foolish, therefore, it is to treat these conditions as causes, when really they are only the result of something else. Of course there are exceptions. Sometimes wild hairs and skin disease affect the eyes. Eye strain should be removed by wearing well-fitting glasses and then these other conditions will disappear. If constant headache is experienced or the eyes itch or become tired easily, there is possibly eye strain.

One way to test the eye is for vision. If you cannot read the first line at 20 feet, the second line at 15 feet, and the third line at 10 feet clearly with both eyes and with each eye separately, consult a first-class oculist.

C L V F O T

E A C F D L O T

D V C L A E O T F

᛫Never buy eye-glasses unless fitted by an expert. Such glasses should be worn in proper relation to the eyes. They should not be permitted to slide forward on the nose or tilt. They may need to be changed often as the eyes grow better.᛫

For reading, a good, steady light is needed. Never sit in front of a window facing it to read. Always have the light come from the rear and over the left shoulder preferably. The book should be held on a level with the face and not too close Sit

erect. Reading when lying down or from the light of a fireplace is unwise.

Care of the Ears

Affections of the ears are exceedingly serious and may lead to grave results. Any trouble with them should be given very prompt attention and a good specialist consulted. Pain in the ear, or ringing or hissing sounds, and particularly any discharge f om the ear, should not be neglected. Any sign of deafness must be heeded. Sometimes deafness occurs in reference to some particular sounds while hearing is normal to others. No matter what the degree of deafness may be, do not neglect to see a physician about it. Ordinarily the tick of a watch can be heard at a distance of thirty inches. If you cannot hear it at that distance and can hear it say at fifteen inches then you are just one half from the normal in your hearing. The test should be made with one ear closed.

Ear troubles are often caused by sticking foreign objects in the ear, such as hair pins, pins, matches, toothpicks, and lead pencils. Never pick the ear with anything. Often the ear drum is pierced in this way. The normal ear does not require anything more than the usual cleansing with the wash rag over the end of the finger.

If wax to any extent accumulates in the ear it should be removed by syringing, but ought to be done by a physician.

In camp an insect might crawl into the ear and if alive cause pain. Putting oil or other fluids in the ear to drown it is unwise. If a foreign body should get in the ear it should not cause great alarm unless attended with severe pain. If a physician is not available at once such objects may remain for a day or two without serious results. Syringing usually removes them, but it should be remembered that some objects like peas or beans swell if made wet. In swimming water is apt to get into the ear and cause annoyance. A rubber ear stop can be secured and placed in the ear at the time of swimming, thus keeping the water out. Cotton should not be stuffed into the ear to keep water out, as it may get inside.

One thing to keep in mind is that catarrh of the nose and throat often extends into the ear passages through a tube which reaches from the throat to the ear and that syringing of the nose and throat frequently causes trouble in the ear.

Care of Nose and Throat

Always breathe through the nose. Air passing through the nose is warmed and moistened and cleansed; thus it gets to the lungs in a better condition. If you cannot breathe clearly through the nose, have it examined. There may be a growth present which needs to be removed. To become a good runner this is important. Adenoids, which are growths far back in the mouth, often interfere with nose breathing and are serious in other ways. Don't stick anything in the nose; and nose picking is not cleanly. If crusts form in the nose, use a little vaseline to soften them. Don't blow the nose too vigorously. It may cause trouble.

Frequent sore throat may be due to enlarged tonsils which either need treatment or removal. To one who has frequent colds in the head, the out-of-door life and morning sponge bath and moderate eating will be of help.

Care of the Feet

This is an important matter with scouts, as they will make frequent hikes and tramps. The first thing to do is to walk right. The straight foot is the normal foot. The normal foot is broad at the ball with space between the toes. How different from the awful feet we see with toes twisted upon each other and crowded together. Walk with feet pointing straight forward. The feet that turn outward are weak feet. Shoes therefore should be straight on the inner border, broad across the ball, and have a low, broad heel.

When a foot is normal, the inner border does not touch the floor. By wetting the foot one can see readily whether he is flat-footed by the imprint made. The following exercises are good to strengthen the arches of the foot if there is a tendency to flat feet: (1) Turn toes in, raise the heels, and come down slowly on the outer borders of the feet; (2) Walk with heels raised and toes pointing inward, or walk on the outer borders of the foot, inner borders turned up.

Shoes should fit the feet comfortably. Tight shoes, or shoes that fit loosely, will cause callouses or corns. The way to get rid of these is to remove the cause — namely, the badly fitting shoes. Soft corns are due to pressure between the toes. The toes in such cases should be kept apart with cotton. Pointed shoes should be avoided. Patent-leather shoes are non-porous and hot. Ingrown toe nails are exceedingly painful. The pain comes from the nail piercing the soft parts. Allowing the nail to grow long and beyond the point of the tender spot will help;

and on the side of the nail and under it cotton should be inserted to protect the soft parts.

Hot foot baths will generally relieve tired feet. Boys should be very careful in trimming corns for fear of blood poisoning. Never buy plates at a store for flat feet. They may not be adapted to your needs. Always consult a foot specialist for treatment and buy plates if needed on his order. Only severe cases need plates.

Many boys are troubled with perspiring feet and are frequently annoyed by the odor resulting. Those who are thus troubled should wash the feet often and carefully, especially between the toes. By dusting the feet with boric acid the odor will disappear. At first it may be necessary to change the stockings daily. In severe cases two pairs of shoes should be used, changing alternately.

Care of the Finger Nails

The chief thing in the care of the finger nails is to keep them clean. Each boy should possess and use a nail brush. Always wash the hands thoroughly before eating, and use the end of a nail file to remove the accumulation still remaining under the nails. Keep the nails properly trimmed. They should not be too long nor too short. If long they are liable to break and if short to be sensitive. Biting the nails is a filthy practice and mutilates the fingers dreadfully and makes them unsightly. It is a very hard habit to overcome ofttimes and will require persistent effort in order to succeed. By keeping the nails smooth the tendency to bite them will to some extent be overcome. A bitter application to the nails will often remind one of the habit, as often the biting is done unconsciously. The nails should never be pared with a knife; a curved pair of scissors is better, as the cutting should be done in a curved direction; but the best method is to use a file. The skin overhanging the nails should be pressed back once a week to keep them shapely. Rubbing the nails with a nail buffer or cloth will keep them polished.

Sleep

One thing a growing boy wants to be long on is sleep, and yet he is most apt to be careless about it. It is during sleep that a boy grows most and catches up. During his waking hours he tears down and burns up more tissue than he builds. Good, sound, and sufficient sleep is essential to growth, strength, and endurance. A boy scout should have at least nine or ten hours' sleep out of every twenty-four. If you lose on this amount on one day, make it up the next. Whenever unusually tired, or when you feel out of trim, stay in bed a few hours more if it is possible. A boy should wake up each morning feeling like a fighting cock. When he doesn't he ought to get to bed earlier that night. Sleep is a wonderful restorative and tonic. It helps to store up energy and conserve strength.

Sleeping Out of Doors

The conditions under which one sleeps are as important as the length of time one sleeps. Many people are finding it wonderfully helpful and invigorating to sleep out of doors. Often a back porch can be arranged, or, in summer, a tent can be pitched in the yard. But, by all means, the sleeping room should be well ventilated. Windows should be thrown wide open. Avoid drafts. If the bed is in such relation to the windows as to cause the wind to blow directly on it, a screen can be used to divert it or a sheet hung up as protection. Good, fresh, cool air is a splendid tonic. In winter open windows are a splendid preparation for camping out in summer.

Conservation

In this chapter much has been said of the active measures which a boy should take in order to become strong and well. We should be equally concerned in saving and storing up natural forces we already have. In the body of every boy who has reached his teens, the Creator of the universe has sown a very important fluid. This fluid is the most wonderful material in all the physical world. Some parts of it find their way into the blood, and through the blood give tone to the muscles, power to the brain, and strength to the nerves. This fluid is the sex fluid. When this fluid appears in a boy's body, it works a wonderful change in him. His chest deepens, his shoulders broaden, his voice changes, his ideals are changed and enlarged. It gives him the capacity for deep feeling, for rich emotion. Pity the boy, therefore, who has wrong ideas of this important function, because they will lower his ideals of life. These organs actually secrete into the blood material that makes a boy manly, strong, and noble. Any habit which a boy has that causes this fluid to be discharged from the body tends to weaken his strength, to make him less able to resist disease, and often unfortunately fastens upon him habits which later in life can be broken only with great difficulty. Even several years before this fluid appears in the body such habits are harmful to a growing boy.

To become strong, therefore, one must be pure in thought and clean in habit. This power which I have spoken of must be conserved, because this sex function is so deep and strong that there will come times when temptation to wrong habits will be very powerful. But remember that to yield means to sacrifice strength and power and manliness.

For boys who desire to know more of this subject we would suggest a splendid book by Dr. Winfield S. Hall, entitled, "From Youth into Manhood." Every boy in his teens who wants to know the secret of strength, power, and endurance should read this book.

CHAPTER VII
CHIVALRY

By John L. Alexander

Ancient Knighthood

A little over fifteen hundred years ago the great order of knighthood and chivalry was founded. The reason for this was the feeling on the part of the best men of that day that it was the duty of the stronger to help the weak. These were the days when might was right, and the man with the strongest arm did as he pleased, often oppressing the poor and riding rough shod without any regard over the feelings and affections of others. In revolt against this, there sprang up all over Europe a noble and useful order of men who called themselves knights. Among these great-hearted men were Arthur, Gareth, Lancelot, Bedivere, and Alfred the Great. The desire of these men was "To live pure, speak true, right wrong, follow the king." Of course in these days there also lived men who called themselves knights, but who had none of the desire for service that inspired Arthur and the others. These false knights, who cared for no one but themselves and their own pleasure, often brought great sorrow to the common people. Chivalry then was a revolt against their brutal acts and ignorance, and a protest against the continuation of the idea that might was right.

Ancient knight

Nowhere in all the stories that have come down to us have the acts of chivalry been so well told as in the tales of the Round Table. Here it was that King Arthur gathered about him men like Sir Bors, Sir Gawaine, Sir Pellias, Sir Geraint, Sir Tristram, Sir Lancelot, and Sir Galahad. These men, moved by the desire of giving themselves in service, cleared the forests of wild animals, suppressed the robber barons, punished the outlaws, bullies, and thieves of their day, and enforced wherever they went a proper respect for women. It was for this great service that they trained themselves, passing through the degrees of page, esquire, and knight with all the hard work that each of these meant in order that they might the better do their duty to their God and country

Struggle for Freedom

Of course this struggle of right against wrong was not confined to the days in which chivalry was born. The founding of the order of knighthood was merely the beginning of the age-long struggle to make right the ruling thought of life. Long after knighthood had passed away the struggle continued. In the birth of the modern nations, England, Germany, France, and others, there was the distinct feeling on the part of the best men of these nations that might should and must give way to right, and that tyranny must yield to the spirit of freedom. The great struggle of the English barons under King John and the wresting from the king of the Magna Charta, which became the basis of English liberty, was merely another development of the idea for which chivalry stood. The protest of the French Revolution, and the terrible doings of the common people in these days, although wicked and brutal in method, were symptoms of the same revolt against oppression.

Pilgrim father

The Pilgrim Fathers

When the Pilgrim Fathers founded the American colonies, the work of Arthur and Alfred and the other great men of ancient days was renewed and extended and fitted to the new conditions and times. With the English settlements of Raleigh and Captain John Smith we might almost say that a new race of men was born and a new kind of knight was developed. All over America an idea made itself felt that in the eyes of the law every man should be considered just as good as every other man, and that every man ought to have a fair and square chance at all the good things that were to be had in a land of plenty. It was this spirit that compelled the colonists to seek their independence and that found its way into our Declaration of Independence as follows:

We hold these truths to be self-evident: that all men are created equal; that they are endowed by their Creator with certain inalienable rights; that among these are life, liberty, and the pursuit of happiness.

The fight of the colonists was the old-time fight of the knights against the oppression and injustice and the might that dared to call·itself right.

American Pioneers

No set of men, however, showed this spirit of chivalry more than our pioneers beyond the Alleghenies. In their work and service they paralleled very closely the knights of the Round Table, but whereas Arthur's knights were dressed in suits of armor, the American pioneers were dressed in buckskin. They did, however, the very same things which ancient chivalry had done, clearing the forests of wild animals, suppressing the outlaws and bullies and thieves of their day, and enforcing a proper respect for women. Like the old knights they often were compelled to do their work amid scenes of great bloodshed, although they loved to live in peace. These American knights and pioneers were generally termed backwoodsmen and scouts, and were men of distinguished appearance, of athletic build, of high moral character, and frequently of firm religious convictions.   Such men as "Apple-seed Johnny," Daniel Boone, George Rogers Clark, Simon Kenton and John James Audubon, are the types of men these pioneers were.

Pioneer

They were noted for their staunch qualities of character. They hated dishonesty and were truthful and brave. They were polite to women and old people, ever ready to rescue a companion when in danger, and equally ready to risk their lives for a stranger. They were very hospitable, dividing their last crust with one another, or with the stranger whom they happened to meet. They were ever ready to do an act of kindness. They were exceedingly simple in their dress and habits. They fought the Indians, not because they wished to, but because it was necessary to protect their wives and children from the raids of the savages. They knew all the things that scouts ought to know. They were acquainted with the woods and the fields; knew where the best fish were to be caught; understood the trees, the signs, and blazes, the haunts of animals and how to track them; how to find their way by the stars; how to make themselves comfortable in the heart of the primeval forest; and such other things as are classed under the general term of woodcraft. And, with all this, they inherited the splendid ideas of chivalry that had been developed in the thousand years preceding them, and fitted these ideas to the conditions of their own day, standing solidly against evil and falsehood whenever they lifted their head among them. They were not perfect, but they did their best to be of service to those who came within their reach and worked conscientiously for their country.

Modern Knighthood

A hundred years have passed since then, and the conditions of life which existed west of the Alleghenies are no more. Just as the life of the pioneers was different from that of the knights of the Round Table, and as they each practised chivalry in keeping with their own surroundings, so the life of to-day is different from both, but the need of chivalry is very much the same. Might still tries to make right, and while there are now no robber barons or outlaws with swords and spears, their spirit is not unknown in business and commercial life. Vice and dishonesty lift their heads just as strongly to-day as in the past, and there is just as much need of respect for women and girls as there ever was. So to-day there is a

Modern knight demand for a modern type of chivalry. It is

for this reason that the Boy Scouts of America have come into being; for there is need of service in these days, and that is represented by the good turn done to somebody every day.   Doing the good turn daily will help to form the habit of useful service. A boy scout, then, while living in modern times, must consider himself the heir of ancient chivalry and of the pioneers, and he must for this reason give himself to ever-renewed efforts to be true to the traditions which have been handed down to him by these great and good leaders of men.   The boy scout movement is a call to American boys to-day to become in spirit members of the order of chivalry, and a challenge to them to make their lives count in the communities in which they live — for clean lives, clean speech, clean sport, clean habits, and clean relationships with others.   It is also a challenge for them to stand for the right against the wrong, for truth against falsehood, to help the weak and oppressed, and to love and seek the best things of life.

Abraham Lincoln

Perhaps there is no better example of chivalry than the life and experience of Abraham Lincoln, the greatest of all our American men.   Every boy ought to read the story of his life and come to understand and appreciate what it means.   Lincoln was born in the back-woods of Kentucky.   He was a tall, spare man of awkward build, and knew very little of the school-room as a boy. He fought for his education. He borrowed books wherever he could.   Many long nights were spent by him before the flickering lights of the log cabin, gleaning from his borrowed treasures the knowledge he longed to possess.   He passed through all the experiences of life that other scouts and pioneers have experienced.   He split rails for a livelihood, and fought his way upward by hard work, finally achiev-

ing for himself an education in the law, becoming an advo-
cate in the courts of Illinois. Wherever he went, he made a
profound impression on the lives and minds of the people, and
won over his political opponents by his strength, sympathy,
and breadth of mind. At the period when storms threatened
to engulf our Ship of State, he became President of our country.
Although Lincoln was an untried pilot, he stood by the helm
like a veteran master. A man of earnest and intense con-
viction, he strove to maintain the glory of our flag and to

keep the Union un-
broken. Hundreds of
stories are told of his
great heart and al-
most boundless sym-
pathy for others.
The generals of the
Civil War were
deeply attached to
him, and the rank
and file of the sol-
diers who fought under
these generals loved
and revered him. He
was familiarly known
as "Honest Abe."
He could always be
relied upon to give
help and encourage-
ment. His smile
cheered the defenders

Using every opportunity

of the Union, and his wise counsel gave heart to the men who
were helping him to shape the destinies of the nation. At the
close of the war which saw the Union more firmly established
than ever, he fell by the hand of the assassin, mourned deeply
both by his own country and by the world at large.

The further we get from the scene of his life and work the
more firmly are we, his countrymen, convinced of his sincerity,
strength, wisdom, and bigness of heart. The two men who
stand out preëminently in history among great Americans are
Washington and Lincoln, the former as the founder of the Union,
and the latter as the man who gave it unbreakable continuity
and preserved it, as we hope and believe, for all time.

Lincoln's life and career should be the study and inspiration
of every boy scout. He became familiar with all of the things

for which the Boy Scouts of America stand. He was a lover of the wild things in the woods, and loved and lived the life of the out of doors. He had a high sense of honor and was intensely chivalrous, as the many hundred stories told about him testify. He did many times more than one good turn a day; he sincerely loved his country; he lived, fought, and worked for it; and finally he sealed his loyalty by giving his life. The path that he traveled from the log cabin to the White House clearly shows that an American boy who has well-defined ideas of truth and right, and then dares to stand by them, can become great in the councils of the nation. The life, then, of Abraham Lincoln should be a steady inspiration to every boy who wishes to call himself a scout.

Challenge of the Present

Thus we see that chivalry is not a virtue that had its beginning long ago and merely lived a short time, becoming a mere story. Chivalry began in the far-distant past out of the desire to help others, and the knights of the olden days did this as best they could. Later the new race of men in America took up the burden of chivalry, and did the best they could. Now the privilege and responsibility comes to the boys of to-day, and the voices of the knights of the olden time and of the hardy pioneers of our own country are urging the boys of to-day to do the right thing, in a gentlemanly way, for the sake of those about them. All of those men, whether knights or pioneers, had an unwritten code, somewhat like our scout law, and their motto was very much like the motto of the boy scouts, "*Be Prepared.*"

Politeness

Good Manners

The same thing that entered into the training of these men, knights, pioneers, and Lincoln, then, must enter into the training of the boy scouts of to-day. Just as they respected women and served them, so the tenderfoot and the scout must be polite and kind to women, not merely to well-dressed women, but to poorly dressed women; not merely to young women, but to old women: to women wherever they may be found — wherever they may be. To these a scout must always be courteous and helpful.

When a scout is walking with a lady or a child, he should always walk on the outside of the sidewalk, so that he can better protect them against the jostling crowds. This rule is only altered when crossing the street, when the scout should get between the lady and the traffic, so as to shield her from accident or mud. Also in meeting a woman or child, a scout, as a matter of course, should always make way for them even if he himself has to step off the sidewalk into the mud. When riding in a street car or train a scout should never allow a woman, an elderly person, or a child to stand, but will offer his seat; and when he does it he should do it cheerfully and with a smile.

When on the street, be continually on a quest, on the lookout to help others, and always refuse any reward for the effort. This kind of courtesy and good manners is essential to success. It was this unselfish desire to protect and help that made these men of olden time such splendid fellows.

Good manners attract and please, and should be cultivated by every boy who expects to win success and make his life interesting to others. In the home, on the street, in the school, in the workshop or the office, or wherever one may be, his relationship to others should be characterized as gentle, courteous, polite, considerate, and thoughtful. These are virtues and graces that make life easier and pleasanter for all.

Cheerfulness

As has been said, whatever a scout does should be done with cheerfulness, and the duty of always being cheerful cannot be emphasized too much.

Why don't you laugh, and make us all laugh, too,
And keep us mortals all from getting blue?
A laugh will always win.
If you can't laugh — just grin.
Go on! Let's all join in!
Why don't you laugh?

Benjamin Franklin said: "Money never yet made a man happy, and there is nothing in its nature to produce happiness. One's personal enjoyment is a very small thing, but one's personal usefulness is a very important thing." Those only are happy who have their minds fixed upon some object other and higher than their own happiness. Doctor Raffles once said, "I have made it a rule never to be with a person ten minutes without trying to make him happier." A boy once said to his mother, "I couldn't make little sister happy, nohow I could fix it, but I made myself happy trying to make her happy."

There was once a king who had a tall, handsome son whom he loved with his whole heart, so he gave him everything that his heart desired — a pony to ride, beautiful rooms to live in, picture books, stories, and everything that money could buy. And yet, in spite of this, the young prince was unhappy and wore a wry face and a frown wherever he went, and was always wishing for something he did not have. By and by, a magician came to the court, and seeing a frown on the prince's face, said to the king, "I can make your boy happy and turn his frown into a smile, but you must pay me a very large price for the secret." "All right," said the king, "whatever you ask, I will do." So the magician took the boy into a private room, and with white liquid wrote something on a piece of paper; then he gave the boy a candle and told him to warm the paper and read what was written. The prince did as he was told. The white letters turned into letters of blue, and he read these words: "Do a kindness to some one every day." So the prince followed the magi-

Cheer up
A scout is cheerful
He smiles whenever he can

cian's advice and became the happiest boy in all the king's realm.

To be a good scout one must remain cheerful under every circumstance, bearing both fortune and misfortune with a smile.

Character

If a scout is cheerful, follows the advice of the magician to the king's son, and does a good turn to some one every day, he will come into possession of a strong character such as the knights of the Round Table had; for, after all, character is the thing that distinguishes a good scout from a bad one. Character is not what men say about you. A great writer once said, "I can't hear what you say for what you are," and another one said, "Your life speaks louder than your words." It was not the words of the knights of old that told what they were. It was their strong life and fine character that gave power to their words and the thrust to their spears.

It is necessary that a boy should live right and possess such a character as will help him to do the hardest things of life. Every boy should remember that he is in reality just what he is when alone in the dark. The great quests of the knights were most often done singly and alone.

Will

Another thing that entered into the make-up of a knight was an iron will. He had staying powers because he willed to stick; and the way he trained his will to do the hard things was to keep himself doing the small things. Not long ago there was a lad whom the boys nicknamed "Blockey" and "Wooden Man." When they played ball in the school playground Blockey never caught the ball. When they worked together in the gymnasium Blockey was always left out of the game because he couldn't do things, and was slow and unwieldy in his motions. But one day a great change came over Blockey and he began to train his will. He worked hard in the gymnasium: he learned to catch the ball, and, by sticking to it, was not only able to catch the ball but became proficient. Then there came a time when the first one chosen upon the team was Blockey; and it all came about because he had trained his will so that when he made up his mind to do a thing, *he did it.*

Thrift

Another thing which entered into the training of a knight was his readiness to seize his opportunities. The motto of the scout is "*Be prepared.*" He should be prepared for whatever opportunity presents itself. An interesting story is told by Orison Swett Marden. He says that a lad, who later became one of the millionaires of one of our great Western cities, began his earning career by taking advantage of an opportunity that came to him as he was passing an auction shop. He saw several boxes of a kind of soap which his mother was accustomed to buy from the family grocer. Hastening to the grocery store, he asked the price of the soap. "Twelve cents a pound" was the reply. On being pressed for a lower figure, the shopkeeper remarked in a bantering tone that he would buy all that the boy could bring to his store at nine cents a pound. The boy hurried back to the auction and bought the soap at six cents a pound. It was in this way that he made his first money in trade and laid the foundation of his fortune.

The knight never waited for opportunity to come to him. He went out looking for it, and wore his armor in order that he might be ready for it when it came. There is a story of a Greek god who had only one lock of hair upon his forehead. The remainder of his head was shining bald. In order to get this ancient god's attention it was necessary to grip him by his forelock, for when he had passed, nothing could check his speed. So it is with opportunity, and the hour of opportunity. A good scout is ready for both and always grips "time by the forelock."

Individuality

If the foregoing qualities enter into a scout's training an individuality will be developed in him, which will make itself known and felt.

Every scout should read over the following list of scout virtues, and should strive at all times to keep them before him in his training, thus making them a part of his life:

Unselfishness: The art of thinking of others first and one's self afterward.

Self Sacrifice: The giving up of one's comfort, desires, and pleasures for the benefit of some one else.

Kindness: The habit of thinking well of others and doing good to them.

Friendliness: The disposition to make every one you meet feel at ease, and to be of service to him if possible.

Honesty: The desire to give to every one a square deal and the same fair chance that you yourself wish to enjoy. It means also respect for the property and rights of others, the ability to face the truth, and to call your own faults by their right name.

Fair Play: Scorning to take unfair advantage of a rival and readiness even to give up an advantage to him.

Loyalty: The quality of remaining true and faithful not only to your principles but also to your parents and friends.

Obedience: Compliance with the wishes of parents or those in places of authority.

Discipline: That self-restraint and self-control that keep a boy steady, and help him in team work.

Endurance: A manly moderation which keeps a boy fit and strong and in good condition.

Self Improvement: The ambition to get on in life by all fair means.

Humility: That fine quality which keeps a scout from boasting, and which generally reveals a boy of courage and achievement.

Honor: That great thing which is more sacred than anything else to scouts and gentlemen; the disdain of telling or implying an untruth; absolute trustworthiness and faithfulness.

Duty to God: That greatest of all things, which keeps a boy faithful to his principles and true to his friends and comrades;

Scout protecting child from mad dog

that gives him a belief in things that are high and noble, and which makes him prove his belief by doing his good turn to some one every day.

This list of virtues a scout must have, and if there are any that stand out more prominently than the others, they are the following:

Courage

It is horrible to be a coward. It is weak to yield to fear and heroic to face danger without flinching. The old Indian who had been mortally wounded faced death with a grim smile on his lips and sang his own death song. The soldier of the

Roman legions laughed in the face of death, and died with a "Hail, Imperator!" for the Roman Cæsar upon his lips.

One of the stories connected with the battle of Agincourt tells us that four fair ladies had sent their knightly lovers into battle. One of these was killed. Another was made prisoner. The third was lost in the battle and never heard of afterward. The fourth was safe, but owed his safety to shameful flight. "Ah! woe is me," said the lady of this base knight, "for having placed my affections on a coward. He would have been dear to me dead. But alive he is my reproach."

A scout must be as courageous as any knight of old or any Roman soldier or any dying Indian.

Loyalty

Loyalty is another scout virtue which must stand out prominently, because it is that which makes him true to his home, his parents, and his country. Charles VIII, at the Battle of Foronovo, picked out nine of his bravest officers and gave to each of them a complete suit of armor, which was a counterpart of his own. By this device he outwitted a group of his enemies who had leagued themselves to kill him during the fight. They sought him through all the ranks, and every time they met one of these officers they thought they had come face to face with the king. The fact that these officers hailed such a dangerous honor with delight and devotion is a striking illustration of their loyalty.

The scout should be no less loyal to his parents, home, and country.

Duty to God

No scout can ever hope to amount to much until he has learned a reverence for religion. The scout should believe in God and God's word. In the olden days, knighthood, when it was bestowed, was a religious ceremony, and a knight not only considered himself a servant of the king, but also a servant of God. The entire night preceding the day upon which the young esquire was made knight was spent by him on his knees in prayer in a fast and vigil.

There are many kinds of religion in the world. One important point, however, about them is that they all involve the worship of the same God. There is but one leader, although many ways of following Him. If a scout meets one of another religion, he should remember that he, too, is striving for the best.

A scout should respect the convictions of others in matters of custom and religion.

A Boy Scout's Religion

The Boy Scouts of America maintain that no boy can grow into the best kind of citizenship without recognizing his obligation to God. The first part of the boy scout's oath or pledge is therefore: "I promise on my honor to do my best to honor my God and my country." The recognition of God as the ruling and leading power in the universe, and the grateful acknowledgment of His favors and blessings, is necessary to the best type of citizenship, and is a wholesome thing in the education of the growing boy. No matter what the boy may be — Catholic or Protestant, or Jew — this fundamental need of good citizenship should be kept before him. The Boy Scouts of America therefore recognize the religious element in the training of a boy, but it is absolutely non-sectarian in its attitude toward that religious training. Its policy is that the organization or institution with which the boy scout is connected shall give definite

Scout helping old lady across street

attention to his religious life. If he be a Catholic boy scout, the Catholic Church of which he is a member is the best channel for his training. If he be a Hebrew boy, then the Synagogue will train him in the faith of his fathers. If he be a Protestant, no matter to what denomination of Protestantism he may belong, the church of which he is an adherent or a member should be the proper organization to give him an education in the things that pertain to his allegiance to God. The Boy Scouts of America, then, while recognizing the fact that the boy should be taught the things that pertain to religion, insists upon the boy's religious life being stimulated and fostered by the institution with which he is connected. Of course, it is a fundamental principle of the Boy Scouts of America to insist on clear, capable leadership in its scout masters, and the influence of the leader on the boy scout should be of a distinctly helpful character.

Work, Not Luck

Life, after all, is just this: Some go through life trusting to luck. They are not worthy to be scouts. Others go through life trusting to hard work and clear thinking. These are they who have cleared the wilderness and planted wheat where forests once grew, who have driven back the savage, and have fostered civilization in the uncultivated places of the earth. The good scout is always at work — working to improve himself and to improve the daily lot of others.

The thing that is to be noticed in all of these men, those of the Round Table, and those of American pioneer days, is the fact that they were ever ready to do a good turn to some one. The knights of the Round Table did theirs by clash of arms, by the jousts and the tourney, and by the fierce hand-to-hand fights that were their delight in open battle. The old scouts, our own pioneers, very often had to use the rifle and the hatchet and the implements of war. However, those days have passed, and we are living in a non-military and peace-loving age; and the glory of it is that, whereas these men took their lives in their hands, and by dint of rifle and sword did their part in helping others, our modern civilization gives the Boy Scouts of America an opportunity to go out and do their good turn daily for others in the thousand ways that will benefit our American life the most. Sometimes they will have to risk their lives, but it will be in case of fire or accident or catastrophe. At other times they will be given the privilege of showing simple deeds of chivalry by their courteous treatment of their elders, cripples, and children, by giving up their seats in street cars, or by carrying the bundles of those who are not as physically strong as themselves. And in it all will come the satisfying feeling that they are doing just as much and perhaps a great deal more than the iron-clad men or the buckskin clothes scouts in making their country a little safer and a little better place to live in. Chivalry and courtesy and being a gentleman mean just as much now as they ever did, and there is a greater demand in these days to live pure, to speak true, and to help others by a good turn daily than ever before in the world's history.

CHAPTER VIII

PREVENTION OF ACCIDENTS, FIRST AID, AND LIFE SAVING

Prepared by the National Safety Council and Major Charles Lynch, Medical Corps, U. S. A., acting for the American Red Cross

Carelessness

More powerful than the combined armies of the universe.

More destructive than all wars of the world.

More deadly than the mightiest of siege guns.

Relentless everywhere: in the home, on the street, in the school and factory, at railroad crossings, on the sea.

Lurking in unseen places, working silently.

Scattering sickness, degradation, and death.

Sparing none: rich nor poor; young or old; strong or weak.

Massacring thousands upon thousands of children and wage earners each year.

Wasting over $300,000,000 annually in the United States.

General

Over two million accidents occur annually, with the great loss and suffering which follows. More than 50 per cent. of these accidents are unnecessary. Census reports give the following statistics for one year:

Deaths by poisoning 2,110
Deaths by fire 5,884
Deaths by gas . . . . 2,271.
Deaths by drowning 7,036
Deaths by firearms 1,572
Deaths by falls, etc. 9,842
Deaths by railroad disasters 8,212
Deaths by street cars 1,998
Deaths by automobiles 2,488
Deaths by other vehicles 2,381
Deaths by coal mines and quarries 2,634

Deaths by machines	2,526
Deaths by landslides	601
Various other causes	6,273

TOTAL LOSS IN ONE YEAR 55,828

During the last sixty years THREE MILLIONS of deaths have occurred, one-half of which were preventable.

Typhoid fever, of which we have heard so much, does not compare with accidents as a cause of death in our country, and while typhoid fever is constantly decreasing, accidents are constantly increasing, and if they continue to do so at the present rate, will soon exceed the annual death rate from tuberculosis.

According to the Interstate Commerce Commission, in 1914 there were 202,964 persons injured in railroad accidents, *of whom 10,302 were killed*. Of the killed, 265 were passengers, 3,259 employees, and 6,788 were other persons or "trespassers," many of them children under 10 years of age. In the same period of time, 192,662 persons were injured on railroads, of whom 15,121 were passengers, 165,212 were railroad employees, and the remaining 12,329 were other persons.

On railroads alone during one year there were 5,284 trespassers killed and 5,687 injured. Think of it! Fourteen trespassers on railroads in this country killed every day, and an equal number injured. Of those injured the majority were seriously maimed or crippled for life.

There has been within the last few years a general awakening, and the result has been a nation-wide movement in which the boy scouts are to play a very important part through the service which they will render along preventive lines.

The Home, the Street, the School

As scouts you will have especial opportunity in this branch of the program to train your powers of observation. To tell you all of the ways in which you would be able to be of service to your home, community, school, and later to your employer would require a book. The following suggestions are given as a help to you and are recommended by the National Safety Council as fundamentals which every boy should observe in his daily life. They are classified under the home, the street, and the school.

AT HOME
Safety Begins at Home

Pick up pins and needles; they cause the death of many babies. Keep medicines out of the reach of small children.

A thoughtful scout will not leave anything on the stairs that may cause others to trip, slip, or fall, thus preventing injury to himself and to others.

Scalding water tipped from the edge of the stove may cause a fatal accident to a small sister or brother.

Be on the "look out" for sharp knives, etc. They should be kept out of reach of small children.

Rugs should lie flat. Serious falls come from tripping over rugs.

Keep your yard free from broken glass, rusty wire, and projecting nails.

To play with matches is dangerous.

Keep matches in a closed metal receptacle.

Break matches before throwing them away.

Let dad's gun alone.

A scout sometimes does his good turn by warning others against the use of kerosene and gasoline when lighting a fire.

Keep all combustible articles, other than fuel for immediate use, away from the stove.

Curtains or woodwork are sometimes ignited by gas jets.

See that the chimneys are examined twice a year to keep the flues clear.

Sixty per cent. of all fires start in closets, cellars, or attics. Keep them clean and free from rags and dry wood.

See that the fire escapes and halls are kept clear of obstruction.

A scout will not carry a lighted match or candle into a closet.

Burn greasy or oily rags and paper immediately after using.

When emptying gasoline or benzine cans, pour the contents on the ground away from buildings, instead of into sinks or drains.

Handling the electric wiring of a house is dangerous and may cost considerable for repairs.

IN THE STREET

It is dangerous to play in the street. Be careful.

Crossing

Cross streets at the corners and at right angles, instead of diagonally.

A scout does not cross the street in front of a moving vehicle.

Always look in both directions before crossing; it never pays to run, you may fall.

Be careful in crossing behind a vehicle, one may be coming in the opposite direction.

Wait for the policeman's signal, that you may not interfere with traffic.

Keep to the right in walking and in entering doorways.

When waiting for a car, stand on the curb, not in the middle of the street.

Get on with right hand and left foot; get off with left hand and right foot.

Get off face forward, retaining firm hold of handle until feet are firmly on the ground. Watch for teams and autos when you get off. Look both ways.

Always wait until the car stops, getting on or off.

The signals for stopping and starting a street car are: one bell —stop, two bells—start, three bells—stop immediately. (Used for emergencies.)

It is dangerous to let any part of your body project from the car window or platform.

The scout is trustworthy; he rides in the car instead of on the bumpers.

Wires

To handle wires of any kind, hanging from poles or trees, or to tamper with them may cause a serious accident or death. They may be live wires.

Report broken wires to Police Department by telephone immediately.

A scout will not fly a kite near wires.

A scout protects property; he will not stone or shoot at the glass insulators on the poles.

A scout knows of better places to play than around arc light poles. He knows that it is dangerous.

A scout knows that to throw a string or wire over a trolley or other wire carrying a current is dangerous, because it is likely to produce a shock.

Fires

Know the location of fire alarms.

Know how to turn in a fire alarm. After turning in an alarm, stay at the box until the arrival of the department to tell them where the fire is.

When you hear a fire alarm, keep on the sidewalk.

A scout will invade the fire lines at a fire only when permitted to do so by the authorities.

Railroad Tracks and Yards

It is dangerous to play along railroad tracks or on railroad bridges. Trains may be expected at any time.

Keep out of railroad yards.

Keep off sidings and cars standing on tracks.

Riding on steps and platforms is dangerous, as is climbing through cars when standing or moving. Wait until the car stops to get on or off.

When crossing railroad tracks stop and listen; look in both directions.

A bell ringing or a moving signal arm indicates a train is approaching.

Notify the station agent, track foreman, or some other official of the railroad whenever you discover a fire on railroad property. As scouts you should put out any fire you may discover, unless instructed differently by railroad employees or officials.

To walk around lowered gates or crawl under them is dangerous.

It is dangerous to let any part of your body project from the car window or platform.

Be careful. In crossing make sure that there is no danger from a train on another track. Wait! It is dangerous to cross in face of a moving or close to the rear of a standing train or car.

A scout plays safe as much for the other fellow's sake as for his own.

He does not jump off moving trains, cars, or engines, and scouting activities are such that he does not care to loiter around railroad stations, or to play on or around turn tables. He reads cautionary signs and rules for safety posted at stations, crossings, etc. He obeys all danger signals and warnings.

General

Accidents due to hitching on wagons with carts or roller skates are very common.

A scout prefers to coast in the open field rather than across a much-traveled highway or across car tracks.

Sling shots, air guns, or "beebee" guns have no place in the scout program. He knows that they are dangerous.

Keep away from excavations and open manholes.

Let strange dogs alone.

A scout knows that sand and stones are very dangerous when thrown.

Use your own sanitary drinking cup in public places.

Have your little scratches and bruises taken care of at once.

Pick up banana peels and deposit them in proper receptacles.

The push-mobile and skate-mobile are dangerous devices; be careful.

AT SCHOOL

Assist your teacher or principal in organizing a safety patrol among the older boys of your school. (The following are some of the duties of the safety patrol.)

Guard street intersections near school as children come to school.

Keep children out of street at dismissal.

Help smaller children over crossings.

Post bulletins of advice to pupils for coöperation in safety work.

Make reports of accidents with suggestions for prevention.

Give notice to principal of any dangerous conditions.

Report open manholes, blocked hallways and fire escapes, protruding nails, or injurious obstructions, broken wires of all kinds; report the building of fires in dangerous places; for example, in the alley, near the fences or buildings.

Doors should open outward.

See that half-doors are not locked.

Doors should have panic bolts; care should be exercised not to rush and cause a jam at the entrance way.

Panics and Their Prevention

Note all exits as you enter a building.

In case of a panic at an indoor assembly, scouts if they live up to their motto, "Be Prepared," will be able to save hundreds of lives.

Distribute the crowd. Use all exits leading to safety.

There is usually time for people to get out of a building if the exits are not blocked by too many crowding them at once. One should, if possible, try to arrange to have the performance go on, and the others could reassure the people and get them to go out quietly through the exits provided, which, according to law, must open outward and be marked by illuminated signs.

Keep crowd moving after passing through exit.

Scouts know how quickly and safely our school buildings are cleared by means of well-organized fire drills.

Keep cool.

FIRES AND THEIR PREVENTION

Fire and fire fighting costs each man, woman, and child $4.56 each year, or over $18.00 per family.

The economic waste by fire in the United States amounts to $250,000,000 yearly, not to mention loss of life. At least 50 per cent. of these fires are preventable.

Fires constitute a danger as great as panics, and scouts should be equally well informed what to do in case of fire. It is the duty of a scout to know how to prevent fires.

Many fires are caused by carelessness.

Smoking is not only a bad habit but a dangerous one as well.

A scout is careful of disposing of a lighted match. He knows that it may fall upon inflammable material and start a fire.

Reading in bed by the light of a lamp or candle is dangerous, for if the reader goes to sleep the bed clothing is likely to catch fire.

A scout may often have to dry his clothes before a fire, and if so they should be carefully watched.

Hot ashes in wooden boxes or in barrels are responsible for many fires.

In camp, dry grass should be cut away from the locality of the campfire; and not to put out a campfire on leaving a camp is criminal. Many of the great fires in our forests have been due to carelessness in this respect.

Fires also result frequently from explosions of gas or gunpowder.

A room in which the odor of gas is apparent should never be entered with a light, and in handling gunpowder a scout should have no matches in his pockets.

How to Put Out Burning Clothing

If your clothing should catch fire do not run for help, as this will fan the flames.

Lie down and roll up as tightly as possible in an overcoat, blanket, rug, or any woolen article.

If nothing can be obtained in which to wrap up, lie down and roll over slowly, at the same time beating the fire with the hands.

If another person's clothing catches fire, throw him on the ground and smother the fire with a coat, blanket, or rug.

Remember that woolen material is much less inflammable than cotton.

What to Do in Case of Fire

A fire can usually be put out very easily when it starts, and here is an occasion when a scout can show his presence of mind and coolness. At first a few buckets of water or blankets or woolen clothing thrown upon a fire will smother it. Sand ashes, or dirt, or even flour, will have the same effect.

If a scout discovers a building to be on fire he should sound the alarms for the fire department at once. If possible he should send some one else, as the scout will probably know better what to do before the fire engine arrives. All doors should be kept closed so as to prevent draughts. If you enter the burning building, close the window or door after you, if possible, and leave some responsible person to guard it so it will not be opened and cause a draught. In searching for people, go to the top floor and walk down, examining each room as carefully as possible. If necessary to get air while making the search, close the door of the room, open a window, and stick the head out until a few breaths can be obtained. Afterward close the window to prevent a draught. If doors are found locked and you suspect people are asleep inside, knock or pound on doors to arouse them. If this produces no results, you will have to try to break down the door. While searching through a burning building it will be best to tie a wet handkerchief or cloth over the nose and mouth. You will get a little air from the water.

Remember the air within six inches of the floor is free from smoke, so when you have difficulty in breathing, crawl along the floor, with the head low, dragging any one you have rescued behind you.

How to Drag an Insensible Man

Tie a neckerchief round the patient's wrists. Drag the patient as indicated. Crawl out on all fours.

Fireman's Drag

Never jump from a window unless the flames are so close to you that this is the only means of escape.

If you are outside a building, put bedding in a pile to break the jumper's fall, or get a strong carpet or rug to catch him, and have it firmly held by as many men and boys as can secure handholds.

In country districts scouts should organize a bucket brigade, which consists of two lines from the nearest water supply to the fire. Scouts in one line pass buckets, pitchers, or anything else that will hold water from one to another till the last scout throws the water on the fire. The buckets are returned by the other line.

PREVENTION OF WATER ACCIDENTS

By Wilbert E. Longfellow, Life Saving Corps of the American Red Cross

The scout's motto, "Be Prepared," is more than usually applicable to the work of preventing water accidents.

Drowning accidents are very common. Every scout should know how to swim and to swim well, but this is not all that is necessary. He should also know how to prevent accidents that may result in drowning. In summer, boating and bathing accidents are common. Remember a light boat is not intended for heavy seas; do not change seats except in a wide and steady boat; and above all things do not put yourself in the class of idiots who rock a boat.

At the seashore, unless you are a strong swimmer, do not go outside the life line, and if the undertow is strong be careful not to walk out where the water is so deep that it will carry you off your feet. Very cold water and very long swims are likely to exhaust even a strong swimmer and are therefore hazardous unless a boat accompanies the swimmer.

Life Buoys

If one is to place a life buoy for instant use in emergencies, it should be hung upon four pegs driven into holes in two pieces of wood nailed together in the form of the diameter of a two-foot square, or three pegs in strips of wood arranged in the form of a "T," about eighteen or twenty inches high, the two pegs at either side of the top bar of the "T" and the other one on the upright near the bottom. Most life buoys used on shore have fifty or seventy-five feet of light line attached to draw the rescued person ashore or to recover the buoy after a faulty throw.

Commencing at the free end of the line, where a small wooden float is often attached, the rope should first be coiled on the pegs, hanging the buoy outside the coil to bind it in place so wind or jars will not loosen it. Then, when the buoy is needed, the ring

Life buoy and ice ball

is grasped by the throwing hand which clasps the buoy itself, and the coil is clasped in the free hand, the end of the rope being secured ashore by standing upon it with one foot. After each use or practice the buoy line should be restored to its pegs for instant use.

Every scout should make himself acquainted with the laws governing the capacity of boats, lights, their colors, position, and use, life boats and drills on steamships and launches.

Swimming

For physical development the breast stroke is useful, for it is one that is used in carrying a tired swimmer, in going to the bottom for lost articles, and in searching for a person who has sunk before help has reached him. It is possible, you know, to get to the bottom, bring a body to the surface, and swim with it to shore before life is extinct, and to restore consciousness by well-directed efforts. The body of an unconscious person weighs little when wholly or partially submerged; in salt water it weighs less than in fresh water, and is consequently more easily carried. Training makes a small boy the equal or superior of an untrained boy much larger and of greater strength, and the way to learn to carry a drowning person is to carry a boy who is not drowning to get used to handling weights. A little struggle now and then lends realism to the work and increases the skill of the scout candidate for life saver's rating.

To save lives, the scout must know first how to swim, to care for himself, and then to learn to carry another and to break the clutch, the "death grip," which we read so much about in the newspaper accounts of drowning accidents. By constant training a boy, even though not a good swimmer, can be perfectly at home in the water, fully dressed, undressed, or carrying a boy of his own size or larger. In fact, one boy expert of twelve or fourteen years can save a man.

Scout Training

The scout should train himself to be as handily and efficiently prepared while in the water as he is on land, so that when the emergency arises he is ready to cope with all difficulties. Swimming is certainly one of the greatest and best sports for all boys, but scouts should train themselves specially to make their ability in swimming count for its usefulness. Speed swimming for itself alone is a very selfish sport so that the scout should develop his ability to make it generally useful to others.

Floating

After the breast stroke is learned, floating on the back for rest and swimming on the back, using feet only for propulsion, leaving the hands free to hold a drowning person, should be learned. The secret of swimming and life saving is to make the water carry the weight, and it will if you let it. This can be readily acquired with a little practice, carrying the hands on the surface of the water, arms half bent, with the elbows close to the sides at the waistline. To carry a man this way the hands are placed at either side of the drowning man's head and he is towed floating on his back, the rescuer swimming on his back, keeping the other away. It is well to remember to go with the tide or current, and not to wear your strength away opposing it. Other ways of carrying are to place the hands beneath the arms of the drowning man, or to grasp him firmly by the biceps from beneath, at the same time using the knee

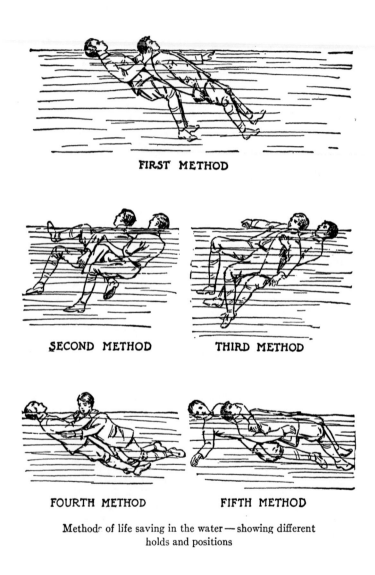

FIRST METHOD

SECOND METHOD   THIRD METHOD

FOURTH METHOD   FIFTH METHOD

Methods of life saving in the water — showing different
holds and positions

in the middle of his back to get him into a floating position, the feet acting as propellers. Develop a back scissor kick and you will find that by using the feet only for propulsion excellent progress can be made with or without a subject. Methods which enable the rescuer's use of one arm in addition to the feet are known as the "German army" and the "cross shoulder." In the first, the swimmer approaches the drowning person from the back, passes his left arm under the other's left arm, across in front of the chest, and firmly grasps the right arm, either by the biceps or below the elbow, giving him control. This leaves the right arm to swim with. Another method, when the patient is unruly, is to approach from the rear, grasp the drowning man by the long back hair, and keep him at arm's length away. I have saved a number of people by swimming toward them, grasping the right arm of the drowning man, tucking his arm under my right armpit, and clasping him with my right hand, thumb up under his armpit. An excellent one-arm hold is one in which the rescuer passes an arm over the shoulder of the one to be carried, approaching from the back as before, and getting a hold under the other's arm, which makes the drowning man helpless. The breast stroke previously mentioned is used only for helping a tired swimmer, and one in possession of his faculties who will not try to grasp the rescuer. The tired swimmer lies on the back and, extending his arm fully in front, rests a hand on either shoulder of the swimmer who rests facing him in the regular breast position allowing the feet of the other to drop between his own. Quite good speed can be made in this way, and all of these methods are practical, as a trial will show. The tired swimmer must not bend his arms at the elbow or he will pull the rescuer's face under the water. A little practice will enable the beginner to see which he can do most readily and then he can perfect himself in it for instant use.

Breaking "Death Grips"

If one uses care in approaching a frightened or drowning person in the water, there will be no use for the release methods; but the best of swimmers get careless at times and all swimmers need to know how to get clear when gripped.

Wrist Grip

Of these the simplest is the one where the wrists of the swimmer have been grasped by the drowning man in his struggles.

The swimmer throws both hands above his head which forces both low in the water and then turns the leverage of his arms against the other's thumbs, breaking the hold easily.

It should be borne in mind that a drowning man grasps what he can see above the surface of the water, so he will not attempt to grasp his rescuer below the points of the shoulders. Remember also that a tall man and a short man would have about the same amount of their body projecting above the surface of the water.

Neck Grip

For the grip around the swimmer's neck from the front, for both arms around the shoulders, and for a grip in which the drowning man had the other over one shoulder and under the other arm, the break is much the same. As soon as the rescuer feels the hold, he covers the other's mouth with the palm of his hand, clasping the nostrils tightly between his first two fingers, at the same time pulling the drowning man to him with the left hand in the small of the back, treading water in the meantime. Then, taking a full breath, he applies his knee in the other's stomach, forcing him to expel the air in his lungs, and at the same time preventing him from getting more by pressure on the nostrils and mouth. Should the pressure of the grip around the body be too great to allow freedom

Break for wrist hold   Breaking back strangle hold

of the arms, the preliminary move in that case would be to bring both arms to the level of the shoulder, thus sliding the other's arms to the neck, leaving the rescuer's arms free to pull the other up and should shut off his wind as previously described.

Back Strangle

The back strangle hold is an awkward one to break and one which must be broken without an instant's delay, or the would-be rescuer himself will be in great need of help. In practice it will be found that, by grasping the encircling arm at the wrists and pushing back with the buttocks against the other's abdomen, room to slip out can be obtained. In a life and death struggle sharper measures are needed, and if the rescuer throws his head suddenly back against the nose of the drowning man he will secure his freedom very readily and have him under control by the time he has recovered from his dazed condition.

Break for front strangle hold

Rescue from Shore or Boat

It is not always necessary to go into the water to attempt a rescue, and in many cases, when some one has fallen off a bridge or dock, a line or buoy can be used to advantage without placing more lives in danger than the one in the water. Discretion in such matters is worthy of recognition rather than too much recklessness in swimming out. Use a boat when possible. Practice in throwing a life buoy should be indulged in where possible, and a good scout should always leave the line coiled over pegs and the buoy hanging on top to bind it in place for instant use in an emergency

Diving from the Surface

When a bather or victim from a boat accident sinks to the bottom of a river or pond of from seven to twenty feet in depth, prompt rescue methods may bring him to the surface, and resuscitation methods, promptly applied, will restore breath. If there is no current in the pond or lake, bubbles from the body will indicate its whereabouts directly beneath the place where it sank. Should there be tide or currents, the bubbles are carried at an angle with the streams and the searcher must go from the spot where the person disappeared and look along the bottom, going with the current. When a drowning man gives up his struggle and goes down, his body sinks a little way and is brought up again by the buoyancy within it and the air is expelled. It sinks again and next rises less high and air is again expelled. This happens several times until enough water is taken into the stomach and air passages to offset the floating capacity. The floating capacity is barely overcome, so the body weighs but little. It is very simple, as almost any youthful

Throwing feet for dive from surface

swimmer knows, to go to the bottom if one can dive from a float, pier, or boat, but to be able to dive down ten feet from the surface requires practice. In most cases to go deeper would require a weight, such as is used by the southern sponge and pearl fishers. Grasp a ten or fifteen pound stone and dive in; to come up the swimmer lets go and rises to the top.

Diving for Lost Objects

In covering a considerable area in search for bodies or lost objects, several ropes can be anchored with the grapnels or rocks in squares and a systematic search thus maintained by divers. Going down from the surface is not so simple and the knack is attained by practice, especially by athletic lads. The secret is to swim to a point where a sound is to be made, and to plunge the head and shoulders under, elevating the hips above the surface to drive the shoulders deep and give a chance for a few strokes—breast stroke preferred—until the whole body in a vertical position is headed for the bottom. The elevation of the feet and lower legs in the air gives the body additional impetus downward, and when the object is attained a push-off from the bottom with both feet sends the swimmer to the surface in quick order. To carry any weight ashore it is necessary to carry it low on the body, hugged close to the waist line, allowing one hand and both feet for swimming, or if on the back hold by both hands using the feet as propellers.

Ice Rescue

To rescue a person who has broken through the ice you should first tie a rope around your body and have the other end tied, or held, on shore. Then secure a long board or a ladder or limb of a tree, crawl out on this, or push it out, so that the person in the water may reach it. If nothing can be found on which you can support your weight do not attempt to walk out toward the person to be rescued, but lie down flat on your face and crawl out, as by doing this much less weight bears at any one point on the ice than in walking. If you yourself break through the ice remember that if you try to crawl up on the broken edge it will very likely break against you. If rescuers are near it would be much better to support yourself on the edge of the ice and wait for them to come to you.

Electric Accidents

For his own benefit and that of his comrades the scout should know how to avoid accidents from electricity. The third rail is always dangerous, so do not touch it. Swinging wires of any kind may somewhere in their course be in contact with live wires, so they should not be touched.

A person in contact with a wire or rail carrying an electric current will transfer the current to the rescuer. Therefore he must not touch the unfortunate victim unless his body is thoroughly insulated. The rescuer must act very promptly, for the danger to the person in contact is much increased the longer the electric current is allowed to pass through the body. If possible, the rescuer should insulate himself by covering his hands with a mackintosh, rubber sheeting, several thicknesses of silk or even dry cloth. In addition he should, if possible, complete his insulation by standing on a dry board, a thick piece of paper, or even a dry coat. Rubber gloves and rubber shoes are still safer, but they cannot usually be procured quickly.

A live wire on a patient may be flipped away with safety with a dry board or stick. In removing the live wire from the person, or the person from the wire, do this with one motion, as rocking him to and fro on the wire will increase shock and burn.

A live wire may be safely cut by an axe or hatchet with dry, wooden handle. The electric current may be short circuited by dropping a crow-bar or poker on the wire. It must be dropped on the side from which the current is coming and not the farther side, as the latter will not short circuit the current before it is passed through the body of the person in contact. Drop the metal bar; do not place it on the wire or you will then be made a part of the short circuit and receive the current of electricity through your body.

What to Do for Electric Shocks

Always send for a doctor, but do not wait for him. Treatment should be given even if the man appears to be dead. Loosen the clothing around neck and body. Proceed to restore breathing by artificial respiration as in drowning. (See pages 371–372.)

Prevention of Gas Accidents

The commonest gas encountered is the ordinary illuminating gas. To prevent such gas from escaping in dangerous quantities, leaks in gas pipes should be promptly repaired. Be careful in entering a room filled with gas to cover the nose and mouth. Be careful in turning off gas to make sure that gas is actually shut off. It is dangerous to leave a gas jet burning faintly when you go to sleep, as it may go out if pressure in the gas pipe becomes less, and if pressure is afterward increased gas may escape into the room. It may also be blown out by a draft.

Coal gas will escape from red-hot cast-iron stoves, and very big fires in such stoves are dangerous, especially in sleeping rooms. Charcoal burned in open vessels in tight rooms is especially dangerous.

In underground sewers and wells other dangerous gases are found. If a lighted candle or torch will not burn in such a place, it is very certain the air will be deadly for any person who enters.

To rescue an unconscious person in a place filled with gas, move quickly and carry him out without breathing yourself. Take a few deep breaths before entering and if possible hold breath while in the place. It is always best for two persons to work together in those cases. Learn method of resuscitation.

What to Do for Gas Poisoning

Proceed to restore breathing by artificial respiration as in drowning. (See pages 371-372.)

Runaway Horses

The method of checking a horse running away is not to run out and wave your arm in front of him, as this will only cause him to dodge to one side and to run faster, but to try to run alongside the vehicle with one hand on the shaft to prevent yourself from falling, seizing the reins with the other hand and dragging the horse's head toward you. If when he has somewhat slowed down by this method you can turn him toward a wall or a house he will probably stop.

FIRST AID FOR INJURIES

General Directions

Keep cool. There is no cause for excitement or hurry. In not one case in a thousand are the few moments necessary to find out what is the matter with an injured man going to result in any harm to him, and of course in order to treat him intelligently you must first know what is the matter. Common sense will tell the scout that he must waste no time, however, when there is severe bleeding, or in case of poisoning.

If possible, always send for a doctor, unless the injury is a trivial one. Don't wait until he arrives, however, to do something for the injured person. A crowd should always be kept back and tight clothing should be loosened. If the patient's face is pale, place him on his back with his head low. If his face is flushed, fold your coat and put it under his head so as to raise it slightly.

In case of vomiting, place the patient on his side. Do not

give an unconscious person a stimulant, as he cannot swallow, and it will run down his windpipe and choke him.

If the injury is covered by clothing, remove it by cutting or tearing, but never remove more clothing than necessary, as one of the results of injury is for a person to feel cold. Shoes and boots should be cut in severe injuries about the feet.

Shock

For example, a scout is riding on a trolley-car. The car runs into a loaded wagon. The wagon is overturned and the driver thrown to the pavement. Part of the load falls upon his body, and when you reach him he is unconscious. So far as you can find out, nothing else is the matter with him. This is called shock. It accompanies all serious injuries and is itself serious, as a person may die without ever recovering from shock. Of course there are different degrees of shock. In severe shock the person is completely unconscious or he may be only slightly confused and feel weak and uncertain of what has happened.

In shock always send for a doctor when you can. Before he comes, warm and stimulate the patient in every possible way. Place him on his back with his head low and cover him with your coat or a blanket. Rub his arms and legs toward his body but do not uncover him to do this. If you have ammonia or smelling salts, place them before the patient's nose so he may breathe them.

This is all you can do when unconsciousness is complete. When the patient begins to recover a little, however, and as soon as he can swallow, give him hot tea or coffee, or a half teaspoonful of aromatic spirits of ammonia in a quarter glass of water.

Warning: Remember always that a person with shock may have some other serious injuries. These you should always look for and treat if necessary.

Injuries in Which the Skin is Not Broken—Fractures

A fracture is the same thing as a broken bone. When the bone pierces or breaks through the skin, it is called a compound fracture, and when it does *not*, a simple fracture.

A scout is in the country with a comrade. The latter mounts a stone wall to cross it. The wall falls with him and he calls out for help. When the other scout reaches him, he finds the injured scout lying flat on the ground with both legs stretched out. One of these does not look quite natural, and the scout complains of a great deal of pain at the middle of the thigh and thinks he felt something break when he fell. He cannot raise the injured leg. Carefully rip the trousers and the under-

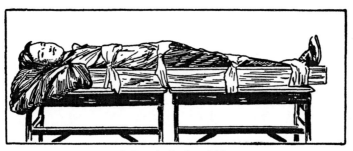

Splints for broken thigh

clothing at the seam to above the painful point. When you
have done this the deformity will indicate the location of the
fracture. You must be very gentle now or you will do harm,
but if one hand is put above where you think the break occurred
and the other below it and it is lifted gently you will find that
there is movement at the broken point.

Send for a doctor first, if you can, and if you expect him to
arrive very soon, let your comrade lie where he is, putting his
injured leg in the same position as the sound one and holding
it there by coats or other articles piled around the leg. But
if the doctor cannot be expected for some time, draw the injured limb into position like the sound one and hold it there

Splints for broken leg

by splints. Splints can be made of anything that is stiff and
rigid. Something flat like a board is better than a pole or
staff; limbs broken off a tree will do if nothing else can be
found. Shingles make excellent splints. In applying splints
remember that they should extend beyond the next joint above
and the next joint below; otherwise, movements of the joint
will cause movement at the broken point. With a fracture of

the thigh, such as that described, the outer splint should be a very long one, extending below the feet from the armpit. A short one extending just below the knee will do for the inner splint. Splints may be tied on with handkerchiefs, pieces of cloth torn from the clothing, or the like. Tie firmly, but not tight enough to cause severe pain. In a fracture of the thigh it will also be well to bind the injured leg to the sound one by two or three pieces of cloth around both. The clothing put back in place will serve as padding under the splint, but with thin summer clothing it is better to use straw, hay, or leaves in addition. Fractures of the lower leg and of the upper and lower arm are treated in the same way with a splint on the inner and outer sides of the broken bone. A sling will be required for a fracture of the arm. This may be made of the triangular bandage, or of a triangular piece of cloth torn from your shirt.

Compound Fractures

The edges of a broken bone are very sharp and may cut through the skin at the time of an injury, but more often after-

Splints and sling for fracture.
of upper arm

ward, if the injured person moves about or if the splints are not well applied so as to prevent movement at the point where the bone is broken. If a compound fracture has occurred, the wound produced by the sharp bone must always be treated first. The treatment is the same for any other wound.

Warning: You will not always be able to tell whether or not a fracture has occurred. In this case do not pull and haul the limb about to make sure, but treat as a fracture. There will always be a considerable amount of shock with fracture and this must also be treated.

Bruises

Everybody has suffered from a bruise at some time in his life and knows just what it is. A slight bruise needs no treatment. For a severe one, apply very hot or very cold water to prevent pain and swelling.

Sprains

A scout slips and twists his ankle and immediately suffers severe pain, and in a little while the ankle begins to swell. The sprained joint should be put in an elevated position and cloths wrung out in very hot or very cold water should be wrapped around it and changed very frequently. Movement of any sprained joint is likely to increase the injury, so this ought not to be permitted. Walking with a sprained ankle is not only exceedingly painful, but it generally increases the hurt.

Dislocation

A dislocation is an injury where the head of a bone has slipped out of its socket at a joint. A scout is playing football. He suddenly feels as though his shoulder has been twisted out of place. Comparison with the other side will show that the injured shoulder does not look like the other one, being longer, or shorter, and contrary to the case with fracture there will not be increased movement at the point of injury but a lessened movement. Do not attempt to get a dislocated joint back in place. Cover the joint with cloths wrung out in very hot or very cold water, and get the patient into the hands of a doctor as soon as possible.

Injuries in Which the Skin is Broken

Such injuries are called wounds. There is one very important fact

Triangular sling for arm

which must be remembered in connection with such injuries. Any injury in which the skin is unbroken is much less dangerous, as the skin prevents germs from reaching the injured part. The princip.e to be followed in treating a wound is to apply something to prevent germs from reaching the injury.

All wounds unless protected from germs are very liable to become infected with matter, or pus. Blood poisoning and even death may result from infection. To prevent infection of wounds, the scout should cover them promptly with what is called a sterilized dressing. This is a surgical dressing which has been so treated that it is free from germs. A number of dressings are on the market and can be procured in drug stores. In using them, be very careful not to touch the surface of the dressing which is to be placed in contact with the wound. The Red Cross First Aid Dressing is so made that this accident

Head bandage

is almost impossible. In taking care of a wound, do not handle it or do anything else to it. Every one's hands, though they may appear to be perfectly clean, are not so in the sense of being free from germs; nor is water, so a wound should never be washed.

It will be a good thing for a scout always to carry a Red Cross First Aid Outfit, or some similar outfit, for with this he is ready to take care of almost any injury; without it he will find it very difficult to improvise anything to cover a wound with safety to the injured person. If no prepared dressing is procurable, boil a towel if possible for fifteen minutes, squeeze the water out of it without touching the inner surface, and apply that to the wound. The next best dressing, if you cannot prepare this, will be a towel or handkerchief which has been recently washed and has not been used. These should be held in place on the wound with a bandage. Do not be afraid to leave a wound exposed to the air; germs do not float around in the air and such exposure is much safer than water or any dressing which is not free from germs. Of course you can bind up a wound with a towel not boiled or piece of cotton torn from your shirt, but you cannot do so without the liability of a great deal of harm to the injured person.

Snake Bites

While snake bites are wounds, the wounds caused by venomous snakes are not important as such because the venom is quickly absorbed, and by its action on the brain may cause speedy death. The rattlesnake and the moccasin are the most dangerous snakes in the United States.

In order to prevent absorption of the poison, immediately tie a string, handkerchief, or bandage above the bite. This can only be done in the extremities, but nearly all bites are received on the arms or legs. Then soak the wound in hot water and squeeze or suck it to extract the poison. Sucking a wound is not dangerous unless one has cuts or scrapes in the mouth. Then burn the wound with strong ammonia. This is not aromatic spirits of ammonia, but what is commonly known as strong ammonia in any drug store. Aromatic spirits of ammonia should also be given as a stimulant.

If you have nothing but a string to tie off the wound, be sure to do that and to get out as much poison as you can by squeezing or sucking the wound. A doctor should of course always be sent for when practicable in any injury as severe as a snake bite. Leave your string or bandage in place for an hour. A longer period is unsafe, as cutting off the circulation may cause mortification. Loosen the string or bandage after an hour's time, so that a little poison escapes into the body. If the bitten person does not seem to be much affected, repeat at the end of a few moments, and keep this up until the band has been entirely removed. If, however, the bitten person seems to be seriously affected by the poison you have allowed to escape into his body, you must not loosen the bandage again, but leave it in place and take the chance of mortification.

Wounds Without Severe Bleeding

These constitute the majority of all wounds. Use the Red Cross Outfit as described in the slip contained in the outfit. The pressure of a bandage will stop ordinary bleeding if firmly bound into place.

Wounds With Severe Bleeding

A scout must be prepared to check severe bleeding at once, and he should then dress the wound. Bleeding from an artery is by far the most dangerous. Blood coming from a cut artery is bright red in color and flows rapidly in spurts or jets. As the course of the blood in an artery is away from the heart, pressure must be applied on the heart side just as a rubber pipe which is cut must be compressed on the side from which the water is coming in order to prevent leakage at a cut beyond. The scout must also know the course of the larger arteries in order that he may know where to press on them. In the arm the course of the large artery is down the inner side of

How to apply first aid dressing

the big muscle in the upper arm about in line with the seam of the coat. The artery in the leg runs down from the center of a line from the point of the hip to the middle of the crotch, and is about in line with the inseam of the trousers. Pressure should be applied about three inches below the crotch. In making pressure on either of these arteries, use the fingers and press back against the bone. You can often feel the artery beat under your fingers, and the bleeding below will stop when you have your pressure properly made. Of course you cannot keep up the pressure with your fingers indefinitely in this way as they will soon become tired and cramped. Therefore, while you are doing this have some other scout prepare a tourniquet. The simplest form of tourniquet is a handkerchief tied loosely about the limb. In this handkerchief a smooth stone or a cork should be placed just above your fingers on the artery. When this is in place put a stick about a foot long under the handkerchief at the outer side of the limb and twist around till the stone makes pressure on the artery in the same way that your fingers have. Tie the stick in position so it will not untwist.

Warning: When using a tourniquet remember that cutting off the circulation for a long time is dangerous. It is much safer not to keep on a tourniquet more than an hour. Loosen it, but be ready to tighten it again quickly if bleeding recommences.

Another method to stop bleeding from an artery when the wound is below the knee or elbow is to place a pad in the bend of the joint and double the limb back over it, holding the pad in tightly. Tie the arm or leg in this position. If these means do not check the bleeding put a pad into the wound and press on it there. If you have no dressing and blood is being lost very rapidly, make pressure in the wound with your fingers. Remember, however, that this should only be resorted to in the case of absolute necessity, as it will infect the wound.

Blood from veins flows in a steady stream back toward the heart and is dark in color. From most veins a pad

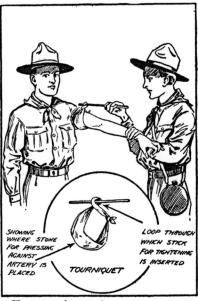

How to apply tourniquet to upper arm

firmly bandaged on the bleeding point will stop the bleeding. If a vein in the neck is wounded, blood will be lost so rapidly that the injured person is in danger of immediate death, so you must disregard the danger of infection, and jam your hand tightly against the bleeding point.

Keep the patient quiet in all cases of severe bleeding, for even if it is checked it may start up again. Do not give any stimulants until the bleeding has been checked unless the patient is very weak. The best stimulant is aromatic spirits of ammonia, one teaspoonful in half a glass of water.

Unconsciousness and Poisoning

Unconsciousness, of course, means lack of consciousness, or, in other words, one who is unconscious knows nothing of his surroundings or of what is happening. A person may, however, be partially, as well as wholly, unconscious.

Unconsciousness may be due to so many causes that, in order to give the best treatment, the scout should first know the cause. Always try to find this out if you can. If you cannot do this, however, you should at least determine whether unconsciousness is due to poison, to bleeding, to sunstroke, or to freezing; for each of these demand immediate, special treatment. If it is not due to one of these causes, and the patient is pale and weak, have him placed with his head low, and warm and stimulate him in every possible way. If the face is red and the pulse is bounding and strong, that patient should have his head raised on a folded coat. No stimulants should be given him and cold water should be sprinkled on his face and chest.

The common causes of unconsciousness are shock, electric shock, fainting, apoplexy and injury to the brain, sunstroke and heat exhaustion, freezing, suffocation, and poisoning. The first two have already been described and the treatment of any form of suffocation in artificial respiration.

Fainting

Fainting usually occurs in overheated, crowded places. The patient is very pale and partially or completely unconscious. The pupils of the eye are natural, the pulse is weak and rapid. The patient should be placed in a lying-down position with the head lower than the rest of the body so that the brain will receive more blood. Loosen the clothing, especially about the neck. Keep the crowd back and open the windows if indoors so that the patient may get plenty of fresh air. Sprinkle the face and chest with cold water. Apply smelling salts or ammonia to the nose, rub the limbs toward the body. A stimulant may be given when the patient is so far recovered that he is able to swallow.

Apoplexy and Injury to the Brain

Apoplexy and unconsciousness from injury to the brain are due to the pressure of blood on the brain so that they may be described together. Apoplexy is of course much harder to distinguish than injury to the brain, as in the latter the scout can always see that the head has been hurt. With both, unconsciousness will usually be complete. Pupils are large and frequently unequal in size, breathing is snoring, and the pulse is usually full and slow. One side of the body will be paralyzed. Test this by raising arm or leg; if paralyzed, it will drop absolutely helpless. Send for a doctor at once. Keep patient quiet and in a dark room if possible. Put in lying-down position with head raised by pillows. Apply ice or cold cloths to head. No stimulants. Drunkenness is sometimes mistaken for apoplexy. If there is any doubt on this point always treat for apoplexy.

Sunstroke and Heat Exhaustion

Any one is liable to sunstroke or heat exhaustion if exposed to excessive heat. A scout should remember not to expose himself too much to the sun nor should he wear too heavy clothing in the summer. Leaves in the hat will do much to prevent sunstroke. If the scout becomes dizzy and exhausted through exposure to the sun he should find a cool place, lie down, and bathe the face, hands, and chest in cold water and drink freely of cold water.

Sunstroke and heat exhaustion, though due to the same cause, are quite different and require different treatment. In sunstroke unconsciousness is complete. The face is red, pupils large, the skin is very hot and dry with no perspiration. The patient sighs and the pulse is full and slow. The treatment for sunstroke consists in reducing the temperature of the body. A doctor should be summoned whenever possible. The patient should be removed to a cool place and his clothing loosened, or better the greater part of it removed. Cold water, or ice, should be rubbed over the face, neck, chest, and in armpits. When consciousness returns give cold water freely.

Heat exhaustion is simply exhaustion or collapse due to heat. The patient is greatly depressed and weak but not usually unconscious. Face is pale and covered with clammy sweat, breathing and pulse are weak and rigid. While this condition is not nearly as dangerous as sunstroke, a doctor should be summoned if possible. Remove the patient to a cool place and have him lie down with his clothing loosened. Don't use anything cold externally, but permit him to take small sips of cold water. Stimulants should be given just as in fainting.

Freezing

The patient should be taken into a cold room and the body should be rubbed with rough cloths wet in cold water. The temperature of the room should be increased if possible. This should be done gradually and the cloths should be wet in warmer and warmer water. As soon as the patient can swallow give him stimulants. It will be dangerous to place him before an open fire or in a hot bath until he begins to recover. You will know this by his skin becoming warmer, by his better color, and by his generally improved appearance.

Frost-bite

Remember that you are in danger of frost-bite if you do not wear sufficient clothing in cold weather, and that rubbing any part of the body which becomes very cold helps to prevent frost-bite, because it brings more warm blood to the surface. The danger is when, after being cold, the part suddenly has no feeling.

The object of the treatment is gradually to restore warmth to the frozen part. To do this the part should be rubbed first with snow or cold water; the water should be warmed gradually. The use of hot water at once would be likely to cause mortification of the frozen part.

Poisoning

For all poisons give an emetic. Send for a doctor at once and if possible have the messenger tell what poison has been taken so that the doctor may bring the proper antidote. Do not wait for him to arrive, but give an emetic to rid the stomach of the poison. Good emetics are mustard and water, salt water, or lukewarm water alone in large quantities. Never mind the exact dose, and if vomiting is not profuse repeat the dose.

Fits

A person in a fit first has convulsive movements of the body, then he usually becomes unconscious. A scout should have no difficulty in making out what is the matter with a person in a fit.

Put the sufferer on the floor or the ground where he cannot hurt himself by striking anything. Loosen tight clothing and do not try to restrain the convulsive movements. A wad of cloth thrust in the mouth will prevent biting the tongue. When he becomes quiet do not disturb him.

INJURIES DUE TO HEAT AND COLD

Burns and Scalds

For slight burns in order to relieve the pain some dressing to exclude the air is needed. Very good substances of this character are pastes made with water and baking soda, starch, or flour. Carbolized vaseline, olive or castor oil, and fresh lard or cream are all good. One of these substances should be smeared over a thin piece of cloth and placed on the burned part. A bandage should be put over this to hold the dressing in place and for additional protection.

Severe burns and scalds are very serious injuries which require treatment from a physician. Pending his arrival the scout should remember to treat the sufferer for shock as well as to dress the wound.

Burns from electricity should be treated exactly like other burns.

Do not attempt to remove clothing which sticks to a burn; cut the cloth around the part which sticks and leave it on the burn.

FIRST AID FOR EMERGENCIES

Besides the accidents which have been mentioned, certain emergencies may demand treatment by a scout.

The commonest of these are described here.

Something in the Eye

No little thing causes more pain and discomfort than something in the eye. Do not rub to remove a foreign body from the eye, as this is likely to injure the delicate covering of the eyeball. First, close the eye so the tears will accumulate, these may wash the foreign body into plain view so that it may be easily removed. If this fails, pull the upper lid over the lower two or three times, close the nostril on the opposite side and have the patient blow his nose hard. If the foreign body still remains in the eye, examine first under the lower and then the upper lid. For the former have the patient look up, press lower lid down, and if the foreign body is seen lift it out gently with the corner of a clean handkerchief. It is not so easy to see the upper lid. Seat the patient in a chair with his head bent backward. Stand behind him and place a match or thin pencil across the upper lid one half an inch from its edge, turn the upper lid back over the match, and lift the foreign body off as before. A drop of castor oil in the eye after removing the foreign body will soothe it.

Eye bandage

Sunburn

This is simply an inflammation of the skin due to action of the sun. It may be prevented by hardening the skin gradually. Any toilet powder or boracic acid will protect the skin to a considerable extent. The treatment consists of soothing applications such as ordinary or carbolized vaseline.

Ivy Poisoning

Poison ivy causes a very intense inflammation of the skin. Better avoid, even though it has not harmed you before. Baking soda made in a thick paste with water or carbolized vaseline are good remedies. In severe cases a doctor should be consulted.

Bites and Stings

Ammonia should be immediately applied. Wet salt and wet earth are also good applications.

Nosebleed

Slight nosebleed does not require treatment as no harm will result from it. When more severe the collar should be loosened   Do not blow the nose.   Apply cold to the back of the neck by means of a key or cloth wrung out in cold water.

Position of hands   Chair carry

A roll of paper under the upper lip, between it and the gum, will also help.   When the bleeding still continues shove a cotton or gauze plug into the nostrils, leaving it there until the bleeding stops

Earache

This is likely to result seriously and a doctor should be consulted in order to prevent bad results with possible loss of hearing.   Hot cloths, a bag of heated salt, or a hot bottle applied to the ear will often cure earache.   A few drops of alcohol on a hot cloth so placed that the alcohol fumes enter the ear will often succeed.   If neither is effective, heat a few drops of sweet oil as hot as you can stand, put a few drops in the ear and plug with cotton.   Be careful that it is not too hot.

Toothache

Remember that toothache indicates something seriously wrong with the teeth which can only be permanently corrected by a dentist. In toothache if you can find a cavity, clean it out with a small piece of cotton or a toothpick. Then plug it with cotton, on which a drop of oil of cloves has been put if you have it. If no cavity is found, soak a piece of cotton in camphor and apply it to the outside of the gum. Hot cloths and hot bottles or bags will help in toothache, just as they do in earache.

Inflammation of the Eye

Cover with a cloth wrung out in cold water and change cloths from time to time when they get warm. See a doctor in order to safeguard your sight.

Cramp or Stomachache

This is usually due to the irritation produced by undigested food. A hot bottle applied to the stomach or rubbing will often give relief. A little peppermint in hot water and ginger tea are both excellent remedies. The undigested matter should be gotten rid of by vomiting or a cathartic.

Remember this kind of pain is sometimes due to something serious and if it is very severe or continues for some time, it is much safer to send for a doctor.

Arm carry

Hiccough

This is due to indigestion. Holding the breath will often cure, as will also drinking a full glass of water in small sips without taking a breath. If these fail, vomiting is an almost certain remedy.

Chills

In order to stop a chill drink hot milk or hot lemonade and get into bed. Plenty of covers should be used, and hot water bottles or hot milk or lemonade help to warm one quickly.

Carrying Injured

A severely injured person is always best carried on a stretcher. The easiest stretcher for a scout to improvise is the coat stretcher. For this two coats and a pair of poles are needed. The sleeves of the coat are first turned inside out. The coats are then placed on the ground with their lower sides touching each

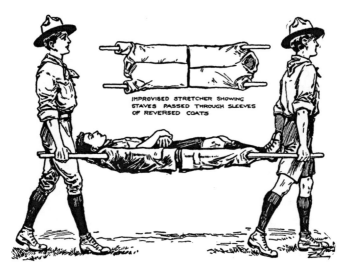

Improvised stretcher

other. The poles are passed through the sleeves on each side, the coats are buttoned up with the button side down. A piece of carpet, a blanket, or sacking can be used in much the same way as the coats, rolling in a portion at each side. Shutters and doors make fair stretchers. In order not to jounce the patient in carrying him the bearers should break step. The bearer in front steps off with the left foot and the one in the rear with the right. A number of different methods for carrying a patient by two bearers are practised. The four-handed

seat is a very good one. To make this each bearer grasps his
left wrist in his right hand, and the other bearer's right wrist
in his left hand with the backs of the hands uppermost. The
bearers then stoop and place the chair under the sitting patient who steadies himself by placing his arms around their necks.

It will sometimes be necessary for one scout to carry an injured comrade. The scout should first turn the patient on his face; he then steps astride his body, facing toward the patient's head, and, with hands under his armpits, lifts him to his knees; then, clasping hands over the abdomen, lifts him to his feet; he then, with his left hand, seizes the patient by the left wrist and draws his left arm around his (the bearer's) neck and holds it against his left chest, the patient's left side resting against his body, and supports him with his right arm about the waist. The scout, with his left hand, seizes the right wrist of the patient

Chair carry

and draws the arm over his head and down upon his shoulder,
then, shifting himself in front, stoops and clasps the right thigh
with his right arm
passed between the
legs (see first posi-
tion), his right hand
seizing the patient's
right wrist (see second
position, next page),
lastly, the scout, with
his left hand, grasps
t h e patient's l e f t
hand, and steadies it
against his side when
he arises. Another
hold is given in the
third illustration.

Fireman's lift. First position

Second position   Fireman's lift   Another hold

Restoring Breathing

Knowledge of resuscitation of the apparently drowned is an important part of the equipment of a first-class scout, and a great many lives could have been saved had it been more general. To be effective no time must be lost in getting the apparently drowned person out of the water and getting the water out of him. The Schaefer or prone method requires but one operator at a time and no waste of time in preliminaries.

When taken from the water the patient is laid on the ground face downward, arms extended above the head, face a little to one side so as not to prevent the free passage of air. The operator kneels astride or beside the prone figure and lets his hands fall into the spaces between the short ribs. By letting the weight of the upper body fall upon his hands resting on the prone man, the air is forced out of the lungs; by relaxing the pressure, the chest cavity enlarges and air is drawn in to take the place of that forced out. By effecting this change of air — pressing and re-

Artificial respiration (*a*)

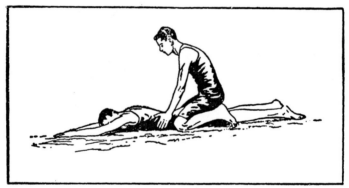

Artificial respiration (*b*)

laxing, twelve to fifteen times a minute (time it by watch at
first, and then count) — artificial breathing is performed.   If the
pressure does not bring the water out at once, clear up the
mouth and pull the tongue forward with the left hand.   Take
care and wedge the teeth apart while doing so, as the bite of the
human teeth is dangerous.   Sometimes it is necessary to work
an hour or two before the flicker of an eyelid or a gasp from the
patient rewards the life saver's efforts, and then he must carefully "piece in" the breathing until natural breathing is re-
sumed.   When breathing starts, then promote circulation by
rubbing the legs and body toward the heart.   Do not attempt
to stimulate by the throat until the patient can swallow.   Give
a teaspoonful of aromatic spirits of ammonia in half a glass of

water. When no water for diluting aromatic spirits of ammonia is available, a small quantity can be placed on the back part of the patient's tongue and it will be readily taken into the system.

Remember that by laying the patient face downward fluids in the air passages will run or be forced out, and the tongue will drop forward and require no holding, always an awkward task.

When there is but one person with the victim, artificial respiration will occupy his whole time. It alone will usually save life.

If a second man is present, his first thought should be the man's mouth — he must be sure it contains no tobacco, gum, false teeth, blood, mucus — it can be cleaned in a moment with a stroke of the finger. He can make sure that the tongue is forward and that no tight collar restricts the neck. If the abdominal muscles are rigid and the jaws tightly closed, both men can exert their whole weight in overcoming the rigidity of the abdominal muscles. The second can then see to providing some form of ammonia for the patient to inhale.

An unconscious patient must not be given any liquids through the mouth, as they will reach the lungs rather than the stomach. Medicines may be administered by inhalation or by hypodermics.

Aromatic spirits of ammonia may be poured on a handkerchief and held within three inches of the nose. If other preparations of ammonia are used, they should be diluted or held farther away. Try it on your own nose first. Spirits of camphor or menthol may be used.

In cases of asphyxiation remove the patient to pure air. The best service a crowd can render is to stand back to allow the patient plenty of air and not interfere. Valuable as drugs and other aids are the prime consideration is continuous, rhythmic, uninterrupted artificial respiration. We must not stop nor permit the patient to stand up until his breathing has become regular. There should be no delay in the attempt to revive the patient, such as removal in an ambulance; he must be revived first or artificial respiration carried on en route.

Treatment After Respiration Begins

The after treatment is important. Put the patient to bed, keep quiet and warm. Always get the services of a physician as soon as possible, but do not wait for him to come. Start work instantly. The patient needs oxygen, so keep spectators away. They are robbing the man of the life-giving properties of the air. For this reason, in all but the most severe weather, it is well to work on the patient in the open.

Grappling Equipment

Scouts doing work around water-front places and especially in camp should be provided with grappling irons, either small anchors or the sort that are called well or bucket grapplings, and be trained in their use. They would render genuine assistance to their community in recovering bodies where there have been fatalities, and also in recovering articles lost in fairly deep water. Large fish hooks alternating with sinkers on clothes-line make a good drag for covering large areas of the bottom. If the bottom is rocky or full of snags, a "trip line" to release the hook or grapple is very necessary and can be of much lighter line than the grapple rope.

In this connection, an excellent thing is a water glass which enables one to see the bottom when the sun is up, in from 10 to 25 feet of water, and lost objects, sunken boats, moorings, lost spectacles, clothing, anchors, cables, etc., are easily located. The "glass" is a tube of galvanized sheet iron, or a long wooden box about eight inches square, with a piece of clear glass set in the bottom and made tight with white lead or putty. By putting the glass end in the water and having the open top well covered where your head does not shut out the light, you can see under water while leaning over the stern of a boat, and being rowed from place to place.

BANDAGES

By Eugene L. Swan, M. D.

The word "bandage" means band, and is an appliance of some sort, made of cloth, folded or rolled up and employed to retain dressings of applications, to make pressure, and to correct deformities.

Bandaging constitutes one of the most necessary things that a scout should know with reference to his assistance to those who are injured. Besides being used to make pressure and to hold dressings in place, they are employed to hold splints in place, and to keep in normal position parts of the body that have been displaced.

The scout may employ bandages of two varieties — the roller bandage and the triangular bandage.

Making of Bandages

The roller bandage should be from one-half to four inches wide and about three feet long. It is made by folding over about six inches of the end, which is then folded upon itself again and again until a firm center, or core, is formed upon which to roll the rest of the bandage. It should be rolled so tight that the center cannot be pushed out of the roll. In a permanent scout headquarters or camp, the hospital squad may construct a bandage roller by running a stiff piece of wire through a cigar box and bending over the end outside the box into a handle like that on a hand-organ. Upon this, firm, well-rolled bandages may be constructed and when completed removed for use by the simple matter of pulling the wire from the center of the roll. They should be pinned or held by an elastic band to prevent unrolling.

Roller bandages may be made of any cloth, though naturally light, pliable material is best, as flannel, unbleached muslin, cheesecloth, or gauze. Unbleached muslin is the best material for general use. Sheets, blankets, underclothing, or shirts may be torn up into strips and used as bandages. Unbleached muslin should be washed to prevent ravelling edges.

Triangular bandages are simply and easily applied. Most nations supply their soldiers with them and they are carried on the field. The same materials may be used as in making a roller bandage.

To make a triangular bandage is simplicity itself. Take a piece of cloth about thirty-two inches square, cut diagonally from corner to corner and you will then have *two* triangular bandages.

There are several ways of folding and applying triangular bandages. The location where it is to be used will determine the method of application. Obviously a bandage around a sprained wrist will take a different form from one used as a sling on the arm.

Arrangements of Triangular Bandages

To arrange a triangular bandage spread out smooth and pass the point of the triangle over to the opposite side, then make two equal folds, forming a cravat bandage.

Cravat Bandage

This is useful where any sort of band is to be applied, as around an arm, wrist, head, eye, throat, or jaw. The method of application and the manner of folding are well illustrated in figures I, II, III, IV. This form of bandage is also useful in checking bleeding when applied snugly with a small roller bandage underneath, or any small, hard substance, as a pebble or coin.

Eye Bandage

With the dressing of cotton or gauze underneath, apply the bandage over eye and tie with a square knot at the back of head. Fig. I.

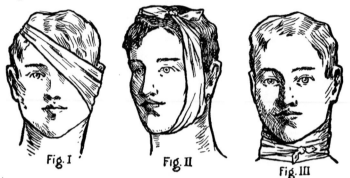

Fig. I   Fig. II   Fig. III

Jaw, or Side of Face, Bandage

One or two cravats may be used. Place one under chin and tie on top of head. If the forehead is to be included or it is desired to assist in holding the jaw bandage in place, fold second cravat around the forehead and tie at back of the head. Pin with a safety-pin where they cross each other. Fig. II.

Bandage for Neck

Place center of cravat with dressing underneath over the injury, carry ends around neck and tie with a square knot. Fig. III.

Bandage for Palm of Hand

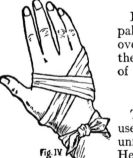

Lay cravat in straight line, placing palm of hand across it. Fold the ends over the back of the hand, carry around the wrist and tie. For injury to the back of the hand, reverse this action. Fig. IV.

Wrist or Hand Sling

The triangular bandage is not always used folded up like a cravat but is applied unfolded as a sling for the wrist or hand. Here it is tied around the neck and the arm slipped through the loop thus made. See

Fig.IV

Fig. V. Do not lift or lower the forearm above or below a right angle unless it is desired to check bleeding in the arm or hand, then elevate the sling until the hand is more nearly opposite the shoulders.

Arm Sling

When a support is desired for the whole forearm or for an injury to the elbow, use the following: throw one end of the bandage over the shoulder on the uninjured side, slip the point of the triangle under the injured arm so that it appears about two or three inches on the outside. Now take the lower end of

Fig. V   Fig VI   Fig VII

the bandage and carry around the back of the neck on the injured side and tie the two ends. To prevent the slipping of this sling, pin the end left around the arm. See Fig. VI.

A sling can also be made by pinning up the tail of a coat or shirt. A pillow slip or piece of blanket may be used to make a sling in an emergency, or the sleeve of the coat or shirt may be pinned to the shirt or coat at a right angle. See Fig. VII.

Where the Entire Hand is to Be Covered

First, lay the bandage down with the point of the triangle pointing away from fingers. Fig. VIII. Fold over the point as in Fig. IX, and passing the ends around the wrist tie in the back as in Fig. X. This is an excellent form of applying a loose bandage to a hand that is suffering from burns, bee stings, or general bruises. Of course some form of application would usually be underneath.

Head Injuries

Any injury to the head above the ears on the side or above the eyebrows in front may have the triangle applied as in Figs. XI and XII. Place the triangle across the top of the head with the point toward the back and the even edge just above the eyebrows, pass the ends around in front and tie or pin the end that is hanging down in back. See Fig. XII.

Side Injuries

For broken collar-bone, broken ribs, sprained shoulder, or any injury to the side, apply dressing in Fig. XIII as follows: Place one end of the bandage over the shoulder with the other end under opposite arm, bring these two ends around and tie in back. Now bring the third end around the body and tie at the back. If any of the ends do not come near enough together to tie comfortably, use a small strip of cloth or handkerchief to increase the length. See Fig. XIV.

For Head

The scout may employ this bandage for an injury anywhere above the ears, to hold a dressing or compress on a cut, or ap-

plication of witch hazel on a bruise or bee sting, or a cold application on the head for heat-stroke.   It may also be used in
place of a hat or cap when sleeping out of doors.   Some boys
catch cold easily sleeping out.

This bandage is applied in the following manner: Lay the
triangle on a smooth surface with the point toward you, fold in
a hem on straight edge, fold the point of the triangle underneath five inches, place this carefully on the head with a folded
hem just above the eyes; now take the ends that are hanging
down over the ears, and carefully pleat them into three or four
small folds so as to lie smoothly, carry around the head, cross
ends at the back and tie at front.   This bandage may also be
applied by not folding the point at the back of the head under,
but permitting it to hang down the neck until the tie has been
made and then pinning it up as in Fig. X.   As a rule, however,
this is not as smooth and of course requires a pin.

Bandage for Foot

Fig.XVI

Place foot on a smoothly laid triangle with the point extending beyond the toes about five inches.
Fold point back on instep, carry ends
around the ankle, cross and tie.   A
safety-pin is not necessary in applying this bandage but may at
times assist in retaining it in place,
i. e., Fig. XVI.   When employing
the triangular bandage, care should
always be used to apply the turns
smoothly by folding the loose ends into pleats and not permitting the bandage anywhere to be "bunchy."

Injury at Back of Head

For an injury at the back of the head, or neck, place the wide
part of the triangle at the base of the head, tie around the forehead.   This same form of bandage may be used tied around
the jaw for dislocation of the jaw.

Injury to the Collar-bone

An excellent use of the triangular bandage where it is desired
to hold a dressing in the armpit or for an injury to the collar-
bone, is as follows: Place the folded triangle in cravat-shape
underneath the arm, cross over the point of the shoulder and
tie underneath the arm on the opposite side.   The youngest

scout can, with very little practice, become sufficiently expert to apply them.

Injury to the Chest

A T-bandage for the chest is helpful where a large area of the chest requires a dressing and is made in the following manner: Take a piece of cloth about a foot wide, carry around the chest exactly in the same manner as a wide belt, pin tightly into place, and at right angles to this carry a strip of roller bandage over the shoulders and pin at the upper edge of the chest bandage, producing the same effect as one side of a pair of suspenders.

Neatness and Cleanliness

There is a vast difference in the appearance of a well-fitting, comfortable triangular bandage, and a rag simply wound around an injured part.

Scouts should be marked on the smooth appearance as well as the correct method of application of bandages. In small injuries to the forehead, hands, fingers, foot, toes, etc., an ordinary handkerchief may be folded in a triangle and used to a better advantage than the longer and bulky regulation triangle.

Roller Bandages

To be applied correctly, these bandages require a little more practice and skill than is necessary in using triangular bandages. They are, however, by far the best fitting and neatest. The youngest scout can, with very little practice, become sufficiently expert to apply them.

General Rule

Place the external surface of the bandage on the surface to be covered. Have the first turn caught by a few more turns. Have the roller unwind *into* the right hand; it will almost surely fall out of the hand if unwound *out* of the hand. Use the same pressure in all parts of the surface bandaged. Almost all beginners bandage too tightly. In removing a bandage, take the unfolded end in the left hand, gather into a wad and pass from the left to the right hand until, in a roughly folded mass, all is removed.

Roller bandages are applied in these ways, depending on the contour or shape of the member injured. They are termed circular, spiral, and reverse.

Circular Roller Bandage

A cylindrical part of the body may be covered by a circular bandage, each turn covering about two thirds of the previous turn and winding along the part being covered.   Fig. XVII.

Spiral Bandage

A conical part may be covered by a spiral bandage, each turn ascending a little higher than the previous turn at a slight angle to the part being covered.   The general appearance of this bandage is very much like that of a wire spring.   As each turn of the spiral bandage is tight at its upper, and loose at its lower edge, when going over a conical surface, the reverse is used to correct this gapping or bulging.   In making this bandage a few circular turns are always made first.   Fig. XVIII.

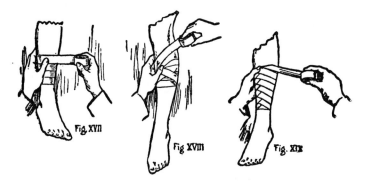

Spiral Reverse Bandage

Take the roller in right hand with not more than four inches slack, make one or two complete circular turns, then one spiral turn, place the thumb across the last turn and fold the bandage down (without any pulling) and continue on around the part in the same direction.   This bandage when finished resembles the leaves on an ear of corn as one husk lies over another.   Fig. XIX.

Spiral Bandage to All the Fingers

This bandage is to be applied where it is desired to have each individual finger bandaged separately, as in a burn, and when completed resembles a gauntlet or glove.   Take a roller one inch wide and half a yard long.   Take two circular turns around the wrist, pass obliquely around the wrist to the base of the thumb by spiral reverses, returning to the wrist; cover in each following finger in the manner just described and finish by two circular turns around the wrist.

If it is desired to bandage the palm or the back of the hand, use a half gauntlet, which is started like the full gauntlet except that instead of going to the end of the fingers, the bandage is carried in between each finger and back to the wrist and finally a spiral carried around the hand to hold these turns in place. If the back of the hand is to be bandaged keep that part uppermost, but if the palm is to be bandaged, the reverse position is used, or the palm up.

General Rules for Bandaging

1. Hold bandage in right hand unless naturally left handed, place fingers on the loose end to prevent slipping, and always catch the first turn by a second or third to anchor the bandage.

2. Unroll bandages always after the manner of a roll of carpet, or so that it will lie flat on the part.

3. Do not wet a bandage before applying it. When drying it shrinks and will become too tight.

4. Do not pull it so tight that it will mark the surface of the skin or impede circulation. Blue fingers or toes always call for a loosening of the bandage. In bandaging arms or legs, do not include feet or hands.

5. Bandage in the position that you desire a patient to remain when completed. For instance, if a knee bandaged with a patient sitting down, keep the leg straight or slightly bent if you desire him to walk after you have finished. If you are bandaging an arm at the elbow, bend it at a right angle before applying the bandage if you desire him to carry it in a sling, or expect him to feed himself with the injured arm.

6. Always bandage *over* a splint and not *under* it, and whenever possible never bandage directly upon the skin, but have some soft dressing underneath, as cotton, etc.

7. Bandage from below upward or in the general direction of the return circulation on a limb. Bandage from the internal surface toward the external, and, as for instance, on the leg, have your bandage go *away* and not toward the opposite leg when starting.

8. Remember when applying a bandage immediately after an injury that swelling may occur later, so apply your pressure accordingly. Always loosen a bandage that is too tight.

CHAPTER IX

GAMES

La Fitte's Treasure Hunt

La Fitte was a famous American pirate of the Gulf of Mexico. Like all pirates, he buried his treasure and made a map of it. La Fitte's actual notes have been found and read as follows:

"Start at the rock in Dead Man's Gulch, near the skull of the Spaniard, travel northwest 70 paces to a cache, where you will find a cask o' rum, from thence, due west 30 paces, where you will find the finger bones of Don Piedro Fiesto. Thence northeast 50 paces, where you will find a cache of coffin nails, thence north 20 paces, where you will find a cache of bullets, thence northeast 40 paces, where you will find a cache of copper coins, thence west 60 paces, where you will find a cache of brass coins, thence southeast 20 paces, where you will find a cache of silver coins, thence southwest 30 paces, where you will find a cache with the keys to the treasure chest, then northwest 30 paces, where you will find a cache containing a brass-bound chest full of bars of gold, bags of doubloons, and pieces of 'eight.'" Fig. 1.

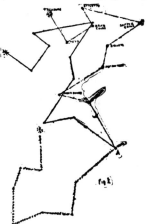

The scoutmaster must carefully lay out the course. At each cache he is supposed to bury the things enumerated, but in reality only marks the spot with a small peg. The treasure may be a pocket compass, scout whistle, knife, axe, cooking outfit, book, or other suitable prize.

The first contestant takes his place at the peg "A" (Fig. 2) with a pocket compass in his hand. "A" is supposed to be the "rock in Dead Man's Gulch." The scout, remembering that the black end of the needle is the north end, adjusts his compass until

A number of these games were furnished by Daniel Carter Beard, Frederick K. Vreeland, Dr. Chas A. Eastman, Jessie H. Bancroft, Ellen H. Wilson, and by scout officials throughout the field. All drawings on pages 383 to 400, inclusive, by Daniel Carter Beard.

the needle points exactly north, then he sights along the north-west point, gets his line of direction, steps off 70 paces, and hunts for the cask o' rum.   He is allowed only a certain time to find each cache, two, three, or five minutes, according to the difficulty of the undertaking.   The scoutmaster starts him with a whistle.

Fig 2.

When played as a game, each cache counts one, and the one finding the treasure makes the biggest score, of course.   The scoutmaster can hand the pathfinder bits of paper or pebbles, one for each peg found.   The pebbles serve as counters for the score.

The distances may be any number of paces you choose, but each direction should be one of the four points of the compass; that is, the four quarters of the compass, north, south, east, and west, or the four eighths of the compass, that is, northeast, northwest, southeast, and southwest.   To go any further into the subdivisions of the compass makes the game too difficult. You will find it hard enough to find the treasure if you stick to quarters and eighths, and you had better practise first simply on quarters; that is, go east so many paces, north so many, south so many, and west so many.

It is allowable for the scout to place his compass on the peg and lie prone on the ground to sight his directions.   A number of boys may play this game at once by laying out several courses from the rock in Dead Man's Gulch, as shown in Fig. 1, the prize being given to the one who reaches the treasure chest first.

The beauty of La Fitte's Treasure Hunt is that it gives one practice and experience in the use of the compass which may serve one to advantage on an occasion of dire necessity.

Let 'er Buck

This is the game of "Busting the Broncho." A troop puts forth its picked scouts for horses and picked scouts for riders, who challenge those of another troop.

The scout as a broncho stoops slightly, places his hands on his knees, grasps firmly his trousers, and dare not remove his hands from there throughout the entire contest. The rider scout mounts on the back of the broncho, clasping his waist with his knees, but not bringing his feet in front of the broncho's waist or legs; they must always be in the rear. With his hands he grasps the shoulders of the broncho, but dare not put his hands or arms about the broncho's neck or head; he must always grasp the broncho's shoulder or back. He dare not even put his arms around the waist or under the armpits of the broncho.

The broncho jumps, bucks, wriggles, squirms, dodges, plunges, and does everything he can think of to throw the rider off his back. If any part of the rider's body touches the ground he is considered thrown and the broncho wins. If the broncho falls or if he removes his hands from his knees he is broken, or if the rider succeeds in staying on his back for three minutes at a time he is broken.

The contest is for three rounds of three minutes each. Should one of them win all three rounds he scores all five points. The winner of two rounds out of three scores three points.

Capture the Flag

This is a competition between two troops or two opposing teams in the same troop, the object being to capture the opponent's flag. The game should be played if possible in the woods or in rough country which gives opportunity for stalking and strategy.

The scouts are divided into two camps, each with a leader and each having its own flag mounted on a light pole or a scout staff. The players of one camp should be marked by a handkerchief or necktie tied around the arm so that a scout can tell at a glance whether another scout is a friend or a foe.

Each camp has its own territory in which its scouts are free to move as they please, but on which their opponents enter at their peril. The two camps are separated by a boundary line, such as a brook or a trail or some other line that can be easily located. Any scout crossing this line may be captured by the enemy.

A starting point is chosen near the center of the line, and the game starts with the two troops or camps assembled close together on opposite sides of the line, each in its own territory. The scoutmaster explains the rules of the game, then blows one blast on his whistle as a signal for the two camps to set up their flags.

The flag may be located at any point within one hundred paces of the starting point. Judgment should be shown in choosing a place where it cannot be easily found or attacked. The staff must be planted in the ground so that the flag can be seen, though it is fair to make it as inconspicuous as possible.

After three minutes the scoutmaster blows the warning signal, three blasts on his whistle, and the game is on. The object is to enter the enemy's territory, capture the flag, and carry it across the line into home territory without being caught.

Scouts may be posted to guard the flag but they must not stand nearer than fifty feet from the flag unless an enemy scout goes within the fifty-foot circle. The guards then can follow him.

Any scout found in the enemy's territory may be captured by grasping him and holding on while the captor says, "Caught, caught, caught!" If he does not hold on long enough to say "Caught" three times, the other scout is not captured.

When a scout is captured he must go to the guard house with the scout who caught him. He is there placed under guard. The guard house is a tree or rock twenty feet from the line at the starting point. The prisoner must keep hand or foot on the tree or rock, otherwise he cannot be released by his friends.

A prisoner may be released by a friend crossing the line and touching him while the prisoner is touching the guard house. If his comrade succeeds in doing this, both are allowed to return free into their own territory. But if the rescuer is caught by the guards before he touches the prisoner, he, too, must go to the guard house.

A scout can rescue only one prisoner at a time.

If the flag is successfully captured it must be carried across the line into home territory. If the raider is caught before he reaches the line, the flag is set up again at the point where it was rescued and the game goes on as before.

If neither side captures the enemy's flag within the time agreed upon, which may be an hour, the scoutmaster calls the game off by blowing the assembly call and the game is won by the camp that has the most prisoners.

This game gives great opportunities for team work and strategy, and for the practice of stalking and various kinds of woodcraft. The game is usually won by the team whose leader is most skilful in placing his scouts and planning stratagems to mislead the enemy and draw the guards away from the flag so that it may be captured by another scout.

The Round-up Hat Relay

A relay team consists of eight scouts. Each lap of the course is 110 yards in length. If a half-mile circular course cannot be obtained use a straightway 110 yard dash course, dividing the relay team into two equal halfs, four scouts at each end of the course. The scouts are numbered 1, 3, 5, and 7 at one end of the course and 2, 4, 6, and 8 at the other end of the course. The scouts lay their hats in a row midway between the ends of the course. This row is laid parallel to the length of the course and the hats are laid in the following order, according to the numbers given to the scouts; the hat nearest to the end of the course at which scouts 1, 3, 5, and 7 are standing will be the hat of Scout No. 1 and the others in order from that one are as follows: 3, 5, 7, 8, 6, 4, and 2 toward the other end of the course at which scouts 2, 4, 6, and 8 have been standing. These hats are laid about six inches apart.

Scout No. 1 starts the race at the signal and in running by the hats picks up his own hat, puts it on his head, and runs to the line at the opposite end of the course. Scout No 2 stands toeing the line, reaching his hand forward to be tagged. No. 1 tags No. 2 and No. 2 starts off back over the same course, picks up his hat, puts it on his head, and runs and tags No. 3, and so on through the relay. Scout No. 8 must cross the tape with his hat on his head. No scout can start his next man in the relay if his own hat is not on his head. If he has dropped it or has picked up the wrong hat he must go back and get the right hat on his head and then start off his next man. The winner, second, and third score, 5, 3, and 1 points respectively. Each troop may enter as many relay teams as it may choose.

Border Scouting

This is a game for two competing patrols. The available play space is divided into two equal parts, the line dividing it being called the boundary or border. A den about 12 feet square is marked off on the boundary line. One patrol stands in the den; the other scatters and hides. As soon as they are all hidden, their patrol leader calls "Ready" and the patrol in the den starts out to find them, one scout being left behind as den keeper. Throughout the game he must stay inside of the den. Each scout of the other side tagged is a prisoner and is brought to the den, where he must stay until the end of the game or until he is freed. A prisoner may be freed by one of his own patrol running through the den and tagging him. The den keeper may make both scouts prisoners by tagging the rescuing scout while he is in the den. The game ends when all scouts of the hiding patrol are tagged.

·Scout Treed by Wolves

One boy is chosen as scout, the rest are wolves. The wolves' den, a circle 25 feet in diameter, is marked off in the center of the field. Around it smaller circles about 12 feet in diameter and 25 yards apart represent trees. When attacked by the pack the scout runs for a tree. He carries a small balloon, representing his "heart," and a stuffed club. The wolves cannot enter the tree rings nor can he enter their den, but all may reach over into the circles.

If the wolves break the scout's heart, he is dead. If he knocks off a wolf's hat with his club, the wolf is dead. If at the end of fifteen minutes the scout is still alive and has not killed all the wolves, a party of rescuers may try to kill the attacking wolves before they can reach their den.

The treed scout scores 20 points for saving himself and 15 for each wolf he kills before the fifteen minutes are up. The rescuers score 15 points for each wolf killed.

A wolf gets 20 points for killing the scout and 15 points for killing one of the rescuing party. The side having the largest total score wins.

Chipmunk Hunt

Each boy taking part provides himself with four lifesize chipmunks made of cotton or rags wrapped in paper. Each selects a tree and fastens his chipmunks lightly to the limbs with long pins or slender nails. Each hunter has a bow and a blunt-headed arrow. A circle with a radius of 25 feet is drawn around each tree, over which the hunter may not step while shooting.

The object is to bring down as many chipmunks as possible in fifteen minutes. The shooting begins at a signal from the referee, who keeps time. A caller keeps score. The hunters having only one arrow apiece, try to shoot so that the arrow will bound back to them. If a hunter clears his own tree before time is called he may shoot at the tree of any other boy who has not finished. Each chipmunk brought down counts ten; if from another boy's tree, it counts fifteen; a chipmunk hit but not knocked off counts five. The boy with the highest score wins.

Douban*

This is a ball game named from the sticks with which the ball is played. These sticks are of hollow bamboo with a striking end of rubber, which make it practicable to play on a smaller field and with more players than may be done with hockey or shinny sticks.

FIELD. This is square or oblong in shape, measuring from 20 to 50 feet in length and breadth. This space is divided into four equal sections by two lines that cross in the center. In each corner a goal area is marked off by the segment of a circle which connects the side and end lines for a distance of 4 feet on each.

Goals: within the goal area, across the corner, a goal line is placed 3 feet long. This may be drawn on the ground, or it may be a stick or rope stretched above the ground.

*By courtesy of the Douban Co., Boston, Mass.

Center Circle: In the center of the field a circle 3 feet in diameter is drawn on the ground. Within this circle the Captains stand to put the ball in play.

PLAYERS. Each team consists of 7 or 11 players. These are a Captain (or "center"), a right "corner," a left "corner," a right and left guard, and right and left forwards. On large courts four rovers may be added.

The corners guard each goal in their home section, and may not go out of the goal area.

The guards stand in the area outside the goal, each being paired off with a forward from the opposite team. Neither guards nor forwards may move from their assigned sections.

The Captains (also called "centers") stand in the center circle at the opening of the game, or whenever the ball is put in play, but during the game may move anywhere on the field on either side of any line except in the goal areas.

Rovers, if used, start the game one from each team in each of the four main sections of the court. They may play anywhere on the field except in the goal areas.

START. The ball is put in play at the opening of the game and after each goal scored, by a "bully-off" in the center by the Captains. For this the ball is placed on the ground; the centers stand, each with his left side toward the opponent's goal, and when the Referee's whistle sounds each taps the striking end of his stick on the ground on his side of the ball, and then touches his opponent's stick with his own over the ball; this is done three times, and then each hits the ball trying to send it toward the opponent's goal.

RULES.

1. Each player must stay in his home section, with the exception of the Captains and the rovers.

2. No player but the corner may enter the goal area.

3. The stick may not be raised higher than the shoulder.

4. No player except the goal tender may touch the ball with anything but the stick.

5. Players may not touch with any part of the body or with the clothing the side lines or corner lines.

6. If the ball goes outside the boundary lines and returns, play shall continue. If it remains out the Referee shall bring it back to the point where it crossed the line and, placing it on the floor between the two players involved, shall put it in play as at the beginning of the game. If one player purposely puts the ball outside, the Referee may bring it back and give the ball to the opponent.

7. When a foul is called the Captain of the offended team may place the ball in the center of the floor and take a free shot for the right corner. In this shot the ball must be hit cleanly, not *scooped* or *pushed*. If a "corner" (goal) is made it counts *one* and the ball is returned to the center and is put into play by the Referee. If the Captain fails to make the "corner" the ball goes at once into play.

8. Any infraction of the above rules is a foul.

SCORE. The game is played in two halves of twenty minutes each with a rest of ten minutes between halves. For young players an additional two minutes' rest may be taken halfway through each half.

Teams change goals in the second half.

One point is scored for a team for each goal made.

The team wins which has the highest score at the end of the second half.

OFFICIAL. A Referee, who is not playing, should be the authoritative official for each game, deciding the score, time limits and fouls, and any disputes.

Tower Ball

A circle is marked on the ground, measuring from 10 to 30 feet in diameter, according to the number of players.

In the center from six to ten staffs are stacked to form a "tower."

From ten to thirty players may play at once. For a large number two balls may be used.

Two or four players stand near the tower as guards, and try to keep a ball from going in or through the tower. This ball (a base ball or tennis ball) is hit by the other players, who stand outside the circle and play the ball with their staffs.

Whenever a ball enters the tower all of the guards are "out," that is, retire from the game, and the same number of circle players take their places as guards. If the players are numbered consecutively before the game begins the succession as guards can be most quickly decided by the numerical order.

The team of guards which holds out the longest wins the game.

The ball must be rolled on the ground and played entirely with the staff, not kicked or played by hand or in any other way with the body.

If the ball stops within reach of a guard or his staff he should quickly hit it out to the circle players.

Circle players may not enter the circle at any time, and may recover a ball that stops out of reach only by hitting it out with a staff, unless a guard can so send it out.

Should the guards knock down the tower, they are not out unless the ball passes within the enclosure that was covered by the tower. The stack should be immediately rebuilt.

An Umpire should decide disputed points and time the periods during which each set of guards holds out.

This game may be played with gymnasium wands or Douban sticks as well as with scout staffs.

Water Tilting

This is a competitive game in boats for two patrols. Four or more boys take part at one time, at least two from each patrol, one boy being armed with a tilting pole, the other at the oars. The combatants stand on the seats of the boats and each tries to force the other overboard. The one who falls overboard is out of the game, his oarsman taking his place and another scout from the same patrol replacing the oarsman. Each boat may have more than one oarsman, numbered and promoted in order of numbers. The side wins which finishes with a combatant still standing in the boat.

Or points may be scored as follows: One point for stepping off the seat with one foot; two points for stepping off the seat with both feet; five points for falling overboard. The patrol scoring the least number of points wins.

Canoe Tag

Any number of canoes or boats may take part. One canoe is "it" and tries to tag another by throwing into it a cork ball, inflated rubber bag or cushion, or any similar article which will float and is light enough not to hurt any one. Each canoe should have the same number of persons, so that odds will be equal. It is best not to use more than three in a boat. Those in the boats pursued must not touch the ball to interfere with its falling into the boat.

The Lost Patrol

This is a game for two patrols, the patrol leaders acting as captains. A goal and a signal station are decided upon. One patrol is chosen as hunters, the other is called the Lost Patrol. The captain of the Lost Patrol hides all of his scouts in the same place. He then goes to the signal station and signals the hunters that his patrol is ready.

The hunters start out separately or in groups, as directed by their captain. At intervals the captain at the signal station tells his scouts by means of signals previously agreed upon where the hunters are. When the hunters are at a safe distance he signals his patrol to return to the goal, at the same time calling, "Lost Patrol!" The hunters immediately start to chase them. If the Lost Patrol reaches the goal first, they win the game and may hide again. If any one of the hunters sees the hiding scouts he calls "Lost Patrol" and they all start to race for the goal. If the hunters reach the goal first, they win and become the Lost Patrol and the game is repeated.

Signals may be given in one of two ways: by signal flags, or by use of the Morse Code. In using the latter a drum, whistle, tin pan, or any other implement of noise-making may be used.

Scouting

One or more patrols may take part in this game.

A number of places equal to the number of scouts competing is selected, all places being about the same distance from the starting point. A scout is sent to each place, returning as soon as possible. He may also be instructed by the leader in charge to report on certain things along the way, such as the number and color of houses, the number or names of streets, the number and direction of roads, the kinds of trees, the kinds of birds, etc.

Points may be scored as follows:

The first scout returning scores as many points as there are scouts competing, less one.

The second scout returning scores one point less than the first scout, and so on.

The last boy returning scores zero. A maximum of five points and a minimum of no points may be given for accuracy of reports. Other points may be scored according to the discretion of the leader in charge. The scout wins who scores the highest number of points, or the patrol wins whose members collectively score the highest number of points.

Blow the Feather

This is an indoor game. The players sit around a long table. A feather is kept in the air by blowing, each player having one count against him if it falls on his right side. Or one side of the table may play against the other side.

The Push O'-War

The push-o'-war is just the reverse of the tug-o'-war. Tie a ribbon in the center of a scout staff and let two boys each grasp an end, while a third boy stands holding a staff upright to show the center of the field. At the word "Set" the boys grasp the staff, the umpire adjusts it so that the ribbon is exactly opposite the upright pole which the third scout is

Push O'-War

holding, then he says, "Go" and the boys begin to push for dear life. The one who succeeds in pushing the other way until he himself stands opposite the upright pole wins the contest and can challenge all comers until he is pronounced victor or loser to some other sturdy boy. Be careful to keep the ends of the staff away from the body so that a sudden thrust will only push it past you and not jab it into you.

The Corral

The Corral is a game played in a field 100 feet square. The corral is a 10-foot square section in one corner of the field. It is formed by planting staves or posts on the boundary lines of the corral about $3\frac{1}{3}$ feet apart.

Two patrols of eight scouts enter the field. One patrol constitutes the Steers and the other the Cow-punchers. The object of the contest is that the Cow-punchers shall herd all of the Steers in the corral within ten minutes' time. The two patrols then change sides, the Cow-punchers become the Steers and the Steers become the Cow-punchers, and contest for ten minutes as before. The patrol leaders make their choice of Steers or Cow-punchers for the first half by flipping up a coin.

The game for the Steers is entirely a defensive one. They may retreat before the on-coming Cow-punchers or they may dodge between them. Should they retreat between the posts of the corral they must remain there and are branded. If in their attempt to dodge between the Cow-punchers they are tagged, they are then considered as lassoed and are sent to the corral to be branded.

The game for the Cow-punchers is a game of team work, spread over as great an area of the field as possible, and working toward the Steers, closing in upon them and forcing them to retreat into the corral. There is no tackling in football fashion, merely tagging the Steers.

The scoring for the contest is done in the following manner: A point is scored by the Cow-punchers for every Steer corraled in ten minutes' time. Also a point is scored by the Steers for every Steer which remains uncaught at the end of the ten minutes' time. Thus if the Cow-punchers succeed in corraling 3 Steers in the ten minutes' time, the score stands 5 to 3 in favor of the Steers. Should all of the Steers be corraled before the ten minutes' time has elapsed, time is called and the balance of the half is not played or considered.

Run, Swim, and Paddle Race

Contestants line up thirty yards from the water's edge, each opposite his own canoe, which is tied or anchored fifty yards from shore. At a signal, the contestants run to water's edge, swim to canoes, climb in and paddle back, jump out, and run back to starting point.

Pyramid Building

1
2 3
4 5 6
7 8 9 10

Ten scouts are numbered according to size, No. 1 being the smallest. They stand at 10 paces from a gymnasium mat. At the word "Go," they rush forward, numbers 7, 8, 9, 10, falling on their hands and knees close together. Numbers 4, 5, 6, hop upon them in the same position, straddling the space between them; numbers 2 and 3 mount the second tier and take their places. Then number one, the smallest, climbs to the top and stands erect. At the word "Down" every scout straightens out his arms and legs and down they come in a nice friendly bunch. There is no danger.

Flag Race

Flag Race

A row of small holes is arranged at the goal line in which flags may be stuck and held upright. The racers run, each carrying a flag, and the one who first plants his flag upright in a hole is the winner.

The Swatter

The "swatter" is a revolving target which you charge at with your scout staff. You must first learn how to hold your staff. Never allow the butt of the staff to come in front of your body or touch any part of your person except the hands and arms, as a thrust from the staff might cause rupture or very serious injury. Grasp your staff as shown in the cut.

The "swatter" is a post set firmly in the ground, like a hitching post, on top of which is a short piece of timber about two inches thick and four inches wide. It is set up on edge and a hole bored through it near the middle so that it will move freely upon a spike or swivel; the spike is driven into the top of the post. On one end of the plank is nailed a square piece of board for a target, painted as shown in the cut. Lash to the other end an old stocking containing cotton which has been saturated with flour, or a big wet sponge may be used.

The Swatter

When all is ready the target man steadies the target by holding the end of the stocking. The scout "couches" his staff and at the command "Attention" fixes himself in position with his eyes upon the target. At the word "Go" he runs full tilt at the target, trying to strike it in the center; of course this spins the target around and "swats" the scout on the back of the neck with the stocking unless he is very spry. If he is marked by the flour or wet by the sponge he scores nothing, but if he hits the target and escapes the stocking he gets ten for a bullseye, eight for the first ring, six for the second, and one for the target outside the rings. Test the swatter before beginning to see if there is danger of the stick striking the scout. If so, this can be remedied by padding the stick with hay, cotton, or excelsior and an old cloth.

The Besieged City

A village or group of farm buildings is surrounded by a circle of scouts who must not approach nearer the town than a certain line agreed upon. These besiegers conceal themselves as best they may and lie in wait for a scout who tries to bear a message from without to some one in the besieged city. The boy must be caught and held to be captured; if he breaks away he is not put out. If he gets through the line it counts one point. If he succeeds in bringing a message back to a point or one of a number of points agreed upon, it scores two. Two or three messengers could be used to complicate the interest.

Antelope Race

This is to be done by teams of eight. The scouts run in single file with at least one hand on the hip or belt of the scout ahead. Falling down or breaking apart throws out the team. The

Antelope Race

distance is fifty yards and return, the turn being made to the left. The team must finish intact. The team wins whose leader first breasts the tape, provided the patrol is unbroken throughout the race.

Cock Fighting

Have two strong sticks, such as broomsticks, cut two feet long and pad one end with a ball of cloth. Each boy sits down inside an eight-foot ring, with his knees over the stick and his arms under it, hands clasped in front of the knees. In this position each opponent tries to upset the other, to make him lose his spur (the pad on the stick) or to push him out of the ring. Whoever does any of these things wins the round and scores one. Any odd number of rounds may be fought.

Tilting

This is a competitive game for two patrols.

Two teams (four boys) take part at a time. Each team is composed of one combatant and one guard. Place two boxes, barrels, or chairs, from six to ten feet apart, according to the length of the tilting poles. One combatant stands on each, his guard standing behind him on the ground to help him in case of a bad fall. Each combatant is armed with a tilting pole (a scout staff with a soft, padded end). Each tries by pushing or thrusting to force his apponent to dismount. If either is pushed off, he is out of the game, his place being taken by his own guard and another scout from his own patrol becoming the new guard. The patrol that finishes with one combatant still mounted wins the tilt.

Score may be kept by counting one point for each scout dismounted, the patrol with the smaller score winning.

Skunk Tag

This game comes from the Sioux Indians. Each player holds his nose with one hand, holds up one foot with the other hand. As long as he keeps this position he cannot be tagged, but if he lets go with either hand he can be tagged by the boy who is "it."

Skunk Tag

Hat Ball, Baby in the Hat, or Roley Poley

All scouts taking part place hats or caps in a row. A throwing line is drawn or is marked 15 or 20 feet from the hats. A soft ball and a supply of marbles, pebbles, or small sticks are provided. These latter are called "babies."

One scout is chosen "it"; the others line up each behind his own hat. "It" throws the ball at the hats. Each time he throws and misses, a "baby" is placed in his hat. When the ball lands in a hat, the owner of the hat takes the ball, while all the other scouts run away. As quickly as possible he throws the ball at one of them. If it hits the scout, a "baby" is placed in that scout's hat and he becomes "it" for the next game. If he misses, a "baby" is placed in his own hat and he becomes "it" for the next game.

As soon as any scout has five "babies" in his hat he is "put through the mill," that is, he must stand with his back to the players and each player is allowed a certain number of throws at him with the soft ball. This number may vary from one to five according to the number of scouts playing.

Where hats are not available, small holes are dug in the

ground and the ball is rolled into them. The game then continues as above. This version is called Roley Poley.

Poison

Mark a circle six or more feet in diameter on the ground. Two patrols form a circle around this, the scouts from the patrols alternating. All scouts join hands and move rapidly around the circle, while each scout tries to force the opponent next to him to step into the inside circle. Any scout stepping into this circle is poisoned and must drop out of the game. The game continues until all scouts except one are out. The patrol to which he belongs wins.

Crab Race

Each boy takes position illustrated on hands and feet, face up, toes on the starting line. The race is run backward in this position.

Crab Race

Hand Wrestling

This is a competitive game for two patrols. Two scouts, one from each patrol, stand facing each other. They place the outside of their right feet together, the left feet being placed backward, knees slightly bent, and join right hands. Each tries to force the other to lift or move one or both of his feet or to lose his balance. The scout who does so loses and must drop out. His place is taken by another of his own patrol. This is continued until all scouts except one are out or until all of one patrol are out. The patrol wins which has the last boy standing.

Leap Frog and Par

Scouts are arranged in line a short distance behind a starting line. The first scout stands on the starting line, his side turned to the line, and makes a Back by placing his feet apart and putting his hands on his knees, the foot nearest the line of boys being on the starting line. The others jump over him in turn. Any scout missing must change places with the Back.

Par. A patrol leader acts as captain. The scout making the

Back stands on the line as before. Each scout in turn jumps over him. The Back moves forward from the starting line a distance equal to the width plus the length of the captain's foot, and the captain tells the scouts some particular way which they are to jump. After each scout has jumped in turn the Back is again moved forward. This continues indefinitely. Any scout missing must change places with the Back. Each time the Back moves forward the captain changes his instructions as to how the jump is to be made. The following are suggested as different methods of jumping:

One step and jump, or one hop and jump.

Two steps and a jump, two hops and a jump, or one hop, one skip, and a jump; or any other combination the captain chooses.

Scouts' Par

This is played as above except that in addition to the various jumps each scout must repeat one point of the scout law while jumping. Scouts must take points of the law in their proper order unless otherwise instructed by the captain, and any scout failing in this, even though he succeeds in jumping, must change places with the Back.

NOTE: Leap frog in any of these or other forms may be played as a competitive patrol game, special rules being agreed upon before the beginning of the game.

Duck on a Rock

Each player has a stone, called a "duck," about the size of a baseball. Bean bags may be used in a gymnasium. A large rock or post is selected and a line drawn twenty-five feet from it for a firing line. First all the players throw their ducks at the goal from the firing line. The one who strikes nearest, or nearest the center, becomes first guard, places his duck on the rock, and stands guard near it. The other players then take turns trying to knock off his duck, throwing from the firing line. After a throw the thrower must recover his duck and run back behind the line. If he is tagged by the guard he must mount guard himself. He may be tagged at any time he is within the line unless he stands with his foot on his duck, where it first fell. He may stand thus until he sees a good chance to run, but if he once picks his duck up he may not put it down again.

If the guard's duck is knocked off, he must not tag a player until he replaces it. Any player tagged by the guard must put his own duck on the rock. The guard must quickly get his own duck and run behind the firing line, as he may be tagged as soon as the new guard gets his duck on the rock.

Lion Hunting*

A lion is represented by one scout, who goes out with tracking irons on his feet, and a pocketful of corn or peas, and six lawn-tennis balls or rag balls. He is allowed half an hour's start, and then the patrol go after him, following his spoor, each armed with one tennis ball with which to shoot him when they find him. The lion may hide or creep about or run, just as he feels inclined, but whenever the ground is hard or very greasy he must drop a few grains of corn every few yards to show the trail.

If the hunters fail to come up to him neither wins the game. When they come near to his lair the lion fires at them with his tennis balls, and the moment a hunter is hit he must fall out dead and cannot throw his tennis ball. If the lion gets hit by a hunter's tennis ball he is wounded, and if he gets wounded three times he is killed.

Tennis balls may be fired only once; they cannot be picked up and fired again in the same fight.

Each scout must collect and hand in his tennis balls after the game. In winter, if there is snow, this game can be played without tracking irons, and using snowballs instead of tennis balls.

Plant Race

Start off your scouts, either cycling or on foot, to go in any direction they like, to get a specimen of any ordered plant, say a sprig of yew, a shoot of ilex, a horseshoe mark from a chestnut tree, a briar rose, or something of that kind, whichever you may order, such as will tax their knowledge of plants and will test their memory as to where they noticed one of the kind required, and will also make them quick in getting there and back.

Throwing the Assegai

Target, a thin sack, lightly stuffed with straw, or a sheet of card-board, or canvas stretched on a frame.

Assegais to be made of wands, with weighted ends sharpened or with iron arrowheads on them.

*The games from Lion Hunting to Hare and Hounds are from Lieutenant-General Sir Robert Baden-Powell.

Flag Raiding

Two or more patrols on each side.

Each side will form an outpost within a given tract of country to protect three flags (or at night three lanterns two feet above ground), planted not less than two hundred yards (one hundred yards at night) from it. The protecting outpost will be posted in concealment either all together or spread out in pairs. It will then send out scouts to discover the enemy's position When these have found out where the outpost is, they try to creep round out of sight till they can get to the flags and bring them away to their own line. One scout may not take away more than one flag.

This is the general position of a patrol on such an outpost:

Patrol Leader

P. P. P.

Flags

Any scout coming within fifty yards of a stronger party will be put out of action if seen by the enemy; if he can creep by without being seen it is all right.

Scouts posted to watch as outposts cannot move from their ground, but their strength counts as double, and they may send single messages to their neighbors or to their own scouting party.

An umpire should be with each outpost and with each scouting patrol.

At a given hour operations will cease, and all will assemble at the given spot to hand in their reports. The following points might be awarded:

For each flag or lamp captured and brought in 5
For each report or sketch of the position of the enemy's outposts up
  to five 5
For each report of movement of enemy's scouting patrols 2

The side which makes the biggest total wins.

The same game may be played to test the scouts in stepping lightly — the umpire being blindfolded. The practice should preferably be carried out where there are dry twigs lying about, and gravel, etc. The scout may start to stalk the blind enemy at one hundred yards distance and he must do it fairly fast — say, in one minute and a half — to touch the blind man before he hears him.

Stalking and Reporting

The umpire places himself out in the open and sends each scout or pair of scouts away in different directions about half a mile off. When he waves a flag, which is the signal to begin, they all hide, and then proceed to stalk him, creeping up and watching all he does. When he waves the flag again, they rise, come in, and report each in turn all that he did, either by handing in a written report or verbally, as may be ordered. The umpire meantime has kept a lookout in each direction, and, every time he sees a scout he takes two points off that scout's score. He, on his part, performs small actions, such as sitting down, kneeling, looking through glasses, using handkerchief, taking hat off for a bit, walking round in a circle a few times, to give scouts something to note and report about him. Scouts are given three points for each act reported correctly. It saves time if the umpire makes out a scoring card beforehand, giving the name of each scout, and a number of columns showing each act of his, and what mark that scout wins, also a column of deducted marks for exposing themselves.

Spider and Fly

A bit of country or section of the town about a mile square is selected as the web, and its boundaries described, and an hour fixed at which operations are to cease.

One patrol (or half-patrol) is the "spider," which goes out and selects a place to hide itself.

The other patrol (or half-patrol) go a quarter of an hour later as the "fly" to look for the "spider." They can spread themselves about as they like, but must tell their leader anything that they discover.

An umpire goes with each party.

If within the given time (say, about two hours) the fly has not discovered the spider, the spider wins. The spiders write down the names of any of the fly patrol that they may see.

Stalking

Instructor acts as a deer — not hiding, but standing, moving a little now and then if he likes.

Scouts go out to find, and each in his own way tries to get up to him unseen.

Directly the instructor sees a scout, he directs him to stand up as having failed. After a certain time the instructor calls "time," all stand up at the spot which they have reached, and the nearest wins.

Demonstrate the value of adapting color of clothes to background by sending out one boy about five hundred yards to stand against different backgrounds in turn, till he gets one similar in color to his own clothes.

The rest of the patrol to watch and to notice how invisible he becomes when he gets a suitable background. E. g., a boy in a gray suit standing in front of dark bushes, etc., is quite visible — but becomes less so if he stands in front of a gray rock or house; a boy in a dark suit is very visible in a green field, but not when he stands in an open door-way against dark interior shadow.

Scout Hunting

One scout is given time to go out and hide himself; the remainder then start to find him; he wins if he is not found, or if he can get back to the starting point within a given time without being touched.

Relay Race

One patrol pitted against another to see who can get a message sent a long distance in shortest time by means of relay of runners (or cyclists). The patrol is ordered out to send in three successive notes or tokens (such as sprigs of certain plants) from a point, say, two miles distant or more. The leader in taking his patrol out to the spot drops scouts at convenient distances, who will then act as runners from one post to the next and back. If relays are posted in pairs, messages can be passed both ways.

Track Memory

Make a patrol sit with their feet up, so that other scouts can study them. Give the scouts, say, three minutes to study the boots. Then leaving the scouts in a room or out of sight, let one of the patrol make some footmarks in a good bit of ground. Call up the scouts one by one and let them see the track and say who made it.

Spot the Thief

Get a stranger to make a track unseen by the scouts. The scouts study his track so as to know it again.

Then put the stranger among eight or ten others and let them all make their tracks for the boys to see, going by in rotation. Each scout then in turn whispers to the umpire which man made the original track — describing him by his number in filing past. The scout who answers correctly wins; if more than one answers correctly, the one who then draws the best diagram, from memory, of the footprint wins.

Smugglers Over the Border

The "border" is a certain line of country about four hundred yards long, preferably a road or wide path or bit of sand, on which foot tracks can easily be seen. One patrol watches the border with sentries posted along this road, with a reserve posted farther inland. This latter about half-way between the "border" and the "town"; the "town" would be a base marked by a tree, building, or flags, etc., about half a mile distant from the border. A hostile patrol of smugglers assemble about half a mile on the other side of the border. They will all cross the border, in any formation they please, either singly or together or scattered, and make for the town, either walking or running, or at scouts' pace. Only one among them is supposed to be smuggling, and he wears tracking irons, so that the sentries walk up and down their beat (they may not run till after the "alarm"), waiting for the tracks of the smuggler. Directly a sentry sees the track, he gives the alarm signal to the reserve and starts himself to follow up the track as fast as he can. The reserves thereupon coöperate with him and try to catch the smuggler before he can reach the town. Once within the boundary of the town he is safe and wins the game.

Shop Window Outdoors in Town

Umpire takes a patrol down a street past six shops, gives them half a minute at each stop, then, after moving them off to some distance, he gives each boy a pencil and card, and tells him to write from memory, or himself takes down, what they noticed in, say, the third and fifth shops. The one who sets down most articles correctly wins. It is useful practice to match one boy against another in heats — the loser competing again, till you arrive at the worst. This gives the worst scouts the most practice.

Similar Game Indoors

Send each scout in turn into a room for half a minute; when he comes out take down a list of furniture and articles which he notices. The boy who notices most wins.

The simplest way of scoring is to make a list of the articles in the room on your scoring paper with a column for marks for each scout against them, which can then easily be totalled up at foot.

Follow the Trail

Send out a "hare," either walking or cycling, with a pocketful of corn, nutshells, confetti paper, or buttons, etc., and drop a few here and there to give a trail for the patrol to follow.

Or go out with a piece of chalk and draw the patrol sign on walls, gate posts, pavements, lamp posts, trees, etc., every here and there, and let the patrol hunt you by these marks. Patrols should wipe out all these marks as they pass them for tidiness, and so as not to mislead them for another day's practice.

The other road signs should also be used, such as closing up certain roads as not used, and hiding a letter at some point, giving directions as to the next turn.

Scout's Nose Indoors

Prepare a number of paper bags, all alike, and put in each a different smelling article, such as chopped onion in one, tan in another, rose leaves, leather, anise-seed, violet powder, orange peel, etc. Put these packets in a row a couple of feet apart, and let each competitor walk down the line and have five seconds' sniff at each. At the end he has one minute in which to write down or to state to the umpire the names of the different objects smelled, from memory, in their correct order.

Scout Meets Scout in Town or Country

Single scouts, or complete patrols or pairs of scouts, to be taken out about two miles apart, and made to work toward each other, either alongside a road, or by giving each side a landmark to work to, such as a steep hill or big tree, which is directly behind the other party, and will thus insure their coming together. The patrol which first sees the other wins. This is signified by the patrol leader holding up his patrol flag for the umpire to see, and sounding his whistle. A patrol need not keep together, but that patrol wins which first holds out its flag, so it is well for the scouts to be in touch with their patrol leaders by signal, voice, or message.

Scouts may employ any ruse they like, such as climbing into trees, hiding in carts, etc., but they must not dress up in disguise.

This may also be practised at night.

Shoot Out

Two patrols compete. Targets: bottles or bricks set up on end to represent the opposing patrol. Both patrols are drawn up in line at about twenty to twenty-five yards from the targets. At the word "fire," they throw stones at the targets. Directly a target falls, the umpire directs the corresponding man of the other patrol to sit down — killed. The game goes on, if there are plenty of stones, till the whole of one patrol is killed. Or a certain number of stones can be given to each patrol, or a certain time limit, say one minute.

Kim's Game

Place about twenty or thirty small articles on a tray, or on the table or floor, such as two or three different kinds of buttons, pencils, corks, rags, nuts, stones, knives, string, photos — anything you can find — and cover them over with a cloth or coat.

Make a list of these, and make a column opposite the list for each boy's replies.

Then uncover the articles for one minute by your watch, or while you count sixty at the rate of "quick march." Then cover them over again.

Take each boy separately and let him whisper to you each of the articles that he can remember, and mark it off on your scoring sheet.

The boy who remembers the greatest number wins the game.

Morgan's Game

Scouts are ordered to run to a certain boarding, where an umpire is already posted to time them. They are each allowed to look at this for one minute, and then to run back to headquarters and report to the instructor all that was on the boarding in the way of advertisements.

Snow Fort

The snow fort may be built by one patrol according to their own ideas of fortification, with loopholes, etc., for looking out. When finished, it will be attacked by hostile patrols, using snowballs as ammunition. Every scout struck by a snowball is counted dead. The attackers should, as a rule, number at least twice the strength of the defenders.

Siberian Man-hunt

One scout as fugitive runs away across the snow in any direction he may please until he finds a good hiding place, and there conceals himself. The remainder, after giving him twenty minutes' start or more, proceed to follow him by his tracks. As they approach his hiding place, he shoots at them with snow-balls, and every one that is struck must fall out dead. The fugitive must be struck three times before he is counted dead.

Hare and Hounds

Two or more persons representing the hares, and provided with a large quantity of corn, are given a start of several minutes, and run a certain length of time, then return by another route to the starting-point, all the time scattering corn in their path. After the lapse of the number of minutes' handicap given the hares, those representing the hounds start in pursuit, following by the corn and trying to catch the hares before they reach the starting-point in returning.

The handicap given the hares should be small, depending on the running abilities of the hares and hounds. The fastest runners are usually picked for the hounds.

Chalk the Arrow

This is usually played in the city streets, one player running and trying to keep out of sight of the others who follow. The runner is given time to disappear around the first corner before the others start after him, and at every corner he turns he marks (with chalk) an arrow pointing in the direction he takes. Those pursuing follow by the arrow the first one seeing him being the runner for the next time.

This may also be played by having any number run and only one follow, the first becoming "it" for the next time.

Dodge-ball

Of any number of players, half of that number form a circle, while the other half stand inside of the ring (center) facing outward. Now, the game for those in the center is to dodge the ball which is thrown by any of those forming the circle with the intention of striking the center ones out. Every time a

Boy Scouts

member is struck he is dead, and takes his place among those of
the circle. Now he has a chance to throw at those remaining
in the center. This arrangement keeps all taking part busy.
Only one is out at a time. This being kept up until finally only
one is left. He is hailed the king. For next round, players
exchange places, *i. e.*, those who were in the center now form
the circle.

Note: If the touch is preceded by a bound of the ball it does
not count.

Prisoner's Base

Goals are marked off at both ends of the playground, the
players divided into two equal divisions, occupying the two
goals. About ten paces to the right of each goal is a prison.
A player advances toward the opposite goal, when one from
that goal starts out to catch him. He retreats, and one from
his side runs to his rescue by trying to catch the pursuer —
who in turn is succored by one from his side, and so on. Every
player may catch any one from the opposite side who has been
out of goal longer than he has. Any player caught is conducted to the prison by his captor and must remain there until
rescued by some one from his side, who touches him with the
hand. The one who does this is subject to being caught like
any other player.

Throwing the Spear

The game is an old Greek and Persian pastime. "Throw
the spear and speak the truth," was a national maxim of the
Persians that we may copy with advantage.

The apparatus required is some light spears and an archery
target. The spears should vary from five to six feet in length;
the point should be shod with a steel tip, having a socket into
which the wooden handle is fitted, and made fast by small
screws passing through holes in the sides of the metal, and then
into the wood itself. The wood, for about a foot above the
barb, should be about three quarters of an inch in diameter,
and from thence gradually taper to about a quarter of an inch
in thickness until the end of the spear is reached.

Some spears are fitted with feathers, like an arrow, but
these are not necessary to obtain a good throw, and soon get
dismantled in continually falling upon the ground. Any
ordinary target will serve. It may be an archery target, a
sack full of straw, or a sod bank.

The object of the contest is to hit the target from a given mark, the firing line. Whoever throws nearest to the center of the target the greatest number of times out of six shots is hailed the winner.

The best form for throwing is with the left foot forward, the leg perfectly straight, body well back, its weight resting on the right leg. Now extend the left arm forward, in a line with the shoulder, and over the left leg; poise the spear horizontally in the right hand, holding at the center of gravity by the forefinger and thumb. Bring the right arm backward until the hand is behind the right shoulder.

Now, inclining the point of the spear slightly upward, make your cast, bringing the right arm forward, followed by the right side of the body, the right leg forward and the left arm backward. Count yourself fortunate if you even hit the target in the first few attempts, but practice will make a wonderful difference. The distance should be mutually agreed upon, but fifty feet for a boy of fifteen and one hundred feet for an adult will be found about right.

To "throw the javelin" is another phase of this pastime. The javelin is four to five feet in length, three quarters of an inch in thickness, and fitted with a barbed end, slightly heavier than the spear end. The "object of the game" is to throw the javelin as far as possible but not at a target; instead, the javelin must stick into the ground.

In throwing the javelin, hold it in the right hand, the left leg and hand being advanced; the barb and arm at this point should be at the rear. Then, describing a semicircle with the arm over the right shoulder, and leaning well to the rear, hurl the weapon as far as possible forward.

Arctic Expedition

Each patrol make a bob sleigh with ropes, harness, for two of their number to pull, or for dogs if they have them and can train them to do the work. Two scouts or so go a mile or two ahead, the remainder with the sleigh follow, finding the way by means of the spoor, and by such signs as the leading scouts may draw in the snow. All other drawings seen on the way are to be examined, noted, and their meaning read. The sleigh carries rations and cooking pots, etc.

Build snow huts. These must be made narrow according to the length of the sticks available for forming the roof, which can be made with brushwood and covered with snow.

Dragging Race

A line of patients from one patrol is laid out fifty feet distant from the start. Another patrol, each carrying a rope, run out, tie ropes to the patients, and drag them in. Time taken of last in. Patrols change places. The one which completes in the shortest time wins. Knots must be carefully tied, and pa·tients' coats laid out under their heads.

Far and Near

Umpire goes along a given road or line of country with a patrol in patrol formation. He carries a scoring card with the name of each scout on it.

Each scout looks out for the details required, and directly he notices one he runs to the umpire and informs him or hands in the article, if it is an article he finds. The umpire enters a mark accordingly against his name. The scout who gains the most marks in the walk wins.

Details like the following should be chosen to develop the scout's observation and to encourage him to look far and near, up and down, etc.

The details should be varied every time the game is played; and about eight or ten should be given at a time.

Every match found	1 point
Every button found	1 point
Bird tracks	2 points
Patch noticed on stranger's clothing or boots	2 points
Gray horse seen	2 points
Pigeon flying	2 points
Sparrow sitting	2 points
Ash tree	2 points
Broken chimney-pot	2 points
Broken window	1 point

Fire-lighting Race

To collect material, build, and light a fire till the log given by umpire is alight.

Follow My Leader

With a large number of boys this can be made a very effective display, and is easy to do at a jog trot, and occasional "knee-up" with musical accompaniment. It also can be done at night, each boy carrying a Chinese lantern on top of his staff. If in a building all lights, of course, would be turned down. A usual fault is that the exercise is kept on too long, till it wearies both audience and performers.

Games in Path-finding

Instructor takes a patrol in patrolling formation into a strange town or into an intricate piece of strange country, with a cycling map. He then gives instructions as to where he wants to go, makes each scout in turn lead the patrol, say, for seven minutes if cycling, fifteen minutes if walking. This scout is to find the way entirely by the map, and points are given for ability in reading.

Mountain Scouting

This has been played by tourists' clubs in the lake district, and is very similar to the "Spider and Fly" game. Three hares are sent out at daybreak to hide themselves about in the mountains: after breakfast a party of hounds go out to find them before a certain hour, say 4 o'clock P.M. If they find them even with field-glasses, it counts, provided that the finder can say definitely who it was he spotted. Certain limits of ground must be given, beyond which any one would be out of bounds, and therefore disqualified.

Knight Errantry

Scouts go out singly, or in pairs or as a patrol. If in a town, to find women or children in want of help, and to return and report, on their honor, what they have done. If in the country, call at any farms or cottages and ask to do odd jobs — for nothing. The same can be made into a race called a "Good Turn" race.

Unprepared Plays

Give the plot of a short, simple play, and assign to each player his part, with an outline of what he has to do and say, and then let them act it, making up the required conversation as they go along.

This develops the power of imagination and expression on points kept in the mind, and is a valuable means of education.

It is well before starting to act a play in this way to be a little less ambitious, and to make two or three players merely

carry out a conversation on given topics leading up to a given
point, using their own words and imaginations in doing so.

The Treasure Hunt

The treasure hunt needs observation and skill in tracking,
and practically any number can take part in it.

Several ways of playing the game are given below:

1. The treasure is hidden and the scouts know what the
treasure is; they are given the first clew, and from this all the
others can be traced. Such clews might be (a) written on a
gate post: "Go west and examine third gate on north side of
stream"; (b) on that gate, scout's sign pointing to notice
board on which is written, "Strike south by south-east telegraph post, No. 28," and so on. The clews should be so worded
as to need some skill to understand, and the various points
should be difficult of access from one another. This method
might be used as a patrol competition, starting off patrols at
ten-minute intervals, and at one particular clew there might
be different orders for each patrol, to prevent the patrols behind
from following the first.

2. The clews may be bits of colored wood tied to gates,
hedges, etc., at about three-yard intervals, leading in a certain
direction, and when these clews come to the end it should be
known that the treasure is hidden within so many feet. To
prevent this degenerating into a mere game of follow my
leader, several tracks might be laid working up to the same
point, and false tracks could be laid which only lead back again
to the original.

3. Each competitor or patrol might be given a description
of the way — each perhaps of a slightly different way; the
description should make it necessary to go to each spot in turn
and prevent any "cutting" in the following way: "Go to the
tallest tree in a certain field, from there go one hundred yards
north, and then walk straight toward a church tower which
will be on your left," etc. All the descriptions should lead by
an equal journey to a certain spot where the treasure is hidden.
The first to arrive at that spot should not let the others know it is
the spot, but should search for the treasure in as casual a manner
as possible.

Will-o'-the-wisp

This game should take place across country at night. Two
scouts set off in a given direction with a lighted bull's-eye

lantern. After two minutes have passed the patrol or troop starts in pursuit.

The lantern bearer must show his light at least every minute, concealing it for the rest of the time. The two scouts take turns in carrying the light, and so may relieve each other in difficulties, but either may be captured. The scout without the light can often mingle with the pursuers without being recognized and relieve his friend when he is being hard pressed. They should arrange certain calls or signals between themselves.

Treasure Island

A treasure is known to be hidden upon a certain island or bit of shore marked off, and the man who hid it leaves a map with clews for finding it (compass, directions, tide marks, etc.). This map is hidden somewhere near the landing-place; the patrols come in turn to look for it — they have to row from a certain distance, land, find the map, and finally discover the treasure. They should be careful to leave no foot tracks, etc., near the treasure, because then the patrols that follow them will easily find it. The map and treasure are to be hidden afresh for the next patrol when they have been found. The patrol wins which returns to the starting place with the treasure in the shortest time. (This can be played on the river, the patrols having to row across the river to find the treasure.)

Horse and Rider Tourney

In playing this game it is necessary to have a soft, velvety piece of grass, or if indoors, in the gymnasium, cover the floor with regular gymnasium mats. It requires four boys to play the game, two being horses and the other two riders. The riders mount their horses and dash at each other with great caution, striving to get a good hold of each other in such a way as to compel the opponent to dismount. This can be done either by dragging him from his mount or by making the horse and rider lose their balance so as to throw them off their feet. A great deal of sport can be gotten out of this game, and boys become very skilful after a little practice.

Mumbly Peg*

First: Hold the right fist with the back to the ground and with the jack-knife, with blade pointing to the right, resting

*From Daniel Carter Beard, National Scout Commissioner.

on top of the closed fingers. The hand is swung to the right, up and over, describing a semicircle, so that the knife falls point downward and sticks, or should stick, upright in the ground. If there is room to slip two fingers, one above the other, beneath the handle of the knife, and if the point of the knife is hidden in the ground, it counts as a fair stick or throw.

Second: The next motion is the same as the one just described, but is performed with the left.

Third: Take the point of the blade between the first and second fingers of the right hand, and fillip it with a jerk so that the knife turns once around in the air and strikes the point into the ground.

Fourth: Do the same with the left hand.

Fifth: Hold the knife as in the third and fourth positions, and bring the arm across the chest so that the knife handle touches the left ear. Take hold of the right ear with the left hand and fillip the knife so that it turns once or twice in the air and strikes on its point in the earth.

Sixth: Do the same with the left hand.

Seventh: Still holding the knife in the same manner, bring the handle up to the nose and fillip it over through the air, so that it will stick in the ground.

Eighth: Do the same with the handle at the right eye.

Ninth: Repeat with the handle at the left eye.

Tenth: Place the point of the blade on the top of the head. Hold it in place with the forefinger, and with a downward push send it whirling down to earth, where it must stick with the point of blade in the earth.

Eleventh to Fifteenth: Hold the left hand with the fingers pointing upward and, beginning with the thumb, place the point of the knife on each finger as described above, and the forefinger of the right hand on the end of the knife handle. By a downward motion, throw the knife revolving through the air so that it will alight with the point of the blade in the sod.

Sixteenth to Twentieth: Repeat, with the right hand up and the forefinger of the left hand on the knife handle.

Twenty-first, Twenty-second: Do the same from each knee.

Twenty-third: Hold the point of the blade between the first and second fingers, and, placing the hand on the forehead, fillip the knife back over the head, so that it will stick in the ground behind the person ready for the next motion.

Twenty-fourth: After twenty-three the knife is left in the ground. Then with the palm of the hand strike the knife handle a smart blow that will send it revolving over the ground for a yard, more or less, and cause it to stick in the ground where it stops. This is called "ploughing the field."

When a miss is made the next player takes his turn, and when the first player's turn comes again he must try the feat over that he failed to perform last. A good player will sometimes go through almost all the twenty-four motions without failing to make a "two finger," that is, a fair stick, each time; but it is very unusual for any one to run the game out in one inning. This is the game in twenty-four motions; many boys play it double that number.

First Aid Game*

This fulfils all the requirements of the really first-class scout game. In its gymnasium form it is simply a race with sides as big as desired, and with each runner carrying another player pick-a-back. But it can be made to take in the whole realm of first-aid work, and the best of it is that every fellow in the patrol has to do the same work as every other fellow, so that the final score shows the efficiency of the whole patrol and not of any particularly clever scout.

Let us suppose that the game is being used as a fireman's lift patrol race and that the contestants are the Stags and the Eagles. Two lines are drawn across the floor of the meeting room as far apart as possible, leaving about six feet between each line and the end wall. One of these lines is the base-line, the other the goal.

Behind the goal the scout master stands to act as umpire, and behind the base-line are the two assistant scout masters or any two disinterested persons who are competent to act as judges. The dotted line in the diagram need not be drawn; it is put here simply to show that each patrol keeps on its own side of the room during the game.

To start the game, stand the two patrols up along the side walls, with the patrol leader, or No. 1, at the base line. At the sound of the whistle No. 2 lies on the floor behind the base-line, No. 1 picks him up with the fireman's lift, and runs down the room with him, depositing him behind the goal. No. 2 then rushes back and finds No. 3 on the floor. He picks No. 3 up with the lift and rushes him to the goal. No. 3 then runs back for No. 4. No. 4 runs back for No. 5, and so on until No. 8 is safely deposited behind the goal. The first patrol to finish is the winner. The scout master and the two assistants

*Additional game suggested by H. M. Neeley.

must watch carefully to see that the boys, in their excitement, do not "edge up" over the lines. They must also see that the fireman's lift is made exactly as it should be, and the assistant scout masters should not allow a boy to start until his patient is placed over his back snugly and safely.

The game can also be played with improvised stretchers. In this No. 3 lies down, Nos. 1 and 2 make the stretcher of staffs and coats and carry him to the goal. No. 1 then recovers his coat. No. 3 puts his in its place and they return for No. 4. At the goal No. 2 recovers his coat. No. 4 takes his place and they return for No. 5, and so on until the whole patrol is across the goal-line.

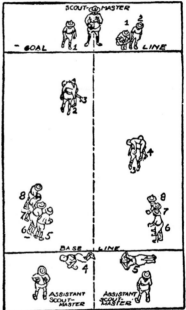

For a further and more elaborate test, let the scout master announce that the patients have broken their left arms or have burned their hands or have dislocated jaws. Then the rescuers must apply the proper bandages before carrying the patients across the goal, and the skill with which the bandages are applied will count in the winning.

This, however, should be done only in a rather elaborate contest, as it takes considerable time and robs the game of the slap-bang excitement which makes it such an ideal wind-up to a regular meeting.

Emergency*

On the wall of headquarters is placed a large map of the city within a radius of half a mile. This can be drawn by the scouts, enlarged from one of the easily available street guides, and should be made large in sections. For one week each patrol is assigned a section. The object is to show on this

---

*Additional game taken from *Boys' Life*.

map the location, name, 'phone number, and important particulars of every doctor, trained nurse, drug store, public telephone, hospital, police station, and policeman's home, fire house, and fireman's home, alarm box and everything of that sort that would be useful in emergency.

Each patrol is to start with a score of 100. At the end of the week the sections are enlarged and all the information gained by one patrol kept secret. After each patrol has worked on each section the scout master compares the reports and for every important bit of data discovered by one patrol and missed by another the latter should be penalized one point. The patrol finishing with the highest score wins.

Take the Hat (For Two Patrols)*

A hat is placed on the floor. One scout from each patrol comes forward. Both lean over toward the hat, each placing

his right hand over and his left hand under the arms of his opponent.

The thing to do is to remove the hat with the left hand and get away with it before the other fellow hits you on the back with his right hand. The one who succeeds in doing this takes his unsuccessful opponent prisoner.

The game is continued until one patrol has made prisoners of all, or half of the opposing patrol.

The Staff Run (Four Patrols)†

Two patrols play together against the other two. We will call them A, B, C, and D.

A and B face each other with a distance of fifty feet between them, the boys standing one behind the other. C and D do the same, taking their position at least fifteen feet to the side of their opponents.

The scout master, or whoever directs the game, stands in the center of the parallelogram which is thus formed. This

---

*Additional game taken from *Boys' Life*.
†Additional game taken from *Boys' Life*.

is shown quite clearly in the picture. He hands a staff to the first boy of each of the patrols standing side by side.

Upon a given signal these two run as quickly as they can to the boys heading the other two patrols, hand them the staves, and retire from the game.

The two who now have the staves return them to the first of the remaining scouts of the other patrols, after which they retire from the game, and so on.

The game is continued until all the boys have run with the staves. The object is to see which two of the patrols can finish first.

The last boy on either side carries the staff to the scout master in the center. Of course, that side wins whose last boy gets to the scout master first.

Naturally, you must remember to have the same number of boys on both sides, and each must stand perfectly still until he has received the staff.

If you play this game outdoors, you can get more fun out of it by arranging so that a ditch, fence, or other obstacle has to be crossed by the boys who run with the staves.

Rabbits*

A space of 30 x 90 feet is outlined on the ground with six cross-lines dividing it into seven sections of equal length. Through the center a long line is drawn parallel to the sides, dividing the ground into two equal halves. Each cross-line represents a track on which alone a hunter may stand or move.

The game is usually played by two teams of nine scouts each, one team being called the rabbits and the other the hunters. One scout of each team is a captain.

For a larger number of players there should be more cross-lines, and for a smaller number of players, fewer cross-lines.

The object of the game is for the rabbits to start at the near end, run through to the opposite or far end, cross over to the other side and run back home without being tagged by a hunter. One such successful run wins a game for the rabbit's team. The object of the hunter is, of course, to tag the rabbits during this run. Five rabbits tagged or "killed" wins the game for the hunters.

The game starts on a signal from the captain of the hunters, who calls "rabbits," when he sees that his scouts are all in position. It is customary for the alternate hunters to stand

*Additional game suggested by Jessie H. Bancroft.

Games

on alternate sides of the center line at the start, but in the course of the play they may cross over from side to side any-where on the specified lines.

While usually but one rabbit starts at a time, any number may be in the field at once, and of course the more there are in the field the more confusing and difficult the game becomes for the hunters. As a hunter may not move away from the cross-line to which he is assigned, the rabbits may rest in between such lines. The captain, however, is at liberty to move on any line in any direction, so the rabbit must keep away from the long lines as well as the cross-lines in his vicinity.

Any rabbit tagged is "dead" and leaves the field.

Five dead rabbits score one game for the hunters.

One rabbit getting back to the starting point, without being tagged, wins the game for his team.

At the close of each game the teams change sides, the rabbits becoming hunters and vice versa.

Swat the Fly*

Two boys are blindfolded and given swatters made by rolling newspapers into the shape of a bat. The boys lie on the ground and each boy places his free hand on a base about five inches square, from which base they must not take the hand during the game. The aim is for the boy to hit an opponent, preferably on the head, but being blindfolded he must judge his whereabouts by hearing his movements. The one who makes the greatest number of hits in a given time wins.

Greek Writing†

The vowels a, e, i, o, u, are numbered 1, 2, 3, 4, 5, respectively. The first letter of the first word of a spoken sentence gives the cue for the consonant in a word. Words of only three letters, such as bee, are selected at first. The vowels are represented by tapping the proper number of times with a stick, and between the vowels flourishes are made on the ground which you pretend is writing. The one who is to read this Greek writing leaves the group and after a word is selected he returns. For example, supposing the word scout is selected. The one with the stick might say, "Sam, don't stand in the light," and taps four times, makes flourishes on the ground and taps five times.

---

*Additional game suggested by Dr. Thomas D. Wood.
†Additional game suggested by Dr. Thomas D. Wood.

He would so have represented the letters S — O — U — and the reader would have guessed scout.

Scout Polo*

Mount two teams of four boys each as for "Mounted Wrestling," meaning eight boys on a side.   A baseball, preferably indoor kind, to be used for ball.   Clubs can be made out of knotted saplings like the old shinney stick, or a broken staff with a small short piece nailed on the end at an angle of about 60 to 120 degrees.   A wrist thong of rawhide or leather through handle end.   Goals about the size of those for lacrosse can be used.   The field should vary according to available space and size of players.

The rules are those of ordinary or bicycle polo, with modifications as suggested after season of play.   Indoors, rubber shoes and padded jerseys would make it very available for board floors.

*Additional game suggested by Samuel T. Stewart.

CHAPTER X

PATRIOTISM AND CITIZENSHIP

By Waldo H. Sherman, Author of "Civics — Studies in American Citizenship

OUR COUNTRY

America is the home of social, religious, and political liberty — "the land of the free and the home of the brave."

As a nation, we have always been rich in land, and for this reason millions of people have sought our shores. We have come into possession of our territory through treaty, purchase, and annexation. In speaking of our territorial area we usually speak of the "original territory" and "additions" to same. When we speak of "original territory" we mean that part of the United States which was ceded to us by Great Britain in the peace treaty of 1783, at the close of the War of the Revolution. This territory, in brief, is described as follows: East to the Atlantic Ocean, west to the Mississippi River, north to the Great Lakes and Canada, and as far south as the northern line of Florida. We sometimes hear it spoken of as the territory of the "Thirteen Original States," meaning the states that formed the Government of the Constitution in 1789. However, if we look at the map we shall see that the original territory includes not only the territory of the thirteen original states, but comprises also land out of which twelve other states have been formed. Looking at this area to-day, however, it seems a small part of our country compared with our present limits

Additions

Louisiana Purchase: What is known as the Louisiana Purchase we bought from France in 1803. It consisted of 875,025 square miles, for which we paid $15,000,000. It is described as follows: west of the Mississippi River to the Rocky Mountains, north to Canada, and south to the Gulf of Mexico, exclusive of Texas. This is a territory greater than the present combined areas of Spain, Portugal, Italy, Hungary, and the Balkan States.

Florida Purchase: In 1819, we purchased Florida from Spain at a cost of over $5,000,000, and this single state is larger in territorial area than the combined territory of Denmark, Netherlands, Belgium, and Switzerland.

Texas: In 1845, Texas came to us by annexation, but the outcome of this annexation later on was our war with Mexico. In territorial area this is an empire in itself — larger than the whole German Empire.

Oregon Territory: In 1846, by treaty with Great Britain, we acquired what is known as the Oregon Territory. This includes the states of Oregon, Washington, and Idaho.

Mexican Cession and Purchase from Texas: As an outcome of the Mexican War, we obtained from Mexico, in 1848, the territory of California, Nevada, Utah, Arizona, and a part of New Mexico at a cost of $15,000,000; and in 1850, we purchased from Texas the remaining part of New Mexico and that part of Colorado not included in the Louisiana Purchase, at a cost of $10,000,000.

Gadsden Purchase: In 1853, we made what is known as the Gadsden Purchase, acquiring thus from Mexico a needed tract of land on the boundary between Mexico, Arizona, and New Mexico, paying for this tract $10,000,000.

Alaska: In 1867, we paid Russia $7,000,000, and added Alaska to our possessions. This purchase is spoken of in history as "Seward's Folly," because the transaction, made while he was secretary of state, was not generally considered a good bargain. Nevertheless it has proved one of our most valuable possessions.

Hawaii: In 1898, we reached out into the Pacific waters and annexed the beautiful Hawaiian or Sandwich Islands.

Porto Rico, Pine Islands, Guam, Philippine Islands: In 1898, the island of Porto Rico with an area of 3,600 square miles came into our possession as an outcome of the Spanish-American War; likewise the Pine Islands with their 882 square miles; Guam with 175 square miles; and the Philippine Islands with a territorial area of 143,000 square miles. But for these latter in settlement of a number of private claims, and to gain peaceable possession of various public lands, we paid Spain $20,000,000.

Samoan Islands: In 1899, we acquired the Samoan Islands, with an area of 73 square miles; and, in 1901, some additional islands in the Philippines.

Patriotism and Citizenship

Land Settlements

The first permanent English settlements in America were made at Jamestown, Va., in 1607, and at Plymouth, Mass., in 1620; and from these two settlements we may trace in large part the growth, character, and development of our national life. The story of the "Pilgrim Fathers" in Massachusetts has been told for generations in literature and in song, and can never cease to be of romantic and thrilling interest.

The story of the settlement and dispersal of other nationalities in America — the Swedes in Delaware, the Dutch in New York, the Spanish and French in Florida and along the banks of the Mississippi and Ohio rivers — all this is summed up in what is known as "colonial history."

In 1763, at the close of the French and Indian wars, England had come into possession of practically all the territory east of the Mississippi — that territory which was ceded in 1783 as the original territory of the United States.

You will sometimes hear it said that thirteen is an unlucky number. Indeed you may have known people so superstitious that they refuse to sit down at a table when the number is thirteen. Again you may know it to be a fact that some hotels do not have a room numbered thirteen, and that many steamboats likewise follow the same custom in state-room arrangement. Strange superstition for Americans! It took thirteen states to make our Union; we have made thirteen additions to our territory; when George Washington was inaugurated as president, a salute of thirteen guns was fired; and, finally, the foundation of the flag of our country bears thirteen stripes.

The American Revolution

The story of the American Revolution (1775-1783) — Declaration of Independence (1776), the adoption of the Articles of Confederation (1781), and, finally, the making and adoption of the Constitution of the United States in 1789 — all is summed up in a period of fourteen years, and may be told and written in the life of George Washington, who was indeed the "Father of His Country."

The cause of the American Revolution was England's oppression of her American colonists; and the injustice of taxation without representation, with other injustices, finally brought about rebellion. The war began in Massachusetts with the battles of Lexington and Concord, April 19, 1775, and ended at Yorktown, Va., October 19, 1781. The treaty of peace was signed at Paris, France, September 3, 1783, and November 25 of that year, known in history as "Evacuation Day," the British took their departure down the bay of New York harbor, and America was free.

Now do we find ourselves at the fireside of American patriotism. Here is Washington. He is a Virginian, and the American people know him at this time as Colonel Washington. It is the 13th day of June, 1775, and the second Continental Congress is in session at Philadelphia. John Adams of Massachusetts has the floor. He is to show himself at this time the master statesman. Justly has he been called the "Colossus of the Revolution." On his way to Independence Hall this morning he meets his cousin, Samuel Adams, and tells him what he is going to do. "We must," he says, "act on this matter at once. We must make Congress declare for or against something. I'll tell you what I am going to do. I am determined this very morning to make a direct motion that Congress shall adopt the army before Boston, and appoint the Virginian, Colonel Washington, commander of it."

Adams is now stating to the Congress the gravity of the situation; he points out the necessity of immediate action — the colonies must be united, the army must be brought together, disciplined, and trained for service, and, under Congress, a fitting commander appointed. "Such a gentleman," he said, "I have in mind. I mention no names, but every gentleman here knows him at once as a brave soldier and a man of affairs. He is a gentleman from Virginia, one of this body, and well known to all of us. He is a gentleman of skill and excellent universal character and would command the approbation of all the colonies better than any other person in the Union."

George Washington is in the hall. The eyes of all Congress have turned toward him. He is surprised, confused, and embarrassed, leaves his seat and hurries into the library.

Congress spent two days considering Adam's motion, for there were other men who had hoped for the appointment; but finally, on the 15th of June, 1775, a ballot was taken, and Washington was unanimously elected commander-in-chief of the Continental Army.

On July 2, 1775, he took command of the army at Cambridge, Mass., and March 17, 1776, the British were expelled from Boston.

We now come to the Declaration of Independence, July 4, 1776. It was written by Thomas Jefferson, at that time a young man of thirty-three. The committee of the General Congress appointed to draft it consisted of the following: Thomas Jefferson, John Adams, Benjamin Franklin, Roger Sherman, and Robert R. Livingston.

The strong feeling of Thomas Jefferson as he wrote the Declaration is indicated by his statement that, "Rather than submit to the right of legislating for us assumed by the British Parliament, I would lend my hand to sink the whole island in the ocean." Here also we get a glimpse of one of the most interesting and delightful characters in the history of this period — Benjamin Franklin. History records that while Thomas Jefferson wrote the Declaration of Independence, a few verbal suggestions were made by Doctor Franklin, as the following conversation reported to have taken place between them would indicate: "Well, Brother Jefferson," said Franklin, "is the fair copy made?" "All ready, Doctor," replied Jefferson. "Will you hear it through once more?" "As many times as you wish," responded the smiling doctor, with a merry twinkle in his eyes. "One can't get too much of a good thing, you know." Jefferson then read to Franklin the Declaration of Independence, which has been pronounced one of the world's greatest papers. "That's good, Thomas! That's right to the point! That will make King George wince. I wish I had done it myself." It is said Franklin would "have put a joke into the Declaration of Independence if it had fallen to his lot to write that immortal document."

The Declaration of Independence went forth to the world signed by one man, John Hancock — which explains the expression you sometimes hear, "Put your John Hancock there." It was, however, signed later by all the members of that Congress — fifty-four in number. This immortal document has been carefully preserved, and the original may be seen at Washington.

The Declaration was a notice to Great Britain and to all the world that the American colonists would no longer be subject to Great Britain; that henceforth they were to be a free and independent people, holding Great Britain as they held the rest of mankind, "enemies in war — in peace friends." This Declaration marks the birth of our nation.

Our government fathers fully realized the step they were taking. They knew it meant a final breaking with the home government of England, but — "with a firm reliance on the protection of Divine Providence," in support of this Declaration, they pledged to each other "their lives, their fortunes, and their sacred honor."

Following the expulsion of the British from Boston, the battle-field of the Revolution changes to New York, moving to Harlem Heights and White Plains; then to New Jersey: Trenton, and Princeton; then to Pennsylvania: Brandywine, Westchester, Germantown, Valley Forge, and on to Monmouth.

But here let us pause. It has been a terrible winter at Valley Forge. While the British at Philadelphia, twenty miles away, have been living in luxury, our Washington and his men have suffered bitterly with hunger and cold; and out of a list of eleven thousand men, three thousand at Valley Forge lay sick at one time. But at last the spring has come and Washington has now been nearly three years in service. Listen! The order has gone forth! At 10:30 o'clock comes the signal, and the firing of a cannon sees all men under arms! At 11:30 o'clock the second signal is given and the march begins. It is May 7, 1778, and Washington is assembling his men. Great news has come and it is fitting to return thanks to Divine Providence — so reads his proclamation.

Now comes the third signal, the firing of thirteen cannon! Another signal! and the whole army breaks into a loud huzza — "Long live the King of France!" followed by a running fire of guns.

On this same day in the afternoon, Washington gives a banquet to his officers, aides, and guests, to which they march arm-in-arm, thirteen abreast. What does it mean? It means that Benjamin Franklin has been heard from, and that an alliance with France, England's bitterest enemy, has been made. Some day when you are in Washington, you may see directly in front of the White House, Lafayette Park, and, knowing the story of the Revolution, you under-stand why it is there. You also understand why Washington's army on that May morning shouted, "Long live the King of France."

But it is not our purpose to tell the whole story: we can only touch the high points. Again the army moves to White Plains and on to Middlebrook and New Windsor; and Washington spends the winter (1781) at Morristown, N. J. The end is approaching. He joins Lafayette at Yorktown, Va., and on October 19th, Cornwallis, the British general, surrenders to George Washington, commander-in-chief of the American Army. Thus the conflict begun in one English settlement is ended in the other. Massachusetts marks the beginning and Virginia the ending of the War of the Revolution.

The War of 1812-1815

The War of 1812 was a naval war.   It was a battle for rights
— the rights of our sailors, the rights of our commerce.   American ships and cargoes were being confiscated.   France and
England and the Barbary pirates were engaged in a profitable
war on our commerce, and last but not least twenty thousand
American seamen had been pressed into service and were slaves
on ships that were foreign, England especially claiming the right
to search American ships and press into service all men found
on board who were English by birth, though American by
choice. and adoption.

"Once a subject always a subject," said Great Britain, but
our answer in 1812 was as it is now any foreigner after five
years' residence within our territory, who has complied with
our naturalization laws and taken the oath of allegiance to our
flag, becomes one of our citizens as completely as if he were
native born.

This war is sometimes spoken of as a "leaderless war," but
great leaders came out of it.   The names of Hull, Perry, and
Lawrence are memorable in its history; it was the war which
made Andrew Jackson, known as "Old Hickory," President of
the United States in 1828.   You will read the story of his great
victory in the Battle of New Orleans.

Some day you will read the life story of David Glasgow
Farragut of whom it is said that, with the exception of Nelson,
the great English admiral, "he was as great an admiral as ever
sailed the broad or narrow seas."   Although the great work
of Farragut was in the Civil War, the story of his life began in
the War of 1812 when he was but ten years old.   Admiral
Farragut is reported as giving this explanation, in the late years
of his life, of his success in the service of his country:

"It was all owing to a resolution that I formed when I was
ten years old.   My father was sent to New Orleans with the
little navy we had, to look after the treason of Burr.   I accompanied him as cabin-boy.   I had some qualities that I
thought made a man of me.   I could swear like an old salt,
could drink as stiff a glass of grog as if I had doubled Cape Horn,
and could smoke like a locomotive.   I was great at cards, and
was fond of gambling in every shape.   At the close of dinner
one day, my father turned everybody out of the cabin, locked
the door, and said to me:

"'David, what do you mean to be?'

"'I mean to follow the sea,' I said.

" 'Follow the sea!' exclaimed my father; 'yes, be a poor, miserable, drunken sailor before the mast, kicked and cuff ?d about the world, and die in some fever hospital in a foreign clime?'

" 'No, father,' I replied, 'I will tread the quarter-deck, and command as you do!'

" ' No, David, no boy ever trod the quarter-deck with such principles as you have, and such habits as you exhibit. You will have to change your whole course of life if you ever become a man.'

"My father left me and went on deck. I was stunned by the rebuke, and overwhelmed with mortification. 'A poor, miserable, drunken sailor before the mast, kicked and cuffed about the world, and die in some fever hospital!' That's my fate is it? I'll change my life, and I will change it at once. I will never utter another oath, never drink another drop of intoxicating liquor, never gamble, and as God is my witness I have kept these vows to this hour."

The Star-Spangled Banner

The sun is slowly sinking in the west. The men of the army and navy are drawn up at attention. At every fort, army post, and navy yard, and on every American battle-ship at home or abroad, the flag of our country is flying at full mast. The sunset gun will soon be fired, and night will follow the day as darkness follows the light. All is ready, the signal is given, the men salute, and the flag to the band's accompaniment of "The Star-Spangled Banner," slowly descends for the night to be folded and kept for the morning's hoisting.

> "And the Star-Spangled Banner in triumph shall wave
> While the land of the free is the home of the brave."

In the cemetery of Mt. Olivet, near Frederick, Md., there is a spot where the flag of our country is never lowered. It is keeping watch by night as by day over the grave of Francis Scott Key, author of "The Star-Spangled Banner." He was born in Frederick County, Md., August 1, 1779, and died in Baltimore, January 11, 1843.

The Congress of the United States has never formally adopted "The Star-Spangled Banner" as a national anthem, but it has become such through the recognition given to it by the army and navy. It is played on all state occasions at home or abroad and is the response of our bands at all international gatherings. In the theatre, at a public meeting, or at a banquet

— whenever it is played, the people rise and remain standing to the end as a tribute to the flag of our country.

The poem itself is descriptive of what the author saw and felt on the night of September 13, 1814, as he watched the bombardment of Fort McHenry by the British during the War of 1812. The city of Washington had been sacked, bombarded, and burned by the British, and now in their march of destruction they were bombarding the fort to gain entrance to Baltimore's harbor, in which city they had purposed to spend the winter. We can well imagine the joy of Key's heart, the son of a Revolutionary patriot, held in custody on a British battleship, to see in the morning "that our flag was still there," and to know, therefore, that there was still hope for our country.

> "Then conquer we must, when our cause it is just,
> And this be our motto, 'In God is our Trust.'"

The Birth of New States

The history of the fifty-six years between 1789 and 1845 is marked by the development of new states formed out of the territorial settlement of the wilderness. The people of our country have always been pioneering, going ahead of civilization, so to speak, but always taking it with them. Scouts they have been in every sense of the word. Following the rivers, clearing the forests, fording the streams, braving the dangers, living the wild life — brave men and women!

The first state to come into the Union of the thirteen original states was Vermont, the "Green Mountain" State (1791); next came Kentucky (1792), the "Blue Grass" State, the home of Daniel Boone, the great hunter and pioneer. Four years later (1796) came Tennessee, the "Volunteer" State, receiving this name because of its large number of volunteer soldiers for the Seminole War and the War of 1812; next comes Ohio (1803), the "Buckeye," so called because of the large number of buckeye trees, the nut of which bears some resemblance to a buck's eye. This is the first state to be formed out of the public domain known at this time as the "Northwest Territory." The land ordinance bill of 1785 and the homestead act of 1862 relate to the development and settlement of the public domain, the first being a plan of survey applied to all public lands owned by the United States government; the other being a law by which the possession of these lands was made possible to settlers.

Following Ohio into the Union came Louisiana (1812), the "Creole" State, whose people were descendants of the original

French and Spanish settlers. This was the first state to be formed west of the Mississippi, and New Orleans, its chief city, known as the "Crescent City," is one of the oldest in our country and full of historic interest.

After the War of 1812 the new states began to come in rapidly. The admission of Indiana (1816), The "Hoosier"; Mississippi (1817), the "Bayou"; Illinois, the "Prairie" (1818); Alabama (1819), the "Cotton," show that the pioneer settlements of our people had been closing in along the banks of the Ohio and the Mississippi rivers.

We now go back to the far East, for the state of Maine, our "Pine Tree" State, has now been developed, and its admission (1820) completes the coast line of states as far south as Georgia. The next state admitted is Missouri (1821), the "Iron," followed by Arkansas, the "Bear" (1836), to be followed in turn by Michigan (1836), the "Lake" or "Wolverine" State, the thirteenth state to be admitted; and the stars in our flag are now doubled.

The first census of the United States was taken in 1790, and the Constitution provided that it must be taken every ten years thereafter. In that year the order of states in rank of population was as follows: Virginia first, Pennsylvania second, North Carolina third, Massachusetts fourth, and New York fifth.

The census of 1820 makes a decided change, we find, in the order of population, and New York comes first, Virginia second, Pennsylvania third, North Carolina fourth, Ohio fifth, Kentucky sixth, and Massachusetts seventh.

The states of Florida and Texas came into the Union in the same year — the one March 3, and the other December 29, 1845; and thereby hangs a tale. It had been claimed by our government that Texas was included in the Louisiana Purchase of 1803; but the Mexicans claimed it also, and in 1819, in order to close the deal for the purchase of Florida, our government was obliged to relinquish its claim to Texas. At this time the possession of Florida was more desirable and necessary to the peace of our country than the possession of Texas; it was under Spanish rule, overrun with outlaws, and a most undesirable neighbor, besides being very necessary to the rounding out of our coast territory.

The Mexican War

The annexation and admission of Texas into the Union in 1845 came about through the pioneering and settlement of our people in her territory; where at first welcomed and encouraged by the Mexicans, they were later deluged in blood. The spirit of Americanism grew rampant under the barbaric and military despotism of the Mexican government, and in 1835 there was an uprising of the settlers led by a pioneer, an ex-governor of Tennessee, Gen. Samuel Houston, the man for whom the city of Houston, Texas, was named. At this time there were about ten thousand Americans in Texas, and on March 2, 1836, through their representatives in convention assembled, these Americans in true Revolutionary spirit declared Texas an independent republic. The Mexican government tried to put down this rebellion, but met with a crushing defeat, and Texas, the "Lone Star" State, remained an independent republic up to the time of her annexation and admission as a state of the Union.

The cause of the war with Mexico, then, was her resentment because Texas began to move for annexation to the United States. The fact that Texas had been for many years an independent republic, and been so recognized by the United States, Great Britain, France, and some smaller countries, gave Texas the right on her part to ask for annexation, and the United States the right to annex her. But in order to bring Texas into the Union and save her people from the Mexicans, the United States was obliged to declare war against Mexico. This she did May 13, 1845, although Texas was not admitted as a state until December 29th of that year. The war lasted nearly three years, peace being declared February 2, 1848. As an outcome of the war the peaceful possession of Texas was secured, and also possession of the territory of California, Nevada, Utah, Arizona, and a part of Colorado and New Mexico, for which territory, however, our government in final settlement paid Mexico, $15,000,000.

New States — 1845-1861

During the Mexican War, Iowa (1846), the "Hawkeye" State, came into the Union, followed by the state of Wisconsin (1848), the "Badger." Next comes the story of the "Forty-niners," and California (1850), the "Golden State," enters the Union; and then comes Minnesota (1858), the "North Star" State, and the Great Lakes are walled in, this state completing the circuit. Oregon (1859), the "Beaver," follows, then the "Garden of the West," Kansas (1861), and the Civil War is upon us. Of course, we do not mean to say that Kansas was the cause of the Civil War, although it had much to do with it.

The Civil War — 1861 - 1865

The Civil War was a war between states in the government of the United States — between states that were slave and states that were free.

The rights of property ownership are involved in state rights, and slaves held as property in slave-holding states were not recognized as such in states that were free. Therefore, the principle of slavery became involved not alone in the individual ownership of slaves, but also in the rights of a state, and the relationship of states to each other in the government of the United States.

At the close of the Revolutionary War one of the first things to be settled was the boundaries as between states of the land comprising the thirteen original states; and as an outcome of this settlement, there came into possession of the United States all of that territory ceded by Great Britain in 1783, which was not included in the boundaries of those states. This territory, in brief, may be described as the territory east of the Mississippi, and north and south of the Ohio River; and out of this territory and that west of the Mississippi added later (1803) through the Louisiana Purchase, most of the new states were formed that came into the Union before the Civil War. And this was the beginning of what is known as the "public domain" — that is, land owned by the Federal Government.

In 1785 Congress passed a law which has become general in its application to all public lands of the United States. It is a law for the uniform survey of public lands into townships six miles square, subdivided into sections containing 640 acres, and quarter sections containing 160 acres. The purpose of the government in making this survey was to make public lands in the territories of the government easy of settlement, and as the townships became settled, to develop in them the local township form of government.

The territory north of the Ohio River was designated the "Northwest Territory." As soon as the public lands in this territory were thrown open to settlers, they began to pour in. Indeed, in many instances, they went ahead of the survey.

The next step taken by Congress was to pass a law, in 1787, for the government and protection of those settlers in this Northwest Territory, and in this law Congress made provision that slavery should be prohibited. Therefore, states formed in this territory had to come into the Union as free states. This was a restriction of slavery, however, which did not apply to the territory south of the Ohio, nor west of the Mississippi; so that when a new state came into the Union, formed out of either one of these territories, it became a great political factor in our government either for or against slavery.

In the passing of the years, many changes were taking place in our government, but there came a time when the people began to realize that slavery was spreading, and that our government was politically divided between states that were slave and states that were free — or, in other words, that in the principle of slavery the peace and preservation of the Union were involved.

And thus it happened that the slave-holding states, not being able to live at peace in the Union, decided to go out of it, and live by themselves. The right of a state to leave the Union was called "the right of secession" — a right which the North held did not exist under the Constitution.

Nevertheless, one by one, under the leadership of South Carolina, December 20, 1860, the slave-holding states announced their secession, either by act of state legislature or in convention assembled; and on February 4, 1861, there had been formed in our government a Southern confederacy. At this time the whole number of states in the Union was thirty-two, and of this number eleven entered the Southern confederacy.

The first shot was fired by the Southern confederacy on April 12, 1861, against Fort Sumter, a fortification of the Federal Government over which floated the stars and stripes. The war lasted four years, ending on April 9, 1865, when Robert E. Lee, commander-in-chief of the army of the Southern confederacy, surrendered to Ulysses S. Grant, commander-in-chief of the Federal army.

Abraham Lincoln

The central figure in the Civil War is Abraham Lincoln — in heart, brain, and character, not only one of our greatest Americans, but one of the world's greatest men.

Lincoln was born February 12, 1809, in Hardin County, Kentucky. His parents had come to this then pioneer state from Virginia, and his grandfather, whose Christian name he bore, moved there as early as 1781, where, a few years later, he was killed by the Indians while trying to make a home in the forest. When Lincoln was eight years old, his people moved to the new state of Indiana about the time it came into the Union, and there he lived until he was twenty-one, when he went to Illinois, from which state, eventually, he was elected President.

In 1859, when he was beginning to gain some recognition as a national figure, he was asked to write a little sketch of his life, and in the letter enclosing it, he said: "There is not much of it, for the reason, I suppose, there is not much of me." In this sketch, which is indeed brief, he tells us he was raised to farm work until he was twenty-two; that up to that time he had had little education; and when he became of age he did not know much beyond reading, writing, and ciphering to the "rule of three." He clerked for one year in a store and was elected and served as captain of the volunteers in the Black Hawk War; later on he ran for the state legislature (1832) and was defeated, though successful in the three succeeding elections. While in the state legislature, he studied law and later went to Springfield to practise it. The only other public office he makes note of is his election to the lower house of Congress for one term (1846). He returned to Springfield and took up more earnestly the study and practice of law; he entered with spirit into the political campaigns, and constantly was growing in public esteem. His public debates with Douglas (1858) made him a familiar figure throughout the state of Illinois, and his profound knowledge and masterful handling of questions debated, his convincing and unanswerable arguments, his clear grasp of the political situation, began to gain the attention of Eastern politicians, convincing them and the country at large that they had a mighty force to reckon with in the prairie state of Illinois.

Although he lost the election to the United States Senate, and Douglas won, the campaign had pushed him to the front as a national figure, and paved the way for his presidential nomination.

In 1860, at the Republican convention assembled in Chicago, Abraham Lincoln was nominated for President. In November he was elected, and March 4, 1861, he was inaugurated. His address at this time was an earnest plea for peace and friendship between the North and South: "We are not enemies but friends. We must not be enemies. Though passion may have strained, it must not break, our bond of affection."

But the war tide was rising and could not be stemmed; four years of bitter conflict ensued. Lincoln's emancipation of the slaves was made only after he had convinced himself it could not be longer deferred and preserve the Union. "My paramount duty," he said, "is to save the Union, and not either to destroy or save slavery. What I do about slavery and the colored race, I do because I believe it helps to save the Union; and what I forbear, I forbear because I do not believe it would save the Union." His Emancipation Proclamation, officially freeing the slaves, was finally issued in September, 1862, to take effect January 1st of the following year.

Lincoln was elected to the Presidency for the second term and inaugurated March 4, 1865, while the war was still on. His second inaugural address closes with these words with which every boy should be familiar, voicing as they do the exalted spirit of a great and good man:

With malice toward none, with charity for all, with firmness in the right as God gives us to see the right, let us strive on to finish the work we are in; to bind up the nation's wounds; to care for him who shall have borne the battle, and for his widow and for his orphan; to do all which may achieve and cherish a just and lasting peace among ourselves, and with all nations.

The war ended on April 9th of this same year, and on April 14th, the President, weary with the cares of state, but with the burden of the war clouds lifted, had gone to Ford's Theatre in Washington for an evening's entertainment and pleasure, accompanied by Mrs. Lincoln. The box which the President occupied had been most elaborately decorated with the flag of the country. His coming had been heralded abroad, and the audience that had assembled in his honor was large, brilliant, and joyously happy over the assured preservation of the Union. In the midst of the play, the assassin, J. Wilkes Booth, entered the box and fired the fatal shot. The body of the bleeding President was taken to a house across the street where the next morning at 7.20 o'clock he died. Thus the emancipator of the slave, the friend of the whole people, and the savior of our country died, a martyr to the cause of freedom.

Washington has been called "the aristocrat," and Lincoln "the man of the people." The one had culture, wealth, and social position; the other lacked all of these in his early years. Lincoln's early life was cradled in the woods, and all of life out of doors had been his in the new and pioneer states of the wilderness. He grew up not knowing many people, but somehow in his up-coming there was developed in his life a great heart full of tenderness and kindly feeling. Doubtless it was the very hardships of life that made him what he was. At any rate, he was one of the greatest and noblest figures in all history. He was called "Honest Abe" by those who knew him because always, even in little things, he wanted to see perfect justice

done; and thus it was, when he came to things of large importance, that the man was only a boy grown tall, not only in
stature but in the things that make for righteousness in a
nation.

The Spanish=American War — 1898

The war with Spain was not of this country's seeking. The
island of Cuba, whose distress had aroused the sympathy of
the whole world, was our near neighbor, and to sit idly by
and witness the inhuman treatment practised by the Spanish
soldiery upon the helpless islanders would hardly be a part
creditable to any people. It was not our intention at first to
do other than to relieve the suffering and distress of Cuba near
at hand, and this we tried to do peaceably in the supplying of
food and other necessities of life.

As the next step, the United States sent a remonstrance to
Spain telling her she should send a more humane governor to
the island. But as matters grew worse instead of better, even
under a change of governors, the sympathy of the United
States became daily more deeply enlisted in the freedom of
the Cubans.

The battleship *Maine* was sent to Havana Harbor to protect, if need be, the Americans and American interests in Cuba.
On the night of February 15, 1898, an explosion occurred,
sinking the ship almost immediately.

With the destruction of the *Maine* — whether by accident
or intent — with the appalling loss of two hundred and fifty-
six men, including two officers, relations with Spain became more
and more strained, until war seemed inevitable. On April 11,
1898, President McKinley in a special message to Congress,
said: "In the name of humanity and civilization, the war in
Cuba must stop."

War indeed was formally declared April 25th, and in the
brief space of one hundred and fourteen days history had added
to its annals: the blockading of Cuban forts whereby the
Spanish fleet was trapped; the invasion and siege of the island
by United States regulars, volunteers, and rough riders; the
destruction of the Pacific Spanish fleet in Manila Bay by Admiral Dewey; and, finally, the destruction of the remainder
of the Spanish fleet under command of Admiral Cervera, Sunday morning, July 3d. The final outcome of this war was the
freedom of Cuba and the possession by the United States of
Porto Rico, Guam, and the Philippine Islands.

Peace

There is no country in the world less warlike than ours, and no country in the world that more potently argues for universal peace. We have never departed from the spirit of our Declaration of Independence, "that all men are created equal; that they are endowed by their Creator with certain inalienable rights; that among these are life, liberty, and the pursuit of happiness." We put it into our Constitution when we said, "in order to form a more perfect union, establish justice, insure domestic tranquillity, provide for the common defence, promote the general welfare, and secure the blessings of liberty to ourselves and our posterity" we "do ordain and establish this Constitution for the United States of America." Such has been, then, and always must be, our program — the chart and compass of all our ways.

The American Flag

"A star for every state and a state for every star."

The flag of one's country is its dearest possession — emblem of home, and country, and native land. This is what one thinks and feels when he sees the flag, and this is what it means. Our flag is the emblem of liberty — the emblem of hope — the emblem of peace and good-will toward men.

There is a story, quite generally believed, that the first flag was planned and made in 1776 by Betsy Ross, who kept an upholstery shop on Arch Street, Philadelphia, and that this, a year later, was adopted by Congress. The special committee appointed to design a national flag consisted of George Washington, Robert Morris, and Col. George Ross, uncle of the late husband of Betsy Ross. The star that the committee decided upon had six points, but Mrs. Ross advised the five-pointed star, which has ever since been used in the United States flag. The flag thus designed was colored by a local artist, and from this colored copy Betsy Ross made the first American flag.

When Washington was in command at Cambridge, in January, 1776, the flag used by him consisted of a banner of thirteen red and white stripes with the British Union Jack in the upper left-hand corner.

The Betsy Ross house has been purchased by the American Flag House and Betsy Ross Memorial Association, and is pointed out as one of the interesting historical places in Philadelphia.

The official history of our flag begins on June 14, 1777, when the American Congress adopted the following resolution proposed by John Adams:

Resolved: That the flag of the thirteen United States be thirteen stripes, alternate red and white: that the Union be thirteen stars, white on a blue field, representing a new constellation.

"We take," said Washington, "the star from Heaven, the red from our mother country, separating it by white stripes, thus showing that we have separated from her, and the white stripes shall go down to posterity representing liberty."

In designing the flag there was much discussion as to the arrangement of the stars in the field of blue. It was thought at one time that a new stripe as well as a new star should be added for each new state admitted to the Union. Indeed, in 1794, Congress passed an act to the effect that on and after May 1, 1795, "the flag of the United States be fifteen stripes, alternate red and white; and that the union be fifteen stars, white in a field of blue. These additional stars and stripes were for the states of Vermont and Kentucky.

The impracticability of adding a stripe for each state was apparent as other states began to be admitted. Moreover, the flag of fifteen stripes, it was thought, did not properly represent the Union; therefore, on April 14, 1818, after a period of twenty-three years in which the flag of fifteen stripes had been used, Congress passed an act which finally fixed the general flag of our country, which reads as follows:

An Act to Establish the Flag of the United States

Sec. 1. Be it enacted, etc., That from and after the fourth day of July next, the flag of the United States be thirteen horizontal stripes, alternate red and white; that the union have twenty stars, white in a blue field.

Sec. 2. Be it further enacted, that, on the admission of every new state into the union, one star be added to the union of the flag; and that such addition shall take effect on the fourth day of July succeeding such admission.

Flag Day

June 14th, the anniversary of the adoption of the flag, is celebrated as flag day in many of our states.

In order to show proper respect for the flag, the following rules should be observed:

It should not be hoisted before sunrise nor allowed to remain up after sunset.

At "retreat," sunset, civilian spectators should stand at attention and on the last four strains of the music uncover, holding the headdress top outward, in the right hand, opposite the left shoulder, right forearm against the breast.

When the national colors are passing on parade or review, the spectators should, if walking, halt, and if sitting, rise and stand at attention and uncover.

When the flag is flown at half staff as a sign of mourning it should be hoisted to full staff at the conclusion of the funeral. In placing the flag at half mast, it should first be hoisted to the top of the staff and then lowered to position, and preliminary to lowering from half staff it should first be raised to top.

On Memorial Day, May 30th, the flag should fly at half mast from sunrise until noon, and full staff from noon to sunset.

(Taken from the "Sons of the Revolution," state of New York.)

The Scout's Pledge to the Flag

"I pledge allegiance to my flag and to the republic for which it stands; one nation indivisible, with liberty and justice for all."

Congress

The Congress of the United States is its law-making body, and is composed of the Senate and House of Representatives. Senators are elected for six years, two from each state; representatives for two years, each state being represented in proportion to its population. The Vice-president of the United States is the president of the Senate, and the presiding officer of the House of Representatives is chosen by the members from their number; he is called the speaker. The salary of the senators and representatives is $7,500 a year and 20 cents per mile is allowed for traveling to and from Washington. The speaker's salary is $12,000 a year.

The President

The President is elected for a term of four years. He lives during his term of office at the White House, where presidential receptions and social affairs of state are held. The President's offices are connected with the White House. Here he receives his callers and here the meetings of his Cabinet are held. The salary of the President is $75,000 a year.

The Cabinet

The members of the Cabinet are the officers and heads of the several departments of the administrative government. They are appointed by the President with the advice and consent of the Senate. The members of the Cabinet are as follows: secretary of state, secretary of the treasury, secretary of war, attorney general, postmaster general, secretary of the navy, secretary of the interior, secretary of agriculture, secretary of commerce and secretary of labor. The members of the Cabinet are such men as the President believes are qualified to serve during his administration of office, and are usually members of the same political party as the President.

United States Courts

The Supreme Court of the United States is at Washington, D. C., but there are other courts of the United States held in the several states, called district courts.

Washington, D. C.

The Capitol at Washington is the home of Congress and the Supreme Court. The Library of Congress, the Treasury, Army and Navy, Pension, Post-office, and many other buildings of public character are located in Washington. These during certain hours are open to visitors.

The Army

The President, in accordance with the Constitution, is commander-in-chief of the army and navy of the United States, and of the militia of the several states when called to the actual service of the United States. The law provides that the total strength of the army shall not exceed at any one time 100,000. As now organized (1910) the total strength of the staff and line is 76,911, not including the provisional force and the hospital corps. These figures include the Porto Rico Regiment of Infantry, the Service School Detachments, the Military Academy (officers, soldiers, and cadets), the Indian Scouts, 5,200 native scouts in the Philippine Islands, 193 First Lieutenants of the Medical Reserve Corps on active duty, and 11,777 recruits, etc. They do not include the veterinary surgeons, the officers of the Medical Reserve Corps not on active duty, nor the retired officers and enlisted men of the army. The appropriation for the maintenance of the army for the year 1913-1914 was $94,266,145, not including the expenditure by the several states on their national guard or expenses for the Military Academy or for fortifications.

Militia

The law of our country states that in time of war every able-bodied male citizen, between the ages of eighteen and forty-five, shall be counted a member of the state militia. The state militia is divided into two classes: one, the organized, known as the national guard; and the other the unorganized, known as the reserve militia.

The membership of the national guard is voluntary. One may join or not, as he chooses, except that in some states the law requires that students at the state university shall receive military training for at least a part of their university course, and during that time they are accounted a part of the national guard of the state. The governor of each state holds the same relationship to the state militia as the President to the army and navy: he is commander-in-chief.

Military Academy

The United States Military Academy is at West Point, N. Y., on the Hudson River. The number of students is limited to 533, and appointments to the academy are made in accordance with the rule which permits each United States senator and each congressman to have one representative, and also gives the President the right to make forty appointments at large. Candidates for appointment must be between the ages of seventeen and twenty-two; must pass the required physical examination; also an examination in English grammar, composition and literature, algebra and geometry, geography and history. The course of instruction is four years; the discipline very strict. Only one leave of absence is granted during the entire four years, and this comes at the close of the second year. The pay is $709.50 per year, and on graduation a cadet is commissioned a second lieutenant. To receive an appointment to West Point one must apply to his United States senator or to a congressman in the state in which he lives, or to the President.

The Navy

The strength of the navy is limited to 51,500 enlisted men and apprentice seamen. This complement is in addition to men detailed as ship keepers of naval militia organizations and court martial prisoners awaiting dishonorable discharge. The maximum enlisted strength of the navy is, therefore, about 52,700. The appropriation for the support of the navy for the year ending July 30, 1915, is $144,417,453.53.

Navy Enlistments

Enlistments in the United States navy are entirely voluntary. The term of enlistment is for four years. The applicant must be between seventeen and thirty years of age. Over twenty-five the applicant must possess some trade, such as machinist, carpenter, coppersmith, and the like. He must be an American citizen of good moral character, of sound physique, and be able to read and write English. All recruits are required to take the oath of allegiance to the United States.

Marine Corps

The Marine Corps is a branch of the naval service of the United States, consisting of about 10,000 men. These "soldiers of the sea" serve on all battleships and cruisers, acting as guards, performing sentinel duty, and manning part of the ship's battery. On shore duty they garrison the navy yards and naval stations in the United States and island possessions. Marines also furnish expeditionary forces for duty beyond the seas when necessary, and in case of disturbance in foreign countries marines from battleships are often landed to protect American interests.

Naval Academy

The United States Naval Academy is at Annapolis, Md. The students are called midshipmen, and candidates for appointment must be between the ages of sixteen and twenty. The appointment of candidates is made as at West Point — through senators and congressmen and the President, the only difference being in the number of appointments that may be made: each senator and representative may be represented by two midshipmen at Annapolis, while at West Point he is represented by but one cadet. The President has the appointment of ten men at large each year to the naval academy and two from the District of Columbia. He may also appoint one from Porto Rico, who must be a native. The midshipman's course is four years. The pay is $600 per year.

Civil Service

In the administration of the government of the United States, thousands of men and women are employed in the various offices at Washington, and are sometimes termed the great "peace army."

In one period of our country's history, it was believed that each President, when he came into office, had the right to turn out of office every person employed by the government in any of its civil departments, should it please him to do so, and to put into office his own friends or the friends of his party. This right was claimed on the ground that "to the victor belong the spoils"— a theory of government administration that has been severely dealt with and reformed through what is known as the "Civil Service Act." The Civil Service Act was passed by Congress January 16, 1883, and by this act a civil service commission was brought into existence. The three members of this commission are appointed by the President with consent of the Senate, not more than two of whom may be members of the same party. Thus, by this civil service act, positions in the government service are now obtained for the most part through competitive examinations, and such positions are not affected in any way by the incoming of a new President or the appointment of a new head of a department.

In some states and in most of the large cities civil service appointments are now made through competitive examinations. Any one interested in learning what positions may be secured in the service of the government may apply to the Civil Service Commission at Washington, D. C., or make inquiry at the local post-office.

Foreign Service

The foreign service of our government is carried on through the diplomatic corps and the consular service. In the diplomatic corps, we have ambassadors, envoys, ministers, diplomatic agents, and secretaries; in the consular service, consuls general, consuls, and consular agents.

Our diplomatic representatives abroad look after our interests as a nation in the family of nations. They represent us socially as well as politically in the great foreign capitals of the world. They are received as our representatives of state, and it is their duty to sustain and promote good-will and friendly feeling between us and other nations.

The consular service is more directly responsible for our trade relationships in the great centers of the world. Through our foreign service, also, Americans abroad, whether as tourists or residents, are protected in person and in property interests. Appointments to the foreign service are made by the President with the advice of the Senate.

As we send our representatives abroad, so the countries to which our representatives go in turn send their representatives to us. In the city of Washington, one may see representatives of all the principal nations of the earth living there as ambassadors, for the purpose of promoting friendly commercial and political relationships. The secretary of state is the representative of our government through whose office the great work of the foreign service is directly carried on, and upon him devolves therefore the great affairs of state relationships with other countries. When our independence as a nation was declared in 1776, it was important to gain as quickly as possible from other nations a recognition of our independence and of our entrance into the family of nations. France was the first to give us recognition, and the first to enter into a treaty relationship. Some of the most thrilling and interesting stories of our national life are to be found in the adventurous determination of our representatives to gain the recognition of our independence as a nation from the great powers of the earth. The name of Benjamin Franklin, sent to the court of France, stands at the head of our diplomatic service; and we may read with interest of the first appearance of our diplomatic representative, John Adams, at the court of Great Britain. When we speak of court in this sense, we mean, of course, the king's court — the place of meeting — usually the throne room. In our country, foreign representatives are received by the President at the White House, or by the secretary of state in his office apartments. Some foreign countries have built for their representatives in Washington palatial and beautiful residences, over which floats the flag of the country to which the palace or residence belongs. Our own country has already begun to make this residential provision for her representatives abroad, and in time will undoubtedly own residences in all of the principal foreign capitals.

State Government

The states of the United States are not all alike either in constitution or government, although there is a likeness at many points. For instance, each state has about the same officers, — a governor, lieutenant-governor, secretary of state, treasurer, auditor, adjutant-general, superintendent of schools, etc.

Each state has its own state legislature: a senate to which state senators are elected, and a house of representatives sometimes called the assembly, to which state representatives or assemblymen are elected. Each state legislature makes laws only for its own state; therefore not all state laws are alike. Indeed, there is a great deal of individuality to each state, and rightly so. As each person has his own individuality, and as each family has its own characteristics, so each state has an individuality and characteristics peculiar to itself. The history of each state reveals its character, so also the climate, the hills, the valleys, the mountains, the plains, the lakes, the rivers, the harbors, the schools, the colleges, the towns, the villages, and the cities within its borders, all help in forming the character of a state.

Towns, Villages, and Cities

The government of the town, or the village, or the city, is called local government. It is government close at hand —

home government. And out of the home government of each town, village, and city in a state must come, by the votes of the people at the ballot-box, the men whom they choose as their representatives in the government of the state and the nation — for the people rule through representatives of their own choosing.

Politics

In every presidential election, the people, through the rule of the majority, as determined by the Constitution, elect their chief magistrate, the President, who becomes the "first citizen" of the nation and is entitled "Mr. President." The people of a state by the same rule elect their chief magistrate and entitle him "His Excellency, the Governor"; he is the state's chief or leading citizen. The people of the city by the same rule elect their chief magistrate and entitle him "His Honor, the Mayor," the city's leading citizen. The people of the town, in the New England States, elect their chief officers — three to five men — and entitle them the "Selectmen," although in towns of the middle and western states they are called "Supervisors."

So likewise, the people in town, village, and city by the same "rule of the majority" elect aldermen, councilmen, state senators, representatives or assemblymen, and congressmen.

And the state legislatures in turn elect, according to the Constitution of the United States, the state's United States senators, two in number. Thus, by the rule of the majority, are all officers of town, village, and city, county and state elected, except such few as are appointed by law to offices by superior officers, heads of departments, bureaus, or districts of supervision or administration.

Property

The ownership of property, both real and personal, and the protection of that ownership, is made possible in the organization of society — termed the government — and in the power of that government to make and enforce its laws. Real property is the kind of property which pertains to land, the ownership of which is transferred from one person to another, either by a deed recorded in the office of the register of deeds in the county court house, or else transferred by descent, or by will through the administration of the county court, usually called the probate court. This latter proceeding is in the case of the owner's death when his property is divided by the court and distributed to the heirs — the family or other relatives according to his will;

or in case no will is left the law provides for the manner of its distribution.

The Register of Deeds: County Court House

The record title, therefore, of all real property is to be found in the office of the register of deeds in the county court house. It makes no difference what kind of real property it is, acre property or city property, here the title of ownership is always to be found, the books of record being always open to the public. Thus when one buys a piece of real property, a home for instance, he should receive from the owner a deed and an abstract of title, which is a paper showing the title as it appears on the records, and this title, when not vouched for as perfect by an abstract title company, should be passed upon by a lawyer in order that any flaw or defect therein may be made right before the deed is passed from one owner to another. In some states, however, the law does not require the owner to furnish an abstract. When the title is proved or pronounced good, the deed should at once be placed on record.

Personal Property

Personal property is that form of property which in general terms is stated as movable, such as animals, furniture, clothing, tools, implements, money, stocks, bonds, mortgages, etc., the transfer of which from one owner to another is not as a rule a matter of public record, although in the case of a bill of sale — sometimes made of some forms of personal property — the county record may give evidence thereof. Therefore it is, that in the matter of taxation, the tax record or assessment comes under two general heads — a tax on real property and a tax on personal property.

Property and Government

It is desirable to be a property owner so long as the government under which one lives protects one in his property ownership. The government must do two things: it must protect the person and his personal rights as a citizen, and it must also protect property and the rights of property ownership from enemies within, as from without. In order that this may be done and done in all fairness and justice, we elect some citizens to make laws and term them legislators. We elect others to enforce or administer the laws, and term them executives — the President, the governor, and the mayor coming under this head. We elect other citizens to enforce and interpret the laws, and we term them judges and officers of the court. In fact, it is a principle in our government that no man or set of men shall have authority in all departments of government, legislative, executive, and judicial. You will see that the Constitution of the United States is divided into these three departments of government,and the state constitutions and city charters are, as a rule, likewise divided.

You will understand that any property you may obtain will be valuable to you only in proportion as you are protected in your rights of ownership by the government, and that the government not only protects your property, it also protects your life and its interest as well as the life and interests of all other citizens.

The building and maintenance of schools and colleges, libraries, art and natural history museums, parks, playgrounds, hospitals, etc., are carried on at the expense of the government by means of taxation, inasmuch as these things are in the interests of mankind and for its upbuilding. In the city the protection of life and property is found in one or the other of these different departments: police, fire, health, street cleaning, parks, water supply, etc.; and every good citizen should lend his hand to help in every way possible the enforcement of law in each department.

Citizenship

In any form of government, problems are continually arising as to the rights of property and the rights of persons, and it is well for us to remember this distinction: that the end of society (and by that term we mean government) is not the protection of property, but rather the upbuilding of mankind. If we bear this in mind and act upon it as a principle in life, we shall find ourselves standing and voting on the right side of public questions. We shall also be able to mark the man in private or public life who shows by his talk or his actions that he thinks more of property rights than he does of the rights of individuals. Any business that does not benefit society, but on the other hand degrades it, whether run by an individual or individuals in a firm, company, or corporation, is a business that ought by the law to be put out of existence. This is why the business of gambling, for instance, is made unlawful; also why the government had the right to make lotteries unlawful; also why some states (for instance New York) have passed laws making book-making at race tracks unlawful. For all of these things degrade and do not upbuild mankind. It is for every one, then, to apply this principle to the town, village, or city in which he lives, and determine just what stand he will take as to endorsing and protecting such business interests in his community. One is likely to find in any community men who seem to care nothing for any interests other than their own. They stand for property rights because it is for their interests to do so; but for the rights of mankind, the rights of society, apparently they care nothing. Here is the distinction, then, between the good citizen and the bad citizen, the desirable and "the undesirable" citizen.

Practical Citizenship

In nearly every town, village, and city of any size or importance, there is at least one individual, and usually groups of individuals, working for the "betterment of society." They are people who take an interest in the people about them and do what they can to improve the conditions of life in the community. If one were to take a survey of the whole country, and make a study of the social workers — the men and the women who give freely of their time and of their money to make the world a better and happier place to live in — he would come to see that such service is a kind of service that grows out of the heart, and is the fruit of the kindly spirit which prompts the "good turn daily."

In doing the "good turn daily," then, one has abundant opportunity to do his part toward the social betterment of the community in which he lives. There are so many ways that one hardly knows what to write down as the most important, because all are important. It is not alone in big things, but in the little things as well, that the really great work is done.

The community — the town, the village, or the city in which one lives — has many problems to solve. The streets in the community are always interesting, and one can do much in the streets to help keep them clean, attractive, and pleasing, as well as safe for the people and horses passing through. In a city where there is a large population the lives of the people are in greater danger at all times than in the country, and that is the reason why the city has to be so organized in its government that it can make special laws, or ordinances as they are called, for its own special protection against the dangers of city life. The policemen of a city, wherever stationed in the daytime or in the night time, are there to protect the lives and property of individuals, at street crossings, at public buildings,

at theatres, in the parks, and on playgrounds; and it is the
privilege as well as the duty of all citizens to help them in
every way possible to do their work well.   In the "good turn
daily," one may be able to help in more ways than one if he is
on the lookout.

"A scout's honor is to be trusted" to obey the laws, and to
see that they are not disobeyed by others.   "A scout's duty
is to be useful and to help others.   He must be prepared at any
time to save life or to help injured persons."   There are often
accidents in the streets — many avoidable ones — due simply
to carelessness. For instance, some boys were careless and threw
broken glass bottles into the street, and a passing automobile
came to a standstill because of a punctured tire.   The man who
owned the automobile and was driving it got out and called
one of the boys on the street to come over to him.   He did not
call this particular boy because he thought he had thrown the
glass, but because he thought he was a boy who would appreciate what he wanted to say to him.   He told the boy that he
had just had a new tire put on his machine and appealed to
him as to whether or not he thought he had been treated right
through the carelessness of the one who threw that glass into
the street.   The boy said no, he didn't think he had been, and,
after a little more talk, added that he would do all in his power
in that neighborhood to see that such things were kept out
of the street in the future.   That boy was in line for the making
of a first-class scout, and the man to whom he had been talking,
being a good scout commissioner, had won the boy, because
instead of being angry, he had been kind, courteous, and
friendly — all qualifications of a good scout.

"A scout is a friend to animals."   "Yes," said a stable keeper,
"I have two good horses laid up, each injured by stepping on a
nail in a board in the street.   You know people are awfully
careless about such things."   There are some people who never
go out of their way to do helpful things, just as some people
never go out of their way to know people, and for that reason
are often alone and lonesome.   It is the little things that count,
just such little things as picking up from the street a board
with a nail in it, and putting it aside — even that is a good turn.

Lincoln once said in speaking of a man whom he thought
lacking in sympathy: "He is so put up by Nature that a lash
upon his back would hurt him, but a lash upon anybody's
else back does not hurt him."   There are many people in the
world who seem to be like that man — not so many who feel
that way toward mankind, possibly, but many who thought-

lessly feel and act that way toward animals. The lash on the
back of an animal — the horse, the cow, the dog — hurts,
and the good scout always takes the animal's part. He is
kind to animals.

In the city, people often become careless as to the necessary
precautions against fire, and for this reason many lives are lost.
In all well-regulated school systems, each school building is
properly provided with fire escapes and the children regularly
disciplined in fire drills. Proper fire precautions are not yet
generally required by law as they should be in great buildings,
factories, or workshops wh re men and women are employed
in large numbers. If a scout should be employed in such a
place, he might make himself very serviceable in case of a fire,
because having thought of it beforehand, he would know what
to do — his motto being, "*Be Prepared.*"

One very important thing in city life is the protection of
one's health: it is essential to have good food, pure water,
plenty of good, fresh air — things not always easily obtain-
able, but always most necessary. The scout learns through the
many activities of scouting something of the market places
and sources of supply for food; he has some idea as to the cost
of living in his own home, and should become a good marketer
himself, making himself competent to judge of the quality and
prices of food. If he is wide-awake and intelligent, he knows
the products of his own country as well as those of the state.
He knows what food products are shipped in and sometimes
finds that it would be cheaper, and more profitable as well, to
produce them in his own community. An industrious scout
may often make his own pocket money in this way or provide
funds toward his own education.

In the Constitution of the United States is written this
law: "No title of nobility shall be granted by the United
States." The purpose of this law is to defeat any attempt to
elevate one citizen above another in rank of social or political
preferment. Ours is a country free from the entanglements
of social distinction such as mark one man or family from
another by way of title or patent of nobility; and yet, in our
country of uncrowned kings and unknighted men, we would
not forget the real deeds of valor, the services rendered, or the
victories won. For it was the purpose in the mind and in the
heart of our fathers who framed the Constitution that each
succeeding generation should rise to the duties and responsibilities of the State; that the virtues of the State should not
descend or be lodged in one family, or any selected number of

families, but rather should be in the keeping of all the families in the care and keeping of all the people.

Thus do we remember our Washington and our Lincoln. They served the generation to which they belonged; they lived and passed out of their generation, having served the State; and all the virtues, cares, and responsibilities of the State — the government that is — they left to the generations that should come after them. And, therefore, each generation as it comes and goes must rise or fall in proportion as it raises or lowers the citizenship standard, for each generation must prove its own worth as must each individual his own virtues.

Practical Citizenship

As set forth in a letter from Colonel Theodore Roosevelt, Honorary Vice-president, Boy Scouts of America:

THE OUTLOOK
287 Fourth Avenue,
New York

Office of
Theodore Roosevelt.

July 20th, 1911.

MY DEAR SIR:

I quite agree with Judge Lindsey that the Boy Scout Movement is of peculiar importance to the whole country. It has already done much good, and it will do far more, for it is in its essence a practical scheme through which to impart a proper standard of ethical conduct, proper standards of fair play and consideration for others, and courage and decency, to boys who have never been reached and never will be reached by the ordinary type of preaching, lay or clerical. I have been particularly interested in that extract of a letter from a scout-master in the Philippines, which runs as follows:

"It might interest you to know that at a recent fire in Manila, which devastated acres of ground and rendered 3,000 people homeless, that two patrols of the Manila scouts reached the fire almost with the fire companies, reported to the proper authorities and worked for hours under very trying conditions helping frightened natives into places of safety, removing valuables and other articles from houses that apparently were in the path of the flames, and performing cheerfully and efficiently all the tasks given to them by the firemen and scout-master. They were complimented in the public press, and in a kind editorial about their work.

"During the recent Carnival the services of the boys were requested by the Carnival officers, and for a period of ten days they were on duty performing all manner of service in the Carnival grounds, directing strangers to hotels, and acting as guides and helpers in a hundred ways."

What these boy scouts of the Philippines have just done I think our boy scouts in every town and country district should train themselves to be able to do. The movement is one for efficiency and patriotism. It does not try to make soldiers of boy scouts, but to make boys who will turn out as men to be fine citizens, and who will, if their country needs them, make better soldiers for having been scouts. No one can be a good American unless he is a good citizen, and every boy ought to train himself so that as a man he will be able to do his full duty to the community. I want to see the boy scouts not merely utter fine sentiments, but act on them; not merely sing, "My Country, 'Tis of Thee," but act in a way that will give them a country to be proud of. No man is a good citizen unless he so acts as to show that he actually uses the Ten Commandments, and translates the Golden Rule into his life conduct — and I don't mean by this in exceptional cases under spectacular circumstances, but I mean applying the Ten Commandments and the Golden Rule in the ordinary affairs of every-day life. I hope the boy scouts will practise truth and square dealing, and courage and honesty, so that when as young men they begin to take a part not only in earning their own livelihood, but in governing the community, they may be able to show in practical fashion their insistence upon the great truth that the eighth and ninth commandments are directly related to every-day life, not only between men as such in their private relations, but between men and the government of which they are part. Indeed the boys even while only boys can have a very real effect upon the conduct of the grown-up members of the community, for decency and square dealing are just as contagious as vice and corruption.

Every healthy boy ought to feel and will feel that in order to amount to anything, it is necessary to have a constructive, and not merely a destructive, nature; and if he can keep this feeling as he grows up he has taken his first step toward good citizenship. The man who tears down and criticises and scolds may be a good citizen, but only in a negative sense; and if he never does anything else he is apt not to be a good citizen at all. The man who counts, and the boy who counts, are the man and boy who steadily endeavor to build up, to improve, to better living conditions everywhere and all about them.

But the boy can do an immense amount right in the present, entirely aside from training himself to be a good citizen in the future; and he can only do this if he associates himself with other boys. Let the boy scouts see to it that the best use is made of the parks and playgrounds in their villages and home towns. A gang of toughs may make a playground impossible; and if the boy scouts in the neighborhood of that particular playground are fit for their work, they will show that they won't permit any such gang of toughs to have its way. Moreover, let the boy scouts take the lead in seeing that the parks and playgrounds are turned to a really good account. I hope, by the way, that one of the prime teachings among the boy scouts will be the teaching against vandalism. Let it be a point of honor to protect birds, trees, and flowers, and so to make our country more beautiful and not more ugly, because we have lived in it.

The same qualities that mean success or failure to the nation as a whole, mean success or failure in men and boys individually. The boy scouts must war against the same foes and vices that most hurt the nation; and they must try to develop the same virtues that the nation most needs. To be helpless, self-indulgent, or wasteful, will turn the boy into a mighty poor kind of a man, just as the indulgence in such vices by the men of a nation means the ruin of the nation. Let the boy stand stoutly against his enemies both from without and from within, let him show courage in confronting fearlessly one set of enemies, and in controlling and mastering the others. Any boy is worth nothing if he has not got the courage, courage to stand up against the forces of evil, and courage to stand up in the right path. Let him be unselfish and gentle, as well as strong and brave. It should be a matter of pride to him that he is not afraid of any one, and that he scorns not to be gentle and considerate to every one, and especially to those who are weaker than he is. If he doesn't treat his mother and sisters well, then he is a poor creature no matter what else he does; just as a man who doesn't treat his wife well is a poor kind of citizen no matter what his other qualities may be. And, by the way, don't ever forget to let the boy know that courtesy, politeness, and good manners must not be neglected. They are not little things, because they are used at every turn in daily life. Let the boy remember also that in addition to courage, unselfishness, and fair dealing, he must have efficiency, he must have knowledge, he must cultivate a sound body and a good mind, and train himself so that he can act with quick decision in any crisis that may arise. Mind, eye, muscle, all must be trained so that the boy can master himself, and thereby learn to master his fate. I heartily wish all good luck to the movement.

Very sincerely yours,

THEODORE ROOSEVELT.

Mr. James E. West,
   Chief Scout Executive
      Boy Scouts of America,
       New York City.

America

MY country, 'tis of thee,
   Sweet land of liberty,
     Of thee I sing;
Land where my fathers died,
Land of the Pilgrim's pride,
From every mountain side
     Let freedom ring.

My native country thee,
Land of the noble free,
     Thy name I love;
I love thy rocks and rills,
Thy woods and templed hills;
My heart with rapture thrills
     Like that above.

Let music swell the breeze,
And ring from all the trees
     Sweet freedom's song;
Let mortal tongues awake,
Let all that breathe partake,
Let rocks their silence break,
     The sound prolong!

Our father's God, to Thee,
Author of liberty,
     To thee we sing:
Long may our land be bright
With freedom's holy light;
Protect us by Thy might,
     Great God, our King.

—Samuel F. Smith, 1832.

The Star-Spangled Banner

O SAY, can you see, by the dawn's early light,
   What so proudly we hail'd at the twilight's last gleaming?
Whose broad stripes and bright stars, thro' the perilous fight,
   O'er the ramparts we watched were so gallantly streaming:
And the rocket's red glare, the bombs bursting air,
   Gave proof thro' the night that our flag was still there!
O say, does that star-spangled banner yet wave
   O'er the land of the free and the home of the brave?

On the shore, dimly seen thro' the mists of the deep,
   Where the foe's haughty hosts in dread silence reposes
What is that which the breeze, o'er the towering steep,
   As it fitfully blows, half conceals, half discloses?
Now it catches the gleam of the morning's first beam,
   In full glory reflected, now shines on the stream—
'Tis the star-spangled banner. O long may it wave
   O'er the land of the free and the home of the brave.

And where is that band who so vauntingly swore,
   'Mid the havoc of war and the battle's confusion,
A home and a country they'd leave us no more?
   Their blood has washed out their foul footsteps' pollution,
No refuge could save the hireling and slave
   From the terror of flight, or the gloom of the grave—
And the star-spangled banner in triumph shall wave
   O'er the land of the free and the home of the brave. ·

O thus be it ever when freemen shall stand
   Between their loved homes and foul war's desolation,
Blest with vict'ry and peace, may the heav'n-rescued land
   Praise the Power that hath made and preserved us a nation.
Then conquer we must, when our cause it is just,
   And this be our motto, "In God is our trust"—
And the star-spangled banner in triumph shall wave
   While the land of the free is the home of the brave.
               —*Francis Scott Key*, 1814.

EVERY BOY'S LIBRARY

Boy Scout Edition

In the execution of its purpose to give educational value and moral worth to the recreational activities of the boyhood of America, the leaders of the Boy Scout Movement quickly learned that to effectively carry out its program, the boy must be influenced not only in his out-of-door life but also in the diversions of his other leisure moments. It is at such times that the boy is captured by the tales of daring enterprises and adventurous good times. What now is needful is not that his taste should be thwarted but trained. There should constantly be presented to him the books the boy likes best, yet always the books that will be best for the boy. As a matter of fact, however, the boy's taste is being constantly vitiated and exploited by the great mass of cheap juvenile literature.

To help anxiously concerned parents and educators to meet this grave peril, the Library Commission of the Boy Scouts of America has been organized. EVERY BOY'S LIBRARY is the result of their labors. All the books chosen have been approved by them. The Commission is composed of the following members: George F. Bowerman, Librarian, Public Library of the District of Columbia, Washington, D. C.; Harrison W. Graver, Librarian, Carnegie Library of Pittsburgh, Pa.; Claude G. Leland, Superintendent, Bureau of Libraries, Board of Education, New York City; Edward F. Stevens, Librarian, Pratt Institute Free Library, Brooklyn, New York; together with the Editorial Board of our Movement, William D. Murray, George D. Pratt, and Frank Presbrey, with Franklin K. Mathews, Chief Scout Librarian, as Secretary.

In selecting the books, the Commission has chosen only such as are of interest to boys, the first twenty-five being either works of fiction or stirring stories of adventurous experiences. In later

Please order through our Book Department

lists, books of a more serious sort will be included. It is hoped that as many as twenty-five may be added to the library each year. Thanks are due the several publishers who have helped to inaugurate this new department of our work. Without their coöperation in making available for popular priced editions some of the best books ever published for boys, the promotion of EVERY BOY'S LIBRARY would have been impossible.

We wish, too, to express our heartiest gratitude to the Library Commission, who, without compensation, have placed their vast experience and immense resources at the service of our movement.

The Commission invites suggestions as to future books to be included in the library. Librarians, teachers, parents, and all others interested in welfare work for boys, can render a unique service by forwarding to National Headquarters lists of such books as in their judgment would be suitable for EVERY BOY'S LIBRARY.

This library contains some of the best stories for boys ever written, and is the only series of books approved by the National Council of the Boy Scouts of America. It is a guaranteed library for boys; the stories are clean, wholesome and vigorous, and have been endorsed by a ⌒ommission of the leading librarians of America.

These books are of full library size, well printed on good paper, and uniformly bound in cloth with the boy scout official stamp on the cover. The wrapper is in four colors and gold, unusually attractive in design. The price is 60 *cents* per volume, or, if sent by mail, 10 *cents* additional.

Following is the complete list of the EVERY BOY'S LIBRARY books. They are for sale wherever books are sold.

EVERV BOY'S LIBRARY

Title	Author
Wells Brothers: The Young Cattle Kings	Adams, Andy
The Horsemen of the Plains	Altsheler, Joseph A.
Yankee Ships and Yankee Sailors	Barnes, James
For the Honor of the School	Barbour, Ralph Henry
Boat Building and Boating	Beard, Dan
Handbook for Boys	Boy Scouts of America
A Midshipman in the Pacific	Brady, Cyrus Townsend
The Cruise of the Cachalet	Bullen, Frederick T.
Jeb Hutton	Connolly, James B.
Cattle Ranch to College	Doubleday, Russell
Along the Mohawk Trail	Fitzhugh, Percy
The Ranch of the Oxhide	Inman, Henry

Please order through our Book Department

EVERY BOY'S LIBRARY

The Call of the Wild........................London, Jack
Redney McGaw............................McFarlane, Arthur E.
Jim Davis................................Masefield, John
Tom Strong, Washington's Scout.............Mason, Alfred Bishop
Pitching in a Pinch........................Mathewson, Christy
Baby Elton, Quarter-Back...................Quirk, Leslie W.
Animal Heroes............................Seton, Ernest Thompson
Tommy Remington's Battle..................Stevenson, Burton E.
Treasure Island...........................Stevenson, Robert Louis
Buccaneers and Pirates of Our Coast..........Stockton, Frank R.
Three Years Behind the Guns................Tisdale, Lieu.
Tecumseh's Young Braves...................Tomlinson, Everett T.

ADDITIONS—1915

Handicraft for Outdoor Boys.................Beard, Dan
Boy Scouts of Bob's Hill....................Burton, Chas. P.
The Wireless Man..........................Collins, F. A.
Be Prepared..............................Dimock, A. W.
The Last of the Plainsmen...................Grey, Zane
Bartley, Freshman Pitcher...................Heyliger, Wm.
The Boy's Book of New Inventions..........Maule, H. E.
The School Days of Elliott Gray, Jr..........Maynard, Colton
The Wrecking Master......................Paine, Ralph D.
Ungava Bob...............................Wallace, Dillon

ADDITIONS—1916

The Last of the Chiefs......................Altsheler, Joseph A.
Danny Fists..............................Camp, Walter
The Wolf Hunters.........................Grinnell, Geo. Bird
To the Land of the Caribou.................Tomlinson, Paul

NEW TITLES ADDED IN 1917

Scouting with Daniel Boone..................Tomlinson, Everett T.
The Half-Back............................Barbour, Ralph. H.
The Cruise of the Dazzler...................London, Jack
The Boy Scouts of Black Eagle Patrol.........Quirk, Leslie W.
The Last of the Mohicans...................Cooper, James Fenimore
Twenty Thousand Leagues Under the Sea......Verne, Jules
A Gunner Aboard the Yankee................Doubleday, Russell
Williams of West Point.....................Johnson, Hugh L.
Ben Hur.................................Wallace, General Lew
Kidnapped ....Stevenson, Robert Louis

Appendix 461

EXTRACTS FROM CONSTITUTION and BY-LAWS
of the BOY SCOUTS OF AMERICA

(II) PURPOSE

The purpose of this corporation (B. S. A.) is as set forth in the original certificate of incorporation under the laws of the District of Columbia, dated February 8, 1910, and restated in Section 3 of the Charter granted by Congress June 15, 1916, as follows—"That the purpose of this corporation shall be to promote, through organization, and coöperation with other agencies, the ability of boys to do things for themselves and others, to train them in scoutcraft, and to teach them patriotism, courage, self-reliance, and kindred virtues, using the methods which are now in common use by boy scouts," by placing emphasis upon the Scout Oath and Law for character development, citizenship training and physical fitness.

(III Sect. 1) PRINCIPLES AND POLICIES

The Boy Scouts of America maintain that no boy can grow into the best kind of citizenship without recognizing his obligation to God. In the first part of the boy scout's oath or pledge the boy promises, "On my honor I will do my best to do my duty to God and my country, and to obey the scout law." The recognition of God as the ruling and leading power in the universe, and the grateful acknowledgment of His favors and blessings, is necessary to the best type of citizenship, and is a wholesome thing in the education of the growing boy. No matter what the boy may be—Catholic or Protestant or Jew—this fundamental need of good citizenship should be kept before him. The Boy Scouts of America therefore recognizes the religious element in the training of a boy, but it is absolutely non-sectarian in its attitude toward that religious training. Its policy is that the organization or institution with which the boy scout is connected shall give definite attention to his religious life.

Only men willing to subscribe to this declaration of principle shall be entitled to certificates of leadership in carrying out the boy scout program.

The activities of the members of the Boy Scouts of America shall be carried on under conditions which show respect for the convictions of others in matters of custom and religion, as required by the twelfth Scout Law, reading, "A scout is reverent. He is reverent toward God. He is faithful in his religious duties and respects the convictions of others in matters of custom and religion."

In no case where a troop is connected with a church or other distinctively religious institution, shall scouts of other denominations or faith be required, because of their membership in the scout troop, to take part in or observe a religious ceremony distinctively peculiar to that institution or church.

Section 2—The Boy Scouts of America shall not, through its governing body or through any of its officers, its chartered councils or members, involve the Boy Scout Movement in any question of a political character, but each official and member shall have freedom of thought and action as an individual.

Section 3—In carrying out the purpose of the Boy Scout Movement as stated herein, technical military training and drill shall not be included for the reason that they are not equal in value or as suitable for boys of scout age in training for good citizenship as the program of scout activities.

(IV) PROGRAM

The program shall be one which recognizes the achievements of boys by the award of degrees and badges designating them progressively as tenderfoot, second class and first scouts, and by the award of special merit badges for proficiency in the subjects of woodcraft, handicraft, civics, etc., as may be determined upon from time to time by the National Council.

The motto of the Boy Scouts of America is "Be Prepared."

(*Art. VI, Sect.* 1)—The program of the Boy Scouts of America shall be carried out through the organization of boys into groups consisting of at least one and not more than four patrols of eight boys each, under the leadership of a man, of clean, virile, and high moral character, to be known as the scoutmaster. Only boys who have passed their twelfth birthday shall be eligible to membership. Authority for enrolling more than thirty-two boys in a troop may be secured from the chartered local council having jurisdiction, or in case the troop is not under the supervision of a council from the National Council.

(XV) FINANCES

Section 2—Contributions shall be solicited in the name of the Boy Scouts of America only through or by the authority of the National Council, or by chartered local councils or troops under an arrangement agreed upon by the National Council. Boys shall not be permitted to serve as solicitors of money to pay any expenses incidental to Scouting.

(Art. XIII) DUES

Section 1—Each troop of Boy Scouts shall pay to the National Council annually, through the local council, if there be one, a registration fee of $3.00, with an additional fee of 25 cents for each member enrolled in excess of twelve either as active or associate scouts. When additional names of new members are added to the troop, they may be registered on the following basis: if the unexpired period for which the troop is registered is more than nine months, the fee of the new scouts shall be 25 cents each; if the period is for more than six and less than ten months, the fee shall be 20 cents; if for a period of six months or less, 15 cents. Scouts re-registering pay the full fee of 25 cents irrespective of the date of payment.

Even though the names of less than twelve boys are submitted with the application for the registration of the troop, additional fees in accordance with the foregoing must be paid for all names added as members of the troop subsequent to the filing of the application.

(Art. XVI) GENERAL REGULATIONS

Section 1—*Commercialism.*

Clause 1—No member of the Boy Scouts of America, troop of scouts, chartered council, or any officer or representative of the Boy Scouts of America shall have the right to enter into a contract or relationship of a commercial character involving the Boy Scouts of America unless duly authorized by the Executive Board and then only in connection with the carrying out of the purposes of the Boy Scout Movement. Nor shall any local council, troop of scouts, or group of boys enter into a contract or business relationship with a business or commercial agency or corporation, or individual which may be construed as using the Boy Scout Movement for commercial purposes. This is not to be interpreted, however, as interfering with any scout earning money for his own scout equipment or for his troop.

Clause 2—In the case of any gift, donation or dedication to the Boy Scouts of America, the Executive Board shall determine whether the same shall be accepted; and then it shall be made clear that the acceptance shall be upon the condition that no attempt will be made to capitalize such gift, donation or dedication in a way which might be construed as commercializing the Boy Scouts of America or securing a profit through the popularity of the Boy Scouts of America by reason of such gift, donation, etc.

Section 2—Soliciting Funds and Tag Days.

Clause 1—Boy Scouts, collectively or individually, shall not be used in the solicitation of money or the sale of tags, or other similar methods of solicitation of money in connection with efforts to raise money incidental to the expenses of Scouting.

Clause 2—Arrangements may be made by the ranking local authorities for scouts to coöperate with well established non-partisan and non-sectarian national movements for the relief of humanity, in undertakings which they may promote to raise money, by giving personal service, provided, however, that this shall not involve the use of the Boy Scouts as solicitors of money.

Section 3—Participation in Public Functions.

The officers and leaders of the Boy Scouts of America shall when practicable, coöperate in connection with civic or other public gatherings of a non-partisan and non-political character in a way which gives scouts an opportunity to render service in harmony with their training as scouts, instead of merely taking part in parades or making a show of themselves in their uniforms.

(Art. IX) UNIFORMS

Section 1—The Boy Scout Uniform. The Boy Scout uniform as specifically authorized by an act of Congress approved June 3, 1916, and protected by the provisions of the federal charter, June 15, 1916, is described on pages 77-78.

The uniform of the official is described on page 76.

Imitation of the U. S. Army, Navy, or Marine Corps uniform is prohibited, in accordance with the provisions of Act of Congress, approved June 3, 1916.

Section 2—Protection. The sale and use of the scout uniform shall be restricted to scouts and scout officials who are registered and in good standing according to the records at the National Headquarters. It shall be the responsibility of all members of the Boy Scouts of America and especially of all commissioned officers and chartered councils to coöperate with the National Council in preventing the use of the official boy scout uniform by those who are not members of the organization in good standing.

Section 3—Distribution. The uniform shall be issued only through the Supply Department of the Boy Scouts of America or through agents recommended and approved by duly chartered local councils of the Boy Scouts of America, or the Executive Board.

Section 4—When to Use. The boy scout uniform is intended primarily for use in connection with the activities of the Boy Scout Movement, but its use may be authorized by local scout officials under conditions and for purposes not inconsistent with the principles of Scouting and the boy scout program provided, however, the uniform shall not be used: 1— When soliciting funds or engaging in any selling campaigns; 2—when engaging in distinctive political endeavor; 3—when appearing upon the stage professionally without specific authority from the Executive Board.

(Art. III) BADGES AND INSIGNIA

Section 1—Badges. All of the badges and insignia of the Boy Scouts of America are specifically protected by the U. S. Patent and Trade-mark Laws and the provisions of the charter granted by Congress June 15th, 1916, and shall be used exclusively by scouts and officials registered and in good standing according to the records at the National Headquarters, who qualify in accordance with the provisions herein set forth, or as may be prescribed from time to time in the official handbooks issued by the National Council.

All badges and insignia shall remain the property of the Boy Scouts of America subject to recall for cause by the National Council or their duly authorized representatives.

(Art. XVI, Sect. 4) SCOUT BANDS

*Clause 1—*Boy Scout bands and fife and drum corps may be organized among members of the Boy Scouts of America and provided with suitable insignia indicating this special membership, provided, however, that the purpose of such organization shall be primarily and distinctively for the development of the boy along lines in harmony with the aims and object of the Boy Scout Movement, and that the members thereof also carry out the regular boy scout program.

*Clause 2—*Under no circumstances shall a fife and drum corps or band made up of Boy Scouts of America enter into a contract as members of the Boy Scouts of America for the sale of their services in competition with any other bands of their own or any other community.

(Art. XVI) ANNIVERSARY WEEK

*Sect. V—*During the week in which occurs the anniversary of the original incorporation of the Boy Scouts of America (February 8, 1910) the National Council, through its various officers and with the co-operation of the officers of the various local councils, shall arrange for a nation wide celebration with a suitable program for the various days of the week, including arrangements whereby every registered scout in good standing, the whole country over, shall be given an opportunity to assemble on the evening of anniversary day and promptly at 8:15, recommit himself to the Scout Oath and Law.

On this occasion it shall be the duty of the scoutmaster and other leaders to bring to the attention of the scouts the extent of the scout brotherhood in our own country and throughout the world, and impress upon their minds the fact that every boy scout the world over is committed to the same obligation and does a "good turn daily."

INDEX

Index of Appendix.

475

ADVERTISEMENTS

National Headquarters invites attention to the advertisements in this Handbook. They have been accepted after careful consideration and merit your patronage.

Are You Prepared?

In camp or on a hike accidents very often occur,—a smashed finger, an accidental cut, a poisonous bite or any of a thousand similar things may happen; if neglected these slight injuries become serious. A pin prick has been known to cause blood poison and the puncture of a rusty nail—lock-jaw.

A bottle of Dioxogen carried in the pack is the surest protection against these risks. Dioxogen prevents infection.

Dioxogen

is a powerful germicide and what is equally important *it is harmless.* It disinfects everything it touches and because of its harmlessness may be used freely for all kinds of accidental hurts, even in the mouth, without the fear which usually accompanies the use of the poisonous germicides.

In the European War, Dioxogen is doing its bit—it is in the first-aid kits and it is used in both field and base hospitals.

Our Emergency Booklet containing valuable first-aid suggestions will be forwarded on request

The Oakland Chemical Co.

10 Astor Place   **New York**

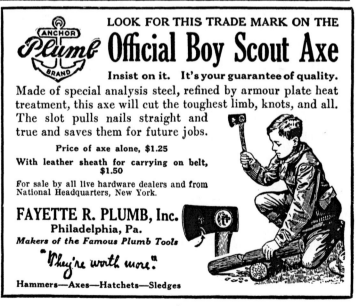
481

Medals for Boy Scouts Who Can Shoot

YOU can win a Gold-Plated Sharpshooter Medal or a Silver-Plated Marksman Medal.

All you need is a Winchester .22-caliber rifle—and the skill to use it.

A Sharpshooter Medal goes to every boy under 18 who makes a first grade score with a Winchester.

The Marksman Medal is awarded every boy who makes the second grade record.

Get a free sample target from your dealer. He will give you a booklet explaining all about the contest and also containing tips on handling your Winchester. The dealer can supply you with packages of targets.

If your dealer cannot supply you, write to the Winchester Repeating Arms Co., Dept. 18, New Haven, Conn.

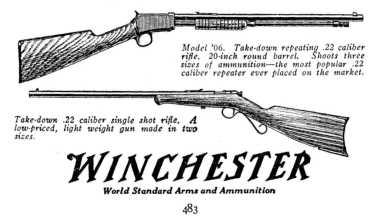

Model '06. Take-down repeating .22 caliber rifle. 20-inch round barrel. Shoots three sizes of ammunition—the most popular .22 caliber repeater ever placed on the market.

Take-down .22 caliber single shot rifle. A low-priced, light weight gun made in two sizes.

WINCHESTER
World Standard Arms and Ammunition

485

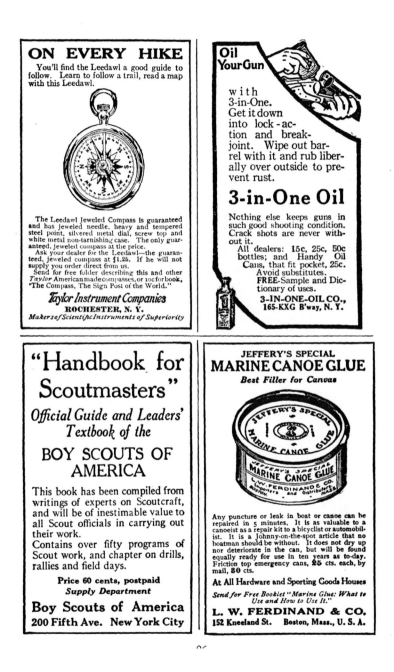

487

BE PREPARED

WITH

COMPLETE SCOUT UNIFORMS and ACCESSORIES

SUGGESTIONS FOR YOUR PERSONAL OUTFIT

No. 503. Regulation Scout Hat..$1.75	**No. 1350.** Khaki Army Blanket.$4.50
No. 564. Special Scout Mackinaw 9.50	**No. 1201.** Aluminum Canteen... 2.00
No. 506. Standard Scout Coat... 2.15	**No. 1200.** Aluminum Cook Kit... 2.25
No. 594. Regulation Scout Sweater 3.75	**No. 1001.** Regulation Mess Kit.. 1.00
No. 509. Standard Scout Breeches 1.85	**No. 1324.** Knife, Fork and Spoon Set .... .75
No. 514. Khaki Scout Shirt— Cotton 1.50	**No. C0100.** Scout Hike Tent.... 4.00
No. 516. Scout Woolen Shirt.... 2.50	**No. 1002.** Scout Axe and Sheath 1.25
No. 591. Scout Canvas Leggings 1.30	**No. 1004.** Regulation Scout Knife 1.25
No. 528. Regulation Cotton Stockings .... .55	**No. 1216.** Scout Lanyard—Khaki .15
No. 529. Scout Web Belt........ .50	**No. 1006.** Regulation Scout Whistle .... .15
No. 568. Scout Neckerchief..... .35	**No. 1276.** Scout Guard Rope.... .35
to	**No. 1061.** Standard Sewing Kit. .65
No. 585. (See catalogue for choice of colors.)	**No. 1273.** Telaway Scout Compass .... .75
No. 536. Waterproof Poncho.... 2.25	**No. 1206.** Litenight (radium) Compass 2.25
No. 540. Waterproof Cape...... 2.50	**No. 1268.** Triumph Scout Watch 1.50
No. 538. Waterproof Middy Hat. .60	**No. 1100.** Individual First Aid Kit .... .40
No. 539. Waterproof Scout Hat. .75	**No. 1058.** Scout Signal Flags... .75
No. 541. Waterproof Ground Blanket 1.50	**No. 1191.** Pocket Signal Disk... .15
No. 592. Regulation Scout Haversack 2.00	**No. 1348.** "Beacon" Electric Belt Lamp 1.50

Prices of garments above are for boys' sizes only; extra charge for all over 18 year age scale.

See Catalogue for illustrations and details.

DEPARTMENT OF SCOUT SUPPLIES
BOY SCOUTS OF AMERICA
200 Fifth Avenue   **New York**

490

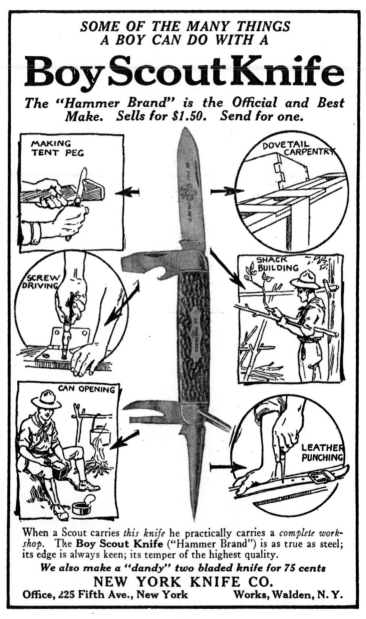
491

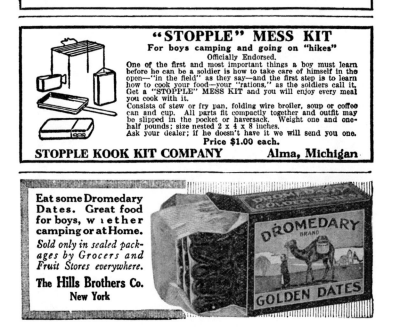
492

Red Blooded Boys

like the Bicycle, and are never satisfied with a wheel that is only "half there."

Pretty nearly everbody who rides knows that the New Departure Coaster Brake is necessary to cycling perfection, because it makes the ride safe, swift and saving of the rider's strength,—enables him to control his mount more completely than does the driver of any other vehicle on the highway,—ideal in service, and will outlast the bicycle itself.

Insist on New Departure equipment for your rear wheel.

The New Departure Mfg. Company
Bristol   Connecticut

493

494

495

BOYS' LIFE

THE BOY SCOUTS' MAGAZINE

OWNED AND PUBLISHED BY THE BOY SCOUTS OF AMERICA

15 cents; $1.50 a Year; Edited by Scout MEN Who Know Boys.

Big Features Here and Coming

Boys, Here's What BOYS' LIFE gives you

Great STORIES Always

Stories of Adventure, Scouting, Camp, Animals, Indians, Pioneers, Explorers, Cowboys, the Sea, Woodcraft, School Life, College, Railroading, Electricity, Stamps, Airships, Government, First Aid, Thrift, Chivalry.

Stories of WAR.

Stories by the greatest writers of boys' stories—Altsheler, Ames, William Heyliger, Walter Walden, Thornton W. Burgess, Ellis Parker Butler, Ralph D. Paine, Irving Crump, Roger Fison, and scores of others.

Contains 48 to 88 pages every issue.

Beautiful cover in colors.

The "Cave Scout," a man of mystery, every month.

Help in passing Scout Tests.

Scouts' questions answered.

"Think and Grin" (what do you suppose that is?).

How to make things (illustrated).

A World-wide Letter Exchange.

Electricity—Stamps—Puzzles.

"A Boys' Life of Roosevelt"

By Hermann Hagedorn

From the start Theodore Roosevelt's life has been packed with adventures that thrill boys. Written especially for boys by Mr. Hagedorn, who was personally selected by Col. Roosevelt. Illustrated with rare photographs, many of which have never before been published.

"Don Strong, Patrol Leader"

A SERIAL

By William Heyliger

Star writer for boys, and author of "Don Strong, of the Wolf Patrol."

"The Mystery of Ram's Island"

By Joseph B. Ames

A Scout story full of snap from the word "go" —every bit as good as his famous "Pete, Cow Puncher."

Series of Scout Articles

By Lt. Gen. Sir

Robert S. S. Baden-Powell

The Founder and Chief Scout of the Boy Scouts' Association of Great Britain.

How to Make and Do Out-Door Things

A Two-Page Illustrated Article Every Month by National Scout Commissioner

Daniel Carter Beard

What Every Scout Wants to Know

A new department giving official information from National Headquarters, by James E. West, Chief Scout Executive. Invaluable to every Scout.

See Premium Offers on Next Page

496

3 Gifts for the Price of 1

This Order Blank Shows You How to Get Them

BOYS' LIFE The Boy Scouts' Magazine for One Full Year

15 cents; $1.50 a Year

Boy Scout Calendar for 1918

New design Six-Sheet Calendar, 5⅛ x 8⅛ inches. Handsomely printed in five colors on heavy card stock; drawings by Mabel Humphrey. Scout Laws and other selections interesting to all Boy Scouts and other Boys. Embodies the Ryte-me post card attached to each page.

Choice of Any One of These Premiums

Eastman Camera, Eveready Pocket Flashlight, Guaranteed Fountain Pen, Scout - Name Knife, Animal Guide Book, Story of Washington, Franklin or Lincoln, the official SCOUT HANDBOOK FOR BOYS, or any book of the EVERY BOY'S LIBRARY, see page 460, or the BOY SCOUT LIFE SERIES.

BOYS' LIFE 1 Year, A Fine Premium, and the BOY SCOUT CALENDAR All for $1.50

The Price of the Magazine alone

These Offers Are Good at Any Time to Anybody

3 Gifts for the Price of 1

Boy Scouts of America,
200 Fifth Ave., New York.

Enclosed find $1.50 in payment of One Year's subscription to BOYS' LIFE, beginning............ number. This amount also to include the BOY SCOUT CALENDAR and........................ (Name of Premium)

....

Magazine, Calendar or Premium can go to separate addresses, if desired. Canadian or Foreign postage extra.

Boy Scout Calendar for 1918

497

COSIMO is a specialty publisher of books and publications that inspire, inform, and engage readers. Our mission is to offer unique books to niche audiences around the world.

COSIMO BOOKS publishes books and publications for innovative authors, nonprofit organizations, and businesses. COSIMO BOOKS specializes in bringing books back into print, publishing new books quickly and effectively, and making these publications available to readers around the world.

COSIMO CLASSICS offers a collection of distinctive titles by the great authors and thinkers throughout the ages. At COSIMO CLASSICS timeless works find new life as affordable books, covering a variety of subjects including: Business, Economics, History, Personal Development, Philosophy, Religion & Spirituality, and much more!

COSIMO REPORTS publishes public reports that affect your world, from global trends to the economy, and from health to geopolitics.

FOR MORE INFORMATION CONTACT US AT
INFO@COSIMOBOOKS.COM

✲ if you are a book lover interested in our
current catalog of books

✲ if you represent a bookstore, book club, or
anyone else interested in special discounts
for bulk purchases

✲ if you are an author who wants to get published

✲ if you represent an organization or business
seeking to publish books and other publications
for your members, donors, or customers.

COSIMO BOOKS ARE ALWAYS
AVAILABLE AT ONLINE BOOKSTORES

VISIT COSIMOBOOKS.COM
BE INSPIRED, BE INFORMED

CPSIA information can be obtained at www.ICGtesting.com
Printed in the USA
BVOW01*1156230816

459905BV00001B/1/P